OXFORD HISTORICAL MONOGRAPHS

GENTLEMEN AND BARRISTERS

The Inns of Court
and
The English Bar
1680–1730

DAVID LEMMINGS

CLARENDON PRESS · OXFORD

1990

Oxford University Press, Walton Street, Oxford OX2 6DP

Oxford New York Toronto
Delhi Bombay Calcutta Madras Karachi
Petaling Jaya Singapore Hong Kong Tokyo
Nairobi Dar es Salaam Cape Town
Melbourne Auckland
and associated companies in
Berlin Ibadan

Oxford is a trade mark of Oxford University Press

Published in the United States
by Oxford University Press, New York

British Library Cataloguing in Publication Data
Lemmings, David
Gentlemen and barristers: the Inns of court and the English
Bar, 1680–1730.—(Oxford historical monographs)
1. England, Barristers, history
I. Title   344.2'0023
ISBN 0–19–822155–X

Library of Congress Cataloging in Publication Data
(data available)

Typeset by Hope Services
Printed in Great Britain by
Courier International Ltd,
Tiptree, Essex

ACKNOWLEDGEMENTS

I HAVE received a great deal of generous help in the course of researching and writing this book, which has developed from an Oxford D.Phil. thesis. Numerous libraries and record offices have facilitated my research, and, although I cannot thank each one individually, I would like to acknowledge my obligations to them all, and in particular to the staffs of the Bodleian Library, the British Library, the Public Record Office at Chancery Lane, the University of London Institute of Historical Research, and the libraries of the four inns of court. I am also grateful to the Masters of the Bench of the Honourable Societies of Gray's Inn, the Inner Temple, Lincoln's Inn, and the Middle Temple for allowing me to use their domestic records, and to the late earl of Harrowby for giving me permission to read a transcript of the diary of his ancestor, Sir Dudley Ryder.

I gratefully acknowledge the help and support which I have received from so many scholars over the years since I first began work on this subject. I owe a long-standing debt of gratitude to Dr Colin Brooks, my former tutor at the University of Sussex, for his inspired teaching and unfailing encouragement, and I am also greatly obliged to the Reverend Dr G. V. Bennett, late of New College, Oxford, for his help in the capacity of my supervisor. I am only sorry that Dr Bennett's tragic death has prevented me from making any recompense for his kindness. My doctoral work also benefited greatly from the generosity of Dr Eveline Cruickshanks and Dr David Hayton, and Chapter 7 is a monument to their own industry as much as it is to my own. Chapter 1 appears by permission of the editor of The *Bulletin of the Institute of Historical Research*, who was kind enough to encourage my work by publishing an earlier version in the issue of that journal which appeared in November 1985. More recently, the process of converting thesis into book has been assisted by Dr Wilfrid Prest, Professor J. H. Baker, and, especially, Dr P. G. M. Dickson. It is a source of great pleasure to me that the original inspiration which I received from their work has been more than matched by their recent friendship. Other scholars have also assisted me with points of special difficulty at all stages of my work, but I leave it to my footnotes to acknowledge their particular contributions. I would like to thank Joyce Sones for help in the preparation of the graphs, and Tania Crow for her expert typing. Of course I am solely responsible for any errors of judgement and fact which remain in the text, just as I am for the interpretation which is advanced there.

D. L.

CONTENTS

LIST OF FIGURES

LIST OF TABLES

LIST OF ABBREVIATIONS

All works cited were published in London, unless specified otherwise. Dates are old style, with the year beginning on 1 January, rather than on 26 March The spelling and punctuation of quotations from original sources in the text have been modernized where necessary to make them intelligible to the modern reader, but the titles of rare books have been rendered in their original forms.

AG	attorney-general
BIHR	*Bulletin of the Institute of Historical Research*
BL	British Library, London
Bodl.	Bodleian Library, Oxford
CGS	commissioner of the great seal
CITR	*A Calendar of the Inner Temple Records*, ed. F. A. Inderwick and R. A. Roberts (1896–1936)
CJ	*Commons' Journal*
CLJ	*Cambridge Law Journal*
CMTR	*A Calendar of the Middle Temple Records*, ed. C. H. Hopwood (1903)
CP	Common Pleas
CRO	County Record Office
CSPD	*Calendar of State Papers Domestic*
DCRO	Devon County Record Office, Exeter
DNB	*Dictionary of National Biography*
Econ. HR	*Economic History Review*
EHR	*English Historical Review*
GI	Gray's Inn
GI Adm. Reg.	*The Register of Admissions to Gray's Inn, 1521–1889*, ed. J. Foster (1889)
GIPB	The Pension Book of Gray's Inn, ed. R. J. Fletcher (1901–10)
HCRO	Hertfordshire County Record Office
HLRO	House of Lords Record Office
HJ	*Historical Journal*
HLQ	*Huntington Library Quarterly*
HMC	Historical Manuscripts Commission
HPT	*History of Parliament Trust* (unpublished drafts)
IT	Inner Temple

IT Adm. Reg.	R. L. Lloyd, 'Admissions to the Inner Temple, 1505–1805' (typescript in the office of the librarian of the Inner Temple, 1954–60)
JBS	*Journal of British Studies*
JMH	*Journal of Modern History*
KAO	Kent Archives Office, Maidstone
KB	King's Bench
KC	king's counsel
KS	king's serjeant
LC	lord chancellor
LCB	lord chief baron
LCJ	lord chief justice
LI	Lincoln's Inn
LI Adm. Reg.	*Records of the Honourable Society of Lincoln's Inn: Admissions and Chapel Registers* (1896)
LIBB	*Records of the Honourable Society of Lincoln's Inn: The Black Books*, ed. W. P. Baildon and others (1897–1977)
LJ	*Lords' Journal*
LK	lord keeper
LQR	*Law Quarterly Review*
MR	master of the rolls
MT	Middle Temple
MT. Adm. Reg.	*Registers of Admissions to the Middle Temple from the 15th Century to the Year 1944*, ed. H. A. C. Sturgess (1949)
MTR	*Middle Temple Records: Minutes of Parliament of the Middle Temple*, ed. C. T. Martin (1904–5)
n.d.	no date
N&Q	*Notes and Queries*
PBA	*Proceedings of the British Academy*
P&P	*Past and Present*
PRO	Public Record Office, London
QC	queen's counsel
QS	queen's serjeant
Rec./CS Lond.	recorder/common serjeant of London
SG	solicitor-general
SCRO	Surrey·County Record Office (Kingston)
TRHS	*Transactions of the Royal Historical Society*
TS Ryder Diary	Sandon Hall, Stafford, Harrowby MSS 3rd ser. A, lxix: TS of diary of Dudley Ryder, 1715–16

INTRODUCTION

THE four inns of court have constituted the principal institutional home of the English common lawyers since medieval times, and to this day they continue to function as professional societies which are the well-spring of the English bar. But they have also taken a larger role in previous centuries. In the early modern period they were often regarded as England's 'third university' for the education of the children of the élite. The history of the inns and their members is therefore of interest for at least two reasons. First, it illuminates some of the basic characteristics and concerns of English society as they were reflected in the educational decisions of the gentry and the lives and activities of individual barristers at law. Secondly, the fortunes of the inns were connected with the structure and development of the common law élite which they nurtured, and inquiry into these societies is therefore an essential foundation for a broader study of the bar itself; the pre-eminent profession of early modern England. These observations are the *raison d'être* of this book, which has the objective of tracing a part of the history of the inns and the bar through a comprehensive analysis of their personnel between 1680 and 1730.

These terminal dates are not a matter of arbitrary choice. They are appropriate because the last two decades have produced a considerable volume of published research which has helped to trace the history of the inns and the bar from their beginnings to the mid-seventeenth century, while other studies have taken up the story from the later eighteenth century and carried it into the Victorian age. The important period of transition between 1680 and 1730 has been neglected at the level of detail.

To set it in perspective, the history of the inns and the bar must be briefly examined. It is now fairly clear that a legal profession existed in England by the end of the thirteenth century. The early *Year Books* (law reports which date from the reign of Edward I) reveal the existence of professional lawyers whose services were tendered to litigants on a regular basis. And around this time pleaders and attorneys—the two classes of lawyers practising in the royal and provincial courts—were first subjected to regulation in respect of their numbers and activities. Pleaders were distinguished from attorneys from the beginning. The former were advocates who spoke for others in court (subject to correction) and therefore addressed the *substance* of an issue, while attorneys acted as agents who stood in the shoes of their principals and acted with the power to bind them at all stages in the *process* of the case. The ancestors of the 'upper branch' of the profession underwent further structural definition in the fourteenth century. After 1318 (at the latest) advocacy in the busiest royal court, the 'Common Bench' (known as the court of Common Pleas in the early modern period), began to be confined to batches of senior pleaders who were admitted or 'called' to practise there at regular intervals by the presiding judges. The importance of this privilege was such that admission came (from 1382) to be sanctioned by royal writ, and the call became an elaborate ceremony, by which the graduand was admitted to the degree of serjeant at law. The serjeants therefore became a distinct order of the profession, distinguished not only by their sole rights of audience in the most important (and most profitable) court in the country, but also by their parti-coloured robes and white linen coifs (caps), and more substantially by their monopoly of promotion to judges' places in the common law courts and on circuit commissions.[1] The 'narratores' or 'countors' in Common Bench, from whom the order of serjeants developed, were already the élite of the pleaders by 1300, but there were also lawyers who attended the Common Bench as students, while pleading themselves in proceedings *coram rege* (the court of King's Bench) and in the circuit jurisdictions. These advocates below the degree of serjeant were known as 'apprentices at law', and they formed a junior wing of the legal profession's upper branch during the late medieval and early Tudor period.[2]

The origins of the four inns of court remain relatively obscure in their details, but it is at least clear that the societies developed from a number of houses which served as places of accommodation for the

---

[1] The serjeants also achieved a monopoly of promotion to the Exchequer bench (excepting places as cursitor barons, who were administrative officers) after 1579.

[2] F. Pollock and F. W. Maitland, *The History of English Law before the Time of Edward I* (2nd edn., Cambridge, 1898), i. 211–17; J. H. Baker, *An Introduction to English Legal History* (2nd edn., 1979), 133–8; id., *The Order of Serjeants at Law* (Selden Soc., suppl. ser. 5; 1984), 8–41; id., 'The English Legal Profession, 1450–1550', in W. Prest (ed.), *Lawyers in Early Modern Europe and America* (1981), 27–8; R. C. Palmer, 'The Origins of the Legal Profession in England, 1450–1550', *Irish Jurist*, 11 (1976), 126–46; G. O. Sayles (ed.), *Select Cases in the Court of King's Bench under Edward I*, (Selden Soc., 55; 1936), pp. xci–xciii.

lawyers attending the courts in London. By the fourteenth century the western environs of the city served as a dormitory area for men of business whose affairs brought them to the capital, and Professor S. E. Thorne has suggested that the legal inns originated when the lawyers who were present during the four law terms clubbed together and took a house and servants for the provision of food and shelter on a communal basis.[3] The judges and serjeants probably kept their own individual houses until the sixteenth century, although the two future serjeants' inns were in existence by 1450, and the majority of serjeants were members a century later. But the apprentices and law clerks (who presumably had more need of economical accommodation) concentrated in their *hospicia*, around twenty of which existed at one time or another, mainly in the area on the western edge of the city, running north from the Thames to Holborn. At least three had come to predominate by 1388—the society of Gray's Inn, and the Inner and Middle Temples. They provided all the apprentices who were admitted to the degree of serjeant at law in that year, and in the fifteenth century the judges and serjeants were invariably drawn from these three houses, together with the society of Lincoln's Inn, which is first heard of in 1422. It is not at all clear why these four houses first achieved their supremacy over the others, but they became the 'great inns' which were the basis of the common law élite and were known by Tudor times as the inns of court (i.e. the inns of the men of court). The other legal societies (ten around 1470, eight by the seventeenth century) declined into inferior inns associated with attorneys and clerks (although some members of the lower branch were members of the inns of court until the nineteenth century), as well as law students who were undergoing basic induction into the formalities of writs before entering the superior inns. They were known collectively as the inns of chancery by the sixteenth century, and in some instances their premises became the property of the inns of court, who assumed rights of governance over them.[4]

It is now generally accepted that the inns of court did not originate as educational institutions, although they subsequently developed an apparatus of legal training which had a profound influence on the

---

[3] S. E. Thorne, 'The Early History of the Inns of Court with Special Reference to Gray's Inn', in id., *Essays in English Legal History* (1985), 137–54.

[4] Ibid.; Baker, *Introduction to English Legal History*, pp. 138–40; id., 'The English Legal Profession, 1450–1550', pp. 19, 31; id., 'The Inns of Court in 1388', in id., *The Legal Profession and the Common Law: Historical Essays* (1986), 3–6.

structure of the English bar. Dr Paul Brand and Professor J. H. Baker
have uncovered evidence of law lectures and disputations which were
taking place (principally in London) during the thirteenth century, but
the way in which the functions of this early law school devolved on the
legal inns is obscure. While there are traces of learning exercises at
the fourteenth-century inns, the system of legal education which
characterized the inns of court during the Tudor and the early Stuart
periods does not become clear until after 1450. From around that time
the four inns of court maintained legal exercises (principally the moot,
a form of case argument) in which all ranks of the membership
participated, and 'readings' (formal lectures on statutes, accompanied
by disputations) were given by senior members.[5] The *hospicia* which
became inns of chancery also developed educational functions (in
some cases before the inns of court), although by the sixteenth century
their parent inns of court sent readers and assistants who presided over
their readings and 'grand moots'.[6]

The system of legal education developed at the inns of court is of
enduring importance, because it gave birth to a hierarchy of ranks
which helped to transform the structure of the profession in the Renaissance period and has survived to the present day. The exercises
at the inns became the basis of their internal order of membership and
governance: junior members participated in moots as 'inner barristers'
who sat within the bar placed in the hall of their inn (perhaps in
imitation of the court of Common Pleas); after several years' study and
further participation in the exercises they became 'utter barristers' who
took a more important role in the moots from their position outside the
bar. The senior members of the inns who presided at moots were
known as benchers, a name derived from the bench they sat upon
during the exercises. They governed the inns and by Tudor times their
enjoyment of authority was associated with their obligation to deliver
the readings which were the most public feature of the inns' educational system. Until the seventeenth century, this hierarchy of barristers and benchers was mainly of internal significance for the inns
of court, although the apprentices who were allowed to practise outside
the court of Common Pleas were normally identical with the readers

[5] For more details of the inns' learning exercises see below, ch. 4.

[6] P. Brand, 'Courtroom and Schoolroom: The Education of Lawyers in England
prior to 1400', *Historical Research*, 60 (1986), 147–65; J. H. Baker, 'Learning Exercises
in the Medieval Inns of Court and Chancery', in id., *The Legal Profession and the Common
Law*, pp. 7–23; Thorne, 'Early History of the Inns of Court', pp. 144–54; E. W. Ives,
The Common Lawyers of Pre-Reformation England (Cambridge, 1983), 39–59.

and benchers of the inns. However, the development of the conciliar courts and a great increase in common law litigation during the reign of Elizabeth I made the inns' rank of utter barrister the primary qualification for audience before the courts of Westminster Hall. Utter barristers may have obtained some work in the lesser jurisdictions before this time, but practice in the superior courts was effectively confined to the apprentices and serjeants. It is reasonable to suppose that these established advocates were not numerous enough to cope with the tidal wave of business which swept over them in the later sixteenth century, and more junior pleaders were therefore given an opportunity to practise. Faced with a need to regulate the numbers and competence of those men appearing before them, the judges and their masters in government naturally resorted to the hierarchy of the inns of court as a means of reference. Utter barristers had been recognized as men 'learned in the law' by an act of parliament in 1532 (23 Hen. VIII, c. 5), and a succession of orders made by the judiciary and privy council from the middle of the century restricted pleading in Westminster Hall to barristers of a certain standing at their inns. Finally, in 1590 the case of *Broughton* v. *Prince* established the rank of utter barrister as the minimum requirement for audience in the superior courts. Henceforth the inns' rank became a public degree, and the 'call to the bar' of an inn of court became the main qualification for admission to the upper branch of the profession.[7]

The 'rise of the barristers' to become the dominant class of advocates in the English superior courts was complete by 1640, after almost a century of continuous expansion in the quantity of litigation and the consequent 'mushroom growth' in numbers called to the bar. The structure of the modern legal profession was becoming clear at this time, and its relationship with the inns of court was also well defined. The inns experienced considerable change during the sixteenth and seventeenth centuries, as their admissions rolls were swelled by sons of the gentry who wished to acquire a little law and complete their education with the culture of the metropolis. The presence of the gentlemen encouraged the benchers and barristers to

---

[7] Ibid.; Baker, *Introduction to English Legal History*, pp. 139–40; id., 'Counsellors and Barristers', in id., *The Legal Profession and the Common Law*, pp. 108–12; id., 'Solicitors and the Law of Maintenance 1590–1640', in id., *The Legal Profession and the Common Law*, pp. 130–5; C. W. Brooks, *Pettyfoggers and Vipers of the Commonwealth: The 'Lower Branch' of the Legal Profession in Early Modern England* (Cambridge, 1986), 48–57; W. R. Prest, *The Rise of the Barristers: A Social History of the English Bar 1590–1640* (Oxford, 1986), 5–6.

take pride in their calling and their societies, with the consequence that there was a progressive campaign to exclude any mere attorneys who were members.[8] The original division between pleaders and attorneys was therefore in the process of being institutionalized by the eve of the English Civil War. On the one hand the attorneys (and their new brethren, the solicitors, general legal agents who also acted as attorneys in the court of Chancery) were being confined to the inns of chancery. The inns of court, on the other hand, were established as the institutional base of the English bar.[9]

The body of published work summarized above carries the history of the inns and the bar no further than the middle of the seventeenth century, and the full story is not taken up again for another hundred years.[10] This leaves a lacuna during the later Stuart and Hanoverian period; years which saw important changes in English society. Professor Geoffrey Holmes has sketched some of the characteristics of the bar between 1680 and 1730 as a part of his general study of the professions, but his work is by no means intended as a full account. On the contrary, his claim that the 'Augustan Age' witnessed a transformation of the professions as a response to economic change can only encourage further research on the common lawyers and their institutions in this period.[11]

In so far as it deals with the professional activities of the barristers, this book concentrates on civil law.[12] It does not deal with crime, a subject which has been much studied by historians recently.[13] Most people who became involved with law in the seventeenth and eighteenth centuries experienced it in its civil capacity, as machinery

[8] See below, p. 150.

[9] Prest, *Rise of the Barristers*, pp. 7–9; id., *The Inns of Court under Elizabeth I and the Early Stuarts 1590–1640* (1972), 5–7, 21–7; Baker, *Introduction to English Legal History*, pp. 140–1; C. W. Brooks, 'The Common Lawyers in England, *c.*1558–1642', in Prest (ed.), *Lawyers in Early Modern Europe and America*, pp. 51–5.

[10] See D. Duman, *The Judicial Bench in England 1727–1875: The Reshaping of a Professional Elite*; id., *The English and Colonial Bars in the Nineteenth Century* (1983).

[11] G. Holmes, *Augustan England: Professions, State and Society, 1680–1730* (1982), pp. x–xi, 3–18, and *passim*.

[12] i.e. law as it applied to purely private rights. This should be distinguished from the Civil law, the collective term for the principles and procedures mastered by advocates and proctors who practised in the ecclesiastical and admiralty courts (for them see B. P. Levack, 'The English Civilians, 1500–1750', in Prest (ed.), *Lawyers in Early Modern Europe and America*, pp. 108–28).

[13] For summaries of this work see J. A. Sharpe, *Crime in Early Modern England 1550–1750* (1984), 9–13 and *passim*; J. Innes and J. Styles, 'The Crime Wave: Recent Writing on Crime and Criminal Justice in Eighteenth-Century England', *JBS* 25 (1986), 380–435.

for resolving disputes or settling accounts between party and party, often arising in the normal course of their affairs. Lawyers, and especially barristers, were therefore preoccupied with the civil law, unless they became judges; crime and the conduct of criminal trials was very much a minority occupation among members of the 'upper branch'.[14] The account of their work presented below therefore offers a different perspective on the role of law in early modern England, as an agency which facilitated the regular progress of life and work.

The chapters which follow present a broad profile of the membership of the inns of court and the bar. They follow recruits to the inns and the legal profession from initial entry to their societies through legal education and practice to maturity in the House of Commons and on the judicial bench. In this way it is possible to observe the general developments of this period from a fresh perspective. Those familiar with the age will recognize the common landmarks of changes in the pattern of landownership, the decline of legal education, the growth of patronage and the development of new methods of parliamentary management. But the primary aim of this book is to tell a new story by showing how the relationship between the inns of court and the English bar was transformed during these years, and to explain how this development paralleled changes in the structure of the bar and its relation to society as a whole. Knowledge of this process is essential to comprehend the way in which the lawyers became attuned to the demands of the world's first proto-industrial nation.

---

[14] Counsel were rarely employed in ordinary criminal trials until the later 18th cent.: before this time only important state trials provided opportunities for them to gain much in reputation and wealth. For counsel in criminal proceedings see J. M. Beattie, *Crime and the Courts in England 1660–1800* (Oxford, 1986), 352–62.

I

THE STUDENT BODY OF THE
INNS OF COURT

In Augustan England, as in modern times, every prospective barrister
was obliged to become a member of one of the four inns of court.
These societies alone enjoyed the *de facto* right to admit men to plead
in the courts which sat in Westminster Hall. But the production of
common lawyers was not their whole function. Not every person
admitted to the inns was called to the bar, and a much smaller number
went on actually to practise as barristers. Indeed, most students had no
intention of becoming active members of the legal profession. As has
been mentioned already, in the later sixteenth and early seventeenth
centuries the inns of court became the fashionable resort of large
numbers of well-born gentlemen who regarded them simply as
'finishing schools', and they had not relinquished this function,
apparently, one hundred years later.[1] It is important to remember
therefore, throughout this study, that the student body of the inns
included 'non-professional' students as well as those men who
intended to become members of the English bar.

This first chapter attempts to define the basic characteristics of the
heterogeneous students who attended the inns between 1688 and
1714, and to compare them with their predecessors of the age of Coke
and Selden. It is concerned principally with variations in the numbers
and social status of those admitted to the legal societies during the later
seventeenth century, and with certain other features of the student
body which may help to illustrate and explain these trends, such as the
'overlap' between attendance at the inns and at the university, the
regional origins of students, and the changing cost of residence at an
inn. This basic information is essential preparatory groundwork for a
full understanding of the place of the inns and the bar in the English
society of the period.

---

[1] Prest, *Inns of Court*, pp. 31–2, 40, 153–4; id., 'Legal Education of the Gentry at the
Inns of Court, 1560–1640', *P&P* 38 (1967), 23; see below, pp. 15–17.

I. NUMBERS AND SOCIAL ORIGINS

In spite of their broad educational function, it is evident that the inns of court had declined in popularity since the earlier seventeenth century. Fig. 1.1 shows that the sixty years following the mid-1680s were a period of steeply falling admissions. The first half of the period, down to the accession of George I, witnessed an almost unrelieved decline in the total number of men admitted to the four inns. There was a rally after 1714, but this was short-lived and after 1730 the numbers admitted to the inns continued to fall, reaching an all time low by the mid-eighteenth century. When total admissions between 1688 and 1714 are compared with those for the thirty years after 1609, there appears a decline of approximately 35 per cent in the average annual intake of students to the inns.[2]

This pattern of decline in total admissions to the inns was by no means evenly spread across the individual societies. Although all the inns, except Lincoln's Inn, were experiencing falling rolls by 1689, the two Temples had actually increased their average annual intake during the Restoration period, and together accounted for over 70 per cent of total admissions between 1688 and 1714.[3] Gray's Inn, on the other hand, went into long-term numerical decline after the Restoration; average annual admissions to this society between the Revolution and the accession of the Hanoverians were 79 per cent down on the intake achieved between 1610 and 1639. Thus it appears that the contraction of student numbers at Gray's Inn was primarily responsible for the aggregate fall in admissions to the inns. This seems even more significant, when it is considered that Gray's may have taken a disproportionate number of the aristocratic 'non-professional' students who had begun to enter the inns during the later sixteenth century, and had accounted for over 40 per cent of total admissions for the three decades preceding the Civil Wars.[4] The post-Restoration decline of Gray's Inn implies not only a quantitative but also a *qualitative* change

---

[2] Comparing figures derived from the sources cited for 1688–1714 in Table 1.1 with those taken from Prest, *Inns of Court*, p. 11. The statistics for 1688–1714 exclude purely honorific and *ad eundem* admissions, and also any other persons identified as having entered previously another inn of court. All subsequent statistics given for admissions 1688–1714 are derived from the sources specified above for those years.

[3] MT showed a 30.5% increase in annual average admissions, comparing 1688–1714 with 1610–39, while IT had increased its average intake by 12.8%.

[4] Prest, *Inns of Court*, pp. 11, 53; but cf. id., *Rise of the Barristers*, Table 1.1.

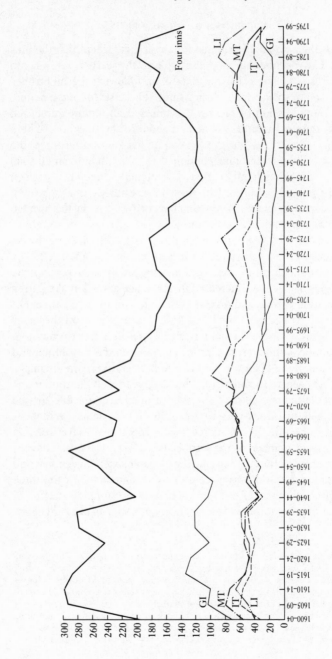

FIGURE 1.1. *First admissions to the inns of court, 1660–1799*

in the student body of the inns of court, and it is to this that we must now turn.

Around the end of the seventeenth century, certain contemporaries voiced their alarm at the apparent decline in the social quality of students attending the inns of court. In 1700 Sir Henry Chauncy, a former treasurer of the Middle Temple, complained that the sons of noblemen and country squires were being supplanted at the inns by the children of 'mechanics, ambitious of rule and government'.[5] A few years earlier Edward Chamberlayne had bemoaned the fact that James I's order of 1603, which commanded the inns to admit only gentlemen by descent, had not been observed, with the result that the offspring of the élite were not provided with employments suitable to their quality.[6]

Analysis of the admissions books between 1688 and 1714 seems to confirm the observations of these commentators. Table 1.1 compares the annual intake of each social group over this period with corresponding statistics for 1610–39 as given by Dr Prest. According to these figures, the decline in total numbers at the legal societies during the later seventeenth century had not been evenly spread across the social spectrum. While admissions from the peer/esquire group had declined by about 42 per cent, the representatives of the bourgeois and professional classes were nearly 70 per cent stronger than they had been in the earlier period. The drop in admissions was greatest among the sons of men calling themselves simply 'gentlemen'; the annual intake of students from these 'mere gentry' was less than half what it had been in the early seventeenth century.[7]

These statistics indicate that the later Stuart period had indeed witnessed a change in the social background of students admitted to the inns of court. The figures should, however, be interpreted with extreme caution. Professor Geoffrey Holmes has suggested that the inns of court were more ready to acknowledge the plebeian origins of

---

[5] H. Chauncy, *The Historical Antiquities of Hertfordshire* (1700), 527–8.

[6] E. Chamberlayne, *Angliae Notitia*, pt. II (7th edn., 1677), 224.

[7] A caveat must be entered here. It is possible that the figures for the number of persons classified by social rank between 1610 and 1639 may be slightly inflated, since Dr Prest has included in his classification persons described by their own rank, where the father's rank is not available. The resultant distortion to the figures for the earlier period may have tended to enlarge slightly the 'gentleman' category. Now if *all* those persons admitted in the later period and classified as unknown are accorded the rank of 'gentleman', then the decline in the annual intake of 'gentlemen' or sons of 'gentlemen' between 1610–39 and 1688–1714 is 44% rather than 57%. Thus, given this over-generous margin of error, our conclusion regarding the declining number of sons of 'gentlemen' is still valid.

TABLE 1.1. *Social origins of entrants to the inns of court, 1610–39 and 1688–1714 (annual averages for aggregate totals)*

Social origins	1610–39		1688–1714		% Change in average annual admissions
	Total admissions	Annual average	Total admissions	Annual average	
Peer/esquire	3942	131.4	2057	76.2	−42.0
Gentleman	3121	104.0	1209	44.8	−56.9
Bourgois/ professional	640	21.3	971	36.0	+69.0
Total classified	7703	256.8	4237	156.9	−38.9
Unclassified and unknown	168		362		

Definition of categories for 1688–1714: Peer/esquire: sons of temporal lords, baronets, knights, and esquires; Gentleman: sons of those described as 'gentlemen'; Bourgeois/professional: sons of clerks in holy orders, including cathedral clergy and bishops; sons of persons described simply as of an inn of court or an inn of chancery, plus sons of judges and serjeants at law; sons of doctors of medicine and of civil law; sons of merchants, civil officials, minor legal officials, tradesmen, artisans, etc.

Sources: 1610–39: Prest, *Inns of Court*, p. 30; 1688–1714: GI, MS Admittance Book ii. 1321–1400; *IT Adm. Reg.*, i. 556–65, ii. 121–217; LI, MS Admissions Book ix, fos. 130–54, x, fos. 1–157; MT, MS Admissions to House and Chambers 1658–95, 514–644; ibid. 1695–1735, 1–216.

students in the early eighteenth century than they had been a hundred years earlier.[8] If this was the case, then the apparent increase in numbers of the middling classes was illusory. Yet there is no evidence to support this contention. On the contrary, there are still many examples of social upgrading in the admissions registers on behalf of students entering the inns between 1688 and 1714.[9] It is also apparent that labels of social rank had been devalued during the seventeenth

[8] Holmes, *Augustan England*, p. 143.
[9] For examples see *IT Adm. Reg.*, ii. 203; MT, MS Admissions 1695–1735, 205 (Peter King); *The Diary of Dudley Ryder, 1715–16*, ed. W. Matthews (1939), 3–4; MT, MS Admissions 1658–95, 263; *DNB* xi. 144 (Dudley Ryder).

century.[10] By 1700 it was generally accepted that many men who lacked the formal qualifications by right of birth might, for a multitude of reasons, yet claim genteel status.[11] If more men were indeed calling themselves 'gentlemen', then the decline in the number of genuine sons of the lesser gentry at the inns over the preceding half-century must have been even greater than the statistics in Table 1.1 show. Correspondingly, there was an even greater influx of persons of bourgeois and professional origins.

The trends described above are important. They did not, however, fundamentally alter the social *balance* of the student body admitted to the inns. Table 1.2 shows that the students who entered the inns of court between 1688 and 1714 were still an élite group of young men. Compared with the University of Oxford, the legal societies included a far greater proportion of students who were derived from the peer/esquire group and a much smaller proportion of men who were of professional or plebeian origins. Moreover, despite the fact that Oxford was numerically a much larger institution than the inns of court over these years, the legal societies actually received more sons of the social élite. The university admitted about fifty-four sons of the peer/esquire group per year over this period, while the inns received about seventy-six.[12] Admittedly, it is doubtful if all these men resided for any length of time. Nevertheless, the import of these figures is striking: they appear to demonstrate that the inns of court still played a central role in the education and cultural formation of the later Stuart gentry.

Although it is evident that students entering the inns of court during these years came mainly from the upper layers of society, it is difficult to be precise about their social origins because of the uncertain meaning of the descriptions of parental status entered in the admission books. No doubt the sons of peers and baronets and many of the knights' children were true representatives of the landed élite. The persons described as being of 'bourgeois' and 'professional' origins were the sons of common lawyers, doctors of civil law or medicine,

[10] See L. Stone, 'The Size and Composition of the Oxford Student Body 1580–1909', in id. (ed.), *The University in Society* (Princeton, 1974), i. 14, 48; L. and J. C. F. Stone, *An Open Elite? England 1540–1880* (Oxford, 1984), 7–8, 234.

[11] See G. Miège, *The New State of England* (1691), pt. II, 226; id., *The Present State of Great Britain* (1707), pt. I, 263–4; D. Defoe, *The Compleat English Gentleman*, ed. K. D. Buldring (1890), 4 [written *c.*1728–9]; E. Chamberlayne, *Angliae Notitia* (18th edn., 1694), 443; J. Chamberlayne, *Magnae Brittaniae Notitia* (23rd edn., 1710), 191–2.

[12] Comparing the statistics in Table 1.2 with those in Stone, 'Oxford Student Body', p. 93.

TABLE 1.2. *Social origins of entrants to the inns of court, 1688–1714*

Social origins	Gray's Inn		Inner Temple		Lincoln's Inn		Middle Temple		Total	
	No.	%	No.	%	No.	%	No.	%	No.	%
Peer	1	0.2	17	1.3	7	1.2	11	0.6	36	0.8
Knight/baronet	39	7.6	91	7.1	45	8.1	120	6.4	295	7.0
Esquire	229	44.4	467	36.5	218	39.1	812	43.1	1726	40.7
Gentleman	149	28.9	360	28.1	156	28.0	544	28.9	1209	28.5
Clerk	13	2.5	57	4.4	14	2.5	93	4.9	177	4.2
Lawyer	56	10.8	169	13.2	112	20.1	155	8.2	492	11.6
Doctor	10	1.9	11	0.9	4	0.7	23	1.2	48	1.1
Bourgeois	19	3.7	109	8.5	2	0.4	124	6.6	254	6.0
Total classified	516		1281		558		1882		4237	
Unclassified and unknown	107		127		103		25		362	

Definition of categories of social origin: Peer: sons of temporal lords; Knight/baronet: sons of knights and baronets; Esquire: sons of those described as esquires or 'armiger'; Gentleman: sons of those described as 'gentlemen'; Clerk: sons of clerks in holy orders including cathedral clergy and bishops; Lawyer: sons of persons described only as members of an inn of court or chancery, also sons of judges and sergeants at law; Doctor: sons of doctors of medicine and doctors of civil law; Bourgeois: sons of merchants, civic officials, minor legal officials, tradesmen, artisans, etc; Unclassified and unknown: all those admissions where the father is not named or identified by rank or occupation, including entrants described simply as 'gentlemen'.

Sources: As specified for 1688–1714 in Table 1.1.

clergymen, and various representatives of the urban commercial classes. Difficulty centres on the place in society of those students admitted as sons of 'esquires', or 'gentlemen', and especially the latter. Rather than treat them all as sons of landed gentlemen, we have to find a means to define their background more carefully. Of those students who entered the inns of court between 1688 and 1714, 161 of the sons of 'esquires' and 257 of the sons of 'gentlemen' had come from English towns which included around 2,000 or more inhabitants. If we regard these 'pseudo-gentry' as men who were not actually of landed origin, then we may conclude that approximately 67 per cent of our students were sons of the landed gentry, while the other 33 per cent were derived from the middle strata of Augustan society.[13]

The decline in the number of gentry students becoming members of the inns of court during the later seventeenth century has induced some historians to think that they had by 1700 largely surrendered their secondary function as academies for the liberal education of socially elevated young men.[14] The experience of Gray's Inn leads one to believe that there had indeed been some weakening of this role. But we must not write off the 'non-professional' student at too early a date. The inns continued to be dominated by the landed élite, and this suggests that not all the men admitted were determined to take up a career at the bar. Moreover, every society included a large majority of eldest sons or heirs among its admissions during our period, and the student body as a whole consisted of over 70 per cent first sons or heirs, as against less than 30 per cent younger sons.[15] This is significant because there are grounds for believing that eldest sons, especially the heirs to landed estates, were less likely to take a serious attitude towards the law than their younger brothers. The records of a contemporary Devonshire family provide us with an illustration of this. Sir Francis Drake, a descendant of the famous sea captain, had two sons at the Inner Temple in the closing years of Anne's reign: his eldest son and heir, Francis, and his second son, Pollexfen. The latter was encouraged to pursue his studies with determination; in August 1713 Sir Francis asked Sir Peter King, who was also a member of the Inner Temple, 'please to acquaint Polly that when I am fully satisfied he is well settled in a studying humour I shall not forget my usual

[13] These figures (and those below, p. 17) supersede the statistics in D. Lemmings, 'The Student Body of the Inns of Court under the Later Stuarts', *BIHR* 58 (1985), 154. For the towns see C. W. Chalklin, *The Provincial Towns of Georgian England* (1974), 5–17 and map 1. 'London' has been restricted to the city of London for the purpose of these calculations.

[14] W. S. Holdsworth, *A History of English Law* (1922–72), xii. 15–16; Prest, *Inns of Court*, p. 44; W. C. Richardson, *A History of the Inns of Court* (Baton Rouge, La., n.d. [1977]), 311; P. Lucas, 'A Collective Biography of Students and Barristers of Lincoln's Inn, 1680–1804: A Study in the "Aristocratic Resurgence" of the 18th Century', *JMH* 46 (1974), 227; id., 'Blackstone and the Reform of the Legal Profession', *EHR* 77 (1962), 465. In fact, non-professional students, although reduced in numbers, were present at MT as late as 1733 (see *Master Worsley's Book on the History and Constitution of the Honourable Society of the Middle Temple*, ed. A. R. Ingpen (1910), 117–18).

[15] Of all entrants to the inns between 1688 and 1714 who were classified by birth order, 2,998 or 70.2% were first sons or heirs, while 1,270 or 29.8% were younger sons, or were described simply as 'son'. (For more detailed figures see Lemmings, 'Student Body of the Inns of Court', p. 155.)

tokens'.[16] Pollexfen's elder brother, however, was not expected to be so persevering in his studies, since his father regarded his sojourn at the Temple as no more than a part of his general education. In March 1712, after Francis had been there for a little over a year, his father informed King that Lady Drake 'begins to be a little impatient and we are determin'd for a little discourse with him to take him into the consult where It is best to set him for another little while next'.[17]

TABLE 1.3. *Correlation of social origins with birth order of entrants to the inns of court, 1688–1714 (totals for all four inns)*

Social origins	First/heir		Son/other		Total classified	Unclassified
	No.	%	No.	%		
Peer	2	5.5	34	94.4	36	—
Knight/baronet	134	45.4	161	54.6	295	—
Esquire	1243	72.1	481	27.9	1724	2
Gentleman	905	75.1	300	24.9	1205	—
Clerk	125	70.6	52	29.4	177	4
Lawyer	348	70.7	144	29.3	492	—
Doctor	36	75.0	12	25.0	48	—
Bourgeois	180	70.9	74	29.1	254	—
Total classified	2973		1258		4231	6
Unclassified and unknown	25		12		37	325

Definition of categories: Social origins: as in Table 1.2; Birth order: First/heir: those described as 'son and heir', 'heir', 'eldest son', 'only son', and 'first son'; Son/other: those described simply as 'son' or some order other than those given above; Unclassified: admissions where birth order is not given.

Sources: As in Table 1.2.

As the eldest son of a baronet, Francis Drake was in an especially elevated social category among the students at the inns. Table 1.3 shows that the cream of the student body—the sons of peers, baronets, and knights—was actually more likely to consist of younger sons than their elder brothers. But even this does not greatly detract from the

---

[16] DCRO, Drake of Buckland Abbey MSS 346M/F78: Drake to King, 6 Aug. 1713; cf. Lady Eliott-Drake, *The Family and Heirs of Sir Francis Drake* (1911), ii. 189.

[17] DCRO, Drake MSS 346M/F76: Drake to King, 1 Mar. 1712; Eliot-Drake, *Family and Heirs*, ii. 188.

evident social exclusiveness of these societies. Even those students who did not enjoy the social cachet of having a father with a title were still highly privileged members of Augustan society and many were likely to inherit a country estate. Referring again to Table 1.3, even if we count the urban dwellers among the heirs (120 of the sons of 'esquires' and 195 of the sons of 'gentlemen') as men whose fathers were not landowners, then we calculate that 47 per cent of our student body enjoyed the rosy prospect of succeeding to an estate in land. Thus it is evident that the inns of court had by no means reverted to their original function as 'associations for practising and would-be lawyers'.[18]

2. UNIVERSITY MEN

By the mid-eighteenth century, however, it would appear that the 'flight of the gentry' which had its beginnings under the later Stuarts, had gone much further, and the student body of the inns included fewer of the landed élite.[19] Confronted with this problem, William Blackstone, the great jurist, attempted to apply what appears at first sight to be an obscure remedy: he appealed to gentlemen at the universities to study the common law of England. Evidently Blackstone believed that an increase in recruitment from the English universities would have the effect of raising again the social quality of students attending the legal societies.[20] Thus it would seem pertinent to examine the relationship between the universities and the inns, and especially the quantity and quality of university men who were also members of the inns during the later Stuart period.

During the fifteenth and sixteenth centuries the inns of chancery had served as preparatory schools for many students who intended to enter one of the four inns of court.[21] On the eve of the Civil Wars, however, the number of students admitted to the houses of court from these satellite inns had declined to a trickle, and this state of affairs had

---

[18] See Prest, *Inns of Court*, p. 44.

[19] Lucas, 'Collective Biography', pp. 230–1, 247.

[20] Id., 'Blackstone', pp. 456–89; W. Blackstone, *Commentaries on the Laws of England* (Oxford, 1765–9), i. 25–6, 30–1.

[21] H. H. L. Bellot, 'The Jurisdiction of the Inns of Court over the Inns of Chancery', *LQR* 26 (1910), 384; *The Pension Book of Clement's Inn*, ed. C. Carr (Selden Soc., 78; 1960), pp. xviii–xix; Baker, *Introduction to English Legal History*, p. 139; A. Harding, *A Social History of English Law* (Harmondsworth, 1966), p. 186; Richardson, *History of the Inns of Court*, pp. 4–6.

not changed fifty years later.[22] Some time between the accession of
Elizabeth and the flight of James II, the universities had largely
replaced the inns of chancery as 'nurseries' for numerous future
members of the greater inns. According to Table 1.4, just under 45
per cent of the student body admitted to the inns of court between
1688 and 1714 had also been admitted to Oxford, Cambridge, or
Trinity College, Dublin. Other students had certainly attended
universities further afield. Protestant dissenters, for instance, preferred to
send their sons to the Calvinist institutions of Scotland and the Low
Countries, especially Edinburgh and Leiden.[23] These universities
currently enjoyed a reputation superior to Oxford and Cambridge for
modern professional and scientific studies, and this may have
persuaded some parents to forsake the more traditional universities.[24]
Thus the figures which represent those students at the inns who
attended a university are clearly underestimated, and it is likely that
about half the student body had enjoyed some kind of university
education.

The distribution of university men across the four inns seems to
have been primarily a function of their regional origins. There were no
formal links between any of the inns and individual colleges or
universities. Oxford was more heavily represented than Cambridge not
only because it was numerically the larger English university at this
time, but also because a large proportion of students at the inns of
court, like alumni of Oxford, came from the south and west of the
country.[25] All the inns except Gray's had a majority of Oxford men
among those of their students who had attended a university. The
large proportion of Cambridge men at Gray's Inn may be explained by
the fact that this inn was unique in attracting great numbers of its
students from the north and east of the country. There were also many
Irishmen at the inns of court; thus Trinity College, Dublin, was well
represented, especially at the Middle Temple.[26]

The statistics presented in Table 1.4 thus suggest that a considerable
number of parents living in Augustan England chose to give their sons

[22] Prest, *Inns of Court*, p. 129; only 2% of all students admitted to the inns of court
between 1688 and 1714 had previously attended an inn of chancery.
[23] e.g. *Diary of Dudley Ryder*, pp. 43–7; *DNB* xi. 144.
[24] N. Hans, *New Trends in Education in the 18th Century* (2nd edn., 1966), 24.
[25] Of students admitted to the inns of court between 1688 and 1714, 45.8%
originated in London and the home counties, the south west or the west midlands.
[26] Of all students admitted to the inns between 1688 and 1714, 10.9% came from
Ireland; 15% of all admissions to MT during these years were of Irishmen.

TABLE 1.4*a*. *Entrants to the inns of court (1688–1714) admitted to a university*[a]

University	Gray's Inn		Inner Temple		Lincoln's Inn		Middle Temple		Total	
	No.	%	No.	%	No.	%	No.	%	No.	%
Oxford	105	16.8	398	28.3	202	30.6	503	26.4	1208	26.3
Cambridge	130	20.9	187	13.3	83	12.6	239	12.5	639	13.9
Dublin	6	1.0	35	2.5	12	1.8	118	6.2	171	3.7
Total admitted to university	241	38.7	620	44.0	297	44.9	860	45.1	2018	43.9
No record of university admission	382	61.3	788	56.0	364	55.1	1047	54.9	2581	56.1
Total	623		1408		661		1907		4599	

TABLE 1.4*b*. *University record of entrants to the inns of court, 1688–1714*

	Gray's Inn		Inner Temple		Lincoln's Inn		Middle Temple		Total	
	No.	%	No.	%	No.	%	No.	%	No.	%
Degree[b]	41	6.6	113	8.0	43	6.5	189	9.9	386	8.4
No degree	200	32.1	507	36.0	254	38.4	671	35.2	1632	35.5
No record of university admission	382	61.3	788	56.0	364	55.1	1047	54.9	2581	56.1
Total	623		1408		661		1907		4599	

[a] Individuals were not necessarily formally matriculated at the university *before* they were admitted at an inn of court. It was advantageous to be admitted to one of the societies of law before departure from the university, or even, in some cases, before matriculation.

[b] Earned degrees only.

Sources: As in Table 1.2; also *Alumni Oxonienses*, ed. J. Foster (Oxford, 1887–92); *Alumni Cantabrigienses*, pt. 1, ed. J. and J. A. Venn (Cambridge, 1922–7); *Alumni Dublinenses*, ed. G. D. Burtchaell and T. U. Sadleir (2nd edn., Dublin, 1935).

an education which combined the benefits both of a university and an inn of court. Of those sons of peers, baronets, knights, and esquires who entered the inns between 1688 and 1714, 1,073, or about forty per year, were also alumni of a university.[27] Given the lack of any formal ties between the legal societies and the universities, this figure seems remarkable, especially when one considers that Oxford University itself received only forty-eight sons of this social group in 1686, and sixty in 1711.[28] Clearly, at a time when institutional education was becoming less popular among the social élite, such a programme of training was still preferred by many gentry families.

The parents of 'non-professional' students may have been encouraged to send their sons to the inns in order to acquire those social attributes which were easily picked up in the capital, but not adequately catered for at the universities.[29] Oxford and Cambridge, however, continued to provide that literary learning and elegance which were considered essential equipment for a gentleman 'of parts'. Thus a university followed by an inn of court may have offered a combination of both academic education and social accomplishment which satisfied the requirements of gentry parents. Moreover, the university could furnish those young men who intended to follow the common law with certain basic skills essential for practice at the bar.[30] Yet both 'professional' and 'amateur' students of the inns of court seemed to enjoy only a brief spell of college life. Many intending barristers remained at the university for no more than a year, and Table 1.4 demonstrates that the vast majority of students who went on to the inns from college left without a degree.[31] Further evidence that such an educational career was common is provided by the fact that two of the legal societies recognized the special relationship between them and the universities by allowing new members to continue at their colleges for a limited period after admission to the inn.[32]

[27] Using statistics derived from Table 1.5.

[28] Stone, 'Oxford Student Body', p. 93.

[29] See G. C. Brauer, *The Education of a Gentleman* (New York, 1959), 116–17, 120; Stone, 'Oxford Student Body', 49–50; *The Prose Writings of Jonathan Swift*, ed. H. Davies (Oxford, 1939–68), xii: *Irish Tracts, 1728–33*, 48–9.

[30] See below, pp. 93–5.

[31] See *The Autobiography of the Hon. Roger North*, ed. A. Jessopp (1887), 14–18; HCRO, Lawes-Wittewrongs MSS D/ELw F41, unfol.: James Wittewronge, personal accounts, 1672–93.

[32] e.g. GI, MS Admittance Book ii. 1321–4; LI, MS Black Book ix, fo. 292; ibid., MS Black Book x, fo. 62.

TABLE 1.5. *Correlation of social origins with university affiliation of entrants to the inns of court, 1688–1714 (totals for all four inns)*

Social origins	Oxford		Cambridge		Dublin		No record of university admission		Total
	No.	%	No.	%	No.	%	No.	%	
Peer	15	41.7	6	16.7	2	5.5	13	36.1	36
Knight/baronet	101	34.2	71	24.1	11	3.7	112	38.0	295
Esquire	498	28.8	268	15.5	101	5.8	859	49.8	1726
Gentleman	279	23.1	115	9.5	19	1.6	796	65.8	1209
Clerk	46	26.0	33	18.6	22	12.4	76	42.9	177
Lawyer	127	25.8	79	16.1	7	1.4	279	56.7	492
Doctor	16	33.3	8	16.7	1	2.1	23	47.9	48
Bourgeois	64	25.2	28	11.0	6	2.4	156	61.4	254
Total classified	1146		608		169		2314		4237
Unclassified and unknown	62		31		2		267		362

Definition of categories of social origin: See Table 1.2.
Sources: As in Table 1.4.

As Blackstone's remedy for improving the social quality of law students recognized, those men who attended both a university and an inn of court constituted the élite of the legal societies. Table 1.5 shows that students of the inns who had attended a university included over 60 per cent of the sons of peers, knights, and baronets, and half the sons of esquires. In contrast, two-thirds of the sons of 'mere' gentlemen and men of 'bourgeois' origins had not enjoyed the benefit of a university education.

Given the correlation of high social status with attendance at a university and an inn of court, a decline in the number of university men at the inns was likely to be a concomitant of any fall in the social quality of the student body. There is evidence that such a trend was already appearing half a century before Blackstone gave his first lectures at Oxford. At Lincoln's Inn, the number of university men admitted fell by over 15 per cent between the 1680s and the second decade of the eighteenth century.[33] Soon the benchers of the inns were

[33] Lucas, 'Collective Biography', p. 247.

providing various incentives for alumni of the universities to enter their societies. As we have seen, two of the inns, Gray's and Lincoln's Inn itself, allowed new members to remain at the university for a limited period after admission. Moreover, after 1711 at least three of the inns of court began calling a few university graduates to the bar *of grace*, thereby excusing them from certain qualifications normally required of those to be made barristers.[34] It is not clear if the benchers actually anticipated Blackstone, intending these favours as part of a deliberate policy designed to counter undesirable trends in the social origins of their students, but it is possible that they may have perceived an alteration in the quality of their recruits, even though the causes of this change were probably beyond their power to remedy or reverse. The most significant of these causes must now be considered.

3. EXPLANATIONS

Although the inns of court and the universities had certain features in common, and some 'overlap' of membership, it is necessary to emphasize the different social compositions of the two types of institution. Oxford and Cambridge were not entirely closed to those persons who did not have the necessary wealth to enter their sons as commoners or pensioners. 'Poor boys' might work their way through college as 'battlers', 'servitors', or 'sizars', or might even be fortunate enough to win a place on the foundation.[35] The inns of court were unable to make such dispensations for their students, because they did not enjoy the resources of the universities. The four inns were not corporations, and they possessed no lands or other endowed revenues.[36] Thus these societies were open only to those who could afford to pay their way. Indeed, the benchers took care to ensure that those persons admitted were able to support the cost of membership of an inn of

---

[34] GI, MS Book of Orders ii. 491, 505; LI, MS Black Book x, fo. 194; MT, MS Orders of Parliament H(8), 43, 47, 64, 89, 197, 204, 212, 232, 240, 285, 293, 303. From 1730 the 4 inns held joint conferences on the subject of qualifications required for call to the bar. These resulted in a common agreement of 1762. Dispensations to university graduates were discussed at these conferences, and were included in the final settlement (Richardson, *History of the Inns of Court*, pp. 313–14).

[35] At the end of the 17th cent., however, scholars' places were increasingly being taken up by students of less humble origins (G. V. Bennett, 'University, Society and Church, 1688–1714', in *The History of the University of Oxford, V: The Eighteenth Century*, ed. L. S. Sutherland and L. G. Mitchell (Oxford, 1986), 365–8).

[36] E. Chamberlayne, *Angliae Notitia*, pt. II. (1st edn., 1671), 418.

court, and they obliged new students to give bonds as a guarantee that they would fulfil their financial commitments to the house.[37]

In fact, the expenses incurred directly by students as a consequence of their membership of an inn were by no means prohibitive. The treasurer of the Middle Temple, writing in 1733, estimated the total sum a student might expend in the course of being called to the bar at only £25.14*s*.8*d*., excluding the cost of a chamber.[38] It was supernumerary expenses which accounted for the main burden of a young gentleman's outgoings at an inn of court. A member of one of these 'honourable societies' was not able to emulate the frugal life-style of a 'poor boy' at the university. Students of the inns, whatever their social origins, seemed to feel obliged to adopt the manners and mode of living commonly associated with English gentlemen. Jacob Wittewronge, for instance, a student of Lincoln's Inn between 1687 and 1693, employed a dancing and a fencing master, retained a personal servant, and ran up large bills at a tailor's shop.[39] Wittewronge may have been accustomed to this life-style, since he was the son of a gentleman, but even Dudley Ryder, the future chief justice and the son of a mere draper, spent some of his allowance on similar extracurricular activities.[40]

There is evidence that such incidental expenses were primarily responsible for the rise in the cost of maintaining a son at the inns of court which was apparent at the end of the seventeenth century. Twenty or thirty years previous to this, students entering the inns had been existing on comparatively modest sums. George Jeffreys was in receipt of only £50 a year when he was a student of the Inner Temple in the mid-1660s.[41] Francis North was allowed a similar sum when studying for the bar, and his brother Roger received £40 per annum in the early 1670s, although he did state that this was inadequate.[42] Thomas Molyneux, however, who was at Gray's Inn between 1685 and 1689, received £80 for each of his last three years, besides about £50

---

[37] e.g. GI, MS Orders ii. 43, 349; IT, MS Acts of Parliament 1665–87, fo. 116; LI, MS Black Book ix, fos. 117, 239; ibid., MS Black Book x, fos. 44, 124.

[38] *Master Worsley's Book*, pp. 209–10.

[39] HCRO, Lawes-Wittewronge MSS D/ELW F41, unfol.: James Wittewronge, personal accounts, 1672–93.

[40] *Diary of Dudley Ryder*, p. 190.

[41] G. W. Keeton, *Lord Chancellor Jeffreys and the Stuart Cause* (1965), 58.

[42] R. North, *The Lives of the Right Hon. Francis North, Baron Guilford; The Hon. Sir Dudley North; And the Hon. and Rev. Dr. John North*, ed. A. Jessopp (1890), i. 40; *Autobiography of Roger North*, pp. 18–19.

extra over the whole period for various extraordinary expenses.[43] Jacob Wittewronge's father expended about £70–80 annually in order to maintain his son at Lincoln's Inn.[44] By 1729 the expense of sending a son to the inns of court seemed to have risen still further. William Mellish, who entered Lincoln's Inn during that year, had been promised £120 per annum by his father, but he requested that he should have £150 in his first year, in order to cover initial expenses.[45]

Thus the annual expense incurred by students at the inns of court may have risen by 50–60 per cent between the 1660s and the end of the seventeenth century.[46] By the early eighteenth century the annual cost of sending a son to the legal societies from the provinces was probably roughly equivalent to that of maintaining a gentleman commoner at the university; that is, around £100 a year. Such a sum was clearly prohibitive for many parents, though it is extremely difficult to relate this level of expenditure directly to the income of different social groups during the later Stuart period, because these incomes were probably fluctuating under the impact of social and economic change.[47] Let us assume, however, that a parent would have to be in receipt of at least £400 a year in order to be able to spend £100 per annum on a single son. Gregory King estimated in 1688 that the most humble social groups able to command such an income were 'merchants and traders by sea' and those middling gentry he identified as 'esquires'. King believed that mere 'gentlemen' were only worth about £280 a year.[48] In fact, his estimates were probably too modest.[49] Edward Chamberlayne, for instance, had assessed the average income of esquires and gentlemen at £400 a year in 1669.[50] But even if we accept Chamberlayne's estimate, *and* also assume that gentry incomes were maintained up to 1700, there is no doubt that the most impoverished gentlemen might have some difficulty in finding the

[43] Guildford Muniment Room, Loseley MSS 1087/2/3/1: Thomas Molyneux, personal accounts, 1680–91.

[44] HCRO, Lawes-Wittewronge MSS D/ELW F41, unfol.

[45] University of Nottingham, Mellish of Hodsock MSS Me 165–104/18: William Mellish to Joseph Mellish, 21 June 1729.

[46] A similar rise in costs had taken place at Oxford (Stone, 'Oxford Student Body', p. 43; Bennett 'University, Society and Church', pp. 373–4).

[47] See below, pp. 29–30.

[48] See King's table of social ranks as printed in D. C. Coleman, *The Economy of England, 1450–1750* (Oxford, 1977), 6.

[49] G. Holmes, 'Gregory King and the Social Structure of Pre-Industrial England', *TRHS*, 5th ser., 27 (1977), 54.

[50] E. Chamberlayne, *Angliae Notitia* (1st edn., 1669), 486.

necessary cash to send their sons to the inns of court. Any deterioration in their financial position would be likely to place the legal societies out of reach of these 'mere' gentry.

Changes in the cost of maintaining a young man at the inns of court were clearly important, but other factors may have contributed towards the trends perceived in the student body of these societies. The most striking feature of the history of the inns during the later seventeenth century was the decline of legal education, and this may have encouraged numerical contraction, although it does not seem to account for the social changes which occurred.

Instruction in the law at the inns ceased during the Civil Wars and Interregnum, but attempts were made to revive it after the Restoration. These were ultimately unsuccessful. After 1684, no more public readings, or lectures, were given by the benchers of the inns of court. Some oral exercises were still being performed in the early eighteenth century, but these had become formal in character, and were not taken seriously by the students.[51] The coincidence between this decline in legal education and falling admissions at the inns would indicate some causal connection. According to Fig. 1.1, although declining rolls were in evidence as early as 1660, the most serious fall in numbers dates from the later 1680s, at a time when it was no doubt clear that the readings were finally extinct. But the link must not be made too firmly. Admissions to the inns had been high in the later 1650s, when they had provided no legal education at all. Moreover, although the legal societies did not offer serious instruction in the law after the Glorious Revolution, they continued to be centres for legal practitioners and students, and they were no less conveniently placed for attendance on the courts. No doubt individuals were still able to acquire a knowledge of law in chambers by private tuition and in conversation with other students. Prospective barristers, of course, still had to be called to the bar of an inn, and 'amateur' students were unlikely to be deterred from admission by any inadequacy of training for the profession.

With the exception of the decline of legal instruction, it is unlikely that changes within the inns of court themselves were responsible for the fall in total admissions to these societies. The explanation is more likely to lie in factors which affected society at large. Dr Prest, the historian of the inns during their 'golden age', has accepted the traditional argument that they suffered a gradual loss of their 'non-

---

[51] See ch. 4.2–3 below.

professional' students after 1660. He has explained this, in the main, by what he sees as a late seventeenth-century reaction against the enthusiasm for institutionalized learning which characterized the age of Elizabeth and the early Stuarts.[52] But, as we have seen, the departure of 'amateur' students from the inns should not be put too early; many were still being admitted between 1688 and 1714, and it is possible that a change in fashion from public education to private tuition with travel abroad has been given too great an emphasis. There is no evidence to show how many gentlemen were having their sons taught at home rather than sending them to the inns of court, but it must be clear that the trough in admissions which characterized the reigns of William and Anne cannot be attributed to the popularity of the Grand Tour, because foreign travel was virtually impossible during the war years of this period.

More positively, the aggregate decline of admissions to the inns parallels evidence of changes in the population history of England with a precision which defies coincidence. It has now been established beyond reasonable doubt that there was a major demographic crisis between 1650 and 1740 which affected the population in general and the landed élite in particular. Among the county élites investigated by Professor Lawrence Stone, for example, declining nuptiality, rising mortality, and reduced fertility in marriage led to frequent failures of the male line which eliminated many families: a comparison between owners of country houses born in the later sixteenth century and those born in the first half of the eighteenth shows that the proportion who died without leaving a son to succeed them increased from 25 per cent to a peak of 43 per cent among the later cohort. Such a contraction on the part of the principal source of the inns' clientele cannot have failed to make some impact on their rolls.[53]

However, the chronology of declining admissions to the inns suggests that England's involvement in continental war was even more important than the demographic crisis as a cause of falling rolls. According to Fig. 1.1, although the decline began before the accession of William and Mary, a deep depression in admissions coincided with

---

[52] Prest, *Inns of Court*, pp. 44–6; id., 'The English Bar, 1550–1700', in Prest (ed.), *Lawyers In Early Modern Europe and America*, p. 77.

[53] E. A. Wrigley and R. S. Schofield, *The Population History of England, 1541–1871* (1981), 162–70, 418, and pull-out 1; T. H. Hollingsworth, *The Demography of the British Peerage* (suppl. to *Population Studies*, 18: 1965), 71; B. G. Blackwood, *The Lancashire Gentry and the Great Rebellion, 1640–60* (Chetham Soc., 3rd ser., 15; 1978), 5, 160–2, and appendix 1; Stone and Stone, *Open Elite?*, pp. 87–104 and Table 3.7.

the long years of struggle against France which dominated the reigns of Anne and her predecessor. The influence of war upon levels of admissions to the legal societies may have been mediated via the burden of war taxation, as we shall see below, but it doubtless had a direct effect too. It is remarkable that Lincoln's Inn, which seems to have been the most 'inbred' and 'professional' of the four societies, was the only inn which manifested a rise in admissions between 1688 and 1714, rather than a decline.[54] This seems to suggest that the sons of lawyers and other students who were destined for the practising bar were not attracted by the opportunities opened to young men as a result of the continental conflict. It is possible that other young men, who were not committed to a legal career, forsook the inns of court for the more glamorous prospects of military or naval service, or for a job in the expanding civil service. Certainly, the opportunities in these fields were greater than ever before. Professor Holmes has drawn attention to a transformation in the service of the crown and of the state after 1680 which was largely a consequence of the demand created by the prosecution of war under William and Anne. In the civil sphere, a full-scale professional bureaucracy developed from the tiny civil service which had existed in the Restoration period. This provided secure careers for an army of public servants, especially in the revenue departments, the Treasury, the Admiralty, and the Navy Office.[55] Of course not all these new clerkships were of high status or remuneration, but opportunities for gentlemanly careers were multiplied because of the expansion and professional development which the armed services of the crown underwent during these years of conflict. The Navy became a better prospect as commissions increased in number and in social status, but, above all, the chance of a glittering career in the swelling officer corps of William and Marlborough's armies must have seduced many of the bolder and more restless young gentlemen from the drudgery of training for the bar.[56]

The wars of King William and Queen Anne no doubt also had a more oblique influence upon the rolls of the inns of court. This is best explained by taking a look at another aspect of the characteristics of the

---

[54] At LI an unusually large proportion of admissions and of calls to the bar were of sons of the legal profession (see Table 1.2 and Table 3.2). This house also attracted more *ad eundem* admissions than any other inn. Most of these migrants were 'professional' students and barristers moving to LI for a practising chamber. Cf. below, p. 68.

[55] Holmes, *Augustan England*, ch. 8.

[56] Ibid., ch. 9.

decline in admissions, and examining the changing regional origins of inns' students. Fig. 1.2 compares the regional origins of men admitted to the inns of court between 1688 and 1714 with the corresponding figures for the fifty years after 1589. As a bench-mark, it is to be noted that there had been an aggregate fall between the two periods of approximately 34 per cent in the number of persons entering the inns and who have been classified by their region of origin. Twelve areas surpassed this norm, in that their representatives at the inns had diminished in number by less than 20 per cent. Of these, no less than nine were located at a considerable distance from London: counties in the north and west of England, Wales, and Ireland. Areas which had

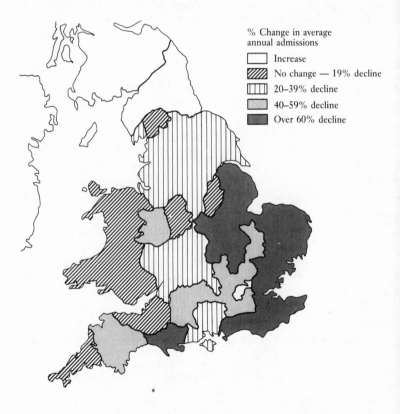

% Change in average annual admissions

- [ ] Increase
- [///] No change — 19% decline
- [|||] 20–39% decline
- [ ] 40–59% decline
- [■] Over 60% decline

FIGURE 1.2. Changes in the regional distribution of students admitted to the inns of court: comparing 1688–1714 with 1590–1639

actually increased their strength at the inns were Middlesex, Ireland, Cumberland, Durham, and Northumberland. On the other hand, eleven counties had experienced a disproportionately large fall in admissions to the inns. All these, with the exception of Dorset, were in the south and east of the country. Thus it appears that the areas which were closely identified with the falling admissions at the inns of court during the later Stuart period were distinguished by their proximity to the capital.

It is possible, then, to describe the changes in the student body at the inns of court with some precision. In social terms there was a marked decline in the number of gentry students, especially the sons of the lesser squires, and a certain limited increase in admissions from bourgeois and professional groups. In geographical terms admissions from counties relatively close to the metropolis fell off, a phenomenon which was only partially compensated for by an increased intake of students from more remote areas. Such features seem remarkably consistent with the thesis advanced forty years ago by Sir John Habbakuk. Habbakuk then maintained that economic difficulties bore heavily on the lesser landowners in England between 1680 and 1730, and many were forced to sell their estates. He identified the increasing burden of taxation, in the form of a grinding land tax imposed to finance the wars of 1689–97 and 1702–13, as the main cause of their problems.[57] This thesis has been modified in the light of subsequent research, but there is no reason to believe that it is not substantially true for those areas in the immediate proximity of the capital, where the land tax seems to have been assessed at a realistic rate.[58] If the lesser gentry in these areas were experiencing a decline in their

[57] H. J. Habakkuk, 'English Landownership, 1680–1740', *Econ. HR*, 10 (1939–40), 2–17. Sir John returned to the subject of landownership in his presidential addresses to the Royal Historical Society (id., 'The Rise and Fall of English Landed Families, 1600–1800', *TRHS*, 5th ser., 29 (1979), 187–207; 30 (1980), 199–221; 31 (1981), 195–217).

[58] B. A. Holderness, 'The English Land Market in the 18th Century: The Case of Lincolnshire', *Econ. HR*, 2nd ser., 27 (1974), 557–76; C. Clay, 'Marriage, Inheritance and the Rise of Large Estates in England, 1660–1815', *Econ. HR*, 2nd ser., 21 (1968), 503–18; id., 'Property Settlements, Financial Provision for the Family, and Sale of Land by the Greater Landowners, 1660–1790', *JBS* 21 (1981), 18–38; J. V. Beckett, 'English Landownership in the Later 17th and 18th Centuries: The Debate and the Problems', *Econ. HR*, 2nd ser., 30 (1977), 567–81. For a summary of the debate see W. A. Speck, *Stability and Strife: England, 1714–60* (1977), 70–4; and J. V. Beckett, 'The Pattern of Landownership in England and Wales, 1660–1880', *Econ. HR*, 2nd ser., 37 (1984), 1–22. For the uneven assessment of the land tax, see W. R. Ward, *The English Land Tax in the 18th Century* (Oxford, 1953), 7–8.

disposable incomes during the later Stuart period, then they would have found it difficult to bear the rising cost of sending their sons to the inns of court. It is reasonable, therefore, to suggest that a fall in the number of the mere squires as a result of land taxation was one of the primary causes of the changing character of the student body at the inns. Indeed, we may tentatively conclude that the decline in admissions to the inns is best explained by the consequences of war— in the form of new opportunities for employment and new fiscal pressures—which may have combined with the demographic crisis to cut a swathe through the rolls of the inns of court.

Thus it appears that the half-century which is the focus of this study may be regarded as a period of numerical depression and change at the inns, in spite of the enduring tendency for the social élite to admit their sons. Moreover, the scale of this decline does not fully appear from an analysis of admissions alone, because it is not certain that all, or even a majority of men who became members of the inns of court, ever attended their societies. In order to assess fully the nature of the transformation experienced by the inns during the Augustan period it is necessary to put flesh on the bones of this possible stage army, and as a first step we must turn to the question of residence.

2

RESIDENCE AND FINANCE
THE TRANSFORMATION OF THE INNS
OF COURT COMMUNITY

THE inns of court were not corporations in the strict legal sense, but they were corporate bodies in so far as they enjoyed a tradition of communal life, by which students and practising barristers were expected to reside and dine together during the four law terms. The benchers of the inns recognized that the maintenance of such a community was basic to the survival of their houses as societies in the true meaning of the word.[1] It is not clear if they had a broader understanding of the importance of regular association for the promotion of a common consciousness among the members of the English bar, but it is probable that professional solidarity was developed and ancient traditions were transmitted by lawyers living and dining together in chambers and halls. Any major decay in the inns of court community which accompanied the fall in admissions might therefore be important both for the inns and for the legal profession. Moreover, the inns' finances were especially vulnerable to institutional decay. Since the societies had no endowments, unlike the universities, they were entirely dependent upon income derived from the active participation of their members in collegiate life. If the residential community contracted too much, it might be impossible to support the expense involved in the maintenance and day to day running of the inns, and the ancient societies would be forced into liquidation.

This chapter measures the vital indices of communal life and finance at the inns of court in the later seventeenth and early eighteenth centuries and shows how the inns were confronted with a serious crisis of non-residence and insolvency. The first section traces the decline of chamber-ownership among students and barristers and the diminishing level of participation in 'commons', or communal dining in hall. Analysis of the inns' surviving accounts then demonstrates the disastrous financial consequences of this exodus on the part of

[1] *MTR* ii. 899.

their members and explains how the benchers only saved their
societies by countenancing the presence of non-members who were
prepared to pay for the privilege of residence. The concluding section
shows how, in this way, the inns of court were preserved through the
Augustan age and beyond at the cost of their transformation into
dormitories and places of business for a diverse community of
Londoners, often not connected with the law and its institutions.

I. RESIDENCE

As seen in the introduction, the four inns of court probably originated
as metropolitan hostels for the accommodation and provision of
counsellors during their termly attendance on the courts at Westminster.[2] This basic function endured as the societies assumed
additional professional and extra-professional roles in late medieval
and Tudor times. Indeed it was institutionalized in the form of
residential orders designed to encourage prospective barristers to
adopt the inns as a base for their future professional activities in
London. Throughout the period covered by this study candidates for
the bar were required to buy a chamber (or part of a chamber) in their
house and to 'continue in commons' for a certain number of terms.[3] In
other words, they were expected to acquire rooms for rest and the
conduct of business and to eat dinners and suppers in hall as part of
the common fellowship of the inn. But these orders were easily evaded,
and even the most committed law students did not flock to their inns
upon first becoming members. Dudley Ryder did not enter into
commons at the Middle Temple until three years after his admission
and, like Philip Yorke, the future lord chancellor, he only acquired a
chamber when he was on the point of being called to the bar.[4]
Moreover, members of the inns who were not committed to the bar
were not bound by any duties of residence. In fact it appears that many
young men who were admitted were simply taking an option on a legal
career which might or might not be taken up later. Like Robert
Walpole, who was admitted to Lincoln's Inn on 21 June 1697 (when he
was aged twenty-one), some of them never resided or played an active

[2] See above, pp. 2–3.
[3] For more details see App. I below and D. Lemmings, 'The Inns of Court and the
English Bar, 1680–1730' (Oxford Univ. D.Phil. thesis, 1986), 43–5.
[4] MT, MS Admissions 1695–1735, 205, 220, 264; ibid., MS Orders H(8), 70, 126;
Diary of Dudley Ryder, pp. 226–7. For evasion of residential qualifications upon call see
below pp. 39–41, 64–6.

role in the societies of which they were nominally members.[5] Given
this state of affairs, the adverse factors which caused the numerical
decline in the inns during the later Stuart period might have affected
residence—which implied a significant commitment of time and
money on the part of members—even more than they influenced
admissions. Sure enough, in his *Discourse on the Study of the Laws*,
written some time after 1709, Roger North described the inns as
'societies, which have the outward show, or pretence of collegiate
institution; yet in reality, nothing of that sort is now to be found in
them'.[6] North's comment raises important questions about the extent
to which students and barristers of the inns of court were active
members of their societies, and these issues have not been addressed
by modern historians. To correct this oversight the quantitative
evidence which relates to residence must now be considered.

The characteristics of the resident population (students, barristers,
and benchers 'in commons') are not easily defined. Dr Prest has said
that there was no uniform pattern of attendance at these societies over
the course of the year.[7] Rather, as Fig. 2.1 demonstrates, members

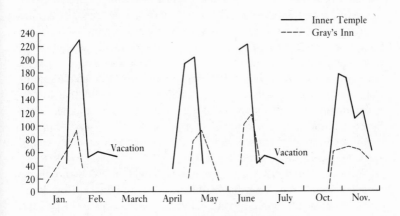

FIGURE 2.1. Attendance at commons in Gray's Inn, 1691, and at the
Inner Temple, 1683–4

drifted in and out of commons according to the dictates of their personal affairs. The peaks of attendance occurred, of course, during the middle of each of the four law terms of Hilary, Easter, Trinity, and Michaelmas. All these lasted approximately three weeks, apart from the last, which was nearly four weeks long. At these times practising barristers no doubt found it convenient to take meals in the common hall of their society, since they were attending the courts in Westminster Hall. Those students inclined to take a serious attitude to their studies also frequented the courts during terms, and were liable to take commons at the inns. When the common law courts closed and the terms ended, a few junior barristers and members below the bar stayed on for a strictly limited period over the vacation, as they were obliged to do by the rules of their houses.[8]

Those in commons were not necessarily present at meals in hall every day. Some were present for only a few days in each week; they were described as taking 'half commons'. Others might enjoy no more than an occasional meal or 'repast'. Dudley Ryder, after entering into commons, seems to have taken dinner or supper in the Middle Temple hall for three days during each week of the term.[9] Those statistics plotted in Fig. 2.1 represent the total number of persons at each inn who, like Ryder, were present in commons on several occasions, at least, in each of the weeks in question. It is doubtful if all of them were ever in attendance on any single day; thus a spot check would no doubt have revealed a lower figure. Bearing in mind that attendance figures were cumulative, the totals given for each inn show clearly that while a maximum of over 200 may have been regularly in commons at the Inner Temple for several weeks of 1683 and 1684, Gray's Inn hall rarely accommodated more than about 100 men during any week of 1691, and generally catered for less.

Thus, as with admissions, aggregate membership was by no means evenly spread across the four societies. Admissions to the Inner Temple averaged double the annual intake of students to Gray's Inn between 1680 and 1700; the former society also catered for approximately twice as many members at its communal meals.[10] If this relationship between admissions and the active population of each inn

---

[8] For junior barristers' obligations to keep vacations, see Lemmings, 'The Inns of Court and the English Bar', p. 55.

[9] Thus in June 1716 Ryder dined in commons on Monday 18 June and Tuesday 19 June, and supped in commons on Wednesday 20 June (TS Ryder Diary, pp. 280–2).

[10] See Fig. 1.1, above.

was also common to Lincoln's Inn and the Middle Temple, the bulk of the inns' community at the close of the seventeenth century must have centred on the Temple, leaving only relatively small groups of men who regularly attended Lincoln's Inn and Gray's Inn.

The surviving evidence about commons suggests that all the inns experienced a decline in active participation by members during the late Stuart and early Georgian periods, although Gray's Inn and Lincoln's Inn suffered the most. In May 1680 the benchers of Gray's Inn noted with consternation that 'commons are declining to the dishonor & great damage of the house'.[11] Worse was to follow. Fig. 2.2 shows that the communal life of this society continued to decay between 1688 and 1730, despite brief rallies in the late 1690s and the second decade of the eighteenth century. Attendance at the commons of the house had been halved by the end of this period, and even the bench table, despite its comforts and luxuries, had experienced a corresponding diminution in numbers.[12] Lincoln's Inn fared no better. As early as 1674 the benchers took action against twenty owners of chambers who had been absent from commons for a number of years.[13] In 1681 one Nicholas Wadsworth was deprived of his chamber

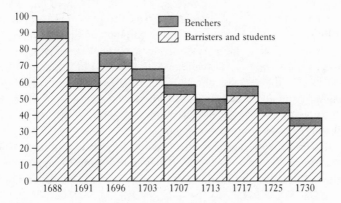

FIGURE 2.2. Average weekly attendance at commons in Gray's Inn, 1688–1730

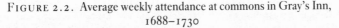

[11] GI, MS Orders ii. 189.
[12] On 8 Feb. 1717 a committee of the bench described the society as 'at present diminished' (ibid. 531). For absenteeism among benchers cf. MT, MS Orders H(8), 149.
[13] LI, MS Black Book ix, fos. 97, 99.

after an absence of eight years.[14] Such draconian measures were certainly lost on his fellows, for in November 1689 the steward petitioned for relief from the bench in compensation for his losses, their being 'but very few gent' in commons in the terme time'.[15]

At the Temple societies signs of a permanent reduction in attendance at commons did not appear until later, although these inns were seriously reduced by the end of the period. In 1708 the benchers of the Inner Temple remarked that there were 'few in commons', and attendance declined further as time passed.[16] Thirteen years later, in 1721, the chief cook of the society, like the steward of Lincoln's Inn, was forced to appeal for relief, arguing that 'of late years the Number of Gentlemen who constantly frequented Commons at the time when your Petitioner first had the Honour to serve your Mastershipps [Nov. 1706], is now very much diminished to his apparent prejudice and Loss.'[17] The Middle Temple was affected in a similar way. As early as October 1667 a committee of the bench had been ordered to look into the 'letts which are the cause of gentlemen not comeing into Commons' and two years later the porter of the society was instructed to present a list of the holders of chambers who *never* came into commons.[18] Things did not become really serious until the very end of the century, however. In February 1690 the bench of the Middle Temple took notice of 'the neglect of the Masters of the Bench to be in Commons that sometimes there have been but two or three masters at the Bench Table in the Terme time & sometimes none at all' and ten years later they complained of 'the small number of Commoners in the Hall in terme time whereby the society is discredited'.[19] Evidently, despite its relatively high level of admissions at the end of the seventeenth century, the Middle Temple, like the other inns, was severely afflicted by increasing non-residence.

This evidence of declining attendance at commons is of considerable significance. Chapter 1 suggested that the decline of admissions to Gray's Inn after the Restoration implies some diminution in the

[14] GI, MS Orders ii. fos. 201–2.

[15] Ibid., fo. 314. In Nov. 1700 the bench contemplated 'the Slender appearance of the Barristers as well as Students of this Society in Commons every Terme' (ibid., MS Black Book x, fo. 103).

[16] IT, MS Orders 1699–1714, fo. 77.

[17] Ibid., MS Orders 1715–33, fo. 30; ibid., MS Miscellanea iii (Letters and Papers of the Inn, 1700–25), fo. 95.

[18] MT, MS Orders E5, 118; ibid. 141. My italics.

[19] Ibid., 375, 473. Cf. ibid. 474.

number of 'non-professional' students entering the inns, although it was argued that the magnitude of this change should not be exaggerated.[20] While the early Stuart 'amateurs' probably had not made a long-term commitment to active participation in the activities of their inns, it is quite likely that they attended the commons of the house on those occasions when they were in London. The subsequent decline of commons may therefore suggest that the inns were more confined to serious law students under the later Stuarts. In order to test this hypothesis more thoroughly, however, it is necessary to identify the degree to which *committed* students and *barristers* were participating in the affairs of their societies, and to assess whether they were more or less involved than their predecessors of the age of Coke and Selden. For this, the evidence of chamber admissions may be adduced.

It is possible that the possession of a chamber was a genuine hallmark of the 'professional' inn student. Prospective barristers, after all, were supposed to enter into residence as a qualification for being called to the bar. Of those students admitted to the inns between 1688 and 1714 who went on to be called to the bar, nearly 75 per cent were at some stage formally admitted to a chamber in their own house.[21] Moreover, it appears that the majority of those who held chambers were actual or prospective members of the legal profession. Records survive which list the owners of chambers in the Inner Temple during the last few years of Queen Anne's reign and the first year of the Hanoverian monarchy. According to figures calculated from these sources, approximately two-thirds of these chambers were in the hands of benchers or barristers during the period.[22] Thus it appears that the *official* residents of this society were mainly lawyers or serious law students in the early eighteenth century.

But global evidence of admissions to chambers does not support the hypothesis that any decline in the active inns' community was a consequence of falling 'amateur' admissions alone. Rather it appears

[20] See above, ch. 1.1.

[21] Sources as in Table 1.2; also GI, MS Orders ii; *CITR* iii, iv; IT, MS General Account Books 1684–94, 1694–1702, 1702–10, 1710–18, 1719–25, 1725–31; LI, MS Black Books ix, x, xi; ibid., MS Red Books i, ii; MT, MS Orders E5, H(8); ibid., MS Admissions 1658–95; ibid., 1695–1735.

[22] In 1709–10 26 chambers were owned by benchers, 149 by barristers, and 85 by students. Corresponding figures for succeeding years were 1710–11: 26 benchers, 147 barristers, 91 students; 1712–13: 27 benchers, 150 barristers, 86 students; 1715: 28 benchers, 149 barristers, 72 students (IT, MS Miscellanea xxx (Chamber Books, 1709–60), fos. 1–7, 9–14, 16–22, 24–32).

that there was a *general* fall in the extent of active participation among members which applied to professional barristers and benchers, as well as to mere students of the inns. For if 'non-professional' students were less likely to take a chamber than young men who intended to study for the bar, any decline in their numbers should have led to an increase in the proportion of entrants to the inns who acquired the title to a set of rooms. In fact, according to Table 2.1, the proportion of those entering three of the inns who were admitted to a chamber was now smaller than it had been in the early seventeenth century, when the inns were at their peak as finishing schools for the gentry. And while these figures may be unreliable, analysis of the orders made by the inns' governing bodies shows that their barristers and benchers were indeed increasingly evading their obligations of residence.[23] In

TABLE 2.1. *Admissions to house and/or chambers of entrants to the inns of court, 1620–9 and 1688–1714*

Inn	1620–9					1688–1714				
	Chamber		No chamber		Total	Chamber		No chamber		Total
	No.	%	No.	%		No.	%	No.	%	
Gray's Inn	—		—		—	238	38.2	385	61.8	623
Inner Temple	183	43.5	238	56.5	421	339	24.1	1069	75.9	1408
Lincoln's Inn	208	47.2	233	52.8	441	212	32.1	449	67.9	661
Middle Temple	229	47.4	254	52.6	483	531	27.8	1376	72.2	1907

Sources: 1620–9: Prest, *Inns of Court*, p. 12; 1688–1714: as in Table 1.2 above; also GI, MS Orders ii; IT, MS General Account Books 1684–94, 1694–1702, 1702–10, 1710–18, 1719–25, 1725–31; LI, MS Red Books i, ii; MT, MS Admissions 1658–95; ibid. 1695–1735.

[23] The figure for admissions to chambers among LI students (1688–1714) is certainly an underestimate, because new buildings were constructed in the late 1690s, and the chamber records for these appear to be lost. Chamber records for the other inns during our period seem to be complete, but there is considerable doubt as to the reliability of these formal records, because it appears that subletting of chambers became increasingly common in the late 17th and early 18th cents. Thus some gentlemen who appear to have

January 1680 the bench of the Inner Temple complained that failures in the performance of legal exercises normally held during term and vacation were caused by 'such Members of the Society who haveing noe Chambers in the House (Contrary to Antient Rules and Orders of this Society) Doe upon their Call to the Barr immediately leave the Society and seldome appear in the house'.[24] In the event, their subsequent exhortations for barristers to lease chambers were relatively ineffectual. Table 2.2 shows that an increasing proportion of men called to the Inner Temple bar between 1690 and 1740 paid £20 in lieu of having a chamber in the house. Similarly, at the Middle Temple, by the 1730s it was common for prospective barristers to purchase only the formal title to a chamber by paying a small sum to the real proprietor. Thus qualified, newly called men generally surrendered their chambers immediately and departed the society.[25] Benchers were also quite likely to be non-resident; in the 1690s several Middle Temple barristers called to the bench were required to deposit £50 in the treasury to compensate for not having a chamber.[26] Lincoln's Inn had already ordered non-resident barristers to pay £100 in default upon promotion to the bench, and Gray's Inn felt obliged to

TABLE 2.2. *Inner Templars paying £20 in lieu of owning a chamber upon call to the bar, 1690–1740*

	1690–9		1700–9		1710–19		1720–9		1730–9	
	No.	%	No.	%	No.	%	No.	%	No.	%
Total called	156	100.0	150	100.0	118	100.0	144	100.0	130	100.0
Number paying £20	75	48.1	78	52.0	56	47.5	89	61.8	97	74.6

Source: IT MS General Account Books 1684–94, 1694–1702, 1702–10, 1710–18, 1719–25, 1725–31, 1732–7, 1737–42.

owned chambers may not have inhabited them, while others who were not formally admitted to a chamber may have, in fact, resided within the society. (For Serle's Court admission book see *LIBB* iii. 1, and for subletting see below, pp. 41, 50–2).

[24] IT, MS Acts 1665–87, fo. 102.
[25] *Master Worsley's Book*, pp. 210–12; for an example of such an arrangement, see Bodl., MS Rawlinson D. 862, fo. 25: bond in £200 to John Scrope of the Middle Temple esquire from Sir Thomas Rawlinson on behalf of his son Thomas, dated 17 May 1705; cf. *The Middle Temple Bench Book*, ed. A. R. Ingpen (1912), 38.
[26] MT, MS Orders E5, 375, 384–5, 387, 392, 436.

insist that no bencher would be qualified to assume the dignity of treasurer of the inn unless he had a chamber and resided in it during his year of office.[27]

The problem of non-residence on the part of *active* members of the legal profession seems to have been most acute at Lincoln's Inn. Faced with the failure of practising barristers to buy chambers and frequent commons, the benchers of this society resorted to drastic action. In October 1674 they resolved to prepare a list of these non-resident practisers, together with details of the courts which they attended, and to present it to those judges who were ex-members of the inn, with a request that they apply pressure to force these counsel to enter into residence.[28] These proceedings came to fruition in November 1675, when a special council of the society, which was attended by three judges, condemned 'those of the Bar that keepe noe chambers and residence in the House, nor continue in commons but practice abroad to the great disparagement of the profession and as well of the decay of Learning therein as of the Society itselfe'.[29] The defaulters were ordered to come into commons and buy chambers, or their names would be given to the presiding judges in their courts of practice, in order that they might be forbidden a voice in Westminster Hall or on circuit. Such draconian measures, if they were ever carried out, were obviously unsuccessful, because similar proceedings were initiated in 1677–8 and in 1690.[30] The problem was clearly beyond remedy.

The experience of Lincoln's Inn demonstrates conclusively that the phenomenon of decaying communal life at the inns of court cannot be attributed entirely to a diminution of 'non-professional' members of these societies. It is manifest that some practising barristers had also forsaken their societies as centres of residence and communal eating. Much of the professional life-blood of the inns seeped away with them, and they entered the Hanoverian period as pale shadows of their former selves. This reduced state of affairs is apparent from the perspective of proceedings at the bench tables of the eighteenth-century inns, where affairs were regulated by the principle of *laissez-faire*, as far as that was compatible with the ease of the benchers themselves. At the Middle Temple, for instance, Charles Worsley, treasurer of the inn for 1733, admitted that the benchers no longer concerned themselves as to whether chambers were inhabited by their

---

[27] LI, MS Black Book ix, fos. 188, 195; GI, MS Orders ii. 424.
[28] LI, MS Black Book ix, fo. 103.
[29] Ibid., fos. 118–19.   [30] Ibid., fos. 151–2, 159, 330.

owners or by others—who might even be strangers to the society—
and that subletting was tolerated on a considerable scale.[31] The
benchers of all the inns also signalled their acquiescence in the decline
of communal eating during these years: between 1710 and 1729
suppers were discontinued, and henceforth commons consisted of
dinner only.[32] At the same time the business of governing the societies
required less time and trouble than it had when they had been full of
students and barristers. Council meetings at Lincoln's Inn during the
1720s were almost entirely a matter of routine, consisting of
maintenance of the fabric of the house, admissions to chambers,
provision of commons, calls to the bar and bench, dispensations for
absence at the university, and the collection of duties.[33] Of course
these formalities did not require the presence of many masters of the
bench: it has been seen that absenteeism was very common among
benchers as well as barristers, and the principle of maintaining a
quorum was allowed to lapse. Indeed, the low ebb of life within the
inns of court during the early eighteenth century is symbolized by a
meeting of the Inner Temple bench which took place on 8 February
1724; for this 'parliament' consisted of only one bencher, who proceeded to attend to a single item of business before adjourning to
another day.[34]

In these circumstances membership of the bench naturally came to
be regarded as an investment for the private advantage and convenience
of senior members of the inns, rather than an obligation of service to
the society or to the legal profession generally. In reality, the inns of
court were no longer societies, and their role in the world inhabited by
professional lawyers was increasingly peripheral. Indeed, a place on
the governing body of an inn was now freely available to men who were
not even active members of the English bar. In 1717 the same Roger
North who complained of the decay of collegiate life at the inns wrote
to his nephew North Foley, a non-practising barrister of the Middle
Temple, and drew his attention to the benefits which would accrue to
Foley if he accepted his recent call to the bench. These consisted of a
free chamber, a perquisite of £100 if he served as treasurer, together
with 'some advantages in Eating, to say nothing of Walking like a

---

[31] *Master Worsley's Book*, p. 144; see below, pp. 50–2.
[32] GI, MS Orders ii, 517; IT, MS Orders 1715–33, fos. 79, 86–7; LI, MS Black
Book x, fo. 184; MT, MS Orders H(8), 223–4.
[33] LI, MS Black Book xi, *passim*.
[34] *CITR* iv. 106.

Magnifico In the Hall. If you have a prospect of spending any time In London, this may be a convenience. . .'[35]

On the admission of North himself, therefore, the corporate existence of the inns of court as collegiate societies where law students and English barristers found their institutional home had decayed to the point where the inns could be regarded as convenient and comfortable clubs for country gentlemen on visits to London. This was a transformation which had very important implications. It is true that the inns had suffered a measure of non-residence under Elizabeth and the early Stuarts, but the high cultural profile of their fellowship is a real testimony to the *esprit de corps* engendered among even 'amateur' students at that time.[36] Their successors, being less involved in the lives of their societies, were comparatively untouched by them: there is no evidence that any of the many laymen who were nominally members of the legal inns between 1680 and 1730 ever acknowledged any debt to their houses. More seriously, the professional lawyers who abandoned the inns as centres of residence and practice may have been equally unimpressed. Alan Brodrick, for example, later lord chancellor of Ireland, wrote in 1685: 'I hold myself so very little obliged by the Middle Temple that I owe the society no service.'[37] Barristers who did not participate actively in the affairs of their inns could not be expected to identify very closely with them, and the residential crisis thus represented a real loosening of the bonds between the Augustan bar and its institutional base. This alienation was an important development in the history of the bar, as the following chapters will show. For the moment, however, it is necessary to remain with the inns of court in order to assess the effects of this change on the financial affairs of the four societies.

2. FINANCIAL CRISIS

The decline of residence among members of the inns of court had serious financial consequences. The inns depended for their income on a significant proportion of their members owning and residing in chambers or attending the commons of the house. This income

[35] BL, Add. MSS 32501 (North Papers), fo. 142: Roger North to North Foley, 25 Nov. 1717.

[36] Prest, *Inns of Court*, pp. 12, 153–73; Richardson, *History of the Inns of Court*, pp. 211–44.

[37] Guildford Muniment Room, Midleton MSS 1248/1/197: Alan Brodrick to St. John Brodrick, 31 May 1685.

consisted of fines paid upon admissions to the house and to chambers, together with various duties or taxes (often appropriated for specific purposes), forfeitures upon failure to perform certain obligations of exercise or attendance, rents for commercial properties or officers' chambers, and 'caution money' paid upon call to the bench or bar.[38] Clearly, receipts from admissions to chambers would decline as the level of residence fell. Moreover, other heads of income were likely to diminish, for many of the duties on which the inns depended were directly linked to the possession of a chamber. 'Absent commons', for instance, the minimum charges made for commons, whether eaten or not, were mainly levied on the owners of chambers, because residents were especially expected to partake of communal meals. Similarly, dues exacted to pay the stipend of the preacher or minister were often connected with the possession of a chamber in the house.[39]

The inns' policy of linking income with residence was realistic, since it was most convenient to exact payment from students or barristers who were present within the house. But the system became highly problematic in conditions of extensive absenteeism. Not only would that large part of income which was linked to the possession of chambers decline as fewer fellows of the inns bought the lease of a set of rooms; even more seriously, *all* the components of normal income were likely to fall in fact, if not in theory, because prevailing non-attendance made collection of money difficult, even impossible. Thus it is hardly surprising that all the inns experienced a severe financial crisis in the later seventeenth and early eighteenth centuries. From the accounts of Gray's Inn and the Inner Temple, which have survived virtually intact for this period, it is possible to trace this in some detail.

Fig. 2.3 charts the aggregate income and expenditure of the Inner Temple for approximate five-year periods between 1685 and 1729, together with the balance remaining in the treasury at the end of each quinquennium. This society clearly experienced serious financial difficulties in these years, especially during the reigns of King William and Queen Anne, when the treasury was frequently empty. Income was very depressed down to 1704; other evidence shows that this was a consequence of diminishing participation in the life of the society on

[38] GI, MS Ledgers A, B; IT, MS General Account Books 1682–4, 1684–94, 1694–1702, 1702–10, 1710–18, 1719–25, 1725–31; *LIBB* iii, p. xv; *Master Worsley's Book*, pp. 136–40, 145–58.
[39] For absent or 'cast-in' commons see IT, MS Acts 1638–64, fo. 153; ibid., MS Acts 1665–87, fo. 143; LI, MS Black Book ix, fo. 160.

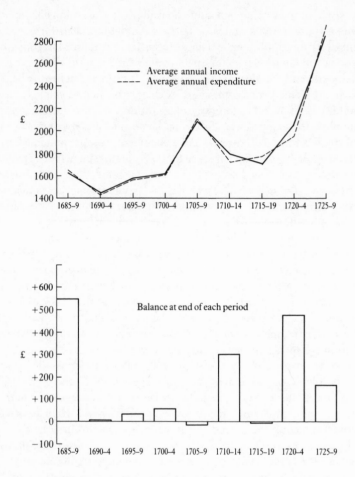

FIGURE 2.3. Inner Temple finance, 1685–1729

the part of the membership. In these years, receipts from purchases and renewals of chamber leases were low, while money due from students and barristers for absent commons and other duties levied upon owners of chambers went unpaid, with the result that large arrears accumulated: by Michaelmas term 1698 the house was owed over £1,321 in duties.[40] This failure of income meant that the benchers

[40] For chamber income see Lemmings, 'The Inns of Court and the English Bar, 1680–1730', p. 96. IT, MS Miscellanea vii, fo. 61; cf. ibid., MS Acts 1638–64, fos. 135,

were unable to meet normal expenditure. In July 1701 they complained that 'severall gentlemen of this Societye doe grow more and more remisse and negligent in payment of their Commons and other Dutyes by reason whereof the House is forced to run in debt to the severall tradesmen for the provisions and necessaryes'.[41] Three years later, faced with extra expenses for repairing the Temple church, and continuing debts which could not be defrayed out of current income, the bench was forced to take drastic action: restrictions were placed on the amount of wine consumed at the bench table, while sixteen of the benchers promised to subscribe £50 each, to be repaid as arrears came in.[42] In fact, this crisis marked the nadir of the Inner Temple's fortunes. Income revived somewhat after 1704 (although this improvement was neutralized by heavy expenditure in 1708–9 for building a library to house books bequeathed by William Petyt), and, despite further setbacks between 1715 and 1719, the finances of the inn had been placed on a firmer footing by the third decade of the eighteenth century, allowing moderate sums to be made available for investment after 1722.[43] The reasons for this recovery will be considered later; at present it is enough to note that the Inner Temple was brought to the point of insolvency by endemic non-residence, despite remaining one of the more popular societies. This implies that inns more seriously affected by depopulation might have suffered even more financially.

Gray's Inn was one of the two societies which bore the main burden of the general decline in admissions and residence at the inns of court under the later Stuarts. Appropriately, its accounts and other records reveal a crisis of insolvency deeper and more prolonged than that experienced by the Inner Temple. Fig. 2.4 traces the financial history of Gray's between 1680 and 1730: the diagrams for income, expenditure, and balance reflect the poor state of the society's finances from 1680 to 1700, and again between 1705 and 1720. Detailed analysis of the accounts show that these problems were largely a result

162; ibid., 1665–87, fos. 9, 61, 66, 76, 96, 109, 125, 141; ibid., MS Orders 1685–91, fos. 7, 43, 60, 110, 143; ibid., 1691–8, fos. 10, 34, 66, 68, 80, 93, 98, 123; ibid., 1699–1714, fos. 4, 12, 15, 22–3, 30, 38, 50, 65, 73, 85, 103; ibid., 1715–33, fos. 1, 20, 36, 44, 55, 62, 79, 96, 103.

[41] Ibid., 1699–1714, fo. 23.

[42] Ibid., MS Miscellanea iii, fos. 18–19; ibid., MS Orders 1699–1714, fos. 43–4, 46, 48; *CITR* iii, pp. lxxv–lxxvi, lxxviii, 386.

[43] IT, MS Orders 1699–1714, fos. 82–3; *CITR* iii, pp. xci–xcii, iv, p. ix. IT, MS Orders 1715–33, fos. 32, 39, 51, 61, 80, 106, 117; *CITR* iv, p. xxxv. At the audit of 19 Nov. 1731, the house held £1,000 South Sea annuities, £1,000 South Sea stock, and £2,000 Bank Stock (IT, MS General Account Book 1725–31, unpag.).

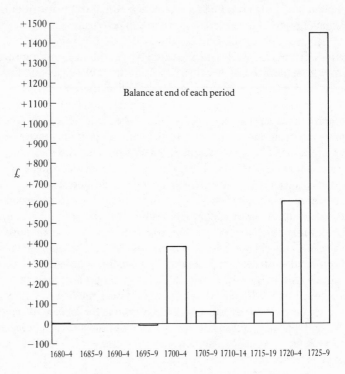

FIGURE 2.4. Gray's Inn finance, 1680–1729

of non-residence and non-attendance by the inn's members. Down to 1720, all the constituents of income which depended upon the membership's participation in the affairs of the society were in decline: fees derived from admissions to the house showed a steady secular drop, fines for admissions to chambers also fell, and even 'caution money', which consisted mainly of substantial sums paid by barristers in lieu of reading upon accepting call to the bench, declined sharply.[44] Members' duties were also not being paid, with the result that large arrears accumulated, such as a debt of £1,400 due to the house for paying the preacher in 1693.[45] The total income of the inn would have been lower if there had not been a rise in irregular receipts due to the sale of investments, together with increased revenue arising from absenteeism from commons and a rise in rents—most probably due to the letting of empty chambers to shopkeepers.[46] As it was, the failure of revenue had consequences which were serious enough, for the society became heavily indebted during the Restoration period, and these incumbrances remained for many years after the Revolution of 1688. By 1673 the house owed nearly £1,800 to tradesmen, workmen, the preacher, and its servants, and in 1690 and 1710 the bench took the drastic step of prohibiting the consumption of wine at the expense of the house until debts were paid off.[47] Some of the inn's financial difficulties were due to extraordinary expenses in the 1680s and 1690s for making repairs necessitated by fire damage and the decay of the chapel.[48] Declining expenditure after the turn of the century therefore made for some improvement, but the recovery was only temporary, and a small surplus which had been accumulated by 1705 was wiped out over the next four years, when disbursements regularly exceeded receipts. In 1716 a committee of the bench which was ordered to inquire into all aspects of the financial state of the inn concluded that, unless measures were taken to reduce expenditure and recover arrears, 'the Society in all probability must sink'.[49] However, like the Inner Temple, Gray's Inn survived the experience of depopulation, although recovery took longer. In 1721 another committee bemoaned 'the great Decay and Ruinous Condition of the Society', but income recovered in the early 1720s, and during the following years the house accumulated sufficient funds for the benchers to turn their attention to

[44] See Lemmings, 'The Inns of Court and the English Bar', p. 89.
[45] GI, MS Orders ii. 335; cf. ibid. i, fos. 542, 559, ii, 4–5, 15–16, 32, 34–6, 59, 64, 125, 164, 176, 233, 274, 295, 305, 331, 363, 386, 408, 432, 453, 473, 496, 514, 533, 555, 603, 675, 702.
[46] Lemmings, 'The Inns of Court and the English Bar', p. 89; for deposits and withdrawals from the Bank of England 1694–1709 see GI, MS Orders ii. 342, 354, 382, 389, 465; ibid., MS Ledger A, 359–97; for shops at the inns see below, pp. 56–7.
[47] GI, MS Ledger A, fo. 97; ibid., MS Orders ii. 238, 315, 478; *GIPB* ii, pp. xviii, 61.
[48] GI, MS Orders ii. 224, 231, 381–2; *GIPB* ii, pp. ix–x, xiii–xiv, 76, 393, 395; N. Luttrell, *A Brief Historical Relation of State Affairs from September 1678 to April 1714* (Oxford, 1857), i. 34, 294, 393.
[49] GI, MS Orders ii. 531.

'Repairing Secureing & Beautifying' their inn, and to invest in securities, as the Inner Temple had done.[50]

In the absence of full accounts, it is not possible to trace the financial history of the Middle Temple, or of Lincoln's Inn, with a similar amount of detail. Nevertheless, enough evidence survives to confirm the pattern of decline, crisis, and recovery which has been established for the other inns. The relationship between depopulation and insolvency can also be demonstrated by the contrast between these two societies. At the Middle Temple, the most popular of the Augustan inns, the benchers did suffer financial difficulties at the end of the seventeenth century, but their problems were less serious, and more easily overcome, than at the other houses. The difficulties experienced were not trivial. In the 1680s the steward was invariably owed at least £500 for commons, by 1700 these arrears had risen to over £900, and in 1733 Charles Worsley calculated that a total of nearly £7,000 was due to the house for duties and absent commons.[51] Moreover, this failure of income coincided with great expenditure to meet fire damage and natural decay in the late 1670s and 1680s, with the consequence that the inn was unable to meet its regular commitments.[52] In January 1680 a parliament of the Middle Temple acknowledged the fact that 'the house is much indebted by meanes of the late sad fire', and five years later several sums due to workmen for building work were added to the 'schedule of debts'.[53] The finances of the house improved during the 1690s, but in 1700 and 1701 it was still necessary to borrow money from the treasurer in anticipation of revenue to meet expenses, and money was taken up at interest for a similar purpose as late as 1709.[54] Nevertheless, only two years later the first regular account reveals that the house had a surplus of over £560 in the treasury, and a reasonable profit was achieved in the subsequent accounting years covered by this study.[55] By 1720 the treasury had a surplus of over

[50] GI, MS Orders ii. 593; ibid. 598, 621, 623, 627, 632, 635, 659, 673, 681, 689, 702; ibid., MS Orders iii. 1. The society was holding at least £800 in South Sea bonds by 1730.

[51] MT, MS Orders E5, 313, 315, 324, 329, 341, 345, 367, 412–13, 430, 438, 441, 469, 478, H(8), 33, 39, 49, 52–3, 71, 75, 83–4, 113, 192; *Master Worsley's Book*, p. 209.

[52] MT, MS Orders E5, 420; *CMTR* 179–84; *Lives of the Norths*, iii. 37–44; Luttrell, *Brief Relation*, i. 7–9; J. B. Williamson, *The History of the Temple*, London (1924), 517–19, 524–7; H. H. L. Bellot, *The Inner and Middle Temple* (1902), 224–7.

[53] MT, MS Orders E5, 292, 340, 343.

[54] Ibid. 473–4, 482, H(8), 32.

[55] *CMTR* 194–9, 201.

£1,300 and during this and the following years quite large sums were invested in money markets.[56]

Lincoln's Inn also had a surplus available for investment at this time, but, like Gray's Inn, this society was more seriously reduced by non-residence than the Temple inns, and it experienced financial problems which threatened its very survival. Arrears of duties amounted to nearly £1,400 in 1698 and over £1,800 in 1704.[57] These problems were compounded by large payments for repairs to the fabric of the inn at the end of the seventeenth century.[58] The coincidence of depressed revenue and high expenditure put the society constantly in debt between the Restoration and 1715. Indeed Lincoln's Inn was able to satisfy some of its creditors, and subsist, only because successive benchers were prepared to borrow money for the inn on their personal security throughout this period.[59] Already by 1697 the masters of the bench had been bound for a sum of £1,400 in all, and, as at Gray's Inn, drastic economics had to be made, for in 1700 it was ordered that one candle was to serve two nights in the hall.[60] As has been seen, Lincoln's Inn had money to spend by 1720, but its penurious circumstances persisted throughout the reign of Queen Anne. It is not certain that the house was free of its debts until 1718, when the accounts showed a healthy balance.[61]

Thus it is clear that all the inns of court went through a period of financial difficulty which coincided with their numerical contraction. The smallest societies barely survived to enjoy the benefits of Georgian prosperity. Yet survive and prosper they all did: in spite of continuing low admissions and a reduced level of corporate activity, each had augmented its income by the second decade of the eighteenth century, with the result that they had money available for investing in stocks and shares and for making improvements to their buildings and

[56] MT, MS Orders H(8), 140–1, 143–4, 173, 180–1, 208, 211, 230, 239, 243, 254, 263, 299, 311; *Master Worsley's Book*, p. 205. By the end of 1731 the house held £5,500 in South Sea annuities (*CMTR* 201).

[57] LI, MS Black Book x, fos. 72, 131. Cf. ibid., viii, fo. 719, ix, fos. 47, 65, 82, 97, 99, 282, 293, 310, x, fos. 72, 84, 87, 166, 179–80, 190, 222, xi. 26, 30, 322.

[58] Ibid. ix, fos. 124–5, 189, 235, 241–2, 244, 250, 282; *LIBB* iii. 154.

[59] LI, MS Black Book viii, fos. 702, 758, 772, ix, fos. 6, 9, 14, 30, 33, 38, 46–7, 56, 68, 79, 87, 256, 260, 262, 265–6, 273, 282, 298–9, 303, 323, x, fos. 14, 17, 20–1, 25, 32, 45, 55, 59–60, 71, 82, 103, 107, 131, 138, 140, 145, 147, 150, 190–1, 196, 213–14; *LIBB* iii. 61–2, 135–6, 154, 166–7, 198, 203, 210–11, 227, 242.

[60] LI, MS Black Book x, fos. 59, 103.

[61] *LIBB* iii. 251. By the end of 1721 LI held £500 South Sea bonds and £1,200 South Sea annuities (LI, MS Black Book xi. 74, 131, 198, 207, 211, 282, 286; *LIBB* iii. 267, 270).

walks. It is necessary now to account for this common recovery, and to examine the methods which the inns employed to escape the threat of liquidation.

The inns' only real financial assets were the premises they occupied, and they depended on revenue derived from those persons whose business obliged them to reside or regularly attend within their precincts. Income was failing in the later Stuart period because students and barristers—the 'official' membership of the inns—were drifting away; but their chambers remained, and there were others, not members of the societies, who were prepared to pay for the privilege of using them. In the past the inns had always resisted the incursion of non-members into empty rooms, but financial circumstances had reached such a pass by 1700 that they were forced to tolerate the presence—and accept the rents—of 'unofficial' residents. Indeed it is evident that the financial recovery of all the inns was founded on revenue derived ultimately from unofficial residents. At Gray's Inn, for instance, income picked up significantly after 1720.[62] This extra revenue consisted mainly of fines paid by members who were owners of chambers for renewing their leases, generally for periods of twenty-one years. Proprietors were taking advantage of special concessions offered by the bench, according to which the fines for renewal were considerably reduced on condition of payment (together with the duties owed on behalf of the chamber in question) within a certain time.[63] However, the proprietors were not resident in person, and this rush to settle dues and renew leases did not mark a revival of residence by members of the society. Many of the orders made by the bench for renewal of leases mention the fact that the chambers in question were inhabited by strangers. The fines for renewal were higher if the chambers in question were occupied by non-members.[64] For their owners, chambers in Gray's Inn thus became a reasonable financial investment because the bench now condoned subletting of chambers to alien residents. Subletting had already been on the increase for some years. An order made by the bench in 1660 prohibited gentlemen from buying up several rooms and farming them out to non-members.[65] The restriction cannot have been effective. In 1688 one Mr Dyose, a member of the society, owned eight chambers, and in 1704 Sir William Williams, the son of James II's solicitor-general,

[62] See Fig. 2.4.
[63] GI, MS Orders ii. 598–711 *passim*.
[64] e.g. ibid. 696–7.   [65] GI, MS Orders i, fo. 538.

possessed seven.[66] Given the abundant evidence of 'foreign' residents in these years, there can be no doubt that some of these rooms were let to strangers, though without sanction by the bench.[67] Then the bench ceased disapproving. In 1730 a fellow of the inn let a set of rooms to the commissioner for licensing hawkers and pedlars. The benchers objected: but they were concerned only because of the potential disturbance from the clients of this officer, not, apparently, because he was not a member of the house.[68] Thus, by the early eighteenth century, a climate had been created in which the letting of members' chambers to strangers was taken for granted. In consequence, the benchers' right to license chamber admissions once again became a valuable asset, which they exploited to repair their crippled finances.

In one way or another, all the inns resorted to the collection of revenue which ultimately derived from resident non-members.[69] From 1715 Lincoln's Inn raised money by allowing absentee owners of chambers to 'compound' for absent commons by paying half the duties owed on their chambers out of the receipts from the true occupiers. The early adoption of this practice at the Middle Temple may have helped that inn overcome the financial consequences of non-residence more easily than the other societies.[70] The Inner Temple, meanwhile, managed to augment its income from chambers after 1705 by selling rooms, which had devolved back to the house at the expiration of leases, at inflated prices; and even more revenue was raised in succeeding years through the device of allowing proprietors to purchase 'concurrent lives' on their chambers from the house.[71] In other words, this society, like Gray's Inn, encouraged owners of chambers to extend their leases; in this case by naming another life interest to succeed to their rooms after their death in exchange for a large fine. As the practice of subletting became acceptable to the benchers, members of the inns and others were no doubt prepared to spend large sums in these ways to acquire or retain chambers because they had become valuable as safe investments, even if they were not

[66] Ibid. ii. 280–1, 426. Cf. ibid. 702, for Robert Fairbard, who had owned 6 chambers before 1730.
[67] For strangers see below, s. 3.   [68] GI, MS Orders ii. 704, 711.
[69] For more details of the financial recovery of IT, LI, and MT see Lemmings, 'Inns of Court and the English Bar', pp. 92–8.
[70] LI, MS Black Book x, fos. 213, 215, 217, xi. 9 and *passim*; *LIBB* iii. 251–2, 254–5, 258, 267, 270, 281–2, 286–7; MT, MS Orders E5, 240; *Master Worsley's Book*, pp. 147–8.
[71] IT, MS General Account Books 1702–10, 1710–18, 1719–25, 1725–31; ibid., MS Orders 1699–1714, fos. 109–12; ibid. 1715–33, fos. 37–8, 42, 44.

needed as centres for residence and practice. In effect, by these means the governing bodies of the inns of court had found a way of taxing farmers of chambers within their houses, and had thereby overcome their problem of insolvency. Thus the inns weathered the storm, but their survival was not ensured without important consequences. By permitting members to sublet their chambers to whomsoever they pleased the benchers accepted the enduring presence of a motley collection of inhabitants who had no connection with the legal profession. The growing incursion of these strangers, and the partial transformation of the resident population of the inns of court from lawyers to laymen, will be considered in the final section of this chapter.

3. 'STRANGERS'

The population of London was continuing to expand throughout this period, and the capital was the acknowledged centre of political, economic, and social life. It is therefore not surprising that as the number of students and barristers resident at the inns of court diminished, vacant chambers became inhabited by a variety of people who desired office or residential accommodation in the metropolis, but were not formally members of the societies of law. The inns had always resisted the presence of an anonymous population of 'strangers' or 'foreigners', but the problem reached epidemic proportions as the 'official' residential communities of these societies contracted.[72]

All the inns found that their precincts had been invaded by large numbers of these unwelcome residents during the Interregnum, when the inns had been half-empty. In accordance with their standing orders, the benchers took steps to evict them after the Restoration, and this traditional policy was maintained until the end of the seventeenth century, although the inns' financial problems must have tempted them to accept any residents who could pay their way, and *laissez-faire* became the norm after 1700.[73] The Middle Temple, for instance, was much afflicted with unofficial residents during the 1670s. In 1671 a debtor was found to be sheltering himself from his creditors by lodging

---

[72] Prest, *Inns of Court*, p. 16; Richardson, *History of the Inns of Court*, pp. 298–9.

[73] For orders against strangers after the Restoration, see BL, MS Harleian 1912, fo. 242; GI, MS Orders ii. 15; *CITR* iii, p. lxxxviii; LI, MS Black Book viii, fos. 678, 690, 701, 713, 754; MT, MS Orders E5, 21, 25–6, 57, 59, 61, 77–8, 80, 117, 141–2.

in a chamber within the house, and in the following year several resident non-members were considered responsible for loss of property sustained by a fellow of the inn.[74] Some of the strangers were certainly a threat to persons as well as property, for in the same year one 'White' was found to have been lodging in another Middle Temple chamber, whence he had fled after committing a violent robbery in Lincoln's Inn Fields.[75] This individual troubled the house no longer, since he was summarily convicted and executed, but the other inns were also turning up many strangers at this time, some no doubt drawn from the many disreputable persons common to the area of London within which the societies were located. Thus, also in 1672, the benchers of Lincoln's Inn ordered three of their number to 'inquire and informe themselves what suspitious persons lie in this house and who keepe families here'.[76] A similar search was undertaken by the benchers of the Inner Temple in 1688, and action was subsequently taken to remove the non-members discovered.[77]

The position did not improve after the Revolution of 1688. Lincoln's Inn was especially troubled with the problem of unofficial residents during the 1690s, because a complete new square of chambers had been built in this society, and the new court was soon plagued by the presence of persons who were not admitted to the house.[78] Similar worries disturbed Gray's Inn, for in 1701 the bench complained that 'Scandalous and loose persons have Intruded into Divers Chambers of this House' and ordered them to depart or be turned out.[79] The Temple, by this time, seems to have been infested with all sorts of persons who were not involved in the practice or study of the law. Samuel Travers, a barrister of the Middle House, complained in 1694 that the bench had refused him permission to collaborate with a natural philosopher in chemical experiments they

---

[74] MT, MS Orders E5, 159, 161. The inns of court claimed immunity from arrest on behalf of everyone (members and non-members) as long as they were within their precincts. Ibid. 173.

[75] Ibid. 175.

[76] LI, MS Black Book ix, fo. 61.

[77] IT, MS Orders 1685–91, fos. 74–5. For other orders concerning strangers at the inns 1670–88 see ibid., MS Acts 1665–87, fos. 111, 124, 132, 135; ibid., MS Orders 1685–91, fo. 38; GI, MS Orders ii. 53, 67, 90, 122, 142–3, 159, 176, 218; LI, MS Black Book ix, fos. 122, 170, 173–4, 210, 217, 219, 224, 248, 286; MT, MS Orders E5, 163, 187, 324, 358.

[78] LI, MS Black Book x, fos. 26–30, 35, 41–2, 44–6, 52–4, 78–80, 86, 96–7, 104, 108, 110, 115, 119, 124–5, 130–1, 135, 177, 182.

[79] GI, MS Orders ii. 406.

had hoped to make in the cellar of his chamber. This man's complaint of injustice conjures up an unexpected picture of the legal inns at this date:

Tis hard that the Temple, which allows free egress and regress to all the dregs of mankind, where perriwig makers, shoemakers, brandy sellers, and fruiterers, keep open shops, should make difficulty of suffering a Member of the Society to receive visits from one of the most learned and ingenious mathematicians and philosophers in England; especially since among the known rules [i.e. precincts] of the Society, the very staircase where the dispute lies, has for many years harboured wives, misses, and costemongers.[80]

As Travers implied, it does appear that, by the end of the seventeenth century, the benchers of the inns of court were exercising a degree of discretion in their policy towards strangers, although they discriminated in a very different way from that suggested by the would-be scientist. After 1700 general searches for strangers initiated by the governing bodies of the legal societies became less common; when the inns took action, it was generally in response to the complaints of resident barristers and students. However, on the rare occasions when the benchers did order searches on their own initiative, their targets, if specifically defined, were 'lewd women', families, and representatives of the low life of the Holborn and Fleet Street area, rather than respectable men who conducted their affairs with prudence and decorum.[81] At Lincoln's Inn, it is significant that many of those persons who managed to obtain chambers in the new buildings, but were not members of the inn, were not summarily turned out of the house; instead they were offered the option of being admitted to the inn and thereby legitimizing their residence. These favoured strangers were by no means 'the dregs of mankind'; a list of twenty persons inhabiting the new court which was presented to the benchers of the society on 26 April 1695 included two 'Mr Harleys'— clearly Edward and his brother Robert, later Queen Anne's first minister. All were ordered to be admitted to the house before the next meeting of the bench.[82] In the case of Robert Harley, there was no sudden compliance: Speaker Harley was not admitted to the inn until

---

[80] HMC, *13th Report*, app. VI, 35–6: S[amuel] Travers to Sir G[eorge] Treby, 12 Sept. 1694. The natural philosopher was one Dr St. Clair, whom Travers described as a former assistant to Robert Boyle.

[81] GI, MS Orders ii. 558; IT, MS Orders 1699–1714, fos. 38, 44; LI, MS Black Book x, fos. 91, 199; MT, MS Orders E5, 502–3, H(8) 21, 26–7, 29–30, 68, 72, 188, 190–1.

[82] LI, MS Black Book x, fo. 41.

1701, but he continued to enjoy his chamber in the meantime, and certainly occupied it when he was in London.[83]

By the beginning of the eighteenth century, the inns of court were ready to abandon their long struggle to prevent non-members from taking up residence in their chambers. Financial pressures were forcing the benchers to accept a more heterogeneous resident population, although their tolerance continued to be limited by occupants' ability to pay. As long as chambers within the inns were inhabited by persons who were prepared to pay for the privilege of residence, it was possible for some of the money received to find its way into the coffers of the societies. Thus the inns discouraged inhabitants who were at the margins of Augustan society, for these persons were probably no more than mere squatters, who paid nothing for their accommodation. Bona fide subtenants, on the other hand, paid rent to the fellows of the inns who were their landlords, and this included sums to cover the duties payable to the house. Lincoln's Inn explicitly sanctioned this type of transaction in 1700, and it is evident that by this time the benchers of all the inns were prepared to tolerate the presence of men of means and good behaviour such as Robert Harley.[84] From 1695 the Middle Temple bench, when instructing the treasurer to act on information of strangers residing within the society, often allowed him to proceed against those 'as he shall see cause' rather than against all the offenders.[85] When the treasurer did act, the objects of his proceedings were of a different stamp from the likes of Harley: in 1704 a 'person of ill fame' was ordered to be removed and in 1711 a tradesman suffered a similar fate. Eleven years later the bench moved rapidly to evict a woman 'big with child' lest the infant become chargeable to the society.[86] Similar discrimination was in evidence at the Inner house, where, after 1695, orders prohibiting the residence of strangers included the qualification 'without leave of the treasurer'.[87] Gray's Inn was also applying double standards; while persons who brought 'Discreditt & Disreputation to the House' were proceeded against, some others were frankly tolerated, as has been seen, and in 1719 the bench of this society ordered non-members who inhabited chambers to pay duties and taxes as fellows of the inn did.[88]

[83] LI, MS Admissions x, fo. 73; HMC, *14th Report*, app. II, 579, 598: letters of 1696 and 1698 addressed to Harley at Serle's Court, LI, and 'New Buildings', LI.
[84] LI, MS Black Book x, fo. 103.
[85] MT, MS Orders E5, 429, 503.   [86] Ibid., H(8), 4, 40, 176.
[87] IT, MS Orders 1691–8, fos. 77, 81, 93; ibid. 1699–1714, fo. 18.
[88] GI, MS Orders ii. 555, 561, 581, 651, 679.

It is therefore clear that the post-1700 decline in the frequency of orders made by the benchers of the inns which prohibited strangers was not due to the fact that non-members had been wholly cleared out of their houses.[89] Rather it was a reflection of their enforced connivance—under the pressure of financial crisis—at a certain level of residence on the part of strangers, as long as they were of a suitable character and financial standing. There can be no doubt that non-members were still present in considerable numbers, right up until 1730 and beyond. In 1727 one Widdington Darby, who resided in the Inner Temple, was robbed and murdered. He was then identified as a clerk in the office of Sir George Cooke, prothonotary of the Court of Common Pleas (and a bencher) rather than a member of the house.[90] A later murder revealed unofficial residents of a different kind: an elderly widow and her two female servants, living in a garret chamber in the Inner house, were found dead in 1733. Subsequent proceedings revealed that the lady had resided in the chamber for nearly forty years, and discovered another widow who was also living in the Temple.[91]

The early eighteenth-century inns of court were clearly dangerous places, and it seems that the incursion of all and sundry into their chambers during this period was one of the causes of increasing insecurity, for, after any violent episode, the benchers of the Temple initiated new proceedings to exclude undesirable strangers.[92] But their efforts to discriminate among resident non-members were bound to fail. The inns became home or workplace to a diverse cross-section of London society. We have seen the extremes, from criminals to ministers of state. There were also common clerks, like Darby, and a wide selection of persons involved in trading activities. Shopkeepers were the most prominent of these; all the inns contained various shops which were let at a yearly rent throughout the period, and the steady rise in the rent-rolls of Gray's Inn and the Inner Temple suggests that their numbers multiplied as empty chambers were leased to tradesmen.[93] Gray's Inn had at least eleven shops within its precincts as early as 1668, and the Inner Temple contained at least twelve by 1700, including a milliner, a barber, and a watchmaker, while it also provided a home for the 'Rainbow coffee house'. By 1729 this inn had acquired

---

[89] *Contra CITR* iii, p. lxxxviii.
[90] IT, MS Orders 1715–33, fo. 65; *CITR* iv, pp. xix–xx; MT, MS Orders H(8), 268.
[91] IT, MS Orders 1715–33, fos. 127, 133; *CITR* iv. 571–7.
[92] IT, MS Orders 1699–1714, fo. 120; ibid. 1715–33, fo. 66; MT, MS Orders H(8), 68, 72, 268–9, 270–2, 278.
[93] See Lemmings, 'Inns of Court and the English Bar', pp. 89–90, 96.

a stationer and a bookseller, as well as another coffee house.[94] At Lincoln's Inn certain shops had been built as part of the fresh construction work carried out at the end of the seventeenth century, and in the 1720s the new square accommodated, among others, a pamphlet seller, at least two barbers, a saddler, a distiller, and a cork-cutter, together with a coffee house.[95] Meanwhile, the Middle Temple was certainly providing more house-room for tradesmen. In 1695 a formal complaint signed by some of the barristers and students of the society specifically accused the benchers of permitting shops and huts to be built, to the damage of the reputation of the inn. By 1733 this most commercial of inns contained no less than twenty-two shops, including several booksellers, stationers, barbers, a hatter, and a shoe-maker.[96]

The presence of a heterogeneous population of Londoners who were not connected with the administration of the law was the price which the benchers had to pay to ensure the continued existence of their societies. In the long term, the inns survived as professional institutions dedicated to the study and practice of the law, but for the moment, the fears expressed by the judges' orders for 1614, 1630, and 1664 had come true, and the inns had degenerated into *diversoria* rather than *hospitia* for lawyers and law students.[97] The benchers' compromises with respect to finance and residence had effected a transformation which represented a major decline in the inns' role as one of the controlling elements of the legal world. Other accommodations were being made at the same time which further reduced the significance of the inns and their customs for men who were committed to a career at the bar, as will be seen in the next chapter.

---

[94] BL, MS Harleian 1912, fos. 255–66; IT, MS Miscellanea vii (accounts and estimates of the inn), fo. 42; ibid. MS Orders 1715–33, fos. 85, 90.

[95] *LIBB* iii. 162, 202, 206, 263–4, 271. Cf. ibid. 3, 53, 69–71, 118, 122, 216, 220–1, 243, 266, 268, 270, 283, 294, 315–16.

[96] *Master Worsley's Book*, pp. 100–2, 148–153; MT, MS Orders E5, 417, 421–2.

[97] See W. Dugdale, *Origines Juridiciales* (2nd edn., 1680), 317, 320, 322.

3

THE QUANTITY AND 'QUALITY' OF BARRISTERS

DESPITE their difficulties, the inns of court continued, during this period, to enjoy a unique privilege. They alone were able to confer upon men the right of audience in the central courts of Westminster Hall, for from the end of the sixteenth century the call to the bar of an inn had been accepted by the judges as a basic qualification for pleading before them.[1] The inns had little control over the size of the practising bar itself, since this was governed mainly by market forces. Their monopoly access to it was a real asset, however. Furthermore, the formal status of a barrister carried some weight in English society, and may also have served as an entrée to various offices of a quasi-legal nature. It was not surprising, therefore, that the inns' right of admission to the bar came to be viewed as a marketable commodity at a time of numerical decline and financial crisis. Qualifications normally required of candidates could be commuted for monetary payment; and this in turn could increase admissions to a particular inn. This chapter traces the development of such strategies by analysing nearly 2,500 calls to the bar between 1680 and 1730; and outlines their consequences for the numerical and social profile of the body of barristers.

I. SUPPLY AND DEMAND

It is necessary first of all to examine the issue of legal numbers. Why did men want to acquire the status of barrister, and how many were being called at the inns during this period? The question of motive is not as simple as it seems because by no means every man called to the bar between 1680 and 1730 had the firm intention of practising in court. Admission to the bar served as a general qualification for a diversity of offices and activities in seventeenth- and eighteenth-

---

[1] Baker, 'Counsellors and Barristers', pp. 111–12; id., 'Solicitors and the Law of Maintenance', pp. 131–5; id., 'The Status of Barristers', *LQR* 85 (1969), 336–7.

century England.[2] There were many comfortable and lucrative berths in the legal bureaucracy which staffed the central and provincial courts, for instance: these were normally sold to the highest bidder, but the majority of prospective purchasers for places as prothonotories, masters in Chancery, or clerks of assize were men who had been called to the bar. Presumably, like Evan Christian, barrister at law, an applicant for the place of 'Register and Clerk' of the proposed Court of Conscience for Tower Hamlets in the later 1690s, their status rendered them 'sufficiently qualified for the said office'.[3] They would have been equally eligible for offices in the civil service, which provided another fertile field of opportunity for the non-practising or part-time barrister. The departments of state furnished positions for men like John Potenger, who purchased the comptrollership of the pipe in 1676 and was appointed secretary to the chancellor of the Exchequer in 1685; while the palace of Westminster had numerous parliamentary clerkships which were regularly occupied by barristers at law. Indeed, the prime place of clerk of the parliaments was practically monopolized by barristers between 1660 and 1740, including William Cowper, nephew of the lord chancellor, who enjoyed its profits and rights of patronage while a deputy performed his duties.[4]

The attractions of a bar gown as a means to gaining a place are clear. More puzzling is the motivation of other members of the inns, who were also called to the bar, but never practised, and never embarked upon an official career. Much has been said on the subject of the 'non-professional student': it is necessary now to consider the 'non-professional barrister'. As late as 1733, at a time when most commentators agree that the 'amateur' element of the inns' membership was reduced in size, the treasurer of the Middle Temple drew attention to the many sons of the gentry 'who take upon the degree of an utter Barrister without any design to practice the law'.[5] The motives

[2] For more details see Lemmings, 'The Inns of Court and the English Bar', pp. 100–2.

[3] KAO, Papillon MSS U101/034/2, 6: papers concerned with prospective courts of conscience for Southwark, Westminster, Tower Hamlets, and Middlesex out-parishes.

[4] *Private Memoirs of John Potenger Esq. . .*, ed. C. W. Bingham (1841), 39–42, 58–61; Sir John Sainty, *The Parliament Office in the 17th and 18th Centuries* (House of Lords Record Office, 1977), 4–10; M. F. Bond, 'Clerks of the Parliaments, 1509–1953', *EHR* 78 (1958), 78–85; HCRO Panshanger MSS D/EP F220, *passim*: papers relating to the office of clerk of the parliaments [1691]– *c.*1723; BL, Add. MSS 35586 (Hardwicke Papers), fos. 139–43: petition of William Cowper with notes of precedents in the grant of the office, 29 Nov. 1738.

[5] *Master Worsley's Book*, p. 118.

which impelled non-professional students to enter the inns are by no means obscure, but it is not evident why they should have taken the trouble to be called to the bar.[6] It does appear that some degree of prestige was a concomitant of a barrister's robe, however, for in February 1685 the bench of Gray's Inn made the following order: 'Ordered that Sir Charles Crofts Read a Knight of an ample Estate and haveing been Long a Member of this Society declareing he doth [not] intend the practice of the Law but to Receive the Honour of the Barr be of Grace Only Called to the Barr. . .'[7] No doubt country gentlemen such as Sir Charles enjoyed greater authority on the local bench as a result of having the status of a barrister at law. In fact this knight was probably no lawyer: calls of grace were made in order to dispense with some qualification normally demanded of a candidate for the bar, usually either seniority or residence and legal exercise, and as Sir Charles was of long standing he was almost certainly a non-resident who had never studied the law seriously.[8] This case would be of little significance, were it not for the fact that such dispensations seem to have been more common during the later seventeenth century, and certain characteristics of the calls suggest that there was an increase in the number of 'non-professional' barristers. The existence of a market for the inns' degree among the gentry should be kept in mind as the supply of barristers during this period is considered.

The various attractions of a call to the bar were, it seems, at their peak during the late Interregnum and Restoration period, when an average of about sixty-five men became barristers in the course of each year.[9] According to Fig. 3.1, from the mid-1680s and especially during the reign of William III, the number of calls tended to fall away, declining to a trough of around forty to fifty on average, which was maintained for each year between 1700 and the third decade of the eighteenth century. However, at the end of the period covered by this study the post-war rise in admissions was beginning to apply some stimulus to the levels of calls to the bar, although their number did not regain the peaks of the 1680s, and, given the mid-eighteenth century depression in admissions, it must be doubted whether this recovery

---

[6] For amateur students see above p. 20.

[7] GI, MS Orders ii. 237; cf. IT, MS Miscellanea ii, fo. 49.

[8] He had been admitted on 1 July 1671, when he was approximately 19 years of age, and had already inherited his father's estate at Bardwell, Essex. He died in 1690, aged 38, and was buried in the parish church at Bardwell (*GI Adm. Reg.*, 312; J. Le Neve, *Monumenta Anglicana 1650–1718* (1719), 166).

[9] Prest, 'English Bar, 1550–1700', pp. 66–8.

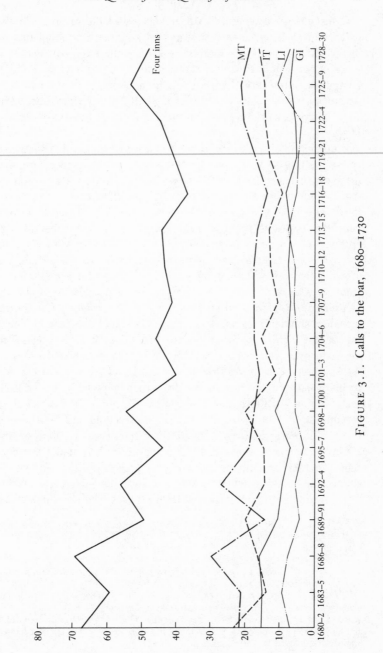

FIGURE 3.1. Calls to the bar, 1680–1730

was sustained.[10] Taking a broad perspective of the seventeenth and early eighteenth centuries, it appears that, after reaching a high plateau in the last years of the Commonwealth and the reign of Charles II, levels of admissions to the bar returned to a point not so very different from those of the early Stuart period, for an average of forty-nine men became barristers every year during the half-century after 1680, while about forty-six had been called to the bar annually between 1590 and 1639.[11]

Students admitted to the inns of court were unevenly distributed across the individual societies, and it is not surprising, therefore, that those who became barristers were not drawn in equal proportions from the four inns. The two Temples, which together received over two-thirds of all the young men who were formally admitted to an inn between 1688 and 1714, also created the greatest number of barristers, providing nearly 70 per cent of all students who acquired the right to wear a bar gown between 1680 and 1730.[12] But there was less of a distinction between the societies in terms of the proportion of students who went on to be called, for at each house around one-quarter of those admitted eventually became barristers.[13] One of the inns does stand out from its sister houses in another respect: at Gray's Inn and the Temple societies, the numbers of new barristers tended to fluctuate over the years, especially during the last two decades of the seventeenth century. In contrast, the benchers of Lincoln's Inn regularly called an average of only five or ten students to the bar each year for most of the period covered by this study. This suggests a certainty and stability on the part of the students and benchers of Lincoln's Inn which were remarkably unaffected by external pressures.

Given the complex of forces which may have determined numbers called to the bar, any explanation of aggregate calls is necessarily an exercise in speculation. Historians have tended to concentrate upon the market for professional legal services when discussing this

[10] See Fig. 1.1. The statistics plotted in Fig. 3.1 are broadly in agreement with those in Holmes, *Augustan England*, pp. 137, 288–9, and id., 'The Professions and Social Change in England, 1680–1730', *PBA* 65 (1979), 325.

[11] There were 2,505 recorded bar calls 1680–1730 (exclusions as in Fig. 3.1), or an average of 49.1 per year. For calls 1590–1639 see Prest, *Rise of the Barristers*, p. 7.

[12] IT made 756 calls and MT 973 1680–1730.

[13] Taking all men admitted 1688–1714 (exclusions as above, ch. 1, n. 2), and identifying those called (including those who migrated to another inn for call), 172 were called of 623 admitted to GI, 338 of 1,408 admitted to IT, 158 of 661 admitted to LI, and 474 of 1,907 admitted to MT. Thus 1,142 were called out of 4,599 admitted originally (sources as in Table 3.2 below).

question.[14] However, the existence of a non-professional market for the status of barrister, and the fact that the benchers of the inns of court determined the qualifications necessary for call, must also be borne in mind. Students who did not intend to practise might be induced to become barristers in name only by relaxing these qualifications, or dispensing with them in exchange for extra fees. Thus it is appropriate to turn to the conventions which the benchers applied in the making of barristers as a means of accounting for the numerical trends observed.

2. QUALIFICATIONS

It was not until the late seventeenth century that the inns achieved independence from external control in their choice of barristers. Between 1557 and 1664 a series of orders were issued for the government of the inns of court and chancery by the crown or its nominees, the Privy Council and judges.[15] Several of these sought to impose conditions on the number and qualifications of men called to the bar.[16] However, the last set of these ordinances was promulgated soon after the Restoration, and after 1689 the inns enjoyed almost absolute freedom of action, although subject to external interference in particular cases.

Appendix I lists the qualifications which each inn prescribed for the assumption of a barrister's robe, together with those laid down by the orders of 1664 and statutory obligations. The inns' conditions centred upon seniority, residence, and the performance of legal exercises: the other requirements were no more than formalities. In the first place, every candidate for the bar was expected to have achieved a minimum 'standing', or 'continuance' in terms of years elapsed since his admission to the house. This was generally stated as seven years, although the Middle Temple prescribed six years during the 1680s and again in the early eighteenth century. At least three of the inns were prepared to count up to two years spent at an inn of chancery towards the standing required for the bar. Secondly, as has been seen, prospective barristers were required to fulfil certain conditions of residence: they should have eaten a minimum number of meals in the

[14] Holmes, 'Professions', p. 326; id., *Augustan England*, p. 130; Prest, 'English Bar, 1550–1700', pp. 77–8.
[15] Richardson, *History of the Inns of Court*, pp. 433–53.
[16] See orders of 1574, 1594, 1596, 1614, 1630, and 1664 (ibid. 436–453).

hall of their society with their fellow students and barristers, and were required to be admitted to a chamber within the house. Besides maintaining the inns' community generally and supporting the finances of the societies, these residential provisos were designed to provide a nucleus of junior and senior members to engage in exercises of legal learning; for the performance of a number of these was another qualification prescribed for admission to the bar. The requirements about exercises varied considerably from society to society and were often altered, especially at the Temple inns, during the later seventeenth century. The profusion and variety of orders on this subject reflected the condition of legal education in this period of change and confusion.

The inns' formal requirements for call to the bar were not much less strict than those which had applied in the early seventeenth century.[17] But there was a considerable discrepancy between the benchers' official policy and the conventions they applied in actually admitting students to the bar. In fact, any of the conditions listed in Appendix I might be dispensed with to the advantage of individual candidates; and calls 'by favour of the bench' became very common after the Restoration. Gray's Inn and the two Temples partially institutionalized this practice in the form of calls described as 'of grace' in the records, by which the beneficiaries received a general dispensation from formal qualifications which they lacked. Between 1680 and 1730 around 15 per cent of all students called at Gray's and the Middle Temple were favoured in this way.[18] Unfortunately most *ex gratia* calls do not give reasons for the benchers' generosity, but all the inns made some special calls which explain the circumstances in which they were prepared to exercise discretion. These fell into two groups. First, the inns accepted the influence of patronage, generally in the form of premature calls of benchers' relatives, or of calls made on the recommendation of judges.[19] Judicial recommendations were often

---

[17] Comparing App. I with Prest, *Inns of Court*, p. 54.

[18] Calls of grace at IT cannot be quantified because *CITR* does not distinguish these calls, and the MS Acts of Parliament are not available for 1688–1730.

[19] GI, MS Orders ii. 88, 153, 286, 288; MT, MS Orders E5, 349, H(8), 60; Downing, *Observations on the Middle Temple*, p. 79. At IT special admissions were reserved for sons of benchers and ex-benchers and these conferred exemption from obligations of attendance at commons (see App. I). GI, MS Orders ii. 217, 222, 226, 239, 251, 276, 287, 291, 299, 323, 326, 333, 343, 380, 553, 635, 668, 671, 681, 686, 705; IT, MS Orders 1685–91, fo. 35; LI, MS Black Book ix, fos. 31, 105–6, 140, xi. 45; MT, MS Orders E5, 346, 369, 415, 434, 443, 451, 504, H(8), 160, 165, 174, 193, 197, 211, 214, 228, 250, 303, 311.

made at the behest of laymen: the future lord chancellor Peter King, for example, was called in 1698 after his patron John Locke had moved Sir George Treby, lord chief justice of Common Pleas, on his behalf.[20] Non-lawyers were not normally allowed to interfere directly in the creation of barristers, however, although the benchers accepted James II's nomination of several catholic barristers.[21] Secondly, the inns acknowledged special circumstances or qualifications as reasons for dispensation. Several men were called prematurely upon their departure to practise abroad or in Ireland, and some university graduates were also exempted from the rules.[22] Students fortunate enough to secure one of the offices in the legal bureaucracy could count upon being made barristers by virtue of their appointment, if they had not been admitted to the bar already. Thus Edward Walpole, master of the Exchequer Office of Pleas, was excused his want of standing and his non-performance of exercises and duly called to the bar at Lincoln's Inn on 6 November 1727.[23]

The benchers were prepared to acknowledge dispensations given in response to patronage which derived from the legal profession or as a recognition of special circumstances. No doubt these were regarded as legitimate reasons for the exercise of discretion, for there were long-established precedents for such practices.[24] Most dispensations made during this period, however, were not acknowledged in the records of the inns. In particular, the legal societies rarely recorded payments made in commutation of qualifications demanded for the bar, although these had become common by the early eighteenth century, at least. An early example of this procedure was recorded at the Inner Temple in 1700, when the bench declared: 'all Gentlemen that shall be presented to the Table for Call of Grace this Terme or any terme hereafter shall pay over and above all other Dutyes into the Treasury of this house the Summe of one pound & tenn shillings from each

---

[20] *The Correspondence of John Locke*, ed. E. S. De Beer (Oxford, 1976–82), vi. 400–1: Locke to [Sir George Treby], 17 May 1698.

[21] LI, MS Black Book viii, fo. 688. The king nominated 8 at GI, 1 at IT, and 6 at LI (GI, MS Orders ii. 256, 260; IT, MS Orders 1685–91, fo. 47; LI, MS Black Book ix, fos. 277, 279, 291, 300, 302; *CITR* iii. 240, 243; Luttrell, *Brief Relation*, i. 388).

[22] GI, MS Orders ii. 215, 514; IT, MS Orders 1685–91, fos. 43, 47; LI, MS Black Book viii, fo. 672, ix, fo. 214, x, fos. 45, 70, 105, xi. 21; MT, MS Orders H(8), 181–2, 264; *CITR* iii. 240–3, 330. For graduates' dispensations see p. 22 above.

[23] LI, MS Black Book xi. 288; cf. ibid., MS Black Book ix, fos. 67, 105, 180; GI, MS Orders ii. 68, 323, 360, 506, 553.

[24] Prest, *Inns of Court*, pp. 56–8.

terme they want in Commons. . .'[25] It is unlikely that this was the first occurrence of such a practice, although the inns generally did not become more open in their acceptance of money in lieu of qualifications for the bar until a few more years had elapsed. On 6 November 1722 William Martin was called to the bar of Lincoln's Inn, having paid £10 in commutation for not performing exercises. A week later John Attwood was also called, having given £15 to compensate for his lack of standing.[26] In the following year the bench of Gray's Inn ordered that the twenty guineas which had been received from Daniel Dolins as an acknowledgement of their favour in calling him to the bar three years earlier should be spent on books for the library; they went on to make a general order that every gentleman called *ex gratia* for want of full standing in future should pay £20 above all other duties.[27] The Middle Temple, meanwhile, had called John Turton to the bar on 3 June 1709, when he was recorded as 'paying' for two exercises, and Lancelot Carr also paid for an exercise which he should have performed at New Inn when he was admitted to the bar of this house in 1710.[28] By 1733 it had long been accepted that fines imposed for failure in carrying out legal exercises at the Middle Temple were not merely looked upon as a punishment for neglect; on the contrary, once the fine was paid, the exercise was counted as over.[29] Obligations of residence were also evaded, as was seen, by the nominal purchase of a formal title to a chamber.[30] By the mid-eighteenth century students of the Middle Temple were able to fulfil practically any of the conditions prescribed for call to the bar by means of a monetary payment, and there is no reason to believe that they were unique in this respect.[31]

It is not possible to assess the full effect these dispensations had in reducing the general requirements for admission to the bar, since there is not complete information on the number of exercises performed, or time spent in commons, for every new barrister. The standing or 'continuance' of men called to the bar between 1680 and 1730 can be tested more precisely. As has been seen, seven years' standing (i.e. statutory membership), was the prescribed continuance required for being called at all the inns, with the exception of the

---

[25] IT, MS Orders 1699–1714, fo. 19; cf. ibid., MS Miscellanea xxix, fo. 11.

[26] LI, MS Black Book xi. 148.   [27] GI, MS Orders ii. 623.

[28] MT, MS Orders H(8), 34, 38.

[29] *Master Worsley's Book*, p. 136. An order of 29 Apr. 1726 enjoined the performance of the 'candle exercise' *or* the payment of a 40s. fine, as an essential qualification for the bar (MT, MS Orders H(8), 245).

[30] See above, p. 39.   [31] *Master Worsley's Book*, pp. 209–10.

Middle Temple, which stipulated six years' standing at various times. In order to assess how far these rules were observed, the dates of admission and call were compared for every student who became a barrister during the period, and their calls classified as 'premature' or 'regular', according to the elapsed time in each case. The results are shown in Table 3.1. Since men were not always sworn formally as barristers immediately upon declaration of their call by the bench, six months are allowed for 'publication' of the call, and 'premature' admission to the bar is defined as any call which took place six and a half or less years after admission.

According to statistics presented by Dr Prest, less than 13 per cent of a sample of barristers called between 1590 and 1639 were called prematurely.[32] However, by 1680–5 early calls were already accounting for over 20 per cent of the total admissions to the bar. If it is assumed that the earlier figure for 'immature' barristers is inflated, because Dr Prest's statistics do not take account of the time which elapsed between call and 'publication', it seems reasonable to conclude that there had been a marked increase in the number of dispensations from the formal requirements for seniority since the early seventeenth century. Moreover, as time passed, there is no doubt that the proportion of premature calls increased still further, for after 1703 they never accounted for less than 30 per cent of the total, and, by the end of the period, a *majority* of men were being called to the bar within six and a half years of first entry into their houses. Over the whole period, at each of the inns the median continuance of new barristers declined from around seven years in 1680 to six years or less in 1730.[33] The significance of this deserves emphasis: by the mid-eighteenth century, not only were many calls taking place a year before their recipients had achieved the *minimum* standing required for the bar, but as many new barristers had not even accumulated six years' continuance as were of greater seniority. It is no wonder that the benchers of the four inns began a series of conferences in 1729–30 with the aim of agreeing on a new set of qualifications for call.[34] The distinction between official

[32] Of a sample of 278 calls classified by continuance 35 were premature (Prest, *Inns of Court*, p. 55).

[33] Median continuance of students called at each inn 1680 and 1730 as follows: GI: 7.5 years in 1680, 5.2 years in 1730; IT: 7.3 years in 1680, 6.3 years in 1730: LI: 7.0 years in 1680, 6.0 years in 1730; MT: 7.0 years in 1680, 6.2 years in 1730 (sources as in Table 3.1).

[34] GI, MS Orders ii. 709, 711, iii. 26; IT, MS Orders 1715–33, fos. 103, 110, 129–30; ibid., MS Miscellanea xxiv, fos. 117–18; LI, MS Black Book xi. 364; MT, MS

demand and actual performance was thus significant at the Augustan inns of court.

It seems likely that the two Temples, especially the Middle house, had made significant accommodations before 1680 in regard to continuance. At each, the number of early calls fluctuated, but showed a persistent increase. Gray's Inn, on the other hand, maintained fairly strict standards of continuance until the second decade of the eighteenth century, when it appears that a decision was taken to call students at an earlier stage. This step was deferred longer at Lincoln's Inn: apart from barristers created at the behest of James II, there were very few premature calls before 1724, when the bench declared publicly that they would in future be prepared to dispense with up to one year of the seven required normally for the bar.[35] Considering aggregate figures for the whole period covered by this study, Lincoln's Inn again shows up as the most 'professional' of the legal societies, since a smaller proportion of its barristers were unqualified, in terms of standing, than at any other inn.

The experience of Lincoln's Inn may point the way to an understanding of the output of barristers from the inns of court during the later seventeenth and early eighteenth centuries. Statistics for admissions and for calls to the bar show that Lincoln's Inn included a higher proportion of barristers' sons than any other society.[36] The other inns, it seems, may have included fewer committed law students among their members. Campbell's *London Tradesmen*, published in 1747, characterized the four societies in the following terms:

> The Temple for Beaus,
> Lincoln's Inn for Lawyers,
> and Gray's Inn for Whore[rs].[37]

It may be significant that Lincoln's Inn, the inn 'for lawyers', called few barristers during the later seventeenth century, and did not seriously reduce its qualifications for admission to the bar, while the Temple societies accounted for the majority of new barristers, and had clearly relaxed their qualifications before the beginning of our period. Is it possible that 'beaus' and other amateur students were the source of that spate of barristers which appeared after the Restoration? A

Orders H(8), 317–18. The common agreement of 1762 reduced the standing required for the bar to 5 years (Richardson, *History of the Inns of Court*, p. 313).

[35] LI, MS Black Book xi. 181.
[36] See Table 1.2 and Table 3.2.
[37] R. Campbell, *London Tradesman* (1747), p. 74.

	Gray's Inn				Inner Temple				Lincoln's Inn				Middle Temple				Total			
	P	%	R	%	P	%	R	%	P	%	R	%	P	%	R	%	P	%	R	%
1680–2	7	15.6	38	84.4	12	18.2	54	81.8	2	9.5	19	90.5	21	32.8	43	67.2	42	21.4	154	78.6
1683–5	5	11.1	40	88.9	9	21.9	32	78.1	—	—	28	100.0	25	39.7	38	60.3	29	22.0	138	78.0
1686–8	12	25.0	36	75.0	13	27.1	35	72.9	6	26.1	17	73.9	42	47.7	46	52.3	73	35.3	134	64.7
1689–91	8	25.0	24	75.0	30	50.0	30	50.0	2	15.4	11	84.6	13	30.2	30	69.8	53	35.8	95	64.2
1692–4	4	14.3	24	85.7	15	34.9	28	65.1	1	5.9	16	94.1	26	32.9	53	67.1	46	27.5	121	72.5
1695–7	2	9.5	19	90.5	18	40.9	26	59.1	1	10.0	9	90.0	22	39.3	34	60.7	43	32.8	88	67.2
1698–1700	—	—	34	100.0	19	31.7	41	68.3	2	11.8	15	88.2	27	51.9	25	48.1	48	29.4	115	70.5
1701–3	3	14.3	18	85.7	12	35.3	22	64.7	2	11.8	15	88.2	12	25.0	36	75.0	29	24.2	91	75.8
1704–6	2	8.7	21	91.3	25	54.3	21	45.7	2	12.5	14	87.5	22	42.3	30	57.7	51	37.2	86	62.8
1707–9	5	23.8	16	76.2	14	43.7	18	56.3	1	5.5	17	94.4	21	40.4	31	59.6	41	33.3	82	66.7
1710–12	11	47.8	12	52.2	16	42.1	22	57.9	1	5.9	16	94.1	32	61.5	20	38.5	60	46.1	70	53.8
1713–15	11	52.4	10	47.6	22	56.4	17	43.6	3	13.0	20	87.0	28	57.1	21	42.9	64	48.5	68	51.5
1716–18	11	45.8	13	54.2	15	53.6	13	46.4	3	18.7	13	81.3	20	48.8	21	51.2	49	44.9	60	55.1
1719–21	8	50.0	8	50.0	19	48.7	20	51.3	3	20.0	12	80.0	24	47.1	27	52.9	54	44.6	67	55.4
1722–4	9	52.9	8	47.1	17	40.5	25	59.5	5	41.7	7	58.3	31	50.8	30	49.2	62	47.0	70	53.0
1725–7	14	66.7	7	33.3	20	47.6	22	52.4	11	34.4	21	65.6	27	42.9	36	57.1	72	45.6	86	54.4
1728–30	11	61.1	7	38.9	21	43.7	27	56.3	13	61.9	8	38.1	32	57.1	24	42.9	77	53.8	66	46.1
Total 1680–1730	123	26.9	335	73.1	297	39.6	453	60.4	58	18.4	258	81.6	425	43.8	545	56.2	903	36.2	1591	63.8
Total calls	458				750				316				970				2494			
Unclassified calls	2				6				—				3				11			

Notes: P = Premature calls; R = Regular calls.

discount in the formal requirements for a barrister's gown would be unlikely to encourage more students to commit themselves to practise, unless prospects for a career at the bar improved, but it might be an incentive for the heirs to landed estates and other 'non-professionals' to acquire the formal status of a barrister, for the sake of prestige alone. From the point of view of the governors of the inns, more barristers implied improved revenue from fines and duties, especially if payments were accepted in lieu of qualifications for the bar, and this may have been attractive as a means of ameliorating their financial problems. Moreover, individual societies, faced with falling rolls during the later seventeenth century as the number of 'non-professional' students diminished, may have regarded the wholesale dispensation of the standard demands for the bar as an obvious means of competing for a bigger share of the 'amateur' cake. If this was the strategy of the Temple inns, it was most successful, for as admissions to Gray's and Lincoln's Inn fell after the Restoration, their own rolls expanded.

Thus it appears that variations in the levels of admissions to the individual inns of court may be partly explained by a relaxation in conventions during the decades after 1660, which brought them in more 'non-professional' students and in turn resulted in an increase of non-practising barristers. Such a policy would have been less effective, however, in the harsher economic climate of the fifty years after 1680, when both admissions and calls to the bar declined, despite the further concessions identified above. The lasting result of this diminution in the demands made for the bar may have been some alteration in the social quality of those who acquired the formal status of a barrister at law, and this is the subject of the next section.

3. SOCIAL PROFILE

Chapter 1 showed that the period covered by this study witnessed a trend towards a more plebeian body of students at the inns of court, although this did not significantly undermine the domination of these societies by the gentry until the mid-eighteenth century. Given this limited change in the social status of students, it would not be surprising if there was a corresponding social change among barristers. Indeed, modern historians claim that barristers were more lowly born in the Augustan age than their predecessors had been, and they have linked this with William Blackstone's mid-eighteenth-century lament

TABLE 3.2a. *Social origins of barristers admitted to the inns of court, 1688–1714*[a]

Social origins	Gray's Inn		Inner Temple		Lincoln's Inn		Middle Temple		Total	
	No.	%	No.	%	No.	%	No.	%	No.	%
Peer	—	—	2	0.6	—	—	2	0.4	4	0.4
Knight/Baronet	8	5.4	17	5.3	9	6.2	24	5.1	58	5.4
Esquire	57	38.5	91	28.5	49	34.0	166	35.5	363	33.6
Gentleman	47	31.8	100	31.4	43	29.9	149	31.8	339	31.4
Clerk	5	3.4	22	6.9	5	3.5	28	6.0	60	5.6
Lawyer	22	14.9	58	18.2	36	25.0	61	13.0	177	16.4
Doctor	2	1.3	2	0.6	2	1.4	8	1.7	14	1.3
Bourgeois	7	4.7	27	8.5	—	—	30	6.4	64	5.9
Total classified	148		319		144		468		1079	
Unclassified and unknown	24		19		14		6		63	

TABLE 3.2b. *Birth order of barristers admitted to the inns of court, 1688–1714*[a]

Birth order	Gray's Inn		Inner Temple		Lincoln's Inn		Middle Temple		Total	
	No.	%	No.	%	No.	%	No.	%	No.	%
First/heir	105	69.1	223	69.5	102	70.8	333	71.0	763	70.3
Son/other	47	30.9	98	30.5	42	29.2	136	29.0	323	29.7
Total classified	152		321		144		469		1086	
Unclassified and unknown	20		17		14		5		56	

[a] Including those who migrated to another inn for call; all other conventions as in Tables 1.2 and 1.3.

Sources: As in Table 1.2; also GI, MS Orders ii; *CITR*, iii, iv; LI, MS Black Books ix, x, xi; MT, MS Orders E5 and H(8).

that the practising bar itself was in danger of being dominated by 'obscure or illiterate men'.[38]

In fact, although there are signs that the *professional* bar was becoming more socially humble in this period, the trend was counterbalanced by the tendency for non-professional inns' students to become barristers.[39] Table 3.2 analyses the social status of those men among 1688–1714 entrants to the inns who went on to be called to the bar. Clearly barristers were by no means collectively lowly born. Nearly 40 per cent were the sons of peers, knights, or esquires, and only around 30 per cent were of professional or lower origin. Moreover, approximately 70 per cent were the eldest sons or heirs of their fathers. If the sons of 'esquires' and 'gentlemen' are divided into urban and rural and the former are counted as non-gentry, the proportion of barristers who were the offspring of men not belonging to the landed élite can be raised to 42 per cent.[40] However, even this higher figure contrasts with Cambridge University, where the sons of men who were not of gentry origin accounted for over 80 per cent of new graduates between 1701 and 1720, and with Oxford, where matriculands below the level of peer/esquire parentage provided 95 per cent of graduates over the same period.[41]

The higher social status of barristers as compared with university graduates to some extent simply reflects the different social composition of the student groups admitted. It is evident, however, that the representatives of the social élite who entered the inns were more likely to become barristers than were the sons of the gentry who attended university to stay on and take a degree. Table 3.3 shows that nearly 21 per cent of the offspring of peers, baronets, knights, and esquires admitted to the inns between 1688 and 1714 were called to the bar, while only just over 13 per cent of the corresponding group among three samples of matriculands to Oxford University became Bachelors of Arts. On the other hand, while the great majority (78 per cent) of socially *humble* matriculands to Oxford graduated eventually,

---

[38] D. Duman, 'The English Bar in the Georgian Era', in W. Prest (ed.), *Lawyers in Early Modern Europe and America* (1981), 91–5; Lucas, 'Collective Biography', p. 231; id., 'Blackstone', pp. 456–89; Blackstone, *Commentaries*, i. 33.

[39] For the social origins of practising barristers, see below, pp. 161–5.

[40] Altogether 45 of the sons of 'esquires' and 89 sons of 'gentlemen' came from towns of approximately 2,000 or more inhabitants. Adding these 134 to those classified as 'bourgeois and professional' gives 449 or 41.6% of the total called (sources as in Table 3.2; Chalklin, *Provincial Towns*, pp. 5–17).

[41] Hans, *New Trends in Education*, pp. 43, 45.

TABLE 3.3*a*. *'Professionalism' of different social groups among students admitted to the inns of court, 1688–1714*[a]

	Total admitted		Called % of admissions		Called % of barristers	
	No.	%	No.	%	No.	%
Peer/esquire	2057	48.5	425	20.7	425	39.4
Gentleman	1209	28.5	339	28.0	339	31.4
Bourgeois/ professional	971	22.9	315	32.4	315	29.2
Total	4237	100.0	1079	25.5	1079	100.0

TABLE 3.3*b*. *'Professionalism' of different social groups among matriculands to the University of Oxford, 1690, 1700, and 1710*[b]

	Matriculands		Graduates % of matriculands		Graduates % of graduates	
	No.	%	No.	%	No.	%
Peer/esquire	129	15.6	17	13.2	17	3.5
Gentleman	301	36.4	161	53.5	161	32.9
Pauperes Peuri, plebians, and clerks	397	48.0	311	78.3	311	63.6
Total	827	100.0	489	59.1	489	100.0

[a] Admissions 1688–1714 classified by social origin as in Table 1.1.
[b] Matriculands to 8 colleges, 1690, 1700, and 1710.

Sources: Inns of court: as in Table 3.2; University of Oxford: Bennett, 'University, Society and Church, 1688–1714', pp. 362, 370. I am indebted to Dr Bennett for allowing me to use his statistics as a basis for comparison.

only just over 32 per cent of students admitted to the inns as sons of men from bourgeois and professional backgrounds became barristers. Thus at the university there was a wide discrepancy, across the social scale, in the proportion of students who stayed on to take degrees. At the inns of court there was far more uniformity, for between 20–30 per cent of each of the major social groups at the inns became barristers.

In other words, graduates of the University of Oxford were a group distinct socially from the rest of the university, while barristers of the inns of court were not so very different in 'quality' from men who were never called. University graduates were, in fact, men committed to a profession, in that most intended to become ordained into the church.[42] This suggests, by way of contrast, that students who were called to the bar of an inn were by no means a coherent professional body. As already suggested, many of them were not destined for the practising bar.

The social profile of barristers called at the inns of court implies that the status of a barrister had become meaningless as a point of demarcation between those men who attended the inns as finishing schools and students who were determined upon joining the legal profession itself. This was a consequence of the late-seventeenth-century benchers' policy of watering down the qualifications their predecessors had demanded for admission to the bar. The graphs for calls to the bar and first admissions are broadly similar in shape between 1660 and 1700, but calls declined less sharply. Comparing the ratio of total bar calls to total first admissions 1688–1714 with the corresponding figure for 1590–1639 shows that a higher proportion of students were going on to be called in the Augustan period.[43] Clearly, many of them were gentlemen who had no intention of becoming professional lawyers. By 1700 at least, admission to 'the degree of utter-barrister' could no longer be regarded as a declaration of intent to enter the lists of counsel in Westminster Hall or on circuit. Still less did it constitute proof of the learning and expertise necessary to become a competent advocate, as shall be seen. In effect, the imprimatur of the inns had been devalued to the point where it was of no real significance to aspiring members of the practising bar.

[42] Bennett, 'University, Society and Church', pp. 369, 371.
[43] Fig. 1.1; Prest, 'English Bar, 1550–1700', p. 68; Figure 3.1. The ratio of total calls to total admissions 1590–1639 was 1 : 5.3, while the corresponding ratio for 1688–1714 was 1 : 3.6 (Prest, *Inns of Court*, p. 52; id., *Rise of the Barristers*, p. 7; sources as in Table 3.2).

4
FORMAL AND INFORMAL LEGAL EDUCATION

THE numerical contraction and general decline which set in at the inns during the later seventeenth century were accompanied by a marked decay in the 'system' of legal education which had flourished in the Renaissance period and been maintained until the Civil Wars. It is well known that the formal lectures or 'readings' ceased before the Revolution of 1688, and the learning exercises became a pale shadow of their former selves.[1] Part of this chapter traces the chronology of this process from the attempted revival of the readings and exercises under Charles II to the collapse of all formal education in the early eighteenth century, and attempts to establish some of the reasons for the failure of the system. Whatever the explanation, it is clear that the inns of court had no significant role in the education of men studying for the bar after 1700. But the decline of institutional legal education did not mean that it was no longer possible for novices to be initiated into the mysteries of English law. Students of the inns continued to become genuine lawyers, and some developed into learned counsel eminent in the courts of common law and equity. The latter part of this chapter is an account of the programme of learning followed by 'professional' law students at a time when their societies accepted no responsibility for their training. First, however, it is necessary to describe the apparatus of formal training which operated at the inns when they were at their peak as places of legal education.

1. THE REGIME TO 1660

The machinery of legal education which operated at the inns of court under the Tudors and early Stuarts consisted of two main elements: readings or formal lectures delivered by senior barristers or benchers; and various exercises, based upon the forms of pleading in the courts, which involved the participation of benchers, barristers, and students.

---

[1] Holdsworth, *History of English Law*, vi. 488–90.

The readings formed the most solemn and sophisticated aspect of the inns' educational apparatus. These were twice-yearly orations on the subject of some statute, chosen by the reader, and delivered during the Lent and autumn 'learning vacations': twenty-four day periods which followed the law terms of Hilary and Trinity. Students who intended to qualify for the bar and junior barristers were obliged (officially at least) to be present during these vacations and, as long as they continued, to attend the readings. In their heyday the lectures also attracted many learned counsel and members of the judiciary. These practitioners, together with the junior members of the audience, would be treated to an exposition of some aspects of the statute, and might participate in the formal arguments which were staged between the reader and his attendant barristers. Their stamina must have been considerable, for the lengthy process of exegesis and disputation continued for three or four days of each week over two or three weeks, and was accompanied by much feasting and ceremony.[2]

Readings were not only important as a means of legal education. As has been seen, the hierarchy of ranks at the inns had evolved out of the educational system, and during the sixteenth and seventeenth centuries the appointment of readers was a fundamental element of the promotional method by which barristers were elected to a permanent place on the governing body. In the Tudor and early Stuart period delivery of a reading was the principal qualification for promotion to full membership of the bench.[3] It is true that the original order of promotion—by which men read before they became benchers—was gradually inverted; and after 1660 senior barristers were admitted to the bench, according to their seniority by date of admission, before they had performed their readings.[4] But they were only called to the bench on condition that they promised to read in due course. At the Middle Temple during Charles II's reign, barristers were summoned to become benchers 'in order to their reading', and at all of the inns failure to read when the time came was often punished by expulsion

---

[2] Dugdale, *Origines Juridiciales*, pp. 159–60, 206–8; Prest, *Inns of Court*, pp. 120–4; Richardson, *History of the Inns of Court*, pp. 101–27.

[3] Ives, *Common Lawyers*, pp. 42–3; id. 'Promotion in the Legal Profession of Yorkist and Early Tudor England', *LQR* 75 (1959), 349–51; Prest, *Inns of Court*, pp. 59–70. Dr Prest may have overstated his argument that promotion to the bench was by no means conditional upon reading during the early 17th cent. for, by his own figures, only a small minority of benchers escaped their obligation to read.

[4] *GIPB* i. 429–59, ii. 2–92; *GI Adm. Reg.*; *CITR* ii. 334, iii. 1–245; *IT Adm. Reg.*, i–ii; *LIBB* ii. 432, iii. 2–156; *LI Adm. Reg.*, i; *MTR* iii. 1145–363; *MT Adm. Reg.*, i.

from the governing body.[5] Thus although senior barristers of the Restoration period might enjoy the comforts of the bench table before they had undergone the trouble and expense attendant upon delivering their course of lectures, their *continued* enjoyment of a bencher's privileges was conditional upon acceptance of the office of reader. This association between promotion to the bench and reading is very important because it meant that any refusal *en masse* among the senior bar to accept their lecturing duties was liable to disrupt the order of government long established at the inns of court.

Although the readings of the inns of court were both spectacular and prestigious, the bread and butter of the inns' system of legal education were rather the disputations upon cases which were held regularly both in the learning vacations and the legal terms. These went under different appellations depending upon their participants and their place of performance. The most commonplace exercise was the moot; a formal argument which involved occasionally all three ranks of the legal societies: students and barristers as counsel and benchers as judges in term-time, and students as counsel before barristers as judges during the vacations. Other exercises were more or less sophisticated, formal, or ceremonious variations on this basic model; from the 'bolt', which involved students only, through the exercise of 'case-putting' which was an informal type of moot, to the elaborate and long drawn out 'imparlance', peculiar to the Inner Temple, which included several stages of argument and ritual carried through on different days. Exercises were not confined to the inns of court themselves: twice-yearly the bench of each inn elected junior readers who were supposed to lecture at their subordinate inns of chancery, and these barristers were accompanied by students who were to participate in 'grand moots' there. Like the readings, the exercises acquired a probationary function as part of the inns' promotional system, but all of them had the same objective: to accustom their participants to formal and public argument and to develop thereby a facility in the 'bablative art' to which they were apprenticed.[6]

There has been some difference of opinion regarding the extent to which readings and exercises were performed conscientiously and

[5] The first e.g. of this wording seems to have been the call of William Booth and Richard Wallop on 9 Feb. 1666 (MT, MS Orders E5, 98).

[6] Prest, *Inns of Court*, pp. 116–19; Richardson, *History of the Inns of Court*, pp. 129–38. For the probationary function of the exercises see p. 64 above and App. I below; cf. W. R. Prest, 'The Learning Exercises at the Inns of Court 1590–1640', *Journal of the Society of Public Teachers at Law*, 9 (1967), 310–13.

effectively down to 1660. Sir William Holdsworth argued that the apparatus of legal education established at the inns went into decline after the mid-sixteenth century and was maintained with difficulty during the succeeding one hundred years.[7] Kenneth Charlton has gone further, dating the beginnings of decay from the later fifteenth century.[8] More recently, however, Wilfrid Prest has challenged these views: he has drawn attention to the fact that the early seventeenth-century inns were always able to find a reader, and has maintained that the lectures of that period were not necessarily of less educational value than their longer mid-Tudor predecessors. Moreover, Dr Prest has insisted that Jacobean and Caroline law students were serious and enthusiastic participants in the moots and other exercises prescribed for their improvement. In fact, while the fundamental causes of educational decay may have been present from the sixteenth century, they did not take full effect, according to Prest, until the normal course of proceedings has been interrupted by Civil War.[9]

The educational apparatus of the inns of court was completely disrupted by the outbreak of hostilities in England. No exercises were performed between 1642 and 1647, and although some moots and bolts were taking place by the 1650s no readings were delivered at any inn during the Interregnum, despite attempts to revive the lectures under the Commonwealth.[10] In effect, there was a decisive break in the continuance of the system of learning. The attempt of the inns to revive their educational machinery after the restoration of the Stuart monarchy is the subject of the following two sections.

2. POST-RESTORATION READINGS

Despite the long interruption in the operation of the machinery of legal instruction at the inns, it is clear that certain senior members of the legal profession were determined to revive it as the return to 'Kingly government' became imminent. As early as February 1660, before Charles Stuart had been invited formally to return to England, the benchers of Lincoln's Inn noted that 'the reviveing of readeing hath

---

[7] Holdsworth, *History of English Law*, vi. 481.

[8] K. Charlton, *Education in Renaissance England* (1965), 177–86.

[9] Prest, *Inns of Court*, pp. 124–36; id., 'Learning Exercises', pp. 301–13.

[10] *GIPB* i. pp. xlv, 365, 401, 413–14, 418, 426; *CITR* ii. 291, 304, 329; *LIBB* ii. 368, 391, 405, 409–10, 412, 422; *MTR* ii. 937, 948, 957, 959, 1019, iii. 1028, 1030, 1050, 1105, 1140–1. W. R. Douthwaite, *Gray's Inn: Its History and Associations* (1886), 76; *CITR* ii, p. cxvi; *LIBB* ii. 422; *MTR* iii. 1093.

been propounded by the Judges to the benchers of the severall Innes of Court', and duly appointed a reader for the following Lent.[11] After conference among the benchers of the four inns, the other societies all appointed readers in November 1660.[12] But while it was a simple matter for a quorum of like-minded benchers to meet together and appoint another (and most likely absent) member of their fellowship to read, it was far more difficult to persuade those so chosen to fulfil their obligation in this regard. Table 4.1 shows that Gray's and Lincoln's Inn both failed to persuade any of their benchers to read in Lent 1661, and it was not until two more years had elapsed that a learning vacation was distinguished by a reading at every one of the four societies. In the meantime, despite various inducements, including a reduction in the length of reading to one week only and preference in the choice of bench chambers, many of the benchers excused themselves from reading or abruptly refused to accept their appointment.[13] At Lincoln's Inn four benchers were unsuccessfully proposed for readers before the society prevailed upon William Prynne to take the duty upon himself, and Gray's received two outright refusals from the two most senior members of the bench before they too found a reader. The Temple societies were initially more successful in their proceedings, for both Francis Philips and Thomas Mundy, who were the first to be called upon to read at these societies after the Restoration, duly delivered their lectures. Subsequently, however, both societies experienced several refusals. In total, at least thirty-two men who were called upon to read at their respective inns down to 1665 did not do so, either by making some excuse, refusing outright, or simply not replying to letters written to them on the subject of reading.[14] Moreover, at the Inner Temple and Gray's Inn a few senior barristers refused flatly to come to the bench upon being summoned.[15]

[11] LI, MS Black Book viii, fo. 668.

[12] *GIPB* i. 434; *CITR* ii. 335; MT, MS Orders E5, 34.

[13] GI, MS Orders i, fos. 541–2, 549; LI, MS Red Book i, fos. 265–6; ibid., MS Black Book viii, fos. 688, 691, 695, 726, 751; MT, MS Orders E5, 35, 39, 49, 55, 60, 63, 67, 74–5. 'Bench Chambers' ('readers' chambers' at GI) were free sets of rooms which were reserved for those elected to the bench (see GI, MS Book of Orders i, fo. 542; *GIPB* ii, p. x; *Middle Temple Bench Book* (1st edn., 1912), 39–40; *LIBB* iii. 20–1, 58).

[14] GI, MS Orders i, fos. 541, 546, 554–6, 558; IT, MS Acts 1638–64, fos. 150, 156, 168, 172; LI, MS Black Book viii, fos. 689, 703, 719, 724–5, 736; MT, MS Orders E5, 35–6, 41, 46, 60, 65, 76. At GI there were still more refusals which do not appear in the pension orders (see BL, MS Harleian 1912, fos. 185–7).

[15] GI, MS Orders i, fo. 559; IT, MS Acts 1638–64, fo. 165.

TABLE 4.1. *Readers at the inns of court, 1660–78*

Year	Gray's Inn	Inner Temple	Lincoln's Inn	Middle Temple
1660 L	—	—	—	—
1660 A	—	—	—	—
1661 L	—	Philips, F.	—	Mundy, T.
1661 A	Armyne, E.	Finch, H. *SG*	—	Lake, T.
1662 L	—	Trevor, A.	Prynne, W.	Hoskins, B.
1662 A	Bacon, F.	Thurland, E. *SGY*	—	Barker, A.
1663 L	Edgar, T.	Yorke, W.	Ashton, R.	Proctor, H.
1663 A	Ellis, W.	—	—	Harvey, F.
1664 L	Hardres, T.	Turbervile, J.	Day, G.	Constantine, W.
1664 A	Willimot, N.	Foster, T.	Atkins, R.	Mountagu, W. *AGQ*
1665 L	Flint, T.	Hopkins, R.	Rich, E.	Turnor, J.
1665 A	—	—	—	—
1666 L	—	—	—	—
1666 A	—	—	—	—
1667 L	—	—	—	—
1667 A	Lehunt, W.	Milton, C.	Powis, T.	Barton, J.
1668 L	—	Shieres, R.	—	Northey, W.
1668 A	Sicklemore, J.	Etherington, R.	Goddard, G.	Bramston, F.
1669 L	Vincent, J.	Goodfellow, C.	Graves, R.	Lechmere, N.
1669 A	Jones, E.	Baldwynn, S.	Howel, J. *Rec.*	Peckham, H.
1670 L	Amhurst, J.	Farrer, T.	Pedley, N.	Conyers, T.
1670 A	Skipwith, T.	Crooke, R.	Churchill, J.	—
1671 L	Lane, W.	Lister, W.	Stote, R.	Wallop, R.
1671 A	Otway, J.	Powell, R.	Aldworth, R.	North, F. *SG*
1672 L	Pickering, R.	Hampson, R.	Goodricke, F. *KC*	Rawlins, T.
1672 A	—	—	—	—
1673 L	—	West, E.	—	Calthorpe, L.
1673 A	Shaftoe, R.	Mosyer, J.	Strode, G.	Staples, A.
1674 L	Rigby, E.	Holloway, C.	—	Ettricke, A.
1674 A	Jones, W. *SG*	—	—	—
1675 L	Holt, T.	Pemberton, F.	—	Barrell, F.
1675 A	Gregory, W.	Trevor, J. *KC*	Atkins, E.	Winnington, F. *SG*
1676 L	—	Holloway, R.	Strode, T.	Johnson, G.
1676 A	—	Poultney, W.	Butler, J. *AGQ*	—
1677 L	Weston, R.	Shuter, H.	—	Whitelocke, W.
1677 A	Baldocke, R.	Dolben, W. *Rec.*	Stedman, J.	—
1678 L	—	Edwards, R.	—	Walcott, T.
1678 A	—	—	—	—

Key: L = Lent vacation; A = autumn vacation; *SG* = solicitor-general; *SGY* = solicitor-general to the duke of York; *AGQ* = attorney-general to the queen; *Rec.* = recorder of London; *KC* = king's counsel.

cont./

Sources: Dugdale, *Origines Juridiciales*, pp. 169, 220, 256, 297, and 'Chronica Series', p. 122; revised with *GIPB* i. 434–59, ii. 1–54; *CITR* ii. 335, iii. 2–118; *LIBB* ii. 432, iii. 4–110; *MTR* iii. 1153–321; BL, Add. MSS 50116 (Legal Reports etc., 1626–80), fos. 144–59; ibid., MS Harleian 1912, fos. 185–7; Bodl., MS North c. 5 (Letters to Lord Guilford, 1663–84), fos. 56–7; *English Legal Manuscripts*, ed. J. H. Baker (Zug, Switzerland, 1978), ii. 177–8; E. Foss, *The Judges of England* (1848–69), vii. 28, 38, 41–2; B. D. Henning, *The House of Commons 1660–1690* (1983), iii. 604; HMC, *5th Report*, app. p. 300.

Clearly, there was considerable reluctance to participate in the revival of readings among many senior members of the legal societies and, despite the support of the judiciary, the lord chancellor, and even of the crown, readings did not get underway without several false starts and interruptions.[16] It is not difficult to see why. The societies of law were wedded to a system of seniority by admission to the house which regulated most aspects of promotion and appointment to their offices. Thus men were called upon to read in strict order of precedence according to their standing. In the early seventeenth century this had meant that men became benchers about twenty-six years after their first admission to the house, and would be called upon to read at a similar stage of their careers, but, as a result of the interruption of readings during the Civil War, those men who were in line to read after the Restoration were uncommonly senior.[17] The average continuance of the benchers who were called upon to deliver their readings between 1661 and 1663 was, in fact, between thirty-five and forty-five years.[18] Some of these men must have been in their sixties or older. The legendary Puritan William Prynne, for instance, who was Lent reader at Lincoln's Inn for 1662, was then sixty-two, and had first become a member of the society in 1621.[19] It is not surprising that some of those who were reluctant to read pleaded their 'weakness & infirmity of body', or their great age, and were sometimes excused in

---

[16] A further conference between representatives of the inns and the judges on the subject of readings was appointed to be held in May 1662 (MT, MS Orders E5, 59), while Clarendon consulted with the benchers of his own society about readings in Feb. 1661 (ibid. 41–2). The judges' orders of 1664, which were issued on the command of the king, promised the support of the judicial bench in dealing with benchers who refused to read (Richardson, *History of the Inns of Court*, p. 450).

[17] For seniority of benchers in the early 17th cent., see Prest, *Inns of Court*, p. 61; cf. id., *Rise of the Barristers*, p. 137.

[18] Average years from admission of those appointed to read in 1661–3 (inclusive) as follows: GI 44.7 years; IT 34.9 years; LI 35.5 years; MT 34.7 years (*GIPB* i. 434–6; *GI Adm. Reg.*; *CITR* ii. 335, iii. 2–13; *IT Adm. Reg.*, i; *LIBB* ii. 432, iii. 4–27; *Ll Adm. Reg.*, i; *MTR* iii. 1153–80; *MT Adm. Reg.*, i).

[19] *DNB* xvi. 432; *Ll Adm. Reg.*, i. 188.

consideration of these disabilities.[20] Moreover, it is clear that some of those who were called upon to read had retired to the country during the Commonwealth period, and had no doubt given up practice at the bar. Despite letters sent to their homes urging their 'continuance & keeping commons & performing the Exercise & duties of the House', they were most unlikely to be persuaded out of their retirement, notwithstanding draconian fines and/or demotion from the bench, as well as the earnest entreaty of their fellows.[21]

Nevertheless, as Table 4.1 shows, by 1664 readings had got into their stride, and from Lent of that year three successive learning vacations featured a course of lectures at every inn of court. However, natural disasters then interposed, for the virulence of the plague in London persuaded most members of the inns to take shelter in more healthy parts of the country, and vacations and readings were cancelled at all the inns. Hardly had the plague abated when fire devastated a large part of the metropolis, including some of the Temple, and although Gray's and Lincoln's Inns were untouched by the conflagration, none of the inns mounted a reading in the autumn of 1666 or in the following Lent.[22]

When readings resumed at the societies of law in the autumn of 1667, there had been an interruption of four learning vacations, and two complete years without law lectures. Despite this lengthy break, readings were revived once more, and from the autumn of 1668 to Lent 1672 an almost unbroken succession was achieved, with one absolute failure, when William Booth neglected to read at the Middle Temple in the autumn of 1670.[23] At Gray's Inn and the two Temples, only one bencher of each society flatly refused to read during these years.[24] It seems that the very senior or retired benchers of these houses had been passed over or disbenched, for those men first called upon to read during the period 1667 to 1671 were of around thirty-two

---

[20] LI, MS Black Book viii, fos. 689, 691, 701; MT, MS Orders E5, 45, 47, 60, 66. Cf. J. H. Baker, 'Readings in Gray's Inn, their Decline and Disappearance', in id., *The Legal Profession and the Common Law*, p. 36.

[21] LI, MS Black Book viii, fo. 699. Cf. ibid., fo. 693; MT, MS Orders E5, 50. GI, MS Orders i, fos. 541, 546, 554–6, 558; IT, MS Acts 1638–64, fos. 150, 165–6, 168, 172; LI, MS Black Book viii, fos. 703, 724–5, 742–3; MT, MS Orders E5, 41, 50, 60–1, 63, 65, 69, 78–9.

[22] GI, MS Orders i, fo. 560; IT, MS Acts 1665–87, fos. 10–11, 13, 15; LI, MS Black Book viii, fos. 756–7; MT, MS Orders E5, 97, 101; Williamson, *The Temple*, pp. 470, 505–11.

[23] MT, MS Orders E5, 153.

[24] Ibid.; GI, MS Orders ii. 20; IT, MS Acts 1665–87, fo. 39.

or thirty-three years' continuance in their societies.[25] Only Lincoln's Inn persisted in calling upon those senior benchers who had already refused to read, with the inevitable result that they refused once more and were fined accordingly.[26] Once they had been passed over, there were no further refusals at this house for three years.

By the second decade of the Restoration period it may have seemed that the solemn lectures which had been the showpiece of the inns of court in their prime had been successfully re-established. In fact, the benchers of the inns were probably aware that serious difficulties were brewing. Although the elderly benchers who were obviously incapable of performing their readings were no longer a problem, and those currently at the bench were reading in regular succession, it must have been clear that there was considerable reluctance on the part of the senior bar to take up their obligation to read, for several had refused to come to the bench recently. At Gray's Inn, by 1668, seventeen senior barristers had refused to accept their invitations to the bench, and in 1669 Sir William Scroggs, the future chief justice, also declined to join the governing body.[27] Meanwhile, at the Inner Temple two barristers were fined for refusing to come to the bench in January 1668, and five more suffered for the same reason in 1670.[28]

The timing of subsequent mass refusals of senior barristers to accept their calls to the bench is of considerable importance. The Middle Temple, for instance, had been comparatively untouched by this problem, for throughout the first decade which followed the Restoration no barrister had flatly refused promotion. In October 1671, however, four barristers 'called to the bench in order to their reading' refused, and all were subsequently fined.[29] Six more were duly called in November, but only three accepted: the others were fined accordingly.[30] No reason was given for this reluctance to accept promotion to the governing council of their house, but it is not necessary to look very far to establish the probable cause. Table 4.1 shows that the autumn reading for 1671 had been delivered by Sir

[25] Average years from admission of those called upon to read in 1667–71 (inclusive) as follows: GI 32.6 years; IT 33.6 years; MT 31.8 years (*GIPB* ii. 1–15; *GI Adm. Reg.*; *CITR* iii. 40–75; *IT Adm. Reg.*, i; *MTR* iii. 1209–50; *MT Adm. Reg.*, i).
[26] LI, MS Black Book viii, fos. 770–1, ix. 4. The average continuance of those called upon to read at this house 1667–71 (inclusive) was 36.2 years (*LIBB* iii. 54–75; *LI Adm. Reg.*, i).
[27] GI, MS Orders i. 23, 32. William Lane, here also listed as having refused the bench, later relented and agreed to read (ibid. 34).
[28] IT, MS Acts 1665–87, fos. 25, 41.
[29] MT, MS Orders E5, 165.   [30] Ibid. 165–6.

Francis North, solicitor-general to the king, and it is well known that the extravagant feasting which distinguished his performance cost nearly £1,000.[31] Attention to the records of Lincoln's Inn shows that this coincidence between ruinously expensive reading feasts and mass refusals of promotion to the bench was not unique to the Middle Temple. At this house in 1673 five men refused admission to the governing council and were fined £40 apiece.[32] It seems that there had been some disinclination to come to the bench among barristers in 1670 but there is no record of any outright refusal before the fines of 1673, and it is remarkable that three of those who then declined had been invited to the bench in the first general call which followed the reading of Francis Goodricke, king's counsel.[33] Goodricke's feast was, like that of North, notable for its extravagance.[34] Without doubt, the escalating cost of reading and providing such lavish hospitality was a major deterrent to senior members of the bar accepting promotion to the governing councils of their societies.

Extravagance in the provision of entertainments which accompanied readings was by no means a new development. The practice of inviting distinguished guests to lavish banquests presided over by the incumbent reader had been well established at the inns under Elizabeth and the early Stuarts.[35] Perhaps, however, in response to the dissipation which characterized the public face of the restored monarchy, readers became still more prodigal in their hospitality after 1660. John Evelyn was present at several of these feasts. In 1668 he recorded:

> Mr Bramstone . . . now Reader at the Middle Temple invited me to his feast which was so very extravagant & greate as the like had not been seene at any time: Here were the Duke of Ormonde; [Lord] Privy-seale, [Earle of] Bedford, [Lord] Belasis, [Viscount] Halifax & a world more of Earles and Lords . . .[36]

The expense necessary to satisfy the appetites of these grandees was clearly a great burden to many of the readers. Mrs John Turnor, wife

---

[31] *Lives of the Norths*, i. 97–8.

[32] LI, MS Black Book ix, fo. 89; cf. ibid., fo. 91.

[33] On 22 Nov. 1670 the bench had appointed 2 of its members to confer with 8 senior barristers, of whom the first 2 that were in town *and would accept* were to be called to the bench (*LIBB* iii. 70).   [34] Ibid. 78–81, 87.

[35] *Middle Temple Bench Book* (1st edn.), pp. 26–7; Richardson, *History of the Inns of Court*, pp. 186–7.

[36] The *Diary of John Evelyn*, ed. E. S. De Beer (Oxford, 1955), iii. 512; cf. ibid. iii. 400, 490, 536–7.

of the Lent reader for the Middle Temple in 1665, was driven to seek the aid of her kinsman Samuel Pepys, from whom she hoped to receive cheap naval victuals. Although Pepys was not disposed to assist her, the feast was duly provided. No doubt Mrs Turnor exaggerated when she told the diarist that it was 'the greatest feast that ever was yet kept by a reader', but it certainly would have cost her husband dearly.[37]

The inns, with the support of the judiciary, had taken steps to curb this improvident extravagance. In November 1661 the bench of the Inner Temple prohibited readers from entertaining any strangers in the hall on any reading day, with the intention that 'noe person may be discouraged from the performance of that Exercise [reading] by the unnecessary & expensive cost & charges thereof'.[38] Evidently this had no effect, since similar orders were issued six years later.[39] Meanwhile in 1664 the judges' orders deplored the fact 'that Readings are grown to so excessive a charge, that many of eminent abilities for learning have been discouraged from undertaking the same, and some which did have been much disabled thereby in their Estates', and limited the charge of readings to no more than £300.[40] Again, these injunctions seem to have been useless, for further and more detailed limitations on the expense of readings were made by command of the king himself (on the advice of the lord chancellor and the judges) in May 1678.[41] By that time it was too late to save the readings.

Why did the prodigal feasts continue, despite the prohibitions against them? The example of the bar élite and the role of the crown are crucial here. Leaders of the bar, that is 'the kinges Queenes and Princes Councell the Recorder of London and such who are allowed to practise within the barr', had been excepted from the injunctions.[42] No doubt they could well afford the expense. Unfortunately ordinary readers such as Turnor and Bramston, although they were not nearly so wealthy as crown counsel of the calibre of North and Goodricke, seemed to feel obliged to go some way towards imitating their extravagance, despite the various orders forbidding them to do so. Half a century later Charles Worsley, who may have known some of the

---

[37] *The Diary of Samuel Pepys*, ed. R. Latham and W. Matthews (1970–83), vi. 28, 49.
[38] IT, MS Acts 1638–64, fos. 151–2; cf. LI, MS Black Book viii, fos. 730, 743–4; MT, MS Orders E5, 132–3.
[39] IT, MS Acts 1665–87, fos. 22–3.
[40] Dugdale, *Origines Juridiciales*, p. 323; Richardson, *History of the Inns of Court*, p. 451.
[41] GI, MS Orders ii. 171–2; LI, MS Black Book ix, fo. 165; MT, MS Orders E5, 227.   [42] IT, MS Acts 1665–87, fo. 23.

surviving readers at the Middle Temple in the 1690s, wrote how 'at length the Readings were made occasions of emulation, each striving to outvie each other in grandeur'.[43] The competition may have become ruinous for the less well endowed after 1670, because more readings were delivered by members of the bar élite. Table 4.1 shows that during the first decade after the Restoration there was only one reading by an incumbent solicitor-general, two by lesser royal counsel, and one by a recorder of London. By contrast, over the next eight years three solicitors-general read, along with three crown counsel and one more recorder. This was a direct consequence of the increased use of royal patronage among the ranks of the legal profession, for the office of solicitor-general changed hands more frequently in the second decade of Charles II's reign than it had done before 1670, and many more men were made king's counsel.[44] It was established practice for law officers of the crown to be admitted to the bench of their society immediately upon their appointment to office, and KCs also secured this right after 1668; these men therefore became eligible to read within a short time of their preferment. Contrary to the view expressed by Sir William Holdsworth, they did not shirk their obligation, but rather turned their readings into orgies of conspicuous consumption designed to secure their favour at court.[45] And they were encouraged by the crown: Charles and his brother had graced Heneage Finch's dinner in 1661 and they were present at Goodricke's feast of 1672, while members of the court were guests on many more occasions.[46] Against this background the royal prohibition of extravagant feasts in 1678 seems more than a little hypocritical: in fact the crown had helped to bring the problem to a crisis since Clarendon's fall by making legal promotion dependent upon favour at court, where flattery and dissipation were the keys to success.[47] Ordinary benchers and

---

[43] He had been admitted 27 June 1690 (*Master Worsley's Book*, pp. 1, 124–5).

[44] Foss, *Judges*, vii. 28, 38. Foss's list of KCs is incomplete; for others appointed 1660–80 see Henning, *House of Commons 1660–90*, iii. 188–9; *CITR* iii. 109, 112; *MTR* iii. 1159, 1278. Five men were made KCs in 1660–70 and 13 in 1671–80.

[45] Holdsworth, *History of English Law*, vi. 490. There is no e.g. of a law officer or KC refusing to read between 1660 and the end of the lectures. In Nov. 1673 Sir William Jones SG excused himself from being Lent reader at GI, but he did read in the following autumn (GI, MS Orders ii. 94; see Table 4.1). Crown counsel may have been less willing to participate in the purely internal affairs of the inns (see below, p. 246).

[46] *CITR* iii, pp. x–xi; *LIBB* iii. 78–81, 87; *Lives of the Norths*, i. 97.

[47] At the level of the judiciary, Charles began to appoint judges with tenure dependent upon his 'pleasure' rather than 'good behaviour' in 1668 (A. F. Havighurst, 'The Judiciary and Politics in the Reign of Charles II', *LQR* 66 (1950), 65).

barristers could not afford to compete in this arena; faced with a choice between improvident expenditure and the humiliation of a parsimonious feast, they increasingly refused to be included among those eligible for the burdensome duty of reading.[48]

The problem of crippling expense, though undoubtedly important, may merely have exacerbated a natural disinclination among members of the bar to participate in the revival of readings and other exercises. The promotional benefits of becoming a bencher and reading were fast diminishing as the track of preferment to the upper levels of the legal profession shifted away from the inns of court and their senior members.[49] Moreover, many Restoration barristers were in their formative years and laid the basis of their later learning at a time when little of the apparatus of formal legal training was functioning at the inns. By 1670, they were the men who were eligible to be called to the bench of their societies, and to read in turn. It seems likely that few had any real interest in the preservation of a system which they had not known as students or junior barristers, and it is therefore hardly surprising that they declined promotion to their governing bodies, as long as the disincentive of reading remained.[50]

The inevitable consequence of the senior barristers' reluctance to accept promotion to the bench was that, after 1670, there were simply not enough benchers available to perform two readings per year at each inn for any considerable period of time. All the inns cancelled their readings in autumn 1672, and Table 4.1 shows that they were held erratically during the next few years.[51] At the Middle Temple there was no reading in autumn 1674, and the autumn 1676 reading was cancelled by the bench.[52] Lincoln's Inn had so far accommodated its demands to the prevailing state of affairs that readers were given the liberty of choosing when they would deliver their lectures.[53] By May

---

[48] For further refusals of barristers to come to the bench and benchers' refusals to read 1671–8 see GI, MS Orders ii. 55; IT, MS Acts 1665–87, fos. 57, 73; LI, MS Black Book ix, fos. 84, 88, 98, 104, 115, 164; MT, MS Orders E5, 183, 194, 197, 206–7, 222, 224, 227–9.

[49] See *The Autobiography of Sir John Bramston, KB*, ed. R. G. Neville, Lord Braybrooke (Camden Soc., old ser., 32; 1845 [written after 1683]), 6; E. Hatton, *A New View of London or, an Ample Account of that City*, (1708), 698; ch. 8.

[50] Those barristers who declined their call to the bench at MT 1671–7 had been admitted between 1646 and 1653 and called to the bar between 1648 and 1661 (*MTR* iii. 1261–314; *MT Adm. Reg.*, i).

[51] IT, MS Acts 1665–87, fo. 60; MT, MS Orders E5, 173.

[52] MT, MS Orders E5, 209.

[53] LI, MS Black Book ix, fos. 116, 123.

1677, the readings were becoming untenable, and the benchers of this inn were forced to recognize the fact:

In regard severall Barristers of this Society of antient standing have refused to come to the Bench, and considering how few there are likely to succeede those that lately came upp, it is thought very expedient, and for the service of this Society, that there be but one Reading from henceforth in every yeare, and likewise but one Reader chosen in each yeare, for this society.[54]

Clearly, the benchers of the inns of court were faced with a stark choice. Either they had to abandon the readings, or accept that many of their senior members would refuse to participate in the government of their societies, with the probable result that the inns would become dominated absolutely by those few who were prepared to read: the privileged barristers who were named king's counsel. The ordinary benchers had struggled to maintain their independence from the crown in the matter of appointments to their governing bodies in 1668, and they reasserted their rights after the Revolution; thus they were unlikely to be pleased by the prospect of their councils being confined to KCs, and they made their choice accordingly.[55]

The year 1678 witnessed the last regular readings to be delivered at the societies of law. Sir William Whitelocke, treasurer of the Middle Temple, gave a single public lecture in the hall of this society in 1684, but there were no more full courses of law lectures.[56] The Temple had been devastated by fire in 1679, and the Middle house took the opportunity to commute the reading of Thomas Smith on payment of £300. At the same time, it was ordered that no bencher who had not read would be allowed to claim a bench chamber until he had paid £200.[57] This pointed the way to the means of dispensing with the benchers' obligation to read, and in June 1680 an order was made to the effect that, for the next four years, those appointed to the office of reader might enjoy full privileges and benefits as if they had in fact read, on payment of £200 into the treasury.[58] The order was not renewed in 1684, but the practice was well established by that time, and benchers continued to pay their £200 apiece upon election to the nominal office of reader throughout the period covered by this study.

[54] *LIBB* iii. 112.

[55] In 1668 MT attempted to deny Francis North promotion to the bench in respect of his appointment as KC (*Lives of the Norths*, i. 50–1). For subsequent refusals to promote KCs see below, p. 247.

[56] Richardson, *History of the Inns of Court*, p. 201.

[57] MT, MS Orders E5, 287.   [58] Ibid. 301.

The arrangement was undoubtedly a convenient one, for the newly promoted 'reader' received a bench chamber and enjoyed the comforts of the bench table without having to endure the effort and greater expense incumbent upon lecturing, while the house, hard-pressed like all the inns to make ends meet at this difficult time, received welcome infusions of cash. All the inns made similar provisions to commute reading on payment of lump sums between 1679 and 1682.[59] In effect, the readings, which had been so prominent a feature of the inns of court during their 'golden age', had been turned into a crude device for raising revenue during their period of decline. There was a clear analogy to the parallel commutation of barristers' residence requirements to cash.

3. POST-RESTORATION EXERCISES

The post-Restoration revival of public readings was only the most conspicuous aspect of a policy designed to reintroduce the old order of institutional legal education in its entirety. Conservative members of the legal profession like Prynne were convinced of the value of the exercises of legal learning which had taxed their developing powers of analysis and argument during their own student days.[60] Thus, at the same time that decrepit benchers were being reminded of their obligation to undertake an extended course of public lecturing, their juniors were enjoined to dispute knotty points of law in a regular succession of moots, bolts, and imparlances.

But it seems that many of the junior barristers who were at the inns of court during the reign of Charles II did not share the opinion of the Inner Temple bench (as expressed in 1683) that 'the said Exercises are very Advantagious for the Learning and Honour of this Society and of great use to such as intend any progresse in the Law', for there was considerable reluctance to participate in them.[61] In February 1661 the governing council of Lincoln's Inn deplored 'severall neglects and faylings of Exercise . . . lately made by the barristers of this society', and expressed amazement 'that there is a consent and combination interteined and owned by some at least of the gentlemen of the Barr to

---

[59] GI, MS Orders ii. 186, 190–1; IT, MS Acts 1665–87, fos. 112–13; LI, MS Black Book ix, fo. 220.

[60] Cf. W. Prynne, *Brief Animadversions on . . . the Fourth Part of the Institutes of the Laws of England . . . by Sir Edward Cooke* (1669), preface, sig. A.2.

[61] IT, MS Acts 1665–87, fo. 127.

abett and justify such defaults . . . and to incourage and countenance the like for the future'.[62] A similar lack of enthusiasm to moot was in evidence among barristers of the Inner Temple in 1664, and the other inns of court also noted that there was 'greate neglect' of performance in exercises during this period.[63]

The disinclination of young barristers to take part in the learning exercises of their societies was a symptom of the general decay of the communal life of the inns described in Chapter 2, and negligence in the performance of moots and bolts increased as this problem became worse. The attendance of students and probationer barristers at vacations was erratic during the later seventeenth century, especially after 1680, when the readings had ceased.[64] In consequence, many of the exercises which were held normally in the learning vacations were not performed owing to the delinquency of the vacationers, and Gray's Inn, at least, found it necessary to reschedule them during term-time.[65] Exercises held during the law terms involved the participation of masters of the bench as judges, and the diminishing attendance on the affairs of the inns by senior members generally could only encourage the gradual collapse of the exercise system.[66] In November 1691 the Inner Temple parliament complained 'That some masters of the bench do from term to term absent themselves from the bench table and do not give their due assistance in the debating and ordering the affairs of the House and upholding the exercise thereof'. The benchers who were present responded by establishing minimum qualifications of residence for the enjoyment of a bench chamber, but this did not reverse the trend.[67]

The cause of the traditionalists who must have been behind such orders was undoubtedly doomed. Until the abandonment of the readings, they may have enjoyed a majority on the governing bodies of the inns, for those senior barristers who were not sympathetic to the revival of the system of education simply refused to join the bench, as we have seen. However, this in itself was a major problem, for it meant that there were not enough benchers to preside over the moots and

---

[62] LI, MS Black Book viii, fo. 681: cf. ibid., fo. 694; ibid. ix. 16.

[63] IT, MS Acts 1638–64, fo. 177; GI, MS Orders ii. 19; MT, MS Orders E5, 138–9.

[64] Lemmings, 'The Inns of Court and the English Bar', pp. 55–7.

[65] GI, MS Orders ii. 175, 177; IT, MS Acts 1665–87, fos. 8, 102; MT, MS Orders E5, 383 [error for 384].

[66] For failures of benchers to sit in on exercises at LI, 1661–8, see LI, MS Black Book viii, fos. 689, 738, ix. 10–12.

[67] *CITR* iii. 276–7.

bolts. The special council of benchers and judges convened by Lincoln's Inn on 18 November 1675 recognized this difficulty, and attempted to dragoon senior barristers into accepting their calls to the bench, besides encouraging residence among the bar generally.[68] But ultimately there was no solution: following the cessation of reading, barristers were indeed more willing to accept promotion to the governing body of their society, but men who had refused to read were unlikely to be very keen participants in the remaining features of the apparatus of education.[69] Indeed, several failures to perform exercises, caused by the negligence of benchers, were recorded during the last two decades of the seventeenth century.[70] The benchers who were committed to the exercise system were a dying breed. The motion made in 1717 to the Middle Temple by its last lecturer Sir William Whitelocke, that his fellow benchers should preside over the exercises in the hall 'according to the ancient useage', was certainly their swan song.[71]

The new generation of late seventeenth-century benchers presided over the inns during a period when the conventions they applied in admitting students to the bar were watered down considerably.[72] The fact that it was by no means difficult for law students of this period to become barristers without fulfilling their obligations in terms of moots and bolts inevitably contributed to the developing erosion of the apparatus of education.[73] Rendered increasingly obsolete as a course of probation for the bar and deprived of adequate support at all levels of the inns' membership, the exercise system was in a state of terminal collapse after the Revolution of 1688, and it was defunct by the beginning of the Georgian era. In 1691 the bench of Gray's Inn appointed a committee to consider 'what is fitt to be done for the Reformeing of the Exercises to be performed by the students and others', but no action seems to have been taken besides the inspection of 'the Ancient orders'.[74] It appears likely that this inn subsequently abandoned any responsibility for the regulation of exercises, because

---

[68] LI, MS Black Book ix, fo. 118.

[69] Individual barristers continued to refuse call to the bench between 1680 and 1730, but there was no recurrence of the 'great failer' to accept promotion which had occurred in the 1660s and 1670s (see below, p. 237).

[70] IT, MS Orders 1685–91, fo. 49; ibid., MS Orders 1699–1714, fo. 27; LI, MS Black Book ix, fos. 285–6, x, fos. 69, 103.

[71] MT, MS Orders H(8), 89. Whitelocke died 6 months later, aged 80 (Henning, *House of Commons 1660–90*, iii. 712). For his lecture (1684) see above, p. 88.

[72] See above, ch. 3.2.

[73] IT, MS Acts 1665–87, fo. 125; ibid., MS Orders 1685–91, fo. 67; LI, MS Black Book ix, fo. 170.   [74] GI, MS Orders ii. 320, 323.

the bench made no further order on the subject throughout the period covered by this study. At the Middle Temple benchers continued to fulminate occasionally against 'the exceeding negligent performance of Mootes & Exercises', both in term-time and in vacation, and deplored the repeated failure of students to participate in 'grand mootes' at New Inn.[75] The Middle house had been fighting a losing battle since the 1660s to preserve some elements of substantive property law as the basis of their exercises, and to counter the growing tendency for students to repeat written pleadings and exercises, rather than perform them in full. But they finally abandoned the struggle against reading from a prepared script in 1714.[76] By this time there was considerable doubt among students at the inns as to whether they were under any serious obligation to perform exercises at all.[77] A few continued to go through the motions, like William Wynne, a future sergeant at law, who performed at least three exercises during the three years he spent in commons prior to his call in May 1718.[78] But even those who did bother to participate in the exercises expended little time and trouble on them. Dudley Ryder, for example, despite his obvious commitment to studying the law, persuaded an attorney to prepare his New Inn exercise for him, and when the time came to perform it he and his fellow students simply recited their answers to the case. Ryder commented that the whole business was 'all mere formality and signifies nothing', and this seems to confirm the opinion of Roger North that exercises at the Augustan inns were performed 'by way of *opus operatum*, as for tale and not for weight'.[79] Thus the 'educational' apparatus developed at the medieval inns of court was entirely irrelevant to the legal education of future barristers and judges by the beginning of the Hanoverian period.

[75] MT, MS Orders E5, 426, 463, 488–9, H(8), 31, 60–1, 66; cf. IT, MS Orders 1699–1714, fo. 23. Inns of chancery moots were moribund at the satellite inns administered by GI and LI (Hatton, *New View of London*, pp. 641, 646–7, 662, 700, 705, 727).

[76] MT, MS Orders E5, 84, 180, 188, 208, 400, H(8), 60–1; *MTR* iii. 1105; Downing, *Observations on the Middle Temple*, p. 85; cf. GI, MS Orders ii. 59.

[77] LI, MS Black Book ix. 46.

[78] BL., Add. MSS 41843 (Middleton Papers), fos. 49–62: accounts of Wynne at MT 1715–18; IT, MS Miscellanea xxix, fo. 53: 'The Manner of doeing Exercise in the Midd: Temple', [c.1709–24]; ibid. xxiv, fo. 113: 'The Manner the Exercise was done in Trinity Term 1735'. Cf. ibid., fos. 114–15; ibid., xxviii, fo. 13; ibid., MS Orders 1699–1714, fo. 103; *CITR* iv. 310, 382; Bodl., MS Rawlinson B. 374, fos. 50–2: 'The Imparlance Exercise 1719'.

[79] *Diary of Dudley Ryder*, p. 528; *Lives of the Norths*, i. 39; cf. ibid. i. 29; North, *Discourse*, pp. 1–2.

4. EDUCATIONAL CAREERS: UNIVERSITY TRAINING
AND APPRENTICESHIP

Having discussed the decline of formal legal education at the inns of court, it is necessary now to consider the ways and means by which prospective barristers learned the tricks of their trade without institutional guidance. Before considering the minutiae of reading in chambers, it may be instructive to take a look at the general pattern of education for the bar during this period.

Despite the moribund state of legal education at the inns of court, it cannot be said that institutions *in general* had no role to play in preparing men for the bar between 1680 and 1730. Edward Chamberlayne, writing in 1671, regarded a spell at the university as *de rigueur* for the future common law pleader. Chamberlayne's views on the subject of legal education were very possibly anachronistic, but there is no reason to doubt that many young men who entered the inns had previously been at a university, and those who went on to become barristers were especially likely to have enjoyed a college education, even if they did not often take a degree.[80] Table 4.2 shows that nearly 54 per cent of all those barristers admitted to the inns between 1688 and 1714 had matriculated at Oxford, Cambridge, or Trinity College, Dublin. This compares with approximately 41 per cent of university men among students admitted to the inns during those years who never went on to receive a call to the bar.[81] Of course it is by no means true that those men who became barristers were synonymous with the practising counsel of Westminster Hall, but the contrast between barristers and non-barristers with regard to their educational background does suggest that 'professional' law students were more likely than the 'amateurs' to spend a year or two at some college before going on to prosecute their legal studies at the inns of court.

At the university, according to Chamberlayne, the intending barrister might have been 'versed in Logick and Rhetorick, both expedient for a Lawyer, and gotten some insight into the Civil Law,

---

[80] Chamberlayne referred to single and *double* readings as if the system of education was functioning with complete efficiency. In fact, the last double reading had been performed in the early 17th cent. (Chamberlayne, *Angliae Notitia*, pt. II (1st edn., 1671), 432–4; Prest, *Inns of Court*, pp. 60–1, 128).

[81] Of 3,457 men admitted to the inns 1688–1714 who were never called, 1,404 or 40.6% were matriculands of Oxford, Cambridge, or Trinity College, Dublin (sources as in Table 4.2).

TABLE 4.2*a*. *University affiliation of barristers among entrants to the inns of court, 1688–1714*[a]

University	Gray's Inn		Inner Temple		Lincoln's Inn		Middle Temple		Total	
	No.	%	No.	%	No.	%	No.	%	No.	%
Oxford	40	23.3	115	34.0	64	40.5	164	34.6	383	33.5
Cambridge	45	26.2	61	18.0	26	16.5	82	17.3	214	18.7
Dublin	1	0.6	6	1.8	1	0.6	9	1.9	17	1.5
Total admitted to university	86	50.0	182	53.8	91	57.6	255	53.8	614	53.8
No record of university admission	86	50.0	156	46.1	67	42.4	219	46.2	528	46.2
Total	172		338		158		474		1142	

TABLE 4.2*b*. *University record of barristers among entrants to the inns of court, 1688–1714*[b]

	Gray's Inn		Inner Temple		Lincoln's Inn		Middle Temple		Total	
	No.	%	No.	%	No.	%	No.	%	No.	%
Degree	19	11.1	37	11.0	11	7.0	58	12.2	125	11.0
No degree	67	38.9	145	42.9	80	50.6	197	41.6	489	42.8
No record of university admission	86	50.0	156	46.1	67	42.4	219	46.2	528	46.2
Total	172		338		158		474		1142	

[a] Including those who migrated to another inn for call.
[b] Earned degrees only.

Sources: As in Tables 1.4 and 3.2.

and some skill in the French tongue, as well as Latin'.[82] He also may have taken part in some of the remaining exercises which took place at Oxford and Cambridge, for participation in these was said to inculcate

[82] Chamberlayne, *Angliae Notitia*, pt. II (1st edn., 1671), 432–3.

boldness, which was 'a necessary ingredient in a Lawyer'.[83] These activities, together with wide-ranging private reading under the direction of a tutor, were the elements of a liberal education which was the preface to the legal training of many an Augustan counsel.[84]

However, despite the evidence of Table 4.2, the comments of contemporaries with regard to legal education in the late seventeenth and eighteenth centuries give the impression that a preparatory spell of liberal studies at a university was less in vogue than it had been. John Evelyn, writing in 1699, bemoaned the prevailing ignorance of ethics and Civil law among students of the inns of court, and their entire absorption in matters of practice, unsupported by any understanding of the principles of jurisprudence.[85] Moreover, although the proportion of university men among barristers may have increased during the first half of the eighteenth century, Blackstone echoed Evelyn's complaint of the severely practical emphasis given to the training of a barrister, and argued forcibly for the educational as well as the social benefits of 'making academical education a previous step to the profession of the common law'.[86]

Blackstone was concerned at the popularity of apprenticeship with an attorney as a means of introducing young men to the mysteries of legal business. That method of training for the bar had become popular during the period covered by this study, because the close supervision which was possible in an attorney's office was regarded as an antidote to the complete lack of guidance given to the student at the inns of court.[87] Thus in June 1689 Lincoln's Inn barrister James Wittewronge was negotiating with 'a very able Attorney' to apprentice his troublesome son Jacob for four years, he being of the opinion that 'if this course be not taken he [Jacob] will never come to any thing in the law'.[88] In the event, Jacob Wittewronge died in 1693, but his father was determined, apparently, to breed up a son in his own professional image, for his second son Samuel, who entered Lincoln's Inn on 15 May 1700, was on 17 April of that year articled to Edward Miller of the

---

[83] Bodl., MS Ballard 10, fo. 102: Simon Harcourt to [Dr Arthur Charlett], 13 Nov. 1697. Cf. ibid., fo. 109: Harcourt to Charlett, 13 Jan. 1698.

[84] G. Jacob, *The Student's Companion* (2nd edn., 1734), p. iii.

[85] *Letters on Various Subjects . . . to and from William Nicholson D.D.*, ed. J. Nichols (1809), i. 140–2.

[86] Lucas, 'Collective Biography', p. 256; cf. Duman, *English Judicial Bench*, pp. 41–3; Campbell, *London Tradesman*, p. 74. Blackstone, *Commentaries*, i. 31–3.

[87] See *Lives of the Norths*, i. 28; Jacob, *Student's Companion*, pp. iii–iv.

[88] HCRO, Lawes-Wittewronge MSS D/ELw F29, unfol.: James Wittewronge to [Sir John Wittewronge], 27 June 1689.

Inner Temple 'gent' for five years.[89] Miller, who was evidently an attorney, covenanted to 'imploy teach and Instruct the said Samuel Wittewronge as his Clerke according to his skill and knowledge' and to provide his diet and lodging for the period in question.[90] Unfortunately, the subsequent course of Samuel Wittewronge's relationship with his master is not known, but the arrangement was, for some reason, ultimately unsuccessful, since Samuel was never called to the bar.[91]

Not all parents were so unlucky in their efforts to prepare their sons for the bar via clerkship to an attorney. Indeed, some must have been very satisfied, because at least one pupil-master, Charles Sanderson or Saunderson, another attorney of the Temple, was able to make a regular business (between 1712 and 1727) of receiving the sons of his fellow north country men into his office in order to train them in the law.[92] Charles Salkeld, a London solicitor, was responsible for the early legal training of Philip Yorke, the future lord chancellor, as well as that of several other future judges.[93] Yorke spent several years in residence with his master, and was immersed in the 'hurry of business' inseparable from the office, thereby gaining valuable experience of the clerical aspect of legal affairs through preparing briefs and settlements with his own hands.[94] Parents were no doubt aware that such an early initiation into the complicated forms and procedures of the 'mechanical side' of the law was of no small advantage to a future counsellor. Dudley Ryder, struggling to come to terms with the complexities of legal forms in 1716, lamented his handicap in this respect:

I could wish I had served a clerkship with an attorney. It would have given [me] the air and manner of business and used me to go through it, [so] that what

[89] HCRO, Lawes-Wittewronge MSS D/ELw F41, unfol.: James Wittewronge, personal accounts, 1672–93. LI, MS Admissions x, fo. 62.

[90] HCRO, Lawes-Wittewronge MSS D/ELw F39: articles of clerkship, 17 Apr. 1700.

[91] Unlike another attorney's apprentice, Richard Turner, who was called to the bar at LI on 19 Nov. 1695 (LI, MS Black Book x, fo. 45).

[92] E. Hughes, *North Country Life in the 18th Century* (Oxford, 1952–65), i. 77, 377; id., 'The Professions in the 18th Century', in D. A. Baugh (ed.), *Aristocratic Government and Society in 18th Century England* (New York, 1975), 188–9.

[93] P. C. Yorke, *The Life and Correspondence of Philip Yorke, Earl of Hardwicke, Lord High Chancellor of Great Britain* (Cambridge, 1913), i. 53–5.

[94] He was at Salkeld's office by Aug. 1707 at least, and was admitted to a chamber at MT on 20 May 1715 (BL, Add. MSS 35584 (Hardwicke Papers), fo. 32: letter to Yorke at 'Mr Salkelds Att^r in Brooks Street in Holburne London', 13 Aug. 1707; MT, MS Admissions 1695–1735, 220). For his work in the office see BL, Add. MSS 35584, fos. 160–1: Yorke to [?] n.d.; KAO, Papillon MSS U1015 C45 (letter book of Philip

now puts me into a hurry and confusion would go off with ease and dexterity. . .[95]

Ryder had followed a different pattern of legal education, having attended the Universities of Edinburgh and Leiden before coming to the Temple.[96] Although some law students attended a university *and* subsequently entered an attorney's office, there was a tendency during this period to view apprenticeship to an attorney as an alternative to a university education, rather than as a complementary aspect of a unified programme of training for the bar.[97] This is not surprising, because the premiums demanded by good attorneys or solicitors were not small. James Wittewronge, for instance, had paid Edward Miller £150 to take his son Samuel in 1700.[98] Coming on top of perhaps £100 a year to keep a son at the university, this was not an insignificant outlay. Thus Philip Yorke, the son of a man who enjoyed an income of only £300 per annum, was faced with a clear choice when, approaching his sixteenth year, he contemplated the first phase of his legal education.[99] Yorke thereupon took the unusual step of composing a letter to Lord Chief Justice Holt for his judgement on the conflicting advice which he had received in the matter:

Some are of the opinion that I ought to be a Clerk for 3 years with some attorney of great note & practice, that I may thereby become acquainted with the methods & proceedings of the Courts of Judicature. Others . . . are wholly averse to my being with an Attorney & advise me to spend those 3 years in some publick university or in any other place where that sort of Learning is read. And those that agree in this point differ yet in the method to be taken in my Law Studys, some are for laying the foundation in Institutes, Reports, & Statutes, others alledge that it is the more commendable & generous way to pry & search into the abstruse parts of antiquity & get acquainted with the Historys & Customes of our British & Saxon Ancestors, as well as those since the Conquest.[100]

Papillon, 1713–14), 32, 148, 153, 186, 226, 350: draft letters of Philip Papillon to various correspondents, 1713–14.

[95] TS Ryder Diary, p. 242: 27 Apr. 1716. Cf. *Diary of Dudley Ryder*, p. 166.

[96] Ibid. 5–7.

[97] Jacob Wittewronge was both apprentice and university student, having been admitted to Magdalene College, Cambridge, on 24 Jan. 1688 (*Alumni Cantabrigienses*, pt. 1, iv. 445).

[98] HCRO, Lawes-Wittewronge MSS D/ELw F39; cf. ibid., D/ELw F29.

[99] SCRO, Somers MSS 01/33: [Sir] J[oseph] Jekyll to [Charles Cocks], 13 May 1718.

[100] BL, Add. MSS 35584, fos. 7–8: [Philip Yorke] to 'my Lord C. J. H[olt]' draft n.d. [?1705]; cf. Yorke, *Hardwicke*, i. 52.

Yorke's doubts as to the best method of preparation for the bar tend to confirm the impression that great uncertainty prevailed during this period with regard to the ideal pattern of legal education.[101] Given the collapse of formal instruction at the inns and the bad reputation of the universities it is no surprise that some parents, especially those of a practical bent, were attracted by the severe discipline of clerkship to an attorney. On the other hand, more traditionally minded men, particularly if they were of gentry stock, may have been repelled by the prospect of subjecting their sons and heirs to the humiliation of executing the orders of a mere 'pettifogger'. Simon Harcourt, for instance, a bencher of the Middle Temple, sent his son Henry to University College, Oxford, and only threatened him with a 'servile' education as an attorney's clerk when he misbehaved.[102] But whichever course was chosen, every prospective barrister had in due course to be admitted to the inns of court, and was bound to grapple with the law literature which provided the main source of a student's legal training. And here, according to the future Lord Hardwicke, still more uncertainty lay in the choice of reading-matter. Apprentices like Yorke no doubt received direction in their reading and other aspects of their training from their masters, but it is likely that the great majority of students were left to shift for themselves. It is necessary now to consider the course of their legal studies, and the expedients they developed as an aid to learning the law.

5. SELF-EDUCATION

Two fundamental points strike any observer of the state of legal education between 1680 and 1730 at first glance. First, one of the long-term causes of the decline of formal instruction was the avail-ability of printed books, and by the mid-seventeenth century the principal means of studying the law was private reading. In the plain words of one post-Restoration law students' guide 'The Means of this Study are books. . .'[103] In the second place, young men who were attending the inns of court at this time with the intention of training to practise the law received no institutionalized guidance in regard to their course of study. As far as the societies of law were concerned

---

[101] Cf. North, *Discourse*, p. 2.

[102] Bodl., MS Ballard 10, fo. 100: Harcourt to Dr [Arthur] Charlett, 21 Oct. 1697.

[103] W. Phillips, *Studii Legalis Ratio or Directions for the Study of the Law* (3rd edn., 1675), 97.

each student was 'left to himself to enter at which end he fancies, or as accident, inquiry, or conversation prompts'.[104] Things had not changed much when Blackstone began to lecture at Oxford, and he bemoaned the situation of the trainee barrister, who, although deprived of supervision, was 'expected to sequester himself from the world, and by a tedious lonely process to extract the theory of law from a mass of undigested learning'.[105] The uncertainty which surrounded legal education and law made the administration of justice seem like an orderless mystery to the uninitiated, whether law student or litigant, rather than the uniform body of doctrine implied by contemporary judges' (and modern historians') declarations about 'the common law of England'.[106]

Given the unprepossessing nature of the mode of legal education during this period, and the absence of any real guidance on behalf of the inns, it was inevitable that many students should be distracted easily by more stimulating pursuits, and many of those who intended to follow the law probably never got started at all. Thomas Burnet, a younger son of the bishop of Salisbury, seemed to spend most of his days at the Middle Temple in writing political pamphlets or carousing with his friends; and he was only induced to resume his legal training, after nine years' absence abroad, by pressing familial responsibilities.[107] Coote Molesworth, who was at the Temple in 1720, found that his parsimony disqualified him from full participation in the gay life of his fellows; he attempted to escape the drudgery of reading in chambers by persuading his mother that he might just as well read the necessary 'quantum' of law books while travelling abroad, for he argued that there was no advantage to be derived from residence at the inns.[108]

Parents knew better, of course, and young men continued to be sent to the legal societies in order to train them for the bar. However, those who were familiar with the state of affairs at the inns generally took the precaution of arranging for some friend or relative who was a barrister to keep an eye on their son and offer informal guidance in the matter of

---

[104] North, *Discourse*, p. 2.

[105] Blackstone, *Commentaries*, i. 31.

[106] Cf. Baker, *Introduction to English Legal History*, p. 147. For the litigants' view of law see *The Law and Lawyers Laid Open in Twelve Visions* (1737), p. xxvii.

[107] He was admitted MT 15 Jan. 1709, and was called 7 Feb. 1729 (*The Letters of Thomas Burnet to George Duckett 1712–1722*, ed. D. N. Smith (Oxford, 1914), pp. xxi–xxxiv and *passim*).

[108] HMC, *Various Collections*, vii. 292–3: Coote Molesworth to [Lady Molesworth] [1720]. I owe this reference to the kindness of Dr R. O. Bucholz, of Loyola University, Chicago.

study. Thus Sir Francis Drake arranged for his friend Sir Peter King to oversee his two sons when they were studying at the Temple.[109] Those families who had a long tradition of affiliation to the inns of court had plenty of contacts among the London legal community whom they were able to rely on in this respect. The Pollexfens of Devon, for example, were by 1691 a well-established legal family.[110] Edmund Pollexfen of Kitley, himself a barrister, must have been reassured at the knowledge that his numerous friends at the inns would watch over his son Edmund, who was enjoined to keep in touch with them during his stay at the Temple.[111] Forty years later, William Mellish of Lincoln's Inn was also relying upon family connections to further his legal studies, for he was obtaining advice in the matter of reading from 'Cousin Baker'.[112] Such guidance was most effective, of course, in the case of law students who were themselves the sons of practising counsel, because these fortunate young men, like John Turner, son of a sergeant at law, could depend upon their fathers to supply the place of law tutor.[113]

Those students who were not the heirs to a family tradition at the inns of court were in a much more difficult position. It was for this reason that Dudley Ryder was constantly on the look out for contacts who might be able to assist him in his studies. Ryder duly benefited from the guidance of 'Mr Bois', a barrister of the Middle Temple, who advised him on the subject of law books, and he also spent much time in conversation with 'Mr Sampson', an attorney, who helped him to understand the complexities of the 'practical part' of the law, and read with him on several occasions.[114] More privileged students probably did not have to work so hard in order to find assistance, and were likely to benefit from guidance of a higher order. Robert Bertie, the son of an earl and himself a member of parliament, was promised the advice and assistance of Sir Bartholomew Shower, the leading Tory lawyer,

[109] See above, pp. 15–16; DCRO, Drake MSS 346M/F71: Drake to King, 19 Nov. 1711.

[110] Sir Henry Pollexfen was at this time LCJ of CP (Foss, *Judges*, vii. 296).

[111] West Devon RO (Plymouth), Bastard of Kitley MSS accession 74/651: Edmund Pollexfen to Edmund Pollexfen [jun.], 15 Sept. 1691.

[112] University of Nottingham, Mellish MSS Me 165–104/16: William Mellish to Joseph Mellish, 24 Aug. 1729.

[113] In 1711 Serjeant Turner promised his son, then at Oxford, that he would supervise his studies at LI (East Sussex CRO, Frewen MSS FRE 1148: Henry Turner to John Turner, 10 Nov. 1711).

[114] *Diary of Dudley Ryder*, pp. 31, 230; TS Ryder Diary, pp. 2, 135, 177, 180, 193, 247: June 1715–May 1716.

without any solicitation on his part.[115] By the mid-eighteenth century, informal and occasional relationships such as these may have developed into a regular convention whereby the bar student was placed under the close supervision of a junior practiser, who read with him and directed his studies generally.[116] Thus it seems that the modern system of pupillage grew out of the *ad hoc* arrangements which law students made to compensate for the absence of any organized system for learning the law.

The course of reading which was recommended to intending barristers did not change greatly, at least in its broad outline, between the Restoration and the reign of George II, although the choice of books to be read must have become more difficult as a greater volume of literature became available.[117] The student was advised to begin his studies with a course of preparatory reading from the legal text-books, or 'institutionary' works, currently available to him. The titles recommended varied according to the present vogue and individual preference, but, before the advent of Blackstone, young men were advised invariably to devote a large amount of time to the study and digestion of *Littleton's Tenures*, which was regarded as the foremost authority on the land law during the period, and was often read with Sir Edward Coke's commentary upon it, known popularly as *Coke upon Littleton*. Other legal textbooks which might be recommended for the initial course of reading included the other parts of Coke's *Institutes*, or later Thomas Wood's *Institute of the Laws of England*, together with secondary works such as John Perkins's *Profitable Book*, Christopher St Germain's *Doctor and Student*, Sir Anthony Fitzherbert's *New Natura Brevium* and Sir John Fortescue's *De Laudibus Legum Angliae*, as well as some books on the criminal law, most likely Sir William Staunford's *Pleas of the Crown*, Hale's book on that subject, and later the *Treatise* of

---

[115] Bodl., MS Ballard 11, fos. 135–6: [Sir] Edmond Warcupp to Dr Arthur Charlett, 23 June 1696. Bertie was a son of James, 1st earl of Abingdon, and was MP Westbury 1695–1702 and Dec. 1702–8. (*HPT* Robert Bertie).

[116] Campbell, *London Tradesman*, p. 75.

[117] For prescriptions as to reading the law *c.*1660–1730 see Jacob, *Student's Companion*, pp. iv–vii; [M. Hale], preface to H. Rolle, *Un abridgement des plusieurs cases et resolutions del common ley* (1668), p. 8; 'Lord Chief Justice Reeve's Instructions to his Nephew Concerning the Study of the Law' [*c.*1720–37], in F. Hargrave (ed.), *Collectanea Juridica*, (1791–2), i. 79–80; Phillips, *Studii Legalis*, pp. 103–21; North, *Discourse*, pp. 10–24; T. Wood, *Some Thoughts Concerning the Study of the Laws of England* (2nd edn., 1727), 43–5, 51–4. The latter work was intended mainly for non-practisers. For details of editions of these and other law books see P. H. Winfield, *The Chief Sources of English Legal History* (Cambridge, Mass., 1925).

William Hawkins. The student was also advised to familiarize himself
with the terms of the law via books such as Cowell's *Interpreter*, Rastell's
Terms of the Law, or Jacob's *Dictionary*. During the Restoration period,
some of these books may have been read in the archaic dialect of
law French, for this was revived after 1660. However, by 1730 many
English translations of works written in the old language were available, and after 1731, when all proceedings of the courts of justice were
confined to English, the vernacular became universal.[118]

Whether he read these textbooks in law French or English, the
trainee barrister may have found that this preparatory reading taxed his
patience and his capacity, for he was expected thereby to grasp the
basic principles of English law, a considerable task which might involve
two or three years of solitary study, according to Chief Justice Hale.[119]
Having got this far, the student was in a position to begin digesting the
mass of precedents which was the foundation of the common law. At
an earlier period, law students had been expected to begin this phase
of their study by reading the *Year Books*, or medieval reports, but by the
later seventeenth century much of the law contained in these ancient
records was obsolete, and even Restoration lawyers such as Hale and
North recommended only certain volumes.[120] North himself confessed
that, when he was a student, he began with the more modern reports,
and this seems to have been common practice in the eighteenth
century.[121] Reading alone was not enough: at this stage of his studies
the young student was expected to begin a commonplace book or
index, in order to aid recall and to facilitate the recovery of various
precedents relating to any point of law.[122] This meant taking a blank
paper book, entering therein certain titles or heads corresponding to
the various divisions of the law, and then laboriously entering under
each head short summaries of cases found in the reports and statutes
which related to it.[123] The operation was by no means a simple task.

---

[118] Phillips, *Studii Legalis*, p. 29; North, *Discourse*, pp. 11–16; Winfield, *Chief Sources*,
pp. 11–13; J. H. Baker, *A Manual of Law French* (Amersham, 1979), 9–14.

[119] Reeve, 'Instructions', p. 81. [Hale], preface to Rolle, *Abridgement*, p. 8.

[120] Ibid.; North, *Discourse*, pp. 20–1.

[121] *Lives of the Norths*, iii. 89; Reeve, 'Instructions', pp. 80–1; Wood, *Some Thoughts*,
pp. 53–4. Dudley Ryder did not mention reading the *Year Books*.

[122] [Hale], preface to Rolle, *Abridgement*, pp. 8–9; Jacob, *Student's Companion*,
pp. vi–vii; North, *Discourse*, pp. 24–9; Phillips, *Studii Legalis*, pp. 151–82; Reeve,
'Instructions', pp. 79–80; Wood, *Some Thoughts*, p. 46.

[123] Various sources were available for collecting these titles. Some students took them
from abridgements; others may have used *An Alphabetical Disposition of all the Heads
Necessary for a Perfect Commonplace* (1680). I have not located a copy of this manual.

On 11 August 1715 Dudley Ryder recorded his efforts in this regard:

Finished entire Lib: of Coke [including] Beverley's Case of Deests [i.e. idiots] and non compos mentis; it being a very long case and variety of things in it I was perplexed about the disposition of it in my commonplace book. I find it requires a large and comprehensive thought to be able to make a complete lawyer.[124]

Here some men may have had recourse to similar digests of the law which had been published as abridgements, but they were enjoined not to rely upon them entirely, and, like Ryder, to essay a commonplace of their own.[125]

Of course, students of the law had to be able to find textbooks and reports in order to prosecute their studies in this manner. All the inns of court had libraries, but it is not clear how much their junior members were able to use the books, and some of the collections may have been of limited scope before the eighteenth century. At Gray's Inn a library had existed since the sixteenth century, but the room in question had been used for moots and other purposes, and in 1684 was destroyed by fire. It was rebuilt subsequently; but the library did not contain many books, for a catalogue made in 1689 listed only 326 volumes, of which 123 were law books.[126] The Inner Temple was no better provided. Here also a library had existed since the sixteenth century, but it too was used for exercises and for the leisure activities of the benchers; and was twice destroyed by fire, once in 1667 and again in 1679, although the books were preserved on the latter occasion. Yet there was no regular provision for the purchase of books, and before 1709, as at Gray's Inn, no permanent librarian.[127]

The libraries of the two other inns of court may have been in a better condition during the seventeenth century. The first proper Middle

---

[124] TS Ryder Diary, p. 50. For Beverley's case see *The Reports of Sir Edward Coke* (1738), pt. IV, 123–8.

[125] For e.g.s of legal commonplace books of the later 17th and early 18th cents., see IT, Barrington MSS 60, 61, 63, 71, 72, 73, 74, 78, 80; BL, Add. MSS 50117: legal commonplace book of William Longueville, counsellor at law (1639–1721); BL, MS Hargrave 319.

[126] *GIPB* i, pp. xlix–l, ii, pp. xiii–xiv, xxvi. 393; GI, MS Orders ii. 27, 224, 231, 290. The catalogue is at the end of the volume, and is unfoliated. At his death in 1691 LCJ Pollexfen had a library of 198 law books (150 separate titles) in his study at IT (DCRO, Drake MSS 346M/F495/17–23: inventory of books of LCJ Pollexfen, 1691).

[127] Williamson, *The Temple*, pp. 125–6, 293, 510, 512, 526–7, 648–9; *CITR* iii. 48, 53, 73, 105, 144–5, 157, 169–71, 351; IT, MS Acts 1665–87, fo. 35; ibid., MS Orders 1699–1714, fo. 43.

Temple library was founded in 1641, as the result of a bequest, and this became a 'public' library with the appointment of a regular library keeper in 1665, who was obliged to attend during certain hours on a regular basis. This officer proved negligent in the performance of his duties and was dismissed, but he was replaced, and although successors in the office were equally remiss, the library received many gifts of books during the Restoration period. After 1680 the bench made several orders to improve it and replace volumes which were missing. In 1700 a catalogue published under the auspices of Sir Bartholomew Shower listed some 220 volumes of English law.[128] At Lincoln's Inn the library had been founded at the end of the fifteenth century, and was opened to all members in 1632.[129] This inn was unique in that there was a regular means of providing for accessions of books as early as the reign of James I, because members paid a standard sum for the purchase of books as part of their duties upon call to the bar or bench, and fines for failures in exercises were also appropriated to the library.[130] On the other hand, there was no permanent librarian, although one of the butlers was obliged to attend; so access to the collections was possible, if not necessarily provided at convenient times.[131] The stock of reading-matter must have grown considerably over the years, for by 1704, on the occasion of a gift of more books, the bencher responsible for the library was forced to acquaint the council 'that the Library of this Societye is now so full of bookes that there is Little roome Left therein to receave more'.[132]

Perhaps as a response to the collapse of formal education at the inns, all the libraries of these societies were improved during the early eighteenth century. The Inner Temple led the way. In 1709 this inn was induced to build a completely new library to house the legacy of books and manuscripts left by William Petyt, the Whig historian and a

---

[128] Downing, *Observations on the Middle Temple*, p. 26; Dugdale, *Origines Juridiciales*, pp. 193, 197; Hatton, *New View of London*, p. 703; Williamson, *The Temple*, pp. 125, 381–4, 435–8, 502–3; MT, MS Orders E5, 83, 91–2, 330–1, 364–5, 370–1, 382, 384–5, 392, 398–9, 402, 408, 430, 432, 439, 447, 452, 456–7, 477, 479; *Bibliotheca Illustris Medii Templi Societatis* (1700), 235–44.

[129] H. H. L. Bellot, *Gray's Inn and Lincoln's Inn* (1925), 189–90; Douthwaite, *Gray's Inn*, p. 173; Richardson, *History of the Inns of Court*, p. 470; R. J. Schoeck, 'The Libraries of Common Lawyers in Renaissance England: Some Notes and a Provisional List', *Manuscripta*, 6 (1962), 156–7.

[130] R. R. Pearce, *A History of the Inns of Court and Chancery* (1848), 202–3; LI, MS Black Book ix, fo. 60; *LIBB* iii, p. xviii.

[131] LI, MS Black Book ix, fo. 62.

[132] Ibid. x, fos. 137–9.

former treasurer. A permanent librarian was appointed, who was to attend at fixed times every day, and from 1713 £20 a year was ordered to be laid out for the purchase of books. In 1728 this was increased to £50. As a result of these regular purchases, and of bequests and gifts, the stock of law books grew steadily. There were approximately 300 in the last year of Queen Anne's reign, 428 in 1715, and some 500 by 1733.[133] Petyt may be regarded as the inspiration for a general improvement in the library facilities of the Temple, for he also bequeathed £50 to the Middle house for the purchase of books.[134] The benchers of this inn continued to pay attention to the condition of their library. During the early Hanoverian period much time and effort was spent in cataloguing and arranging the books to improve security and facilitate ease of access, and in 1722 the library keeper's hours of attendance were extended.[135] In the meantime Lincoln's Inn had continued to augment its stock of books via bequests and regular purchases, while Gray's Inn, having solved its financial difficulties, also set up a 'public' library in 1725, and allocated specific sums of money to 'Compleat the Law Books of such Library'.[136]

Although by 1730 the libraries of the inns of court were well stocked and accessible, it is evident that law students of the early eighteenth century, no less than their predecessors, found it necessary to have their own supply of essential texts. Dudley Ryder, for instance, was advised 'to get a good study of law books' as a means of reference, and William Wynne, his contemporary at the Middle Temple, made several purchases of textbooks and reports.[137] These outlays must have been a considerable burden to the less well endowed among the

---

[133] *CITR* iii, pp. xci–xcii, 411–13, 417–20, 424–5, 438, 441, iv, pp. ix–x, 11, 13–14, 48, 88, 98–9, 101, 118, 131–2, 152, 169, 185, 210, 230, 232–3; IT, MS Orders 1699–1714, fos. 82–3, 86, 88, 91, 95, 108–9, 111, 114–15, 118, 120; ibid. 1715–33, fos. 3, 9, 13, 22, 35, 62, 64, 74, 76, 89; ibid., MS Miscellanea xi (Library Papers, 1708–1842), items 1, 3, 6, 7, 9, 10, 11, 12, 14, 15: receipts, bills, and accounts of books given and purchased, 1708–29; ibid., Miscellaneous or Additional MSS iv, item 1, fos. 13–27, item 3, fos. 14–22, item 4, fos. 2–15: library catalogues, *c.*1709–13, 1715, and 1733.

[134] MT, MS Orders H(8), 32, 56, 59. He had previously given this society books (mainly non-legal) in 1698 (Williamson, *The Temple*, p. 502).

[135] MT, MS Orders H(8), 179–80, 219, 258–9, 262, 271, 273, 275, 278, 306–7, 309, 328, 352; *Master Worsley's Book*, pp. 107, 195–6; *Catalogus Librorum Bibliothecae Honorabilis Societatis Medii Temple Londini* (1734), *passim*; HMC, *Portland*, v. 552–3: Henry Carey to the earl of Oxford, 1718.

[136] LI, MS Black Book x, fos. 163–4, 167, 170, xi. 42, 44, 129, 142, 152–3, 173, 206, 258. *GIPB* ii, pp. xxvi–xxvii, 401–2; GI, MS Orders ii. 643, 645, 648, 650–3, 656, 685, 690, 709, iii. 15.

[137] TS Ryder Diary, p. 292: 2 July 1716; BL., Add. MSS 41843, fos. 53–61: expenses of William Wynne for Mar. 1716–Feb. 1719.

trainee barristers. Even William Cowper, son of a highly successful barrister and nephew of the former lord chancellor, found them onerous. By 1711 he had completed the first phase of his reading, and was about to venture upon a commonplace, but he was unable to afford the purchase of the necessary reports, and was compelled to appeal to his eminent uncle. While less well-connected students like Ryder and Wynne had to manage as best they could, Cowper was more fortunate, for the ex-chancellor sent his nephew his own set of Coke's reports, together with a promise of further aid.[138]

Reading and commonplacing were clearly of vital importance to law students such as Cowper, Wynne, and Ryder, but there were other less cloistered aspects to their legal studies which were designed to supplement their grounding in the theory and practice of the law. Observation of the administration of justice was regarded as being of particular value to intending counsel. Men born into the ranks of the landed gentry may have taken the advice of Roger North and, like him, presided over courts leet or courts baron as a means of gaining a practical insight into the operation of the law at grass-roots level.[139] Sons of merchants or professional men probably did not have the connections necessary to enjoy this experience, but every law student, whatever his social origins, was able to attend the central courts of Westminster Hall or the London sessions at the Guildhall and the Old Bailey, and this was considered an essential part of training for the bar. Having grasped the main principles of the law via his preparatory reading of textbooks, the student was enjoined to supplement his indexing of reports and statutes by making notes of the arguments which he was able to witness in these courts.[140]

Philip Yorke was assiduous in his visits to Westminster Hall during his student days, as his reports of proceedings in King's Bench throughout the period 1711 to 1716 show.[141] However, the primary aim of attending the courts of law was not to increase the student's stock of precedents, but to familiarize him with the procedures and

---

[138] HCRO, Panshanger MSS D/EP F58/85–8: letters of William Cowper to Lord Cowper, 31 May 1711 and 5 July 1711.

[139] North, *Discourse*, pp. 38–9; *Lives of the Norths*, iii. 106–10; cf. ibid. i. 29–31.

[140] [Hale], preface to Rolle, *Abridgement*, p. 8; North, *Discourse*, pp. 31–8; Phillips, *Studii Legalis*, pp. 184–5; Reeve, 'Instructions', p. 80; Wood, *Some Thoughts*, p. 6.

[141] BL., Add. MSS 35988, 35989, *passim*, 35990, fos. 1–143. Not all the reports in the Hardwicke papers are the work of Yorke himself (C. E. Croft, 'Philip Yorke, 1st Earl of Hardwicke: An Assessment of his Legal Career' (Cambridge Univ. Ph.D. thesis, 1983), 18–22).

language common to the courtroom. Dudley Ryder found the experience beneficial in this respect:

> It is good to attend the courts constantly, though one does not find one's self much the better for every particular time one goes, for it insensibly habituates one to think in their manner and accustoms one to their style and practice. I intend therefore to be very constant in my attendance upon them.[142]

Indeed, Ryder kept to this, for he recorded regular morning visits to Westminster (sometimes every day of the week) right through the law terms which fell between June 1715 and November 1716, and even went to the trouble of gaining admission to the House of Lords in order to witness the trials of the Jacobite peers.[143]

Unlike reading in chambers, attending the courts was not a solitary activity, for early eighteenth-century students invariably went down to Westminster in groups, either sharing a coach or a boat from the Temple steps.[144] This company was no doubt a welcome antidote to being sequestered alone with a pile of books, and it also provided an opportunity for conversation on the subject of their studies. Indeed, students were recommended to discuss their reading with their peers (or their superiors) as a means of fixing it in the memory, rectifying misunderstandings, and, most of all, developing a facility of ready speech.[145]

The institutional expression of this practice had virtually disappeared by 1700, because the inns' exercises were to all intents and purposes defunct, as was seen earlier. It is clear, however, that certain serious students realized the value of such activity, and that it was continuing in the form of unofficial mooting and case-putting in the coffee houses in and around Fleet Street. Thus a correspondent of Dr Arthur Charlett, upon finding a mutual friend who was a law student 'hard linked to Cooke upon Littleton' in his study, 'obliged him to come to Mainwarings Coffee house, for there he will meete many students of his owne Standing, who comonly moote cases, besides . . . many other Barristers and some Benchers'.[146] Dudley Ryder gave a more detailed description of a law club of nine students which he had from John Bowes, a friend of Philip Yorke, and himself a member of the club.

---

[142] TS Ryder Diary, p. 171: 28 Jan. 1716.
[143] Ibid. 9–442 *passim*; *Diary of Dudley Ryder*, pp. 168–9, 179–80, 196–9.
[144] TS Ryder Diary, pp. 12, 117: 25 June and 27 Oct. 1715.
[145] North, *Discourse*, pp. 29–31, 38; Phillips, *Studii Legalis*, pp. 182–4.
[146] Bodl., MS Ballard 11, fos. 135–6; [Sir] Edmund Warcupp to Dr Arthur Charlett, 23 June 1696.

Bowes and his associates were each assigned a different topic of the law which they were to describe in detail to the company, who thereupon discussed the points raised. In this way the club would proceed in the exposition and discussion of several branches of the law. Moreover, each week two members were assigned to prepare arguments on some theoretical case which they were to dispute before their fellows on the next occasion they met. Ryder perceived that such practice was of great use in the development of those powers of oratory essential to a successful lawyer, and lamented the fact that he was unlikely to gain admission to this élite society.[147] But the diarist himself was not entirely deprived of the benefits of informal disputation with his fellow students. Much of his time was spent in several local taverns and coffee houses where he met and conversed with a wide circle of acquaintances on a variety of subjects. Furthermore, Ryder was a member of a 'civil law club': he and several other young men who were training for the bar met weekly at 'Sue's' in order to discuss aspects of the Civil law and jurisprudence. Like Bowes and his associates, these students took their proceedings seriously, for they adhered to some kind of regular agenda at their meetings, and Ryder invariably took the trouble to read specific texts in preparation.[148]

Thus, although they had no institutional guidance, students of the inns of court showed considerable enterprise in developing their own apparatus for oral exercise. This individual initiative was the characteristic feature of legal education in the early eighteenth century. Unless they entered into apprenticeship with an attorney, students like Ryder learned the law according to a programme which was not greatly dissimilar from that of their early Stuart predecessors, for they too had been occupied in solitary reading and commonplacing, and they also attended the courts.[149] But by 1700 training for the bar had reached the end of a process of development by which it became almost entirely a matter of self-help, and had no official connection with the inns of court. Whether left to his own devices entirely, or having the benefit of guidance from an attorney or practising barrister, the Augustan law student learned his trade by determined personal application to his severe diet of study, and his activities in this regard were quite separate from his obligations as a member of one of the societies of law. After

---

[147] *Diary of Dudley Ryder*, pp. 363–4; TS Ryder Diary, p. 435: 15 Nov. 1716.

[148] *Diary of Dudley Ryder*, pp. 10–11; TS Ryder Diary, pp. 133, 135, 141–2, 146, 157, 161, 179, 183, 187, 219: Nov. 1715–Mar. 1716.

[149] Prest, *Inns of Court*, pp. 131, 137–49.

several years spent in this way, he would be duly called to the bar, but this was not a recognition of his successful conquest of the mysteries of the law; rather it was a sign that he had eaten the requisite number of dinners in commons and paid for a sufficient number of exercises.[150] Still, it was at this point that informal training and formal qualification finally coincided for the 'professional' student, and he was thereby in a position to contemplate the next crucial step in his forensic career, that of beginning practice as a counsellor at law.

---

[150] The very limited biographical material cited above suggests that students spent 3 or 4 years in 'residence' before call (Bertie 1696–9, Ryder 1715–19, Wynne 1715–18).

5

THE PRACTISING BAR
PRACTICE AND PROFESSIONAL
DEVELOPMENT

EXAMINATION of the upper branch of the English legal profession between 1680 and 1730 yields depressingly negative results if confined to the inns of court. During these years, as has been seen, the inns experienced falling admissions and reduced levels of residence, together with financial difficulties, the devaluation of the qualifications prescribed for the bar, and the decline and collapse of their educational apparatus. However, the point has now been reached where the focus of attention can be shifted from the institutional structure of the bar to the profession itself and its members, and this presents a more positive picture. It is true that the bar, like the inns, underwent numerical contraction, but for the profession this represented an invigorating purge, rather than a symptom of decline. The increasing irrelevance of the inns to active barristers and judges was in fact one aspect of an important development by which the bar began to respond to the demands of a society which was becoming more sophisticated and more prosperous as the pace of economic activity accelerated. It is the purpose of this and the following chapters to adumbrate and explain this development.

The present chapter focuses upon the professional characteristics and activities of the men who made advocacy at the bars of the courts in Westminster Hall and on circuit the principal element of their careers. Alternative or supplementary careers available to barristers have already been considered, if only in outline.[1] Owing to limitations of space the discussion is concerned mainly with the bar as it appeared at the centre. This may give insufficient emphasis to the provincial aspects of legal practice, although there was no *purely* provincial bar of any significance after the Restoration, or until the early nineteenth century.[2] The analysis below concentrates upon the quantitative

---

[1] See above, pp. 58–9.
[2] Duman, 'English Bar in the Georgian Era', pp. 97–8; see below, pp. 169–70.

'anatomy' of the bar, in terms of its size and professional structure, and the distribution of business among advocates in the central courts. But first it is necessary to describe and classify the salient features of *beginning* practice at the bar.

I. STARTING OUT

For the newly called barrister of the Renaissance and early seventeenth century, it is possible that the acquisition of a bar gown was not the signal for immediate entry into the lists of counsel pleading in Westminster Hall. From 1559 orders promulgated on behalf of the crown, the Privy Council, and the judges had regularly insisted upon a period of probation after call, during which the junior barrister was not to appear at the bar of any of the central courts. This period was originally set at ten years, but it was reduced to five years in 1574, and then to three years from 1614.[3] Throughout this time of enforced silence the fledgling counsel was expected to continue his study and engage in exercises to perfect his understanding of the law, for 'the over-early and hasty practice of Utter Barristers doth make them less grounded and sufficient, whereby the Law may be disgrac'd and the Clyent prejudiced'.[4]

This injunction not to practise for three years after call was included among the judges' orders of 1664.[5] How much notice was taken of it by young counsel and the presiding judges themselves is not clear: Francis North, the future lord keeper, did not immediately rush to practise upon his call to the bar in 1661, but continued to attend the courts and report, although he was prepared to accept briefs if they came his way.[6] His brother Roger saw Guilford as a model in this as in so much else, and recommended young counsel to follow the same course for a few years after their calls.[7] But it is likely that this advice was out of step with the times, for there is no evidence that new barristers of the late seventeenth and early eighteenth centuries abstained from practice for any significant period of time. William Cowper, the future lord chancellor, made his first motion at the King's Bench bar only a month after he had been called in May 1688, and ten

---

[3] Richardson, *History of the Inns of Court*, pp. 435–6, 443, 447.
[4] Orders of 1614 and 1630 (Dugdale, *Origines Juridiciales*, pp. 317, 320; Richardson, *History of the Inns of Court*, pp. 443, 447).
[5] Ibid. 450.   [6] *Lives of the Norths*, i. 39–40.
[7] North, *Discourse*, pp. 34–5, 37.

years later Peter King, another future occupant of the woolsack, waited no longer to make his first appearance, despite the advice of his patron, John Locke, to bide his time.[8]

Nevertheless, the majority of young barristers, no matter how precocious they were, could not expect to gain much business for a few years after they had been called to the bar. During these early stages of their careers they were no doubt forced to continue much as they had while mere students: like North, attending the courts, reading, and, if they were lucky, taking a motion when given the opportunity to do so. Since they could not hope to gain much in the way of fees at this time, they must have continued to be reliant upon their parents or patrons, unless, like Roger North, they earned a small income via court keeping, or enjoyed some other remuneration, perhaps from a college fellowship, or illicit practice as an attorney.[9] However, throughout these early years, although they may have continued to study, they were also laying the foundations of a regular legal practice.

First of all, this meant acquiring and furnishing suitable accommodation for the reception of clients: attorneys, solicitors, and, to a diminishing extent, litigants themselves. Traditionally, the new barrister sold his student's garret or third floor chamber at his inn, and took a more accessible set of rooms, preferably upon the first floor, no doubt as a compromise between 'health' and 'wealth': in other words escaping the bustle and smell of street level, while relieving the legs of prospective clients.[10] But as has been seen, many students did not take any chamber until they were on the point of being called; only then did they set up as resident members of the inns.[11] The benchers' complaints about non-resident barristers show that some never did so: these men must have established their chambers elsewhere.[12] Yet all who were seriously intent upon practice in the metropolis must have found some form of professional accommodation in London, and a majority probably preferred to be established in the legal quarter, close to the precincts of the inns, and near to the attorneys' offices. Once

---

[8] HCRO, Panshanger MSS D/EP F81/19: Cowper to Judith Cowper [his wife], 28 June 1688. Cowper was called 25 May 1688 (MT, MS Orders E5, 363); *Correspondence of Locke*, vi. 437, 442; Locke to King, 27 June and 3 July 1698. King was called 3 June 1698 (MT, MS Orders E5, 451).

[9] *Lives of the Norths*, iii. 106–10; Duman, 'English Bar in the Georgian Era', p. 95.

[10] *Lives of the Norths*, i. 41–2; *The Law and Lawyers Laid Open in Twelve Visions* (1737), p. 78.   [11] See above, p. 32.

[12] Sir Bartholomew Shower had chambers in Chelsea during the 1690s (BL, MS Lansdowne 1105, fo. 154: brief notes of Shower's life in his own hand).

having found such a base, the young counsel busied himself in making it ready to receive clients. Thus Philip Ward, a barrister of the Inner Temple who was called in 1710, worried about the appearance of his newly acquired chambers, and appealed to the young Philip Yorke for assistance, insisting that: 'Cou'd you but help me to furnish the Inside of them [his chambers] with a little of your Spirit I am satisfied that wou'd best answer the purpose of tempting Suitors'.[13]

No matter how sumptuously he furnished his rooms, it was not sufficient for the aspiring young barrister simply to sit within, waiting for attorneys to knock on his door with lucrative briefs. In early modern England counsel found business and made their way in the world by creating and exploiting connections in society generally and among lawyers in particular. Their most direct source of employment, of course, was the attorneys themselves, those 'pettifoggers' of the law who were the objects of so much derision among the pamphleteers of the early eighteenth century. Barristers on the make could not afford to despise them. Dudley Ryder, for instance, even before he was called to the bar, was making plans 'to get as much acquaintance among the attornies as possible and cultivate what I have already'.[14] As usual Ryder was forced to shift for himself while others were rendered valuable assistance by family and friends. Peter King was assured of the patronage of John Locke and his numerous friends and allies from all walks of life in post-Revolution England. Only six months after King became a barrister he must have been encouraged to receive this proof of the efforts of Locke's circle to establish him in practice:

I have sent you your booke by this bearer Mrs Lane. She has an Uncle in town an Attorney of Stafford Shire a man of credit & practise in that Country. My Lady Masham has spoke to her to recommend you to her Uncle & I believe she will not forget it, for she told my Lady that she intended it her self.[15]

King doubtless acquired much of his early practice in Westminster Hall from his acquaintance with Locke's friends, who included several Whig politicians, together with some of the judges and the lord chancellor, Somers.[16] Like most young barristers, however, a large part

---

[13] Ibid., Add. MSS 35584, fo. 180: Ward to Yorke, n.d. Ward was called at IT on 26 June 1710, and had been admitted to a chamber by 19 Nov. 1710 (*CITR* iii. 421; IT, MS General Account Book, 1702–10, unpag.).

[14] TS Ryder Diary, p. 327: 7 Aug. 1716.

[15] Bodl., MS Locke c. 40, fo. 31: Locke to King, 11 Feb. 1699; cf. *Correspondence of Locke*, vi. 562.

[16] See ibid. v–vii, *passim*.

of his early business (especially on circuit) was probably derived from connections acquired in his county of origin. Among the manuscripts in the care of Devon County Council is a collection of legal papers in the hand of the future lord chancellor. These include documents of 1700–1 relating to a private act of parliament on behalf of Rawlin Mallock, a Devonshire country gentleman, and a series of Exchequer bills and answers, together with some Chancery bills, covering 1700–5, all of which relate to the affairs of King's fellow west countrymen.[17] His activities on behalf of these local connections did not cease as his reputation grew and his career developed an important parliamentary aspect. In 1701 Henry Pollexfen, son of the late lord chief justice, was employing Counsellor King to draw up a strict settlement in order to entail his estate, and the rising barrister continued to advise and represent friends and acquaintances of Sir Francis Drake, his patron in parliament, for many years.[18]

The exploitation of local connections was only one way for a young counsel to begin to build up a successful practice, although it was probably a very common strategy. The ambitious barrister had to be ready to exploit any natural advantages which accrued to him, and these varied according to the relationships which he or his family had established with society at large. For James Harrington, a young man called to the bar at the Inner Temple in 1690, his closest ties were with the world of scholars and divines in the ancient University of Oxford, where he had received his education and, in return, bestowed his allegiance.[19] Harrington's opportunities for employment lay in his college connections and their legal affairs. During the 1690s Oxford was involved in a series of disputes which gave rise to litigation, and Harrington, as a faithful son of the university who was also a London-based lawyer, was useful as a general agent and later as an advocate. In 1689–90, before he had been called to the bar, he was employed to oversee and act as solicitor in the celebrated case of Henry Wildgoose, which was a dispute between the university and the city of Oxford.[20]

---

[17] DCRO, Exeter City Library MSS 49/11/1–214: 'Manuscripts relating to Somersetshire, Devonshire etc.' in the hand of Peter King. Cf. Exeter City Library MSS 48/13/5/78: P[eter] King to Rawln Mallock [?] Nov. 1700.

[18] Ibid., Drake MSS 346M/F83–101: correspondence between King and Pollexfen, Oct.–Nov. 1701, and legal documents; cf. Elliot-Drake, *Family and Heirs*, ii. 147–9; DCRO, Drake MSS 346M/F37, 40, 41: Sir Francis Drake to King, 13 Jan. 1704, 23 Mar., and 3 Apr. 1706.

[19] Matriculated Christ Church 17 Dec. 1683 (aged 19); graduated BA 1687, MA 1690; called IT 2 June 1690 (Foster, *Alumni Oxonienses*, i. 653; *CITR* iii. 266).

[20] BL, Add. MSS 36707 (Harrington Papers), fos. 73, 77–80: letters from Thomas

During 1690 Harrington was also negotiating with the Stationers' Company on behalf of the university in a dispute as to its privilege of receiving a copy of every book published.[21] By January 1691, having been called to the bar, he was sufficiently trusted to make routine motions on behalf of his *alma mater* in King's Bench, relating to the affair of Exeter College, which involved a quarrel between the rector and the visitor.[22] The case dragged on for some time and, besides continuing to act for the university in this and other matters, by 1692 the young advocate gained the confidence of his clerical clients so far that he was employed to argue at a hearing before Lord Chief Justice Holt and his puisnes, with no less an advocate than the solicitor-general, Sir Thomas Trevor, as his opponent.[23] Thus only two years after his call, James Harrington was well on the way to becoming one of the principal legal representatives of the university: in addition to being employed as an advocate, he was approached for legal opinions on college business, and he continued to be consulted on the university's legal affairs generally.[24] Having established such a secure base for his practice in such a short time, it is likely that he would have gone on to make a brilliant figure at the bar, and it must have been a matter of regret and disappointment to his friends and employers alike that he died prematurely in November 1693.[25]

Harrington's exploitation of his university connections was a variation on the general pattern by which young barristers took advantage of whatever contacts were available to them in order to establish the beginnings of a practice. For many, this simply meant

Newey, Arthur Charlett, and G[eorge] S[malridge] to [James Harrington], 3 Nov. 1689, 23, 26, and 28 Jan. 1690; Bodl., MS Ballard 22, fo. 3: Harrington to Mr [Arthur] Charlett, 30 Jan. 1690. Wildgoose was an Oxford tradesman who attempted to avoid undertaking city office by being matriculated as a privileged servant of the university. The affair led to a Common Pleas suit between the city and the university (G. V. Bennett, 'Against the Tide: Oxford under William III', in *The History of the University of Oxford*, V: The Eighteenth Century, ed. Sutherland and Mitchell, p. 33).

[21] BL, Add. MSS 36707, fos. 83, 98–100: correspondence of Harrington with Dr Jonathan Edwards and G[eorge] S[malridge], 19 June 1690 and n.d.; Bodl., MS Ballard 22, fos. 8–11: Harrington to Charlett and Smalridge, 23 Sept. and 11 Dec. 1690.

[22] Bodl., MS Ballard 22, fos. 12–13, 17–18, 20–2: Harrington to Charlett, 29 Jan., 12 and 14 June 1691, 18 Feb. 1692. For the Exeter College affair see C. E. Mallet, *The History of the University of Oxford* (1924–7), iii. 78–9; W. R. Ward, *Georgian Oxford* (Oxford, 1958), 21.

[23] Bodl., MS Ballard 22, fos. 16–17, 29–30, 40–1: Harrington to Charlett, 9, 23, and 31 May 1692, and n.d.

[24] Ibid., fo. 27: opinion of James Harrington, 29 Mar. 1692. BL Add. MSS 36707, fos. 115–18, 120–3: Charlett to [Harrington], 25 Dec. 1692, 2, 3, 5, and 17 Jan. 1693.

[25] Bodl., MS Ballard 22, fo. 43: note of Harrington's death in an unknown hand.

taking opportunities opened up by parents and other relatives: William Wynne, for example, later a serjeant at law, was a permanent beneficiary of his family's general involvement with a particular section of Augustan society.[26] Wynne's father, Dr Owen Wynne LL D, undersecretary of state during with reign of James II, seems to have been well connected with the Church establishment, to the extent that, at his death, the bishop of Bangor solemnly promised to assist his children as far as it was in his power to do so.[27] The young William Wynne was also a relative of John Wynne, bishop of Asaph; thus he already enjoyed good connections in the Church when he was called to the bar in 1718, and it is no surprise that he seems to have turned to the ecclesiastical establishment for employment.[28] By 1723, only five years after he had first put on a bar gown, he was eminent enough to be retained as one of the counsel to Francis Atterbury, bishop of Rochester, upon the trial of the bishop for high treason.[29] Although this cannot have done much to improve his prospects of employment by the government, the young barrister's ties to the upper echelons of the Church were strengthened by his marriage (in 1728), for his father in law, William Brydges, serjeant at law, was friend and counsel to successive bishops of Hereford.[30] In future years Wynne was the trusted adviser of some of the leaders of the Church, while he continued to be employed generally in matters of an ecclesiastical nature. In 1735–6 he was involved in a case of tithes on behalf of the Bathurst family; and a decade later he was consulted by Edmund Gibson, bishop of London, in order to settle the marriage articles of Gibson's daughter.[31] No doubt Serjeant Wynne also found business in other spheres of the law, but it seems that the clerical connections

[26] Called MT 23 May 1718; serjeant 1736 (MT, MS Orders H(8), 104; Baker, *Serjeants*, p. 210).

[27] For Owen Wynne see *DNB* xxi. 1176. BL, Add. MSS 41843 fo. 9: H[umphrey Humphreys, bishop of] Bangor to [Dorothy Wynne], 3 Dec. 1700.

[28] Ibid., fos. 88, 98, 102: J[ohn Wynne, bishop of] Bath and Wells to William Wynne, 14 June 1729, 22 Jan. 1732, and 5 May 1735; *DNB* xxi. 1177–8.

[29] BL, Add. MSS 41843, fo. 93: [Francis Atterbury, bishop of Rochester] to [William] W[ynne], [1723].

[30] He married Grace, daughter and co-heiress of William Brydges on 30 Sept. 1728 (*DNB* xxi. 1176); BL, Add. MSS 41843, fos. 20–1, 64–5: letters of H[umphrey Humphreys, bishop of] Hereford and P[hilip Bisse, bishop of] Hereford, to William Brydges, n.d. and 24 Apr. 1718.

[31] Ibid., fos. 104–8: letters and memoranda from H[enry] Bathurst to Mr Serjeant Winn, 1735 and n.d., and from [Allen, 1st Baron Bathurst to the Revd Mr Jackson, 6 Mar. 1736; ibid., fos. 109–12: Edmund [Gibson, bishop of] London to [William Wynne], 21 and 26 Apr. 1746.

established by his relatives provided him with early opportunities to make his way at the bar, and gave his practice a bias towards the affairs of the Church and its ministers which was never entirely abandoned.[32]

Although connections derived from family, university, or locality might give a young counsel the opportunity to take his first steps in practice, this support could not assist him when he came to plead his client's cause in open court. Unless he was fortunate enough to be patronized by some judge, the young barrister had only his natural talents to depend upon, and his first motion was likely to be a considerable ordeal. Roger North, who enjoyed the singular good fortune to open his career at the bar before his brother as chief justice, described the experience as 'a crisis like the loss of a maidenhead', and even Lord Chancellor Cowper, who was noted in his maturity for the eloquence of his advocacy, at his maiden motion had to resort to much 'self persuasion & reasoning with myself' in order to get through without the 'bashfulness' to which he was naturally inclined.[33]

Cowper began his career as an advocate in the court of King's Bench, before Lord Chief Justice Holt, and many new barristers looked to this court as a forum for their first motion.[34] Table 5.1 is an analysis of the barristers pleading in the central courts of Westminster Hall in 1680 and in 1720, according to their seniority by date of call to the bar. This shows that in 1680 the King's Bench, and especially the pleas side of that court, was indeed heavily populated with relatively junior counsel, who formed nearly 42 per cent of the barristers who have been identified at that bar. The Chancery was also popular among young counsel, and by 1720 it is clear that the chancellor's court had replaced King's Bench as the favourite court for the junior practitioners. Like Dudley Ryder, they may have found 'the Chancelry business more agreeable to my nature as it depends less upon precedents and more upon good sound reason and sense'.[35] Common Pleas, of course, was closed to all but the serjeants, and the Exchequer was regarded as 'mysterious' to the point that it required some degree of experience and specialization, especially in 1680.[36] The House of Lords involved practice of an even more 'exquisite' nature, and it

---

[32] For an e.g. of Wynne's *non*-clerical business see App. XI below.

[33] *Lives of the Norths*, iii. 90; HCRO, Panshanger MSS D/EP F81/19: Cowper to Judith Cowper, 28 June 1688.

[34] *Lives of the Norths*, iii. 90–1; M. Hale, 'A Discourse concerning the Courts of King's Bench and Common Pleas', in F. Hargrave (ed.), *A Collection of Tracts Relative to the Law of England* (1787), 371.

[35] TS Ryder Diary, p. 427: 9 Nov. 1716.   [36] *Lives of the Norths*, iii. 140.

TABLE 5.1*a*. *Seniority of practising counsel by court, 1680*

Standing (years)	KB Crown bar		KB Pleas bar		Exchequer Pleas bar		Exchequer Equity bar		Common Pleas bar		Chancery bar		House of Lords bar	
	No	%	No.	%	No.	%	No.	%	No.	%	No.	%	No.	%
0–9	41	36.9	70	41.7	20	30.8	35	31.8	—	—	70	37.8	2	9.1
10–24	46	41.4	69	41.1	32	49.2	53	48.2	7	19.4	77	41.6	15	68.2
25–39	22	19.8	26	15.5	12	18.5	21	19.1	24	66.7	36	19.5	5	22.7
40–54	2	1.8	3	1.8	1	1.5	1	0.9	5	13.9	2	1.1	—	—
Total classified	111		168		65		110		36		185		22	
Unknown	53		88		31		60		—		106		2	

TABLE 5.1*b*. *Seniority of practising counsel by court, 1720*

Standing (years)	KB Crown bar		KB Pleas bar		Exchequer Pleas bar		Exchequer Equity bar		Common Pleas bar		Chancery bar		House of Lords bar	
	No.	%	No.	%	No.	%	No.	%	No.	%	No.	%	No.	%
0–9	29	33.3	35	30.4	11	35.5	28	28.6	1	3.8	76	39.6	6	35.3
10–24	36	41.4	46	40.0	10	32.3	39	39.8	3	11.5	70	36.5	3	17.6
25–39	19	21.8	30	26.1	10	32.3	28	28.6	17	65.4	37	19.3	7	41.2
40–54	3	3.4	4	3.5	—	—	3	3.1	5	19.2	9	4.7	1	5.9
Total classified	87		115		31		98		26		192		17	
Unknown	30		57		13		43		—		66		4	

Sources: See Appendix II for the sources of this data and the methodology of quantification.

tended therefore to be dominated by the élite of the bar, who were generally men of some maturity in practice, although in 1720 a remarkable crop of relatively young barristers, including Philip Yorke and Charles Talbot, were beginning to make some impression in the peers' house.[37]

In King's Bench or in Chancery, the junior barrister could expect to be employed alone in making small motions which were regarded as a matter of course and were not likely to require great learning or

---

[37] *Lives of the Norths*, iii. 168; in 1720 Philip Yorke appeared twice in the House of Lords, while Talbot appeared 7 times (sources as in App. II).

oratorical skills. Roger North began his bar practice with work of this nature.[38] However, even if he had some briefs, it might be difficult for the young counsel to obtain a hearing, for these courts were furiously competitive, and the senior barristers had priority when it came to making motions, beginning with the law officers and crown counsel.[39] But there were specific opportunities for junior members of the bar to secure a hearing. The Chancery at least recognized the difficulties of young counsel by establishing the custom that they should have the privilege of moving first on the last day of the law term. Thus in Michaelmas 1725 the Honourable John Finch, a barrister of only six years' standing, was proposed by a solicitor to make a motion on behalf of the duchess of Marlborough, and the solicitor-general was nominated merely to second him.[40] There were also openings for junior counsel in making motions at the 'side bar' of one of the courts: judges regularly heard these lesser matters while robing themselves, and young barristers tended to move them, even in Common Pleas.[41] Such scraps were not likely to bring in much in the way of fees, nor to gain much credit for the counsel, however. No doubt greater opportunities for making a figure at the bar were provided by being retained as junior counsel in more important cases, where a team of barristers was engaged. Here the leader had the right to argue the cause, but if a junior hit upon an important point, and dutifully communicated it to his senior, then he might be favoured with the privilege of moving it himself in court. Lord Keeper Guilford had taken advantage of such openings to establish his reputation when he was a junior barrister in the Restoration period, and there is no reason to believe that later generations of advocates did not do likewise.[42]

For most common lawyers, advocacy in the central courts was only one aspect of beginning a career at the bar. Young barristers with

---

[38] *Lives of the Norths*, iii. 90–1, 103–4; cf. BL, Add. MSS 61469 (Blenheim Papers), fo. 156: J[ohn] Waller to [Sarah] duchess of Marlborough, 20 Dec. 1729.

[39] D. Veall, *The Popular Movement for Law Reform 1640–1660* (Oxford, 1970), 46.

[40] BL, Add. MSS 61469, fos. 129–30: J[ohn] Waller] to [the duchess of Marlborough], 27 Nov. 1725. Finch was called 5 Feb. 1719, and became KC 1727 (*CITR* iv. 50; information from Sir John Sainty).

[41] BL, Add. MSS 32510 (Recollections of Lord Keeper Guilford), fos. 85–6: R. North's account of the 'dumb day' in Common Pleas; cf. *Lives of the Norths*, i. 132–3, iii. 104–5; Shropshire CRO, Bishop of Shipton MSS 3385/2/13: [Sir] Littleton Powys to Henry Mitton, 12 July 1698.

[42] For a good description of the proper roles of junior counsel in trials at common law, *temp.* Charles II, see BL, Add. MSS 32508 (MS Life of Lord Keeper Guilford), fo. 92; cf. Add. MSS 32509 (Recollections of Lord Keeper Guilford), fo. 13; *Lives of the Norths*, i. 53–4.

strong provincial connections generally concentrated their attention on
the circuit, or on some other local jurisdiction, as an important field of
opportunity for the establishment of a practice which encompassed
both local and central business. Indeed, litigation which began at the
assizes might end up in London, a symbiosis which was summed up by
the aphorism of Francis North, to the effect that 'the circuit found
buissness for Westminster hall, & that for the Circuit'.[43] It was usual
for a barrister to ride the circuit which included his home county,
for there he might take the greatest advantage of the support and
patronage of friends and relatives. Thus Peter King, an Exeter man,
followed the long Western circuit, while William Cowper rode the
Home, which took him in due course to the assizes at Hertford, the
place of residence of his family.[44] Special circumstances, however,
might induce some lawyers to follow circuits which took them far away
from their place of origin. James Harrington, for instance, rode the
Oxford circuit, although he hailed from Essex; presumably he did this
in order to take advantage of his university connections.[45] Roger North
simply followed his brother the lord chief justice on whichever circuit
the latter agreed to preside over, and he thereby derived much profit
from his privileged position as the judge's 'friend' or favourite, for he
was not only regularly employed by the local attorneys, but was even
retained by Exeter City Corporation on a permanent basis, as one of
their standing counsel.[46]

North clearly owed a great deal of his success on circuit and in
Westminster Hall to the advantage of having a brother who was highly
placed in the profession. Indeed, although individual competence and
talent were essential to gain a share of the glittering prizes available at
the bar, patronage was a significant element in the careers of many
successful barristers of the late seventeenth and early eighteenth
centuries. It has been seen how personal connections in the world at
large might facilitate the establishment of an embryo practice. It is no
less certain that contacts within the profession itself might have the

[43] BL, Add. MSS 32509, fo. 15; cf. *Lives of the Norths*, i. 60.

[44] *Correspondence of Locke*, vii. 668–9: Locke to King, 17 Aug. 1702; HCRO,
Pangshanger MSS D/EP F81/50–1, 74, 80–2: letters of William Cowper on circuit to his
wife Judith, 1693 and 1696–7.

[45] Bodl., MS Ballard 22, fos. 24–5: Harrington to Charlett, 21 Feb. 1692; Foster, *Alumni
Oxonienses*, i. 653.

[46] *Lives of the Norths*, iii. 90, 129–36. The published editions of North's autobiography
are in error here, for the MS reads 'at Exeter I was made of their counsell', rather than 'at
Easter . . .' (BL, Add. MSS 32506 (MS Autobiography of Roger North), fo. 131; cf. *Lives of
the Norths*, iii. 137; *Autobiography of Roger North*, p. 139).

same effect. Maundeford Bramston, for instance, son of a master in Chancery, thereby found himself in 'good practice' in that court in the 1680s, and thirty years later Dudley Ryder recorded how a barrister acquaintance of his who was practising as an equity draftsman was also obtaining business via his father, who had an office in Chancery.[47]

These were only minor beneficiaries of favour from within the profession; some counsel were more fortunate in that they obtained grace and favour from more eminent sources. One aspect of this was the practice by which a junior barrister might 'devil' for a distinguished counsel and thereby obtain briefs which the senior practitioner did not have time or inclination to argue himself. In the Restoration period Francis North fulfilled this role *vis-à-vis* the invalid attorney-general, Sir Geoffrey Palmer; his appointment as king's counsel was a direct result of an opportunity to argue in the House of Lords which came by the attorney's patronage.[48] North also received favour and encouragement from the judicial bench itself, in that he was acknowledged as 'cousin' in open court by his kinsman Lord Chief Justice Hyde.[49] There is no doubt that marks of favour bestowed by judges on individual counsel who appeared before them were of major importance in the professional success of certain barristers during the period covered by this study. Indeed, they were actively sought after. In March 1710, when it was well known that Sir Thomas Parker was to be appointed lord chief justice of King's Bench in place of the deceased Sir John Holt, the judge-elect received the following request from his former patron, the duke of Devonshire: 'Sir I have bin so sollicited in behalf of Mr [Alexander] Denton of the house of Commons, that I can not forbear recommending him to your favour at the bar. . .'[50] Parker, the future Lord Macclesfield, seems to have become notorious for the partiality he displayed towards certain individuals in King's Bench and Chancery. On 8 February 1716

---

[47] *Autobiography of Sir John Bramston*, p. 29; TS Ryder Diary, pp. 29–30: 18 July 1715. Ryder referred to his acquaintance as 'Mr Mills'; he was probably Edward Mills, called IT 13 June 1714. By 1720 he had a fair practice as an advocate at the Chancery bar (*CITR* iii. 437, and Chancery records as listed in App. II).

[48] BL, Add. MSS 32511 (Collections for the Life of Lord Keeper Guilford), fos. 6, 8; cf. *Lives of the Norths*, i. 47–9.   [49] Ibid. 47, 59.

[50] BL, Stowe MSS 750 (Macclesfield Papers), fos. 13–14: [William, duke of] Devonshire to Sir Thomas Parker, 'Friday morning', endorsed 10 Mar. 1710. Cf. a letter of 1733 recommending Sidney Stafford Smythe, a barrister of 5 years' standing, to Sir Philip Yorke, who was very soon to be LCJ of KB (ibid., Add. MSS 35585 (Hardwicke Papers), fos. 193–4: [Lionel, duke of] Dorset to [Yorke], 22 Sept. 1733; *DNB* xviii. 606–7).

Dudley Ryder was in King's Bench when 'a young man Mr Yorke made a very good long argument and my Lord Chief Justice [Parker] commended it very much'.[51] Parker's continued favour towards Philip Yorke in Chancery, although it was clearly well deserved, disgusted Sir Thomas Pengelly to such an extent that he threatened never to appear in the court again.[52] Yorke was not the only object of Parker's patronage, for he also consistently favoured John Fortescue-Aland, sometime solicitor-general and later a judge, to the point where Fortescue-Aland virtually begged him to preside on the Western circuit; without such advantage the counsel claimed that he could offer no competition to the many serjeants who practised on that circuit.[53]

Lest it should be thought that Parker, as a judge who was later convicted of corruption, was exceptional in his patronage of individual barristers, it is necessary to mention one more example of this practice. Among the papers of the Cowper family is an incomplete copy of a letter from the wife of Charles Talbot, later lord chancellor, which describes Talbot's early career at the bar:

'Lord Harcourt[54] for several years had been an intimate friend of his [Charles Talbot's] father's, and promis'd to make Mᵣ Talbot his favourite in the Court of Chancery provided he wou'd follow that Profession; The Law was a study he had applied himself to, & upon that Encouragement [he] put on his Bar Gown, & received Favours from my Lord till he publickly avow'd his Principles by appearing Council for Mᵣ Ridpath[55] & in Committing other Crimes of the like Nature, which turn'd Lord Harcourt's smiles into Frowns, & the Sollicitor's,[56] & all the Tory Party, in whose Power he experienc'd it was to procure him Business from that time deserted him, & were very active in doing him Prejudices.[57]

[51] TS Ryder Diary, p. 179.

[52] R. Cooksey, *Essay on the Life and Character of John Lord Somers, Baron of Evesham: Also Sketches of an Essay on the Life and Character of Philip Earl of Hardwicke* (Worcester, 1791), 72.

[53] Fortescue-Aland was called MT 3 May 1695 (as J. Fortescue), was SG 1715–17, baron of Exchequer 1717–18, justice of CP 1718–27 and 1729–46 (MT, MS Orders E5, 415; Foss, *Judges*, viii. 99). Foss erroneously dates his call as 1712. BL, Stowe MSS 750, fos. 17–18, 28–9: Fortescue-Aland to Parker, 12 Mar. 1710 and 20 Mar. 1711. For earlier judicial favourites cf. Prest, *Rise of the Barristers*, pp. 27–30.

[54] Successively LK and LC in the Tory ministry of 1710–14.

[55] A Whig political journalist, prosecuted by the government in 1713 (*DNB* xvi. 1178–81).

[56] Sir Robert Raymond SG.

[57] HCRO, Panshanger MSS D/EP F230 ('Family Book' of Lady Sarah Cowper, 1714–16), 9–10: part copy of Cecill Talbot to Lady Essex Robarts, 27 Sept. 1714; cf. BL, Add. MSS 4472 (Dr Birch's Memorandum Book), fo. 33. I owe the last reference to the kindness of Professor J. H. Baker.

It has to be understood that the period of this study was the age of Danby and Walpole, not that of Peel and Gladstone: even lawyers and judges of the capacity of Talbot and Yorke competed for and later dispensed personal favour with a facility which demonstrates the general recognition of patronage as an accepted feature of the profession, rather than a species of corruption. At the level of the bar, which was subject to the full blast of market forces, judicial patronage probably only reflected the natural inequalities among those who aspired to professional eminence. The characteristics of the practising bar and its members, and in particular their unequal capacities and advantages, are the subject of the following two sections.

2. THE STRUCTURE OF THE BAR

Young counsel of the seventeenth and eighteenth centuries who were beginning practice at the bar were joining a relatively small body of men. Although the annual average output of barristers from the four inns of court did not drop much below forty between the accession of James I and the demise of George I, it is almost certain that the practising bar itself never included more than 500 individuals at any time during either century.[58] Upon the eve of the Civil War, according to Dr Prest, the professional bar included a minimum of approximately 440 individuals, and a century and a half later Dr Duman has estimated the number of practitioners at around 150 counsel.[59] For the period which is the focus of this study it is possible to give minimum figures for the size of the bar based upon a detailed examination of the central court records for all proceedings which took place during the years 1680 and 1720.[60] In the former year, during a period when the output of barristers from the inns was at its pre-industrial peak, the bar has been found to include a minimum of 424 counsel; forty years later, by which time average annual bar calls had declined by over a third, a minimum of 338 barristers were employed as advocates in these

---

[58] Prest, *Rise of the Barristers*, p. 7; id., 'English Bar, 1550–100', p. 68; Fig. 3.1.

[59] Prest, *Rise of the Barristers*, pp. 79, 331; Duman 'English Bar in the Georgian Era', p. 88. Dr Duman gives a minimum figure of 121 barristers for 1785, but his sample is excessively narrow, and the figure of 155 derived from the Chancery reports and assize circuit lists is more reasonable as a lower estimate for comparison with the other minima derived from the original records. Dr Prest's figure may also be a slight underestimate, since he has examined the records for one term only. All these figures (and my own below) take no account of any barristers who practised solely as chamber counsel (see Prest, *Rise of the Barristers*, pp. 66–71; Duman, 'English Bar in the Georgian Era', p. 88).

[60] For the sources and methodology of this exercise, see App. II below.

courts. Thus, on the basis of these unevenly distributed and rather crude snapshots, it may be suggested that the practising bar had reached a numerical peak in the mid-seventeenth century from which it diminished in size between the Revolution of 1688 and the accession of the Hanoverians; and subsequently experienced further contraction up to the mid-eighteenth century.

Of course it is easier to establish this trend than to account for it. The size of the practising bar was (and is) determined by the balance between the supply of barristers and the demand for their professional services. Dr Prest has suggested that this balance was turning against aspiring counsellors after the Restoration.[61] The decline in the output of barristers from the inns during the reigns of William and Anne after the mid-seventeenth-century peak does indeed imply that the bar may have reached saturation point.[62] The number of barristers was no doubt being reduced by those forces which led to a decline in admissions to the inns of court; a combination of static population, hard times among lesser landowners, rising costs of qualifying for call, and better career alternatives.[63] But there is also the important question of whether there was a significant change in the level of demand for lawyers' services. Prest has argued for a decline in the volume of litigation which began in the seventeenth century and may have continued after 1660, accompanied by a contraction in the vocational sphere of the bar.[64] On the other hand, Professor Holmes has written of a 'mounting volumes of cases' coming before the courts after 1680, and a demand for 'a greater range and variety' of legal services.[65] In the light of this disagreement it is necessary to review the available evidence of changes in the amount of litigation and the range of the barristers' activities, as essential background to important shifts in the structure of the bar itself.

Turning first to the question of the volume of business transacted in the late Stuart and early Hanoverian central courts, recent research carried out by Dr Christopher Brooks has established a clear pattern. Although the common law courts and the Chancery experienced a temporary increase in litigation from 1650, this probably represented only a reaction to the jurisdictional changes and disruption caused by the Civil Wars. After 1680, the courts of King's Bench and Common

[61] Prest, 'English Bar, 1550–1700', p. 78.
[62] See above, pp. 60–2.   [63] See above, ch. 1.3.
[64] Prest, *Rise of the Barristers*, pp. 78–82; id., 'English Bar, 1550–1700', pp. 77–8.
[65] Holmes, *Augustan England*, p. 130; id., 'Professions', pp. 326–7.

Pleas went into decline and this developed into a general collapse in the eighteenth century. The pattern was not the same in every jurisdiction, but the net result was that by 1750 the number of bills filed in Chancery had fallen by over 60 per cent since the 1670s, while King's Bench and Common Pleas were reduced to a level where together they heard only about a tenth as many causes as they had at the beginning of that decade.[66] This picture of a spectacular drop in the aggregate of litigation during the late seventeenth and early eighteenth centuries confirms earlier impressions derived from statistics for some assize circuits and the equity side of the Exchequer court.[67] The causes of the decline cannot be identified with any precision, but the social and economic changes which the country experienced during these years were clearly important, especially stagnating population and the declining fortunes of some landowners in the agricultural areas which had generated so much litigation under Elizabeth and the early Stuarts.[68] Whatever the reason for the drop in the number of law suits was, it must have resulted in a contraction in the amount of court work available for barristers. It is true that in the common law courts the decline in litigation was accompanied by some substantive changes which meant that more causes went for trials at *nisi prius* involving judges, barristers, and juries.[69] But on the other hand analysis of the number of appearances made by advocates before all the central courts in 1680 and 1720 shows that only two of the tribunals in Westminster Hall (Common Pleas and the equity side of the Exchequer) did not suffer a decline in activity among counsel.[70] These trends must have had serious implications for men considering a career at the bar in the early eighteenth century, and their probable impact goes a long way towards explaining the fall in the number of practising barristers between 1680 and 1720.

This picture of a shrinkage in the traditional market for barristers' services is confirmed by changes in the vocational sphere of the practising bar. Fresh fields of opportunity may have opened before some specialist barristers in the early eighteenth century, but these

---

[66] C. W. Brooks, 'Interpersonal Conflict and Social Tension. Civil Litigation and Court Usage in England, 1640–1830' (forthcoming). I am grateful to Dr Brooks for allowing me to read this important article in advance of publication.

[67] Cockburn, *Assizes*, pp. 137–9; W. H. Bryson, *The Equity Side of the Exchequer* (Cambridge, 1975), 16, 160, 168; id., 'The Equity Jurisdiction of the Exchequer', in D. Jenkins (ed.), *Legal History Studies 1972* (Cardiff, 1975), 118–19.

[68] Brooks, 'Interpersonal Conflict'; see below, pp. 166–8.

[69] Brooks, 'Interpersonal Conflict'.   [70] See Apps. III–X below.

probably did not compensate for a marked contraction in the range of services encompassed by counsel generally, as distinct from lesser legal practitioners.[71] The separation of functions between the two 'branches' of the legal profession was not yet fully established, but it may have reached a crucial stage in this period; old-fashioned Restoration barristers like Roger North and Sir Henry Chauncy complained that attorneys and solicitors were taking over 'mechanical' legal functions, such as conveyancing, court keeping, and the preparation of briefs after consultation with clients.[72] The eminent and aged Serjeant Sir John Maynard was probably one of the last counsel to meet clients and witnesses regularly in the first instance and prepare legal documents without the intervention of an attorney: henceforth barristers were more likely to confine themselves to advocacy and the provision of specialist advice, rather than provide the full gamut of legal services.[73] This increasing distinction between inferior and superior lawyers can only have diminished the chances of establishing a firm footing in practice, because younger or less able counsel may formerly have depended upon 'mechanical' activities to supplement their incomes, and such a deterrent was bound to reduce the number of young men who resorted to the bar to seek regular employment.

A diminution in the aggregate of opportunities for practice does not only help to explain the observed reduction in the number of Westminster Hall advocates. It also implies a more profound qualitative change in the characteristics of the bar, by way of a trend towards greater 'professionalism' and a movement away from the inns of court and the medieval structure of the profession generally. Looking first at the question of professionalism, Table 5.2 shows that the bar in 1720 included a smaller proportion of junior practitioners than its predecessor of 1680. For the earlier sample slightly more than 70 per cent of the counsel identified were of less than twenty years' seniority from call, whereas in 1720 only around 60 per cent of the bar were practitioners of this vintage. Evidently, at the same time as the bar was becoming smaller and more closely identified with specific legal services, the balance of experience among counsel was shifting towards

---

[71] See below, ch. 6.4, cf. Holmes, 'Professions', p. 327.

[72] BL, Add. MSS 32508, fo. 28; ibid., Add. MSS 32509, fo. 7; *Lives of the Norths*, iii. 139; Chauncy, *Hertfordshire*, p. 528.

[73] Baker, 'Counsellors and Barristers', pp. 221–2; cf. M. Miles, ' "Eminent Practitioners": The New Visage of Country Attorneys c.1750–1800', in G. R. Rubin and D. Sugarman (eds.), *Law, Economy and Society 1750–1914* (Abingdon, 1984), 485–7.

TABLE 5.2. *Seniority of practising barristers, 1680 and 1720*

Standing (years)	1680 practisers		Cumulative total		1720 practisers		Cumulative total	
	No.	%	No.	%	No.	%	No.	%
0–4	66	23.2	66	23.2	53	20.7	53	20.7
5–9	48	16.8	114	40.0	49	19.1	102	39.8
10–14	49	17.2	163	57.2	32	12.5	134	52.3
15–19	38	13.3	201	70.5	24	9.4	158	61.7
20–4	30	10.5	231	81.0	31	12.1	189	73.8
25–9	27	9.5	258	90.5	27	10.6	216	84.4
30–4	15	5.3	273	95.8	18	7.0	234	91.4
35–9	7	2.5	280	98.3	10	3.9	244	95.3
40–4	3	1.0	283	99.3	6	2.3	250	97.7
45–9	1	0.3	284	99.6	5	1.9	255	99.6
50–4	1	0.3	285	100.0	1	0.4	256	100.0
Total classified	285				256			
Unknown	139				82			

Sources: See Appendix II.

more senior men, who were no doubt career barristers, rather than part-time pleaders.

An occupational squeeze puts a premium upon flexibility as well as experience. It is therefore appropriate that the Augustan age witnessed a trend by which the practising bar became less bound to, and restricted by, its ancient institutions. The tendency for the bar to become alienated from its institutional base has been remarked upon earlier.[74] It is confirmed by an analysis of the affiliation of practitioners to the inns of court for the two sample years. Table 5.3 shows that in 1680 three societies, Gray's Inn, the Inner Temple, and the Middle Temple, had provided the majority of barristers who were practising in Westminster Hall. Gray's Inn was most prominent, both with respect to quality as well as numbers, for several Gray's Inn men were among the greatest counsel of the day, especially at the King's Bench.[75] Lincoln's Inn was not well represented. By 1720 the picture had

[74] See above, p. 42.   [75] See Apps. III and IV below.

TABLE 5.3*a*. *Inns' affiliation of practising barristers, total bar, 1680 and 1720*

	Gray's Inn		Inner Temple		Lincoln's Inn		Middle Temple		Total	Unknown
	No.	%	No.	%	No.	%	No.	%		
1680 practisers	93	31.1	84	28.1	45	15.0	77	25.7	299	125
1720 practisers	35	13.5	88	34.0	47	18.1	89	34.4	259	79

TABLE 5.3*b*. *Inns' affiliation of practising barristers, individual bars, 1680*

	Gray's Inn		Inner Temple		Lincoln's Inn		Middle Temple		Total	Unknown
	No.	%	No.	%	No.	%	No.	%		
KB Crown	31	27.9	36	32.4	11	9.9	33	29.7	111	53
KB Pleas	47	27.2	55	31.8	21	12.1	50	28.9	173	83
Exchequer Pleas	26	39.4	14	21.2	8	12.1	18	27.3	66	30
Exchequer Equity	34	30.6	29	26.1	15	13.5	33	29.7	111	59
Common Pleas[a]	10	27.8	15	41.7	6	16.7	5	13.9	36	—
Chancery	54	28.1	57	29.7	35	18.2	46	24.0	192	99
House of Lords	4	18.2	7	31.8	2	9.1	9	40.9	22	2

[a] Inns' affiliation before accepting the coif and leaving the inns of court.

TABLE 5.3*c*. *Inns' affiliation of practising barristers, individual bars, 1720*

	Gray's Inn		Inner Temple		Lincoln's Inn		Middle Temple		Total	Unknown
	No.	%	No.	%	No.	%	No.	%		
KB Crown	7	8.0	32	36.8	14	16.1	34	39.1	87	30
KB Pleas	12	10.4	38	33.0	18	15.7	47	40.9	115	57
Exchequer Pleas	4	12.9	12	38.7	5	16.1	10	32.3	31	13
Exchequer Equity	9	9.2	32	32.6	22	22.5	35	35.7	98	43
Common Pleas[a]	2	7.7	8	30.8	3	11.5	13	50.0	26	—
Chancery	24	12.3	61	31.3	45	23.1	65	33.3	195	63
House of Lords	2	11.8	5	29.4	7	41.2	3	17.6	17	4

[a] Inns' affiliation before accepting the coif and leaving the inns of court.

Sources: See Appendix II.

changed very significantly. It is true that Lincoln's Inn barristers were still a small minority, although this society was already beginning to foreshadow its later renown with regard to equity, since its counsel had achieved a high profile in Chancery and the House of Lords.[76] More remarkably, the numerical decline of Gray's Inn had devastated its contingent of practising counsel, while the two Temple societies were quite dominant, at least in the common law courts. Now it will be recalled from Chapter 3 that the two Temple societies had led the way in the matter of making accommodations with respect to the seniority required of candidates for the bar, while Gray's Inn and Lincoln's Inn had more or less maintained their official requirements for full standing until the early eighteenth century.[77] Thus, although the body of practitioners in 1720 were more senior men than their predecessors of 1680, the predominance of men from the Temple societies suggests that they were less likely to have fulfilled the traditional obligations for call, and in consequence were not as thoroughly steeped in the ancient customs and orders of the profession.

Table 5.4 tends to corroborate this deduction via a breakdown of the customary ranks of the profession. Given the greater maturity of practitioners in 1720, one would have expected them to have included a higher proportion of benchers and serjeants than the sample of 1680, since these were distinctions which recognized maturity in practice rather than eminence. In fact there was a clear trend towards reduced representation from the order of the coif and the governing bodies of the inns, both proportionately and in terms of absolute numbers. Indeed, by 1720, in every court except the Exchequer and the House of Lords there were proportionately more utter barristers, men who were dignified neither by a coif nor inclusion among the benchers of their society, than there had been in 1680. Thus it appears that the early eighteenth-century bar was not only more 'professional' in the ways we have noticed: it was also more distinct from the institutional base of the profession, not only with regard to residence, but also in the matter of government, and was less identified with the medieval structure of the profession generally. This latter point will recur later in this study, but for the moment it is necessary to concentrate upon the developing 'professionalism' of the bar as it appeared in the activity of barristers at Westminster.

---

[76] See Apps. VIII and X below.
[77] See above, p. 68.

TABLE 5.4*a*. *Professional ranks of practising barristers, total bar, 1680 and 1720*

	Serjeants		Benchers		Utter barristers		Total	Unknown
	No.	%	No.	%	No.	%		
1680 practisers	36	12.2	44	15.0	214	72.8	294	130
1720 practisers	26	10.0	28	10.8	206	79.2	260	78

TABLE 5.4*b*. *Professional ranks of practising barristers, individual bars, 1680*

	Serjeants		Benchers		Utter barristers		Total	Unknown
	No.	%	No.	%	No.	%		
KB Crown	18	16.2	18	16.2	75	67.6	111	53
KB Pleas	22	12.9	25	14.7	123	72.4	170	86
Exchequer Pleas	9	13.8	12	18.5	44	67.7	65	31
Exchequer Equity	16	14.4	23	20.7	72	64.9	111	59
Chancery	28	14.7	35	18.3	128	67.0	191	100
House of Lords	2	9.1	10	45.4	10	45.4	22	2

TABLE 5.4*c*. *Professional ranks of practising barristers, individual bars, 1720*

	Serjeants		Benchers		Utter barristers		Total	Unknown
	No.	%	No.	%	No.	%		
KB Crown	15	17.4	11	12.8	60	69.8	86	31
KB Pleas	17	14.8	10	8.7	88	76.5	115	57
Exchequer Pleas	7	22.6	3	9.7	21	67.7	31	13
Exchequer Equity	13	13.4	14	14.4	70	72.2	97	44
Chancery	17	8.7	24	12.3	154	79.0	195	63
House of Lords	2	11.8	9	52.9	6	35.3	17	4

Sources: See Appendix II.

3. ACTIVITY IN THE COURTS

It had long been a feature of practice at the English bar that a few very successful advocates enjoyed a surfeit of business while the majority of barristers had to struggle along with an occasional brief.[78] In 1717 Thomas Kilpin, a barrister of ten years' standing, wrote phlegmaticaly to a friend: 'The last general seal was on Tuesday but it lasted all the next day, Your neighbour Brown had no less than 45 Breifs, your most humble servant, no more than two.'[79] The fortunate Counsellor Brown was John Brown, a bencher of Lincoln's Inn, and the gulf between this leading Chancery practitioner and poor Kilpin was indeed great, for in 1720 Brown's name appeared 411 times in the Chancery records, signifying 411 separate appearances, while Kilpin was mentioned only nineteen times.[80]

Such inequalities were natural, given the inevitable variations in energy, advantages, and ability among barristers. However, the developing changes in the characteristics of barristers during the period covered by this study, in terms of contraction in numbers and the trend towards a higher proportion of senior counsel, suggest that the profession was in the process of becoming confined to men who were committed to a full-time career at the bar as the aggregate of available work declined, and this may have affected the scale of inequality. At all times there have existed barristers like William Cowper, nephew of the lord chancellor, who combined a very slight practice at the bar (one appearance in Chancery during 1720) with enjoyment of office, in this case as clerk of the parliaments.[81] If part-time junior counsel such as Cowper were becoming less common in the early Hanoverian period, this might show up in the courts by way of a more even distribution of work. In order to test this hypothesis, and to elucidate some of the features of practice and practitioners in the

[78] Prest, 'English Bar, 1550–1700', pp. 71–2; id., *Rise of the Barristers*, pp. 58–61. An echo of the briefless barrister is provided by the charity dispensed to unsuccessful counsellors throughout this period by the inns of court (GI, MS. Orders ii. 613, 637, 648; IT, MS Acts 1665–87, fo. 158; ibid., MS Orders 1685–91, fo. 29; ibid. 1691–8, fos. 68, 74, 79; ibid. 1699–1714, fos. 35, 42, 47; ibid. 1715–33, fos. 33, 42–3, 45, 95; MT, MS Orders E5, 44, 48, 75, 89, H(8), 37).

[79] East Sussex CRO, Frewen MSS FRE 1150: Kilpin to John Turner, 10 Aug. 1717. Kilpin was called MT 23 May 1707 as T. Gilpin (MT, MS Orders E5, 23).

[80] Brown was called 14 Nov. 1698, bencher 2 July 1717 (LI, MS Black Book x, fo. 71; *LIBB* iii. 199). Sources as in App. II below.

[81] Cowper was called MT 8 Feb. 1712; clerk of the parliaments 1716–40 (MT, MS Orders H(8), 49; Sainty, *Parliament Office*, p. 9). Sources as in App. II below.

different courts, it is necessary to analyse the activities of the barristers at Westminster with some precision.

The primary sources for such an exercise are preserved at the Public Record Office in the form of the records of the central courts.[82] The rule books of the court of King's Bench, the minute books of the plea side of the Exchequer, and the remembrance rolls of the Common Pleas contain records of motions made by named counsel for interlocutory orders in the causes which they were pleading. They might take many forms; in these common law courts motions were made regularly for writs, for attachments against individuals, for converting fictional actions into real ones, for giving parties time to answer the proceedings against them, for references to examining officers, or for appointing days for hearings or for judgements. For the equity courts records of motions and the counsel who moved them are found in the Chancery registers' minute books and the common minute books of the King's Remembrancer in the Exchequer. Besides the common orders for time or for reference to officers, interlocutory orders peculiar to these courts included orders for subpoenas to parties, orders for commissions to take evidence in the country, and injunctions restraining parties or other jurisdictions. Unlike the common law records, the equity records used also include some brief minutes of hearings, in addition to simple motions. All these sources, together with the manuscript minutes of the House of Lords, which contain similar records of proceedings in judicial appeals, have been utilized to analyse the activities and personnel of the practising bar during the sample years: 1680 and 1720. As explained more fully in appendix II, the names of counsel have been extracted and used for a prosopographical exercise which appears throughout this and the following chapter, and the frequency of each name's occurrence has been recorded as the basis for the following analysis of activity among barristers pleading in each of the central courts.

Two caveats must be considered before proceeding to examine the data. First, there is some evidence to suggest that very simple motions did not require the presence of counsel in court, although they were formally moved by barristers: in the equity side of the Exchequer, for example, at the end of the eighteenth century 'orders of course'— simple motions which the court would grant for the asking—were

---

[82] For a complete explanation of the sources and methodology employed in this exercise, see App. II below.

made upon the submission of motion papers signed by counsel.[83] Thus it may be that an unspecified number of the 'appearances' recorded in this analysis represent work undertaken by counsel in name only, rather than in person. But this was business for which barristers were retained and fee'd, and it therefore seems reasonable to argue that it is a legitimate component of any analysis of their activity. Secondly, it may be objected that the data do not fully reflect the activity of juniors at the bar, since motions might be attributed to the senior barrister appearing, and his juniors would not be named in the order. In fact, it does not appear that this is a serious objection. As has been seen, simple motions of the type included in this data were often entrusted to one barrister only in all the courts; moreover, the Common Pleas remembrance rolls sometimes give the names of serjeants who supported a motion, as well as their opponents on the other side, and the equity records frequently cite junior counsel who seconded a motion or were members of a team retained for a hearing.[84] It remains possible that there is some underrepresentation of the work of junior counsel in the data for the King's Bench and the plea side of the Exchequer, but this is unlikely to affect the conclusions drawn below, because the data have been used to measure changes in the spread of business between the two sample years, and any possible bias must be common to the evidence for 1680 and 1720.

Bearing these points in mind, it is appropriate to turn to the results of this investigation, presented in Appendices III–X and Figs. 5.1–5.4. Appendix III is an analysis of those barristers who appeared in the crown side of King's Bench during the two sample years of 1680 and 1720, according to the frequency of appearance of their names in the records of that court. In the former year, sixty-eight barristers appeared only once, while one man appeared forty-four times, and in 1720 thirty barristers made only a single appearance as against the thirty-eight appearances of the leading counsel. This was not an extreme case of uneven activity: for both years the aggregate number of barristers who appeared in this court was less than 40 per cent of the *minimum* established for the total bar, and this minority interest implies that advocacy in KB crown may have involved some special expertise, no doubt with regard to the affairs of corporations and the

---

[83] D. B. Fowler, *The Practice of the Court of Exchequer upon Proceedings in Equity* (1795), ii. 272, 392. I am grateful to Professor Henry Horwitz of the University of Iowa for drawing my attention to this manual.

[84] For junior counsel making simple motions, see above, pp. 118–19.

criminal law. This would have mitigated against the extreme contrasts in the workloads of counsel typical of some other courts. Nevertheless, there were clear leaders, and most of them are well known as regular combatants in the state trials of this period. But the name of William Scroggs junior seems obscure by contrast with the other leaders, and his presence among them is another reminder that favouritism was an important ingredient in success, for Scroggs was the son of Scroggs CJ and enjoyed rapid promotion at Gray's Inn as a consequence of his father's position.[85] Whatever the reason for their eminence these leading counsel was fortunate men, for barristers who were prominent in this politically sensitive court had a good chance of being preferred to the highest stations in the administration of the common law, especially in the late seventeenth century, when there were frequent removals. Thus, of the 1680 leaders, Saunders, Jeffreys, Holt, and Pollexfen all went on to become chief justices, and even in the more stable conditions of forty years on, two of the leaders, Serjeant Pengelly and Thomas Reeve, were future chiefs in Westminster Hall.

Pengelly, Reeve, and their fellow top practisers were no less learned or talented than their predecessors who were leaders at King's Bench in 1680. However, if the bar was becoming more generally 'professional' in the eighteenth century their ascendancy ought to have been less marked than that of the common lawyers who had dominated proceedings at the time of the Exclusion Crisis. Some simple calculations based upon the data derived from the original court records will demonstrate this point, and facilitate a comparison between the two sample years in terms of the spread of business.[86]

In Appendix III the barristers who were pleading in KB crown during the years in question have been ranked according to the number of appearances they made. Thus in 1680 twenty-three counsel appeared twice and three appeared nine times. It is possible, therefore, to calculate the total of appearances made by each rank at the bar simply by multiplying the figures: for example, the seven counsel who appeared four times each were together responsible for an aggregate of twenty-eight appearances. The figures for all ranks can be summed to give the total number of appearances made by all barristers during the two years; 781 in 1680 and 547 in 1720. We may then calculate the proportion of the total appearances for which each rank was

---

[85] *GIPB* ii, pp. xvi, 42, 50–1, 65, 69.
[86] I am very grateful to Professor Roderick Floud of Birkbeck College, London, for his advice regarding the processing of this data.

responsible: in 1680 the sixty-eight barristers who appeared once accounted for 8.7 per cent of the total appearances cited in the records. From here it is but a short step to demonstrate the distribution of appearances, or business, across the bar, for the proportion of appearances accounted for by each rank is simply expressed in cumulative figures, beginning with the lowest rank and ending with the top practitioner, and these figures are compared with the cumulative proportion of the bar represented by each rank. In other words, for 1720 fifty-nine barristers (30 + 29), being 50.4 per cent of the total bar for KB crown, accounted for eighty-eight appearances (58 + 30), or 16.1 per cent of the total business, while seventy-seven barristers (30 + 29 + 11 + 7), being 65.8 per cent of the bar, were responsible for 149 appearances (30 + 58 + 33 + 28), or 27.2 per cent of the total. These data are plotted in graphical form as Fig. 5.1*a*.

Clearly, if the distribution of business at the bar was absolutely even, the graph in Fig. 5.1*a* would simply be a straight line at forty-five degrees to the axis, for in such an ideal world 10 per cent of the practitioners should take 10 per cent of the business, 15 per cent should take 15 per cent, and so on. In fact, the further the line deviates from this ideal, the greater was the inequality of appearances among counsel. It has already been established that a severely uneven distribution of work was characteristic of the bar at all times, and it is no surprise, therefore, to see that the graph is far from the ideal. More interestingly, however, there was some movement towards a more even spread of work in the early eighteenth century, for in 1720 the middling ranks of the bar (represented by the middle portion of the horizontal axis) were accounting for a higher proportion of the total business than they had in 1680, and the leaders were, as expected, slightly less dominant. Calculation of the gini coefficient for each sample, a measure of inequality which might vary between zero and one, confirms this shift, for in 1680 the inequality in activity across the bar was 0.60, while by 1720 it had declined to 0.54.[87] Of course the magnitude of the change should not be exaggerated, but for this court at least, it does appear that the Hanoverian period was characterized by a tendency towards greater equality in the share of business which fell to each barrister.

---

[87] For the gini coefficient see C. M. Dollar and R. J. Jensen, *Historian's Guide to Statistics: Quantitative Analysis and Historical Research* (New York, 1971), 124.

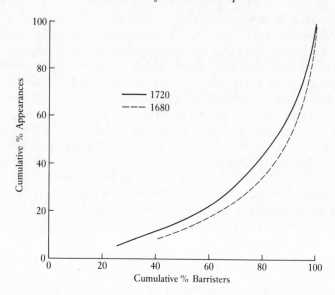

FIGURE 5.1*a*. King's Bench (crown side) bar: dimensions and distribution of business, 1680 and 1720

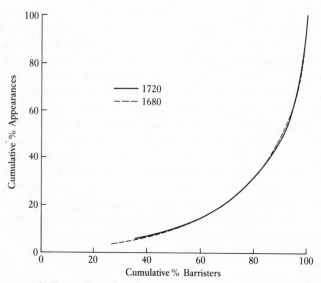

FIGURE 5.1*b*. King's Bench (plea side) bar: dimensions and distribution of business, 1680 and 1720

This trend was not apparent on the plea side of the court of King's Bench. Fig. 5.1*b*, which has been drawn using the data from Appendix IV, shows that there was very little difference between the two sample years in the distribution of business among the practitioners on this side of the court. As has been seen, junior barristers naturally flocked to this bar for their first employment, and this probably accounts for the large number of men who appeared very infrequently. Indeed, this court was regarded as the natural place of employment for the majority of common lawyers, especially in 1680, because in that year the total number of barristers who appeared here accounted for 60 per cent of the minimum bar. By 1720 KB pleas had become slightly less popular, but there was still a large proportion of occasional practitioners, which meant that the leaders at this time were no less dominant than their predecessors: during both sample years the top 10 per cent of practitioners accounted for over 50 per cent of the appearances noted in the records, making for considerable overall inequality in the workloads of counsel.[88]

Turning to the Exchequer courts, here it was again the case that a few leading counsel were overburdened with briefs, while the majority enjoyed very small pickings. This was true even of the Exchequer of Pleas, a court of obscure practice which was confined to a few specialists; a handful of leading counsel were able to gain the ascendancy even though a total of only ninety-six barristers appeared in 1680 and no more than forty-four were named in the records for 1720 (Appendix V).[89] However, according to Fig. 5.2*a* the fall in the number of practitioners was accompanied by a more even distribution of business, as it was in KB crown, for in 1720 the middle ranks of pleaders were reponsible for a larger proportion of the activity in this court than their predecessors of Charles II's time, even though one man, Thomas Bootle (a barrister of only seven years' standing), had achieved a dominance over the whole of the bar which was quite unparalleled in any other court. Whether this barrister enjoyed any special patronage among the Exchequer judges is not clear, although his subsequent career suggests a talent for gaining favour from politicians and courtiers by a succession of offices and professional distinctions.[90]

---

[88] Gini coefficients: 1680: 0.64; 1720: 0.63.

[89] For the 'mysterious' nature of the Exchequer see above, p. 117.

[90] Gini coefficients: 1680: 0.68; 1720: 0.62. Bootle was called IT 21 June 1713 (*CITR* iii. 433); for his career see R. Sedgwick, *The House of Commons 1715–1754* (1970), i. 473–4.

Bootle was also one of the leading practitioners on the equity side of the Exchequer, where only the elderly former lord chancellor of Ireland, Sir Constantine Phipps, was more active in 1720.[91] The decline in the quantity of bills filed in this court did not become really marked until the reign of George II, and it clearly provided rich pickings for many counsel in both the sample years, to the extent that in 1680 the leaders included Edward Ward, the future lord chief baron, and Sir Robert Sawyer, soon to be made attorney-general (Appendix VI).[92] Figure 5.2*b* shows that these men were marginally more dominant than their successors as leaders in 1720, but this was compensated for by the fact that the lesser practitioners in 1720 were responsible for an even smaller proportion of the total activity than the occasional pleaders of 1680. Thus overall there was little difference between the two samples in terms of the apportionment of work in the court.[93]

So far it has appeared that, comparing 1720 with 1680, courts in the later period were characterized by lower numbers and either a slightly more even spread of the workload across the bar, or no change. But there were two exceptions to this pattern. These were the court of Common Pleas and the House of Lords in its judicial capacity. In fact, both may be discounted as special cases, because neither was truly open to the bar at large. The Common Pleas was, until the nineteenth century, confined to those barristers who had been created serjeants at law by the crown. Accordingly, Appendix VII shows that only thirty-six men appeared at the Common Pleas bar in 1680, and just twenty-six serjeants were pleading there forty years later. This represents only about 8 per cent of the minimum total of barristers for each sample year. Of course all these counsel were men committed to a career at the bar and with great experience in practice. Reference back to Table 5.1 shows that, in both years, roughly two-thirds of the serjeants identified who appeared in Common Pleas had attained between twenty-five and forty years' seniority from call, and several were still more mature. Clearly then, serjeants at law were at *all* times highly experienced and relatively successful counsel, and it is therefore unlikely that as a body they would reflect any change in the balance of the profession generally towards a greater proportion of career barristers and a more equal distribution of business. Fig. 5.3*a* confirms this: on the contrary, the Common Pleas bar in 1720 was characterized

[91] *DNB* xv. 114–15.   [92] Bryson, *Equity Side of the Exchequer*, p. 168.
[93] Gini coefficients: 1680: 0.77; 1720: 0.78.

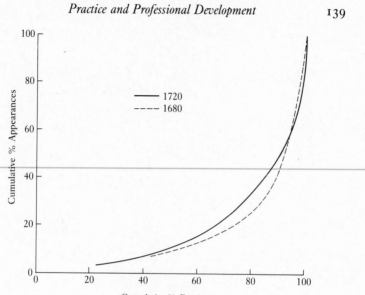

FIGURE 5.2*a*. Exchequer (plea side) bar: dimensions and distribution of business, 1680 and 1720

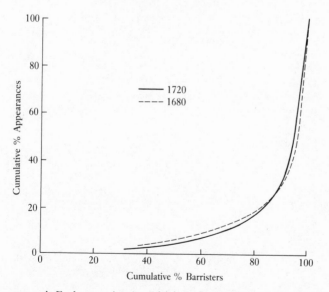

FIGURE 5.2*b*. Exchequer (equity side) bar: dimensions and distribution of business, 1680 and 1720

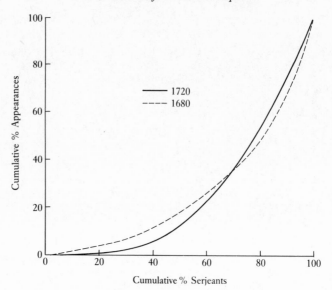

FIGURE 5.3*a*. Common Pleas bar: dimensions and distribution of
business, 1680 and 1720

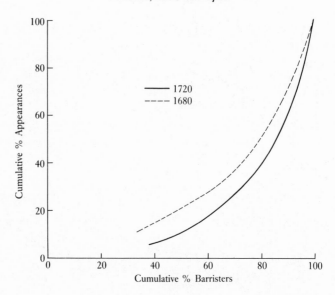

FIGURE 5.3*b*. House of Lords bar: dimensions and distribution of
business, 1680 and 1720

by a slightly less even apportionment of work compared with the pattern which was manifested in 1680. Moreover, the graph clearly demonstrates the general maturity in practice which was peculiar to the bar in this court, for the absence of a large group of junior barristers who might gain only a single brief meant that the inequality of work across the body of practitioners was much less marked than it was in those courts which were open to all comers.[94]

A similar point may be made in relation to those barristers who were active as counsel before the House of Lords (Appendix VIII). These men were not necessarily of great seniority, but they were the cream of the Chancery bar, because much of the litigation in this court involved appeals on behalf of wealthy clients who were prepared to pay for the best counsel in order to overturn a Chancery decree.[95] Thus, as in Common Pleas, there were really no juniors among the barristers who appeared before their lordships, and there was less opportunity for absolute dominance on the part of a few leaders. It is not surprising, therefore, that although some counsel were very prominent, especially in 1720, activity here was always more evenly distributed than in the more regular courts of Westminster Hall.[96] Fig. 5.3*b* demonstrates the concomitant of this, for the Lords' bar, like Common Pleas, did not reflect any change in the profession towards greater equality.

A rather different pattern was characteristic of the court of Chancery. At the head of this court were the great counsel who often saw causes through to appeal in the House of Lords: men who were every bit as eminent as the leaders of the King's Bench, although they often had to be content with wealth rather than power, since Chancery specialists were rarely preferred to the common law judiciary.[97] But Chancery was a popular court among early modern barristers because its proceedings required the services of counsel more frequently than litigation in the common law courts, and its fees were higher than elsewhere in Westminster Hall.[98] Moreover, as has been seen, equity was more palatable to some junior barristers than the common law

---

[94] Gini coefficients: 1680: 0.48; 1720: 0.50.   [95] See above, pp. 117–18.

[96] Gini coefficients: 1680: 0.43; 1720: 0.57. The first analysis of the Lords' bar does not rest on secure foundations because parliament was disrupted by the Exclusion Crisis in 1680, and the Lords therefore transacted very little judicial business.

[97] HMC, *14th Report*, app. II, pp. 464–5: Robert Harley to Sir Edward Harley, 5 May [16]81.

[98] Brooks, *Pettyfoggers and Vipers of the Commonwealth*, p. 104; G. Norburie, 'The Abuses and Remedies of Chancery', in F. Hargrave (ed.), *A Collection of Tracts* (1787), 437–43; *Lord Nottingham's 'Manual of Chancery Practice' and 'Prolegomena of Chancery and Equity'*, ed. D. E. C. Yale (Cambridge, 1965), 66; see below, pp. 152–5.

administered in King's Bench.[99] As a consequence of these various attractions, a large proportion of the bar restored to Chancery for employment: in 1680 291 counsel, or nearly 70 per cent of the minimum deduced for the profession, made some appearance here, and in 1720, having become even more popular than KB pleas among newly called men, this court provided some employment for 76 per cent of the bar. Given such a wide spectrum of ability and experience, it is no wonder that the inequality of work was extreme: the gulf between men like Anthony Keck in 1680 and Samuel Mead in 1720, who were each mentioned hundreds of times in the records, and the humble barristers who appeared only once, was unmatched in any other court (Appendices IX and X). Nevertheless, Fig. 5.4 shows that, as with the crown side of King's Bench and the Exchequer of Pleas, there was a tendency towards a slightly more even distribution of business, for the later sample again shows that middling barristers of the early eighteenth century were accounting for a higher proportion of the total activity at the bar than their later Stuart counterparts.[100]

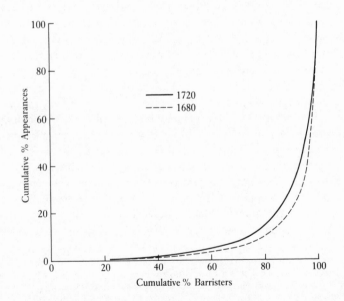

FIGURE 5.4. Chancery bar: dimensions and distribution of business, 1680 and 1720

---

[99] See above, p. 117.   [100] Gini coefficients: 1680: 0.83; 1720: 0.80.

Thus, for three of the central courts, there is evidence to support the hypothesis that the shrinkage of the bar between 1680 and 1720 may be partly explained by a tendency for the profession to become less congenial for the occasional practitioner—a man who might combine some minor office or occupation with the odd brief—who was being deterred by the increasing difficulty of establishing a practice at a time when 'mechanical' activities of a supplementary nature were becoming incompatible with a barrister's gown, and when the volume of court work available was declining. The data presented in this chapter suggest that changes in the volume and nature of barristers' work were tending to restrict the profession to men who were willing and able to establish a full-time career as a busy advocate and counsellor. In other words, barristers were experiencing a process of 'natural selection' as a consequence of changes in the market for their professional services. The smallness of the changes observed makes it necessary to conclude that the trend towards enforced 'professionalism' or 'careerism' was only developing rather than fully-fledged, but its existence is confirmed by parallel changes in the barristers' public reputation and remuneration and in the social context of their lives and work. The following chapter addresses these developments.

6

THE PRACTISING BAR
REPUTATION, WEALTH, AND SOCIAL
DEVELOPMENT

ENGLISH barristers today have an elevated professional and social identity. They are sharply demarcated by dignity and function from solicitors and other lawyers as members of the 'upper branch' of the legal profession, and they are distinguished in society as élite members of a profession which confers high status. Wealth and prosperity are also aspects of this image: barristers are associated with sectors of society able to afford high fees, and success at the bar is identified with large incomes and social mobility. It would be naïve to claim that this reputation was achieved completely in the Augustan period, but its origins and development could well be connected with the changes identified in the last chapter, for the occupational squeeze may have reduced the number of incompetent and unambitious, as well as part-time, barristers. The more even spread of business in court might therefore represent the increasing dominance of barristers dedicated and imaginative enough to adapt to the new conditions of practice; men who achieved wealth and status as valued servants of the community. The present chapter traces the signs of this evolution through an analysis of the barristers' image and reputation, and individual counsellors' incomes and wealth, together with the social background to their lives and work.

I. IMAGE AND REPUTATION

Historians of the bar have drawn attention to developments in the sixteenth and early seventeenth centuries by which barristers began to evolve a coherent professional identity, and these form the background to changes in the image and reputation of the bar during the subsequent period. At the end of the middle ages Sir John Fortescue, sometime chief justice of England, had praised his fellow judges, serjeants, and inns of court men in his influential eulogy, *De Laudibus*

Legum Angliae. This commendation was based on the lawyers' status—especially their social status—rather than their function. Fortescue pointed out that they mingled with the landed élite at the inns, drew attention to the similarity between the serjeants' degree and university doctorates, and even suggested that judges were blessed with divine benediction.[1] Deference to aristocratic values continued to constitute an element of the barristers' self-image in the early modern period, but Tudor and Stuart humanists began to develop a professional identity based upon their vocation as individual counsellors, rather than their ascribed social status as part of the inns' community. In his *Boke Named the Gouernour*, first published in 1531, Sir Thomas Elyot, son of a judge and himself a former clerk of assize, argued for a more liberal programme of legal education, by which he believed counsellors would be raised to the level of the *prudentes* of ancient Rome, as men whose accomplishments would enable them 'to serve honourably theyr prince, and the publike weale of their contray'.[2] This image of the socially useful lawyer was taken up by Sir John Davies in 1615. In the preface to his reports the future chief justice lauded the 'worthie Professor of the lawe' as 'a Starr in the firmament of the common-wealth', who was honoured for his commitment to the ideal of justice and his service to the community. Moreover, in a famous passage Davies elaborated the stereotype by arguing that the lawyer's vocation placed him above the dependent role of wage-earner, and beyond the mere pursuit of lucre, for his fees were not 'duties certaine, . . . [which] . . . grow due by contract for labour or service, but that which is given to a learned Counsellor is called *honorarium* & not *merces*, being indeede a gift which giveth honor as well to the *Taker* as to the *giver*'.[3] According to this humanist model of the 'good lawyer', then, the ideal professor of the common law was distinguished by his liberal education and ennobled by his vocation as a counsellor and advocate who placed his learning and oratorical skills at the disposal of justice and the public in a disinterested fashion, merely accepting fees as honoraria freely given in recognition of his services.[4]

[1] Sir John Fortescue, *De Laudibus Legum Angliae*, ed. S. B. Chrimes (Cambridge, 1942 [written *c.*1468–71]), 117–27, 129–31.
[2] Sir Thomas Elyot, *The Boke Named the Gouernour*, ed. H. H. S. Croft (1880), i. 132–62.
[3] Sir John Davies, *Le Primer Report des cases and matters en ley* (Dublin, 1615), sigs. *7ᵛ–*10.
[4] Cf. W. Prest, 'Why the History of the Professions is not Written', in Rubin and Sugarman (eds.), *Law, Economy and Society 1750–1914*, pp. 313–18; id., *Rise of the*

The honorarium doctrine became an established part of the etiquette of the bar by the early eighteenth century, and the neo-classical ideal of the 'good lawyer' continued to occur in popular literature.[5] But it is not possible to say how many barristers aspired to live up to the model, and it is therefore difficult to judge whether there was a parallel development in terms of improving standards of practice as the stereotype became established. Certainly, every age has had its share of practitioners who were guilty of malpractice or corruption. Dr E. W. Ives has uncovered evidence of bribery among pre-Reformation lawyers and 'a large-scale conspiracy to influence the course of the law' among a group of judges and counsellors who rode the Northern circuit in 1502, whilst Dr Prest has concluded that 'judicial corruption was a fact of life in pre-Civil War England', and shown how 'barristers played an integral role as go-betweens in the corrupt relationships of judges with litigants'.[6] Augustan England also had its share of delin-quent barristers and judges. At the very top of the profession, Lord Chancellor Macclesfield was found guilty of corruption for selling masterships in Chancery at exorbitant prices: a practice which encouraged the purchasers to recoup their losses by speculating with suitors' money which they held in trust. Admittedly, Macclesfield argued that his behaviour was legitimized by prescription, and there is some suspicion that the reason for his successful prosecution was partly political, rather than being motivated entirely by public outrage at his breach of trust.[7] But there are other testimonies to dubious practices which are not complicated in this way. John Evelyn recorded the following anecdote in his diary for 26 November 1686:

I din'ed at my Lord Chancelors, where being 3 other Serjeants at Law, after dinner being cherefull & free, they told their severall stories, how long they had detained their clients in tedious processes, by their tricks, as if so many

---

Barristers, pp. 314–19; C. W. Brooks, 'The Common Lawyers in England, *c.*1558–1642', in W. Prest (ed.), *Lawyers in Early Modern Europe and America* (1981), 54–5; id., *Pettyfoggers and Vipers*, pp. 179–80; Baker, 'Counsellors and Barristers', pp. 118–22.

[5] Ibid. 122; H. C., 'The Character of an Honest Lawyer' (1676), in *Somers Tracts* (1748), pt. I, iv. 305–8; *Corona Civica: A Poem to the Right Honourable Lord Keeper of the Great Seal of England* (1706), 1–5, 10.

[6] E. W. Ives, 'The Reputation of the Common Lawyers in English Society, 1450–1550', *University of Birmingham Historical Journal*, 7 (1959–60), 150–1; id., *Common Lawyers of Pre-Reformation England*, pp. 309, 311–12; Prest, *Rise of the Barristers*, pp. 310–11.

[7] *DNB* xv. 208–1; Foss, *Judges of England*, viii. 49–52; J. H. Plumb, *Sir Robert Walpole* (1956–60), ii. 110.

highway thieves should have met & discovered the severall purses they had taken. This they made but a jeast of: but God is not mocked.[8]

Evelyn's outrage suggests that this behaviour was not acceptable by the ethical standards of contemporary laymen, although it is not clear if other lawyers would have been equally offended, and Lord Chancellor Jeffreys may be regarded as an exceptional member of his profession. Dudley Ryder was a member of the legal fraternity, however, and in 1715 he was almost as offended as Evelyn when he became aware that it was common 'for lawyers and attorneys to entangle and perplex a case on purpose to make more work for themselves'. Ryder singled out William Branthwaite, a recently created serjeant at law, as a man who resorted to this kind of practice often.[9] He also identified two judges who were guilty of a more serious offence, the details of which are worth relating in full.

It is, it seems, a practice common to some of the judges to encourage the bringing cases to a hearing before them at their chambers, by which very considerable fees come to their clerks, but which they are accountable to the judges themselves for by agreement. But yet these judges (as Littleton Powys and [Robert] Tracey who attend this kind of practice very much) will sometimes in favour to an attorney that is wont to bring matters before them go beyond their bounds. They don't do it directly, but when a judge advises a party to do so and so and one of them thinks it hard upon him, [and] refuses to consent, the judge tells him if he won't he must move it in court the next term, but it had been better for him to consent. When a motion is made the judge tells the court he had heard the matter at his chambers and had advised them to agree so-and-so. The court is generally so partial to the opinions of a particular judge that instead of entering into the merits of the case they scarce ever fail to order the rule according to the judge's opinions and perhaps commit the attorney for refusing to comply before. This is a partiality that is very dishonest and unjust. . .[10]

In other words, according to Ryder, certain judges were prepared to favour individual attorneys and their clients in order to increase their earnings from fees, irrespective of the burden of justice, in cases which these attorneys brought before them. This is sufficient proof that some

---

[8] *Diary of Evelyn*, iv. 530.

[9] *Diary of Dudley Ryder*, pp. 106–7. Branthwaite was called GI 27 Nov. 1691, serjeant Jan. 1715 (*GIPB* ii. 112; Baker, *Serjeants*, p. 206).

[10] *Diary of Dudley Ryder*, p. 107; Powys was baron of Exchequer 1695–1701, judge of KB 1701–26; Tracy was baron of Exchequer 1700–2, judge of CP 1702–26, and commissioner of the great seal 1710 and 1718 (Foss, *Judges of England*, viii. 52–5, 62–4).

Augustan lawyers were very far from the neo-classical ideal of the disinterested and public-spirited practitioner.

However, while experience may have bred cynicism and contempt for common values among some, there is no reason to suppose that the process was general. Indeed, for every 'bad' lawyer one might cite the example of a 'good' one whose conduct implied adherence to a code of professional ethics. Lord Chancellor Cowper, for example, refused to accept the gifts commonly tendered to the occupant of the woolsack on New Year's Day; and he also rejected the recommendation of his brother as solicitor-general (in 1715) because he wanted to make it clear that he had 'no designs of interest' in making appointments to legal offices.[11] Cowper's well-deserved reputation for 'Noble principles of Integrity' was one reason why his political opponents tried to persuade him to stay on as lord chancellor after the fall of the Whig ministry in 1710.[12] Serjeant Thomas Pengelly, the future chief baron of the Exchequer, was also a man of principle. A complaint commonly levelled against barristers was that 'to shew the Brightness of their Parts, few of them even vouchafe to look upon their Briefs, till the Cause is call'd: and some of them look upon it as an Affront, to be ask'd to peruse 'em before.'[13] How far this accusation was generally true is not clear, but Pengelly, at least, took his clients' causes seriously. According to a short life of the judge published just after his death, he preferred, when practising as a counsel, to spend the evenings mastering his briefs rather than wining and dining with friends and colleagues. Moreover, the same source suggests that Pengelly genuinely lived up to the spirit of the honorarium doctrine, for it describes how he agreed to appear gratis for a client who had exhausted her funds in a suit which had been depending for more than three years, after counsel who had been retained previously refused to argue at the final hearing without a further fee. The fact that Pengelly bequeathed several sums to discharge poor men imprisoned for debt lends credence to this story.[14]

---

[11] HCRO, Panshanger MSS D/EP F23/20: Cowper to Sir William Cowper [his father], 2 Jan. 1706; ibid., D/EP F205/23: diary of Mary, Countess Cowper, Jan. 1716; ibid., D/EP F57/122: draft letter [Cowper to ?Bernstorff, autumn 1716].

[12] Ibid., D/EP F55/25: [John, duke of] Newcastle [to Lord Cowper], 2 Sept. 1710; ibid., D/EP F55/13–14: R[obert] Monckton [to Cowper], 28 Aug. 1710.

[13] *The Law and Lawyers Laid Open in Twelve Visions*, p. 213.

[14] *Some Private Passages of the Life of Sir Thomas Pengelly, late Chief Baron of the Exchequer, written by a Lady, his Intimate Friend* (1733), 2–6, 10–12, 30–44.

It would be fruitless to attempt to judge whether Pengelly was more typical of his fellow barristers and judges than the lawyers criticized by Evelyn and Ryder. But there are reasons to believe that standards of practice may have been improving among members of the law's upper branch in the later seventeenth and early eighteenth centuries. At least Augustan barristers had earned a fund of public credit which set the standards for the conduct of individual practitioners. In 1627 the barrister Henry Sherfield felt that he had transgressed against God, rather than his profession, when he acknowledged taking part in a corrupt transaction between a former client and the lawyer who had decided his case.[15] A century later the signs are that barristers were judged, and judged themselves, by totems and taboos associated with their calling. Thus Sir Thomas Pengelly commended another serjeant at law as 'an Honour to the Bar' for dedicating himself to his clients, and Campbell's *London Tradesman* warned against the danger of the poor barrister being tempted 'to prostitute his Profession by dirty Jobs, or demean his Character by espousing causes in themselves vilainous'.[16] It is evident that early Georgian barristers enjoyed a positive public reputation which they were expected to live up to, and this implies that their stock had risen since the sixteenth and seventeenth centuries.

The lawyers had always served as popular targets for indiscriminate abuse, and this kind of criticism did not cease in the eighteenth century.[17] Dr Prest has concluded that 'the vehemence and volume of recorded anti-lawyer comment . . . appear to increase steadily from the late sixteenth century onwards', but it is likely that this reached a peak during the Interregnum, when the opportunity for converting popular sentiment into action threatened to sweep the legal profession away entirely.[18] While the debasement of the judiciary under Charles II and James II did nothing to improve the image of the profession, Professor Holmes has remarked upon the way in which the new-found stability of the bench under William and Anne gave judges an image of dignity and impartiality which inevitably rubbed off on to members of the bar. Indeed, by the early eighteenth century barristers had established their right to bear the title 'esquire', irrespective of social origins; an appellation which had certainly been assumed by most for a hundred

[15] Prest, *Rise of the Barristers*, p. 310.

[16] *Life of Pengelly*, p. 5; Campbell, *London Tradesman*, p. 77; cf. ibid. 74.

[17] Ives, 'Reputation of the Common Lawyers', *passim*; id., *Common Lawyers of Pre-Reformation England*, pp. 308–21; Prest, *Rise of the Barristers*, pp. 283–91.

[18] Ibid. 286; Veall, *Popular Movement for Law Reform*, pp. 74–96.

years or more, but had been challenged by the College of Arms as recently as 1681.[19]

Changes in the constitutional position of the judiciary, although they are important, do not fully account for the evident rise in the status of barristers. Other factors were certainly involved. For one thing, before the Civil War the barristers were tarred with the same brush as attorneys and solicitors, who may have been the real source of a majority of the charges that lawyers were unlearned, inefficient, or corrupt. The developing separation of functions between the two branches of the profession after 1660 was accompanied by a further phase in a long drawn out process by which attorneys were excluded from the inns of court, and this growing distinction on the part of their institutional base and functions allowed the barristers to insist on their intellectual and social superiority over other legal practitioners. Attorneys and solicitors were therefore relegated to an inferior place in the legal firmament just as they came between counsellors and the public, and popular criticism was henceforth concentrated on these 'caterpillars of the nation', rather than being applied to lawyers in general.[20] Moreover, it is very probable that there was a genuine rise in standards of practice among members of the 'upper branch', for the conditions of legal practice were quantitatively different in 1700 from those which had pertained a hundred years earlier. English society was especially litigious under Elizabeth and the early Stuarts, and bad practice was no doubt encouraged as the proliferation of law suits provided business for an increasing number of barristers.[21] By contrast, after 1680 the decline in the volume of litigation must have made the law a buyer's market. Casual and incompetent counsellors would have found it more difficult to find work, and it is reasonable to suppose that a majority of those who did establish a regular practice were able to satisfy their customers as to their efficiency and probity, although it is obvious that malpractice and corruption were not eradicated. The rise in status and public reputation enjoyed by the bar in this period implies that the decline in the aggregate of available work did indeed operate as a purge. Those who succeeded in spite of the squeeze were not only probably more competent than the average practitioner of a century earlier; they were also rewarded with higher

[19] Holmes, *Augustan England*, p. 117.

[20] H. H. L. Bellot, 'The Exclusion of Attorneys from the Inns of Court', *LQR* 26 (1910), 140–3; *Private Memoirs of John Potenger*, p. 38.

[21] Cf. Prest, *Rise of the Barristers*, p. 296.

incomes which set the seal on their elevated status, as the following section will show.

2. FEES AND INCOMES

The most concrete evidence of the heightened public appreciation of barristers and their services is provided by an analysis of changes in the levels of their remuneration during the seventeenth and early eighteenth centuries. Only a decade after the Restoration, Edward Chamberlayne drew attention to a marked rise in the fees given to counsel:

Antiently, the fee expected by a Sergeant from his Client for Advice given, at his Chamber, or for pleading in any Court of Judicature, was no more than 20s and the fee of a Barrister 10s . . . but, at present it is become, almost ordinary, to give some Sergeants £10 and sometimes £20 and, to a Barrister half as much, at the hearing of any considerable Cause.[22]

Thus, according to the author of *Angliae Notitia*, barristers' fees had risen tenfold during the time of his experience. Evidence presented by Dr Prest tends to identify Chamberlayne's 'antient' fees as sums normally paid to barristers and serjeants during the early seventeenth century, when 10–20s. was the regular unit of remuneration.[23] By the 1680s there had indeed been some inflation of barristers' fees, as Professor Holmes has pointed out, although this should not be exaggerated: Roger North, describing his practice in Chancery, mentioned receiving ten guineas in 'very great' causes and five in the 'better sort', although two and three guineas were the staple of his practice, with only one guinea for simple motions and defences.[24] It is true that Edward Turner, later solicitor-general, had taken higher fees in the 1660s, when his receipts for advocacy were quite frequently in units of £5, but he must have been exceptional, for North himself was one of the leaders of his profession: indeed he was writing of his practice under his brother as lord keeper, when he enjoyed the double advantage of being the 'favourite' of the court and king's counsel.[25] If it is reasonable to compare the Restoration barrister with the barristers and serjeants of Dr Prest's study, it appears that fees for advocacy had

[22] Chamberlayne, *Angliae Notitia*, pt. II (1st edn., 1671), 339–40.
[23] W. R. Prest, 'Counsellors' Fees and Earnings in the Age of Sir Edward Coke', in J. H. Baker (ed.), *Legal Records and the Historian* (1978), 171.
[24] *Lives of the Norths*, iii. 167.
[25] Holmes, *Augustan England*, p. 131.

risen perhaps fivefold over the half-century which divided them (although only two- or threefold, if inflation is taken into account).[26]

But variations in the eminence of counsel and the wealth of litigants make generalizations on the subject of fees extremely dangerous. On the one hand, as North remarked, highly important cases might be extremely rewarding. Thus in 1688 the Seven Bishops paid out large sums to their counsel for advice and learned argument: £2.3s. (three times) and £5.7s.6d. (three times) as retainers; £2.3s. (twice), £3.4s.6d. (three times), £5.7s.6d. (three times), and ten guineas (three times) for advice and consultations; £2.3s. (once) and £3.4s.6d. (once) for simple motions; and the princely sum of twenty guineas (five times), which was probably given for arguing the case. Of course this was one of the most celebrated trials of the period, and the barristers involved were the cream of their profession: Sir Francis Pemberton, Sir Robert Sawyer, Henry Pollexfen, Heneage Finch, Sir George Treby, Sir Cresswell Levinz, and John Somers being the most notable, all of them former or future judges or law officers.[27] By contrast, fees tended to be much lower in more run of the mill cases, especially if second-rank counsel were retained. An instance of this is provided by an attorney's bill of 1701–2, which records discrete payments of only £1.1s.6d. (ten times) for arguments, motions, and other appearances made by counsel representing his client in a King's Bench case. These barristers, who included one 'Mr Weld' and the common serjeant of London, were paid even less for their out of court work, since they received only 10s. (three times) for signing documents.[28]

Levels of remuneration also varied according to the court concerned. Inferior jurisdictions generally gave rise to small fees; for example, at the Sheriffs' court in the city of London, counsel were normally paid only 5s. each for their appearance, which was regarded as less than a quarter of the charge to the litigant in the courts of Westminster Hall.[29]

[26] It should be noted that North was appearing in Chancery, where fees were generally high, while many of Dr Prest's examples are drawn from common law litigation (*Lives of the Norths*, iii. 166–7; Prest, 'Counsellors' Fees and Earnings', pp. 168–71 and apps. II and III, pp. 179–82).

[27] Bodl., MS Tanner 28/1/106: 'Fees to the Counsell' in Archbishop Sancroft's hand [1688].

[28] Guildford Muniment Room, Midleton MSS 1248/1/339: attorney's bill, 1701–2. The common serjeant was Duncan Dee of IT, who was called 12 Feb. 1682. 'Mr Weld' was probably J[oseph] Weld, called MT 30 May 1679 (B. R. Masters, 'The Common Serjeant', *Guildhall Miscellany*, 2 (1967), 387; *CITR* iii. 172; *MT Adm. Reg.*, i. 187).

[29] BL, Add. MSS 22263 (Strafford Papers), fos. 94–5: papers concerning a bill for the removal of suits out of the inferior courts, n.d.; cf. *LJ* xxiv. 253, 267, 276, 284, 301, 305: proceedings of 2 May–9 June 1733.

At the opposite extreme were the court of Chancery and that most expensive of all jurisdictions, the House of Lords. A Chancery case of 1694 involved payments to counsel (who included Sir Bartholomew Shower and Sir Thomas Powys, two very eminent barristers) ranging from £1.2s. (twice) to twelve guineas (once), with around two guineas being the standard fee.[30] Thirty years later, a respondent to an appeal in the Lords was expected by her solicitor to give her counsel (the solicitor-general, Charles Talbot) four or five guineas for 'settling the case' and ten guineas to Talbot and William Hamilton of Lincoln's Inn for arguing it. Fortunately this great expense was not in vain, since the appeal was dismissed and the lady had her decree affirmed.[31]

Edward Chamberlayne's statement on the subject of rising barristers' fees clearly included an element of hyperbole, but notwithstanding the variations cited above, it is apparent that the remuneration of barristers did increase significantly during the mid-seventeenth century, and by 1688 the two or three guineas mentioned by Roger North was a common unit of payment among leading counsel in the regular courts of Westminster Hall. The House of Lords acknowledged this rise in 1690, when they proposed legislation 'for the restraining extraordinary charges and fees to counsel' pleading at Westminster, in the Duchy Courts, or at the Great Sessions in Wales. When it came to preparing a bill, the peers resorted to the professional expertise of the chief justices, who set upper limits for fees at £3–5 for a full argument and £1 for arguing a demurrer—sums which seem reasonable in the light of North's comments. The judges were probably less realistic, however, when they stipulated no more than 10s. (20s. was crossed out in the draft) for a simple motion. Whether these restrictions on the free market would have got past the legal lobby in the House of Commons, or could have been enforced in the courts, is very much open to doubt; but in fact they were never put to the test, for the bill was lost with the end of the parliamentary session.[32]

In the absence of executive control and despite relative price stability generally, it is very likely that the rise in barristers' fees was

[30] PRO, C113/38: 'Exceptions taken from the Books, Jornall of the Convex Light', 23 Aug. 1694; cf. *LJ* xv. 527–8: proceedings of 29 and 30 Mar. 1695. I owe this and the previous reference to the kindness of Mr Clyve Jones of the Institute of Historical Research.

[31] Guildhall Library, London, MS 18760/1, unfol.: Nathaniel Cole to David Wilson, 3 Oct. 1727 and 30 Apr. 1728. Hamilton had been called LI 17 Nov. 1714 and was one of the leaders of the Lords' bar by 1720 (LI, MS Black Book x, fo. 202; App. VIII below).

[32] HMC, *13th Report*, app. v, 23–4: amended clause for the Lords' abortive law reform bill, 14 Apr. 1690.

maintained over the following half-century. Appendix XI is an abstract of the fees paid to counsel by solicitors on behalf of Viscountess Carrington in a Chancery suit which she maintained during the 1720s. This shows that while one guinea was the standard fee paid to junior counsel for retainers, motions and defences, and settling documents, with two guineas for arguments and advice, the leading barristers, such as Sir Thomas Pengelly, the king's premier serjeant, Nicholas Fazackerley, John Willes KC, and Talbot the solicitor-general, commonly received two to three guineas in lesser matters, and five or even ten guineas for arguments.[33] What is more, there is no reason to believe that this was an outstandingly 'great' case, for the breviates were relatively low compared to some which were given to Sir Thomas Pengelly. In 1717 Pengelly received a brief in a Chancery case marked seven guineas, and in 1722 a King's Bench brief with his name on the cover was endorsed ten guineas, while four years later he had a breviate of twenty guineas in a Common Pleas case.[34] On this evidence, it appears that fees payable to top barristers had indeed continued to rise during the later Stuart and early Hanoverian period to a point where they were virtually double what they had been in the 1680s.

The rise in the standard units of payment for the services of counsel inevitably meant that the aggregate incomes of the leaders changed correspondingly. Advocacy in the central courts may have provided employment for a diminishing body of men in the period covered by this study, but the rewards of success were becoming more substantial. Dr Prest has shown that the earnings of some successful barristers under the first two Stuarts varied between approximately £150 and £450 per annum, with a maximum of no more than £600 a year.[35] Some time during the Commonwealth period there seems to have been a quantum jump, for Professor Holmes has provided evidence which suggests that leading counsel of the 1660s were able to gain £1,000 to £2,000 from a single year's practice.[36] Further research into the fee books of mid-seventeenth-century barristers confirms this conclusion: in the later 1650s Heneage Finch, the future lord

---

[33] Although the anomaly of the low fees paid to Sir Constantine Phipps, who was leading counsel in the case 1722–3, is puzzling.

[34] BL, Add. MSS 19773 (Pengelly Papers), fos. 112, 215: briefs of 1717 and 1722; ibid., Add. MSS 19774 (Pengelly Papers), fo. 239: brief of 1726. For similar fees paid to Sir Philip Yorke as SG and AG see Croft, 'Philip Yorke', pp. 58, 69–70.

[35] Prest, 'Counsellors' Fees and Earnings', pp. 183–4.

[36] Holmes, *Augustan England*, p. 127.

chancellor, being then of eleven to fifteen years' standing at the bar, earned between £1,000 and £1,800 a year from his practice, and during the ten years when he was solicitor-general, he received an average of £4,000 per annum. Even this was not the peak of his income, for between May 1670 and July 1673, when he was attorney-general, his receipts averaged £6,700 a year.[37] The fee book of Sir Francis Winnington shows the same pattern of increasing income with the acquisition of office: over four terms during 1671–2, when Winnington was a barrister of eleven years' standing, he received a total of £1,791, exclusive of circuit work and vacations; while during 1673 and 1674, as solicitor-general to the duke of York, he took nearly £3,500 a year, rising to £3,637 (exclusive of office fees) in 1675, when he was solicitor-general to the king.[38] Sir John King, the leader of the Chancery bar in 1676, might have done better than any of his contemporaries if he had lived, for in that year, having succeeded Winnington as solicitor-general to the duke of York, he made £4,700 from his practice, and in Trinity term 1677 he received £40–50 *per day* in fees, despite being in the grip of an illness which was to prove fatal.[39]

As in the case of Roger North, who earned up to £4,000 a year at the Chancery bar in the early 1680s, the incomes of these Restoration barristers had been inflated by their appointment as royal counsel.[40] Given the continuing rise in fees, it is likely that the bar élite of Queen Anne's reign, especially law officers such as Sir Simon Harcourt, Sir Edward Northey, Sir Robert Raymond, and Sir James Montague, enjoyed even greater emoluments than the cream of the bar under Charles II. Indeed, by the time of the accession of the Hanoverians, it appears that the levels of remuneration attained by Finch, Winnington, *et al.* were quite within the reach of leading counsel who were not distinguished by major office, while the law officers were earning even more. Thus Sir Thomas Powys, a former attorney-general and incumbent queen's serjeant, was said to have earned nearly £4,000 a year from his practice during the last years of Anne's reign, while Sir John Cheshire, king's serjeant under George I, received an average of £3,241 from his practice before various courts each year between 1719

[37] *Lord Nottingham's Chancery Cases*, ed. D. E. C. Yale (Selden Soc., 73; 1957), pp. xiv–xv.

[38] *N&Q*, 2nd ser., 7 (1859), 65. For Winnington's career see Henning, *House of Commons 1660–90*, iii. 746.

[39] *A Memoir of the Life and Death of Sir John King, Knight*, ed. G. H. Sawtell (1855 [written 1677]), 11.

[40] *Lives of the Norths*, iii. 166–7.

and 1725.[41] A few years earlier John Comyns, a future lord chief baron of the Exchequer, had been establishing a practice which brought him £3,000 per annum prior to his appointment to the bench in 1722, and Lord Chancellor Talbot later declared that he earned the enormous sum of £7,500 a year when he was solicitor-general between 1726 and 1733.[42] Clearly, as Lord Chief Justice Parker pointed out in a memorial to his new monarch in 1714, rising prosperity in the nation at large over the previous decades had created a situation where successful counsel were conspicuous by their wealth:

Le Commerce l'étant augmenté, et L'argent devenu plus abondant, Les Fees ou Emoluments des Advocats practiciens ont aussi augmente, De sorte que leurs Gains sont a present fort grands . . . Les proportions sont a present, presques sur ce pied; Savoir un Avocatt de distinction gaigne £1500, £2000, £3000 ou £4000 par an, Et quelques uns plus.[43]

Incomes on this scale placed the top barristers on an equal footing with some of the 'great commoners' among country landowners, who received between £2,000 and £15,000 a year at the beginning of the eighteenth century.[44]

The steady rise in the fees and aggregate incomes of leading counsel provides an eloquent testimony to the rising public reputation of the bar. It also had important implications for English society, because wealth on the scale of that acquired by the bar élite during this period could be a powerful solvent of social bonds. But the social consequences of the barristers' riches depended upon their social mores, and these are not certain. Admittedly, counsellors were traditionally 'gentlemen' and formally 'esquires' by the early eighteenth century, but did this mean that they adhered to the 'aristocratic' values and aspirations expressed by Chief Justice Fortescue three hundred years earlier? If so, they would no doubt have spent their surplus income on landed estates and country houses in order to become members of the gentry élite in their own right. Or was the counsellors'

---

[41] HCRO, Panshanger MSS D/EP F147/19: Lord Cowper's advice to George I on the appointments of the judges [1714]; *N&Q*, 2nd ser., 7 (1859), 492–3.

[42] BL, Add. MSS 35585, fo. 309: J[ohn] Comyns [to Lord Hardwicke] 3 Jan. 1736; ibid., Add. MSS 4472, fo. 33: memorandum of Dr Birch, 1758. For Comyns see Sedgwick, *House of Commons 1715–54*, i. 569–70; for Talbot see *DNB* xix. 307–8.

[43] HCRO, Panshanger MSS D/EP F147/21: memorial on the salaries of the judges [1714]. Ibid., D/EP F57/126: draft letter [Lord Cowper to ?Baron Bernstorff, autumn 1716] cites Parker as the author.

[44] Holmes, 'Gregory King and the Social Structure of Pre-Industrial England', p. 55 n. 64.

pride in their vocation sufficient to make them content with their status as professional men, rather than aspiring to join the landed gentry? These and related questions have to be addressed in order to judge in what sense the subjects of this study were really 'barristers and gentlemen', and to assess how far the evolution of the bar in this period affected its traditional role as an agency of social mobility.

3. WEALTH AND SOCIAL ORIGINS

It was a truism in seventeenth-century England that rich lawyers 'in a few years purchase Estates fit for Lords', and in 1684 Henry Philipps embellished the platitude with his *Grandeur of the Law*: a catalogue of 'those illustrious families of our Nation, which have been raised to Honor and Wealth by the Profession of the Law'.[45] But Philipps exaggerated their number; moreover, the advent of war and heavy government borrowing under William and Anne created other, possibly more attractive, forms of investment. Nevertheless, it will be shown that for most lawyers land remained the favoured investment, not only because of its security, but also for the social status it conferred, in addition to its financial returns.[46]

There is no doubt that in simple terms of return upon investment, land purchase was not the most rewarding way of laying out surplus capital between the Revolution of 1688 and the accession of George I. Profits from estates were reduced by agricultural depression and a grinding land tax levied to pay for the continental campaigns of William III and Marlborough. Moreover, the necessities of war finance had created alternative forms of investment which were superficially more attractive than land, at least in the short term. Dr P. G. M. Dickson's analysis of the 'Financial Revolution' in England has shown that money invested in government stocks during the war years might yield 6–14 per cent return, and the rate of interest in the private sector financial institutions was at an equally appealing level.[47] Thus it is no surprise that some of the rich and successful barristers and judges of the period invested money in these funds. To give a few examples: Sir Joseph Jekyll, master of the rolls under George I, was one of the

[45] Chamberlayne, *Angliae Notitia*, pt. II (1st edn., 1671), 340; H. Philipps, *The Grandeur of the Law* (1684), preface, sig. A.2.

[46] For Philipps's exaggerations see the criticial annotations which Anthony Wood made in his copy of *Grandeur of the Law* (preserved in the Bodleian Library, Oxford, at pressmark Wood 251 (4)).

[47] P. G. M. Dickson, *The Financial Revolution in England* (1967), 470–2.

original subscribers to the Bank of England, and he was still listed among the public creditors in 1707, while he was also a major holder of East India Company stock by 1709.[48] Jekyll's predecessor as chief justice of Chester, Sir Job Charlton, had also been a heavy subscriber to the same fund, for a list of East India Company stockholders shows that in 1689 he was one of the largest investors outside the London merchant community, with a holding of £5,350.[49] Sir Ambrose Phillips, serjeant at law and one of the leaders of the Chancery bar as early as 1680, likewise dabbled in the funds: according to the will which he made in 1704 he then owned £1,000 Bank stock, which he duly bequeathed to his son.[50] Finally, Sir Littleton Powys, a puisne common law judge throughout the war years, had an enduring penchant for investing in government securities, for he loaned £750 in 1707 in anticipation of the land tax, and in 1720 he advanced £6,950 on security of the same fund, while four years later he was listed as the owner of £15,000 Bank stock.[51]

Admittedly, all these men, with the exception of Phillipps, were public servants who might have privileged knowledge of, or access to, the funds. Their investments, however, do not seem to be untypical of the élite of the legal profession generally, for barristers such as Peter King, Thomas Vernon, Sir Bartholomew Shower, Sir Thomas Powys, and Serjeants Henry Turner and Nathaniel Mead, to take a few names at random, were all investors in the financial markets at a time when they enjoyed no legal office.[52] But while it is clear that the money markets were recognized as a profitable means of investing surplus money by wealthy lawyers of this period, it is equally sure that for most

---

[48] *A List of the Names of all the Subscribers to the Bank of England* [1694], broadsheet; Dickson, *Financial Revolution*, p. 267; *A List of the Names of the Members of the United Company of Merchants of England, Trading to the East-Indies, who are also Members of the General Society, the 7th of April, 1709* (1709), broadsheet.

[49] BL, Add. MSS 22185 (Johnson Papers), fos. 12–13: list of East India Company stockholders, 15 Apr. 1689. For Charlton, see below, p. 159.

[50] See App. IX below; PRO, PROB11/489/152: will of Sir Ambrose Phillipps, made 17 Dec. 1704, proved 13 July 1706.

[51] Dickson, *Financial Revolution*, pp. 279, 428, 431.

[52] *Correspondence of Locke*, vii. 536–7: Peter King to John Locke, 13 Jan. 1702; *List of Subscribers to the Bank of England; List of Members of the East India Company*; Dickson, *Financial Revolution*, p. 267; East Sussex CRO, Frewen MSS FRE 557: receipt for £600 East India Company Stock purchased by Henry Turner, 2 Dec. 1717. I gratefully acknowledge the advice of Dr P. G. M. Dickson with regard to Sir Nathaniel Mead's holdings of Bank stock (in 1720 and 1724) in particular and financial records in general. For the careers of King, Vernon, Shower, and Powys see *DNB* xi. 144–7, xvi. 269, xviii. 161–2, xx. 282–3. For Turner and Mead see Baker, *Serjeants*, pp. 525, 541; Sedgwick, *House of Commons 1715–54*, ii. 249–50.

of them the funds were by no means a permanent alternative to the traditional pattern of buying land. Exceptions to this rule there were, but they were generally men who had special reasons for neglecting the land market. A good number of barristers were sons of country gentlemen, and many were heirs to their fathers' estates; men such as these may have been more interested than most in non-landed forms of investment for their accumulated wealth. Some of the regular legal operators in the money markets were certainly among this group: Sir Littleton Powys, for instance, was the heir to an estate in the Welsh Marches, as was Sir Job Charlton, who inherited his father's manor of Ludford in Herefordshire only ten years after the Restoration.[53] Sir Joseph Jekyll, on the other hand, was not the son and heir of a landed gentleman, but he was fortunate enough to inherit the estate of Brookmans, including Bell Bar in Hertfordshire, from his friend and political ally Lord Chancellor Somers.[54] Like Jekyll, Lord Cowper, Somers's successor on the woolsack, was very active in the financial markets (indeed he was the heaviest investor of all the lawyers) and did not purchase much land during his professional career; but he also had good reason to prefer non-landed investments, since he was the first son of a baronet and heir to an estate in Kent.[55]

In fact, despite the superior rates of return produced by paper securities, most successful barristers dabbled in the stock market only as a supplement to more permanent and significant expenditure on real estate. It cannot have escaped contemporary notice that land was a more secure investment, especially after the débâcle of the South Sea Bubble, and it continued to confer status and power in Augustan society to an extent which was as yet unchallenged by stocks and shares. This explains the eagerness of men from urban bourgeois or professional backgrounds to purchase estates and build great houses. Among other examples of barristers and judges who bought land from the fruits of their professional success, Professor Holmes has shown how Peter King, the son of an Exeter tradesman, purchased the manor of Ockham in Surrey within ten years of his first sallies in practice, and how a Staffordshire attorney's son, the future Lord Chancellor Thomas Parker, early in his career began to accumulate land which

[53] B. and A. P. Burke, *A Geneological and Heraldic History of the Peerage and Baronetage* (89th edn., 1931), 1490; Henning, *House of Commons 1660–90*, i. 44.
[54] *HPT* Sir Joseph Jekyll.
[55] Holmes, *Augustan England*, p. 132; *Victoria History of the Counties of England: Hertfordshire Genealogical Volume*, ed. D. Warrand (1907), 138–9.

formed the basis of an estate fit for an earl.[56] Although socially obscure counsel like King and Parker may have been more eager than most to find a place in landed society, perusal of the will of almost *any* leading counsel of the later seventeenth or early eighteenth centuries reveals the general desire among the cream of the bar to establish or improve the position of their families in the gentry élite. For example, Sir William Jones, the second son of a minor country gentleman, left substantial landed property in tail to his eldest son, with clear instructions for his executors to lay out the residue of his personal estate in further purchases of land as additions to the patrimony.[57] Similarly, Sir Anthony Keck, late Stuart Chancery counsel *par excellence* and lord commissioner of the Great Seal under William III, left land in three counties to his son with provision to spend £29,000 on more real estate.[58] Thomas Vernon, another eminent Chancery barrister, was even more obsessed with land; he had already inherited a small estate before he began to practise at the bar, but between 1685 and 1717 he spent a further £62,000 on additions to his inheritance in Worcestershire and purchases elsewhere, and he erected a magnificent mansion where his family house had stood.[59] Unfortunately, Vernon did not have a son to whom he could leave this great estate, but he intended to found a major county family all the same, and his will tied up the bulk of his land in a strict settlement designed to preserve it for ever in name and family via a collateral branch.[60]

Thus it appears that Augustan counsel generally were no less keen than their predecessors to follow the traditional pattern and use their wealth as a means to acquire or enhance a stake in the land. The bar was developing some elements of professional self-consciousness, but this did not mean that judges and counsellors accepted social and economic values quite different from the dominant mores of landed society.[61] Such conservatism had important consequences for social

---

[56] Holmes, *Augustan England*, pp. 133, 135.

[57] PRO, PROB11/370/58: will of Sir William Jones, made 18 Oct. 1681 with codicil 30 Apr. 1682, proved 24 May 1682.   [58] *HPT* Sir Anthony Keck.

[59] Hereford and Worcester CRO, Vernon MSS 705:7 BA 7335/115 (ii) 2: list of purchases of land in the hand of Thomas Vernon, 1685–1717. For Vernon's house, Hanbury Hall, see N. Pevsner, *The Buildings of England: Worcester* (Harmondsworth, 1968), 184–6.

[60] Ironically, the great equity counsel's will was the subject of an action in Chancery and subsequent appeal to the House of Lords (Hereford and Worcester CRO, Vernon MSS 705:7 BA 7335/51 (i) 1: printed papers in *Acherley* v. *Vernon*, to be heard before the Lords, 4 Feb. 1726).

[61] Cf. Duman, *English Judicial Bench*, pp. 167–8, 172.

mobility; the increasing wealth of successful lawyers meant that it was now possible for even 'mere' barristers—men who did not attain high legal office—to accumulate wealth on a scale sufficient to propel them into the upper reaches of the landed gentry. This novel state of affairs is reflected in Lawrence and Jeanne Stone's recent study of three county élites. Between 1700 and 1759, at a time of limited social mobility generally, legal wealth was the single most important source of infiltration into the cream of the squirearchy in these counties from outside landed society. And more lawyers were joining the élite during this period than in the sixteenth and seventeenth centuries, despite the contraction of the bar.[62] These are remarkable findings, because the Stones' élite is narrowly restricted to the very wealthiest of the gentry, and they imply even more mobility of a less restricted kind. For if the prosperity of the bar was able to carry eminent barristers like Vernon into the topmost ranks of landed society, then it is very likely that lesser counsel were making more modest improvements to their circumstances of life and social standing in even greater numbers.

The extent to which the bar was able to function as a ladder of ascent between different sectors of Augustan society was of course dependent upon the collective social origins of its recruits. One generation leaps from 'rags to riches' like that of Sir Edmund Saunders (who was born into poverty but became lord chief justice of England under Charles II), cannot have been common, but there are more examples of ascents from the middling ranks of society (Peter King and Thomas Parker are cases in point), and there were no doubt numerous instances of mobility over two or three generations which owed something to legal wealth.[63] Any progressive downward shift in recruitment to the bar might have increased its importance as an instrument of this kind of social change, and for this reason it is appropriate to analyse the origins of practising barristers. Table 6.1 is a limited exercise of this nature, based upon the labels of social rank the inns of court registers accorded to the fathers of barristers found to be practising in 1680 and 1720. Admittedly, the large proportion of 'unknowns' tends to devalue the statistics, but it does appear that there may have been a small but decisive shift towards greater recruitment of counsel from the lower ranks of society, because representation of the peer/esquire group fell from 44 per cent to around 37 per cent over

---

[62] Stone and Stone, *Open Elite?*, pp. 200–1, table 6.2.
[63] Foss, *Judges of England*, vii. 160–4; for King and Parker see above, pp. 159–60.

TABLE 6.1. *Social origins of practising barristers, 1680 and 1720*

Social origins	1680 practisers		1720 practisers	
	No.	%	No.	%
Peer	4	1.8	1	0.4
Knight/baronet	18	7.9	11	4.5
Esquire	78	34.4	77	31.7
Gentleman	74	32.6	87	35.8
Clerk	10	4.4	8	3.3
Lawyer	35	15.4	39	16.0
Doctor	1	0.4	2	0.8
Bourgeois	7	3.1	18	7.4
Total classified	227		243	
Unclassified and unknown	197		95	

Note: All conventions as in Table 1.2.

Sources: See Appendix II.

the period, while the proportion of 'gentlemen' and men of 'bourgeois' origins increased correspondingly.

It has already been remarked, however, that data derived from the inns' admission registers must be used with caution because of the uncertainty which attaches to some of the status descriptions employed there.[64] For this reason an attempt has been made to get beyond the labels by selecting two random samples of fifty barristers from each year group and then searching for information on their origins in a variety of standard geneological and local historical sources. As expected, the results of this exercise reveal that some of the sons of 'esquires' and 'gentlemen' were not members of the landed gentry. Among the 1680 sample, Serjeant Cristopher Goodfellow had been admitted to the Inner Temple in 1634 as the son of a London 'esquire', but his father was in fact a girdler, and there is no evidence that he had a landed estate.[65] And James Lightbowne, whose father was described as a Manchester 'gentleman' when his son entered Gray's Inn in 1662, was really the son of a woollen draper, although his

---

[64] See above, pp. 11–15; cf. Prest, *Rise of the Barristers*, pp. 87–8.

[65] *IT Adm. Reg.*, i. 44; *London Visitation Pedigrees 1664*, ed. J. B. Whitmore and A. W. Hughes (1940), 69.

father did acquire an estate by marriage.[66] Similarly, among the barristers practising in the central courts during 1720, Serjeant James Glyde's father was an alderman of Exeter, although he was described as 'esquire' on his son's admission to the Middle Temple in 1684, while counsellor Marmaduke Horseley was the son of a Caernarvon brewer who was elevated to 'gentleman' in the Gray's Inn admission register for 1710.[67] But when all the pseudo-gentry identified have been reclassified according to their proper social origins, and men from large towns have also been counted as non-gentry, analysis of the samples continues to suggest that the bar's recruits were becoming more socially humble during this period.[68] Of course the absolute numbers are too small for percentages to be of any significance, but there was a clear drop in the number of sons of 'esquires' and above. Moreover, although the rise in the number of men from 'bourgeois/ professional' groups does not appear to be significant, the increase in the number of 'gentlemen' by 1720 probably implies the presence of more pseudo-gentry, rather than offspring of the landed élite, because the sons of 'gentlemen' were frequently found to be non-gentry, and it is less easy to weed these imposters out of the later sample as a consequence of the lack of heraldic visitations. It is difficult to give a precise estimate of the social quality of barristers in these years, but more intensive research would no doubt reduce the number of possible gentry further; perhaps to as little as 40 per cent of the total or less. This guess may be compared with Dr Prest's estimate of an outside maximum of 50 per cent sons of landed gentlemen among barristers in the half-century before 1640.[69] The clear trend towards decreasing recruitment from the landed élite is confirmed by the work of Daniel Duman, who has shown how Middle Temple barristers and the judiciary were progressively colonized by the middling classes in the course of the eighteenth century.[70]

[66] *GI Adm. Reg.*, p. 293; *Victoria History of the Counties of England: Lancashire* (1906–14), iv. 268.

[67] *MT Adm. Reg.*, i. 214; Henning, *House of Commons 1660–1690*, ii. 398–9; J. J. Alexander, 'Exeter Members of Parliament, Part III, 1537 to 1688', *Report and Transactions of the Devonshire Association*, 61 (1929), 204, 213; *GI Adm. Reg.*, 357; K. Evans, 'Eighteenth-Century Caernarvon, II, Burgesses—Resident and Non-Resident', *Carnarvonshire Historical Society: Transactions*, 8 (1947), 79.

[68] The adjusted figures are as follows. 1680 sample: peer/esquire 12; gentleman 7; bourgeois/professional 17; total classified 36; unclassified and unknown 14. 1720 sample: peer/esquire 9; gentleman 10; bourgeois/professional 19; total classified 38; unclassified and unknown 12.   [69] Prest, *Rise of the Barristers*, p. 91.

[70] Duman, 'English Bar in the Georgian Era', pp. 91–3; id., *English Judicial Bench*, pp. 50–2.

Analysis of the birth order of practitioners in 1680 and 1720 serves to define the changing social background of the bar more closely. It seems that there were more first sons and heirs among practitioners in 1720 than there had been forty years earlier; for while around 60 per cent of the barristers identified by birth order in 1680 were eldest sons, by 1720 the proportion had risen to nearly 70 per cent.[71] Table 6.2 explains the social dimensions of this change by correlating the birth order of the barristers with their fathers' social status as recorded in the inns' admission books. The figures show that the proportion of sons and heirs among the offspring of baronets, knights, and esquires at the bar was diminished between the two sample years, while there was an enhanced representation of eldest sons among the children of 'gentlemen' and other inferior social ranks. In other words, bearing in mind the limitations of the inns' registers, the analysis suggests that the gentry were less inclined to commit their heirs to the law in the early eighteenth century; but this was more than compensated for by the increased enthusiasm for a legal career among the professional men and urban bourgeoisie, who were keener than ever to send their eldest sons to the bar.

Such a trend was entirely appropriate, because Augustan England was experiencing economic and social changes which are now recognized as symptoms of the early stages of industrialization, and they may have encouraged recruitment to the bar from the dynamic sectors of English society. The aggregate of business available to barristers was decreasing in the eighteenth century, and this caused a contraction in the number of practitioners. At the same time, however, there were important changes in the nature of litigation and in the propensity of different social groups to resort to the courts, and these provided opportunities for barristers who were versatile and imaginative. The bar was not only leaner and wealthier in the early eighteenth century than it had been a hundred years earlier; it was also becoming 'fitter' in the sense of being dominated by men who were adaptable enough to respond to the demands for legal services created by a society increasingly complex and variegated in its interests and occupations.

[71] The statistics are as follows. 1680 practisers: first/heir 140 (60.9%); son/other 90 (39.1%); total classified 230 (100.0%); unclassified and unknown 194. 1720 practisers: first/heir 169 (69.0%); son/other 76 (31.0%); total classified 245 (100.0%); unclassified and unknown 93. (Conventions and sources as in Table 6.2.)

TABLE 6.2a. *Correlation of social origins with birth order of practising barristers,*
1680

Social origins	First/heir		Son/other		Total classified	Unclassified
	No.	%	No.	%		
Peer	—	—	4	100.0	4	—
Knight/baronet	6	33.3	12	66.7	18	—
Esquire	49	62.8	29	37.2	78	—
Gentleman	51	69.9	22	30.1	73	1
Clerk	5	50.0	5	50.0	10	—
Lawyer	21	63.6	12	36.4	33	2
Doctor	1	100.0	—	—	1	—
Bourgeois	4	57.1	3	42.9	7	—
Total classified	137	61.2	87	38.8	224	3
Unclassified and unknown	3		3		6	191

TABLE 6.2b. *Correlation of social origins with birth order of practising barristers,*
1720

Social origins	First/heir		Son/other		Total classified	Unclassified
	No.	%	No.	%		
Peer	—	—	1	100.0	1	—
Knight/baronet	2	18.2	9	81.8	11	—
Esquire	47	61.0	30	39.0	77	—
Gentleman	69	80.2	17	19.8	86	1
Clerk	5	62.5	3	37.5	8	—
Lawyer	29	74.4	10	25.6	39	—
Doctor	2	100.0	—	—	2	—
Bourgeois	12	66.7	6	33.3	18	—
Total classified	166	68.6	76	31.4	242	1
Unclassified and unknown	3		—		3	92

Note: All conventions as in Table 1.3.

Sources: See Appendix II.

4. LAW AND SOCIETY: NEW OPPORTUNITIES

The half-century which is the focus of this study was a period of considerable social and economic development. Admittedly, overall growth was by no means spectacular compared with the classical era of industrialization, but there was important progress all the same. Industry was not yet the motor force of the economy, but individual areas of manufacturing grew considerably and the industrial sector as a whole expanded in an atmosphere of investment and enterprise. The pace of internal trade quickened as communications were improved by turnpike and river navigation projects, and overseas commerce grew at an unprecedented rate, to the extent that trade generally was 'transformed' by 1750. The financial sector of the economy was transformed in its wake; new banking and insurance companies were established in London, while the City began to assume its modern form as the home of great institutions, such as the Bank of England, the United East India Company, and the South Sea Company: only the largest among a proliferating breed of joint-stock ventures which were the basis for an infant market in stocks and shares. All this amounted to a 'commercial revolution' which left its marks upon society, most obviously in the form of numerical and cultural development in the urban areas generally and in London particularly, as more people concentrated in the centres of wealth and vitality.[72] But what effect did these changes have on the barristers and their work?

It will be recalled that Lord Chief Justice Parker attributed the rise in barristers' fees to an increase in the nation's commerce and the abundance of 'money'.[73] Clearly, England was more wealthy and prosperous in 1714, when Parker was writing, then it had been half a century earlier. The improvement had not been uniform, however, as his words implied. Many urban merchants and financiers, professional men, craftsmen, and artisans, had surplus wealth to spend or invest, but prosperity was less even in the countryside.[74] It is true that static

---

[72] M. Berg, *The Age of Manufactures: Industry, Innovation and Work in Britain 1700–1820* (1985), ch. 1 *passim*; Coleman, *The Economy of England*, chs. 8–10 *passim*; W. R. Scott, *The Constitution and Finance of English, Scottish and Irish Joint-Stock Companies to 1720* (Cambridge, 1910–12), i, chs. 15–22 *passim*; Dickson, *Financial Revolution*, ch. 1 *passim*; A. McInnes, *The English Town, 1660–1760* (Historical Association, 1980) *passim*; P. Borsay, 'The English Urban Renaissance: The Development of Provincial Urban Culture *c.*1680–*c.*1760', *Social History*, 2 (1977), 581–603.

[73] See above, p. 156.

[74] Borsay, 'Urban Renaissance', pp. 591–3; Dickson, *Financial Revolution*, pp. 301–2.

agricultural prices induced some landowners and farmers to adopt new methods of cultivation and new crops, and thereby enabled them to pay higher wages to their labourers. On the other hand, there was no general increase in profitability, and there were many years of depression. The lesser gentry and yeomen were especially hard pressed, and some were forced to sell up completely.[75] High war taxation was one cause of their difficulties, as has been seen, and many declining gentlemen focused their discontents on city business men who were doing well out of war finance. Although the extent to which the new 'monied interest' grew fat at the expense of the squires was exaggerated for political purposes, the financial revolution did result in a transfer of wealth from the land and some of its owners to the urban financiers and psuedo-gentry who invested in the funds.[76] The differing fortunes of these groups were translated into a marked shift in the pattern of litigation conducted in the central courts. Dr Brooks's work on the legal records shows that a large proportion of the boom in litigation during the late sixteenth and seventeenth centuries had been derived from the mainly agricultural Norfolk assize circuit, and the decline in business which dominated the Augustan age was characterized by a considerable fall in litigation from this area. And it is very likely that there was a corresponding drop in the proportion of litigants from the gentry élite of landed society, because members of this group accounted for approximately a third of the suitors in Common Pleas during Easter term 1640, but provided only 14 per cent of a sample of that court's customers in Trinity 1750.[77]

According to Brooks, these trends suggest that 'the work of the courts was being concentrated increasingly on the affairs of merchants, tradesmen and artisans' as the volume of litigation declined. The transition is substantiated by a significant rise in the proportion of litigation in Common Pleas and King's Bench which took the form of actions on the case, the type of law suit which became common among merchants seeking to enforce bills of exchange, instruments by which

[75] B. A. Holderness, *Pre-industrial England: Economy and Society 1500–1750* (1976), ch. 3 *passim*; Coleman, *Economy of England*, ch. 7 *passim*; *The Agrarian History of England and Wales*, V: *1640–1750*, ed. J. Thirsk (Cambridge, 1984–5), ii. 1, 3–4, 8–9, 57–8, 61, 118, 162–3, 170–1, 175.

[76] See above, p. 29; G. Holmes, 'The Achievement of Stability: The Social Context of Politics from the 1680s to the Age of Walpole', in id., *Politics, Religion and Society in England, 1670–1742* (1986), 270–1; Coleman, *Economy of England*, p. 195.

[77] Brooks, *Pettyfoggers and Vipers*, pp. 63–4, 283; id., 'Interpersonal Conflict', tables III and V.

they credited each other with money employed in trade.[78] What was happening, it seems, was that the courts were changing their procedures to become more congenial to the custom of merchants as the commercial sectors of society developed and the volume of litigation generated by the rural areas declined. In the area of contract, for example, the common law courts had formerly enforced the conditional bond (by which individuals contracted to pay debts, or to perform certain actions, within a given time) absolutely, without taking any notice of the merchants' need for flexible contracts and negotiable instruments of credit to allow cash flow and liquidity. By the seventeenth century, the court of Chancery was acting to relieve debtors from the penalties of the bond if they could show good reasons for defaulting, or if the principal, interests, and costs were paid. The common law courts followed suit after the Restoration by forcing plaintiffs suing on bonds to accept reasonable damages, rather than the full penalty specified by the instrument. These changes were recognized by statutes of 1696–7 and 1705. Moreover, during the tenure of Lord Chief Justice Holt (1689–1710), the court of King's Bench developed rules for the enforcement of bills of exchange as negotiable instruments, and promissory notes also became negotiable by act of parliament in 1704. These were perhaps the most important of a series of measures taken by the legislature and the courts in the late Stuart and early Georgian period which consolidated the commercial revolution by accommodating the increasing demands for justice created as a consequence of the growth of overseas trade, banking and insurance, joint-stock enterprise, and business failures.[79] Between 1690 and 1750 136 cases on negotiable instruments and forty-eight on marine insurance were heard which found their way into the published law reports; while at least 120 cases of bankruptcy were reported between 1737 and 1754.[80] Many more cases on these and other mercantile affairs must have gone unreported, and they represented the ever-increasing body of raw material from which the commercial law was developed. The enunciation of a system of principles was not achieved until Lord Mansfield presided in King's

[78] Brooks, 'Interpersonal Conflict', and table VI. For bills of exchange and litigation thereupon see [Sir Geoffrey Gilbert], *The Law of Evidence* (1761 [written before 1726]), 113–21.

[79] Brooks, 'Interpersonal Conflict'; A. W. B. Simpson, *The History of the Common Law of Contract: The Rise of the Action of Assumpsit* (Oxford, 1975), 118–22; Holdsworth, *History of English Law*, vi. 337–9, 519–21, 634–7, viii. 160–300, xi. 444–9; J. M. Holden, *The History of Negotiable Instruments in English Law* (1955), chs. 3–4.

[80] C. H. S. Fifoot, *Lord Mansfield* (Oxford, 1936), 13–14.

Bench; but even by the early eighteenth century, according to Sir William Holdsworth, 'the foundations of English commercial and maritime law had been laid', and the law merchant had been established as a 'rival' to the land law which would eventually attain supremacy over it.[81]

Changes in the law and in the substantive balance of central court litigation could not but have an effect on the barristers. In respect of their clientele and their conditions of practice they became a more exclusive body of men in the Augustan age: a relatively small group whose wealth and status was earned increasingly from the most prosperous members of the community at the centre of national life. It has already been remarked that the bar tended to relinquish general counselling, conveyancing, and clerical business after the Restoration.[82] This basic legal work was generated at the grass roots of society, in the countryside where the majority of the population lived, and the barristers abandoned it to a growing number of country attorneys and solicitors. The manorial and borough courts which might have provided local opportunities for small-time advocacy had decayed rapidly in the sixteenth and early seventeenth centuries; in consequence there was less reason for counsellors to reside in the rural towns.[83] Indeed, one of Lord Chief Justice Hale's motives for proposing (in the 1660s or 1670s) the establishment of a network of county courts to replace the existing moribund jurisdictions was that 'by this means the students and professors of the law, who are now generally driven or drawn up to London, so that there are scarce any left in the country, will have some encouragement to reside in the country, and the country not left to the management of attornies and solicitors'.[84] Hale may have exaggerated the extent and the speed of the barristers' flight from the countryside; but the process was no doubt accelerated after he wrote by the fall in the volume of central court litigation generated in the rural areas which the results of Dr Brooks's researches imply. Increasingly, it seems, barristers tended to be based in and around London, where they could be reached by agents acting for attorneys all over the country whose clients required expert counselling or the services of an advocate.[85]

---

[81] Holdsworth, *History of English Law*, viii. 298–9.

[82] See above, p. 126.   [83] Brooks, *Pettyfoggers and Vipers*, pp. 96–101.

[84] M. Hale, 'Considerations Touching the Amendment or Alteration of Lawes', in F. Hargrave (ed.), *A Collection of Tracts* (1787) 284.

[85] M. Miles, '"Eminent Attorneys": Some Aspects of West Riding Attorneyship, *c*.1750–1800' (Birmingham Univ. Ph.D. thesis, 1982), 317, 353–67.

It is true that some of the less ambitious practisers established themselves in the major provincial cities: Professor Holmes has identified barristers who maintained practices in Coventry, Manchester, and Chester between 1680 and 1720, and there were counsellors who were resident practitioners in the West Riding of Yorkshire during the later eighteenth century.[86] There are good reasons to doubt whether these provincial counsellors were very numerous, however. Throughout this period, barristers continued to be employed in the Duchy and palatinate jurisdictions, but the abolition of the council for the North in 1660 and the council for the Welsh Marches in 1689 (described as 'Probably the busiest, and certainly the most extensive, regional jurisdictions' before 1640) must have severely limited the opportunities for permanent practice in the provinces.[87] Moreover, although Hale's plea for a fresh system of small local courts was partially heeded over the following century by the establishment of a few courts of request or 'conscience' in the major urban centres for dealing with small debt claims, in practice these new tribunals adopted irregular forms of equity procedure and were generally disapproved of by the common law establishment.[88] Growing urbanization and the development of provincial culture in the eighteenth century should have created more central court work for barristers in the towns, but in the prosperous textile towns of West Yorkshire at least the attorneys who had become the lawyers of first resort tended to discourage their clients from going to law at all.[89] The Law List of 1785 certainly overestimated the extent to which the bar had become an exclusively metropolitan profession, but the absence of a single provincial barrister suggests that the capital was the primary workplace for the overwhelming majority of counsellors and advocates.[90]

London, of course, was the centre of the commercial revolution. For barristers who were serious about a full-time career the long-standing attractions of the metropolis were no doubt enhanced by the decline in their traditional areas of practice and the success of the 'monied men'

---

[86] Holmes *Augustan England*, pp. 139–40; id., 'Professions and Social Change', pp. 314–15; Miles, 'West Riding Attorneyship', p. 317.

[87] Prest, *Rise of the Barristers*, p. 51.

[88] W. H. D. Winder, 'The Courts of Request', *LQR*, 207 (1936), 369–94. Cf. Brooks, 'Interpersonal Conflict'.

[89] Miles, 'West Riding Attorneyship', pp. 333–50. In Preston, the source of much of Dr Borsay's evidence for the development of provincial urban culture, the 1742 guild rolls list 15 resident attorneys, but only 2 counsellors. Rolls for 1702 and 1722 list no attorneys or counsellors (Borsay, 'Urban Renaissance', p. 602).

[90] Duman, 'English Bar in the Georgian Era', p. 97.

and merchants in the capital. The prosperity of these people created work for them in a variety of ways. Pleading commercial cases in the courts was an obvious area of growth, as more and more financiers, merchants, and tradesmen brought their business disputes to the King's judges for settlement. For example, the historian of the tobacco trade between Britain and her American colonies has recently traced the long drawn out case of *Sheffield* v. *Starke*, a dispute between a London merchant trading to Maryland and the executors of his former business partner which proceeded through the courts of Common Pleas and the equity side of the Exchequer between 1706 and 1713. The action brought in the Exchequer was simply a device for settling accounts between the parties, but it ran the gamut of motion, counter-motion, bill, and cross-bill for seven years, and provided work for counsel which must have been converted into a considerable sum in fees.[91] This was not an isolated example of Exchequer litigation arising from overseas trade. In February 1680 a case was argued by the two leaders, Edward Ward and Thomas Jenner, which originated in a disagreement between the parties over profits made from exporting wine and an ensuing suit at common law on a bill of exchange. And in the Hilary term of 1720 no less than six counsel took part in the hearing of an action brought by the owner of a Baltic merchantman against the ship's master, alleging fraud in respect of money expended for refitting and cargo.[92] Four of these counsel were among the half-dozen busiest barristers in the Exchequer, and it is therefore difficult to avoid the conclusion that, in this court at least, successful advocates were men who kept abreast of developments in commercial law.[93]

Opportunities for advocacy which originated in the commercial sectors of society did not only arise in the supreme courts at Westminster. The growth in the number and variety of speculative ventures which reached a peak in the orgy of the South Sea Bubble during 1719–20 had an interesting offshoot in the form of numerous references to the law officers for their recommendations on petitions to

---

[91] J. M. Price, 'Sheffield v. Starke: Institutional Experimentation in the London–Maryland Trade *c.*1696–1706', *Business History*, 28: 3 (1986), 19–26.

[92] PRO, E126/13/200–1: decree in *Baker* v. *Denham et al.*, 5 Feb. 1680; ibid., E126/21/366–7: decree in *Bateman* v. *Grove*, 24 Feb. 1720. I am grateful to Professor J. M. Price for drawing my attention to the Exchequer Decree Books, and to Professor Price and Professor Henry Horwitz for their advice on these records.

[93] The counsel named were Sir Edward Northey, Mr [Thomas] Bootle, Sir Constantine Phipps, Mr [?John] Ward, Mr [?Paul] Foley, and Mr [Marmaduke] Alington. For the leaders see App. VI below.

the crown for monopoly charters, or for amendments to existing charters. These created work for barristers because interested parties were at liberty to enter a challenge to the proposed grant before letters patent passed the great seal, and these caveats were heard by the attorney- or solicitor-general, when proponents and opponents were able to present their arguments by their counsel.[94] Most of the challenges involved grants for joint-stock financial organizations, and their number must have declined after June 1720, when the government passed the 'Bubble Act', which was designed to limit the boom in stock-market speculation.[95] Records which survive among the Hardwicke manuscripts in the British Library show that the hearings did not cease altogether, however, and their details demonstrate some of the continuing links between the activities of Augustan speculators and the work of leading barristers. Sir Philip Yorke, later Lord Hardwicke, presided over many of these hearings during the 1720s in his capacity as a law officer. In October 1721, for example, Serjeant Pengelly, Sir Constantine Phipps, and Thomas Bootle argued the pros and cons of the proposed charter for the Equivalent Debentures Corporation (a venture for incorporating the obligations of public creditors who had been given 'equivalent debentures' in 1707 in exchange for a loan to the government) before Yorke. On this occasion, Pengelly represented the directors of the Bank of England, who opposed the grant as an infringement of their monopoly, and the other counsel spoke on behalf of the Equivalent Company.[96] Yorke also heard a petition around this time from the Royal Exchange Assurance Company, which was seeking a new charter, when Bootle and Serjeant Comyns argued on behalf of the petitioners, while Serjeant John Cheshire and Charles Talbot spoke for the Sun Fire Office, another insurance company which was seeking to defend its interests.[97] A further hearing on an insurance charter took place in 1728, but these financial ventures were not the only projects which

[94] C. MacLeod, 'Patents for Invention and Technical Change in England 1680–1753' (Cambridge Univ. Ph.D. thesis, 1982), 31–2; A. B. DuBois *The English Business Company after the Bubble Act 1720–1800* (New York, 1938), *passim*.

[95] Ibid. 2–3; MacLeod, 'Patents for Invention', pp. 46–7; Scott, *Joint-Stock Companies*, i. 417–18.

[96] BL, Add. MSS 36134 (Hardwicke Papers), fos. 64–5: notes of hearing, 5 Oct. 1721; cf. DuBois, *English Business Company*, pp. 14, 107.

[97] BL, Add. MSS 36134, fos. 22–3: notes of hearing, n.d. [before 1728]. Serjeant Comyns was probably John Comyns, created serjeant in June 1705 (Baker, *Serjeants*, p. 205).

were argued in front of the law officers.[98] The development of the manufacturing sector of the economy was reflected in a crop of applications for monopoly patents which were the subject of hearings. In March 1720 four counsel argued over the merits of an 'invention' for salvaging wrecks at sea which the author desired to patent, and in 1722 applications for patenting an unspecified 'machine' and an 'Engine for making thread' were argued before the solicitor-general.[99] A hearing of 1721, when counsel for two parties (Bootle, Mr [Charles] Coates, Mr [John] Floyer, and Mr [?] Rowlandson) contested the right to a monopoly over the new method for smelting iron with coal, shows how closely the work of this 'patent bar' mirrored the progress of industry.[100] It is therefore a pity that the surviving records of its activities appear to cease with the appointment of Yorke to the judiciary in 1733. But it is reasonable to suggest that barristers must have done more of this kind of work as industrialization gathered pace, although its forum must have changed after 1753 when the Privy Council renounced jurisdiction over patents and it passed to the common law courts.[101]

The growth of commerce and industry did not merely create opportunities for barristers to appear as advocates. It also gave rise to a considerable quantity of chamber work, in the form of specialist opinions written by counsel at the behest of business men. The large financial institutions employed their own standing counsel, of course, and they commissioned a steady stream of opinions on the legal implications of their activities. Thomas Bootle was standing counsel to the South Sea Company in the early 1720s; he and his successor James Gambier were naturally called upon for advice very frequently as a consequence of the nervousness of the directors who inherited the company after the crash.[102] The estates of their predecessors, the

[98] BL, Add. MSS 36137 (Hardwicke Papers), fos. 4–5; notes of hearing on the petition of the Amicable Society, 19 Jan. 1728; cf. DuBois, *English Business Company*, p. 343.

[99] BL, Add. MSS 36134, fos. 39–40, 71, 89; notes of hearings, 11 Mar. 1720, 14 Apr., and 24 Nov. 1722.

[100] Ibid., fos. 51–3: notes of hearings, 7 and 9 June 1721. Cf. ibid., fos. 16–17, 47: papers and correspondence relating to the case, July 1720 and 28 Apr. 1721; MacLeod, 'Patents for Invention', pp. 35–6. Coates was called MT 4 July 1712 (*MT Adm. Reg.*, i. 260); Floyer was called IT 8 July 1709 (*CITR* iii. 414); Rowlandson may have been Richard Rowlandson, whose call is not recorded, but who had a chamber in IT 1716–22 (ibid. iv. 18, 35, 39–40, 89).

[101] MacLeod, 'Patents for Invention', p. 4.

[102] BL, Add. MSS 25500 (South Sea Company Directors' Minutes, vol. vii), fos. 38, 40, 51, 54–5, 57–8, 61, 63, 73, 114, 117, 125; ibid., Add. MSS 25503 (South Sea

delinquent directors, were vested in trustees who also retained standing counsel, Serjeant Pengelly and Charles Talbot.[103] And Pengelly was one of the permanent counsel to the Bank of England, which was not much less importunate than the South Sea Company in addressing its counsel for advice at the time of the Bubble.[104] The fortunate survival of his opinion book reveals that this busy lawyer was also called upon by a variety of other business companies who desired his opinion in 1720–1 as a consequence of the Bubble Act. This ambiguous statute erected dire penalties which might apply to a broad range of ventures, and business men therefore had to resort to counsel for their advice as to how they could continue with their activities without falling foul of its barbs.[105] In the immediate aftermath of the act Pengelly was called upon to deliver opinions on its implications for no less than twenty-seven organizations whose activities covered the whole range of trade and industry, including mining, metalworking, manufacturing, colonial development, river navigation, insurance, steam power, and land drainage.[106] No doubt all the London counsel who were expert in the commercial aspects of corporation law benefited from the increased demand for advice, but this barrister was surely one of the most active among the regular commercial counsellors.

On the basis of this evidence, the historian of English companies after the Bubble Act has credited Pengelly and his fellow barristers with a large share of the responsibility for the organization and development of eighteenth-century business.[107] The flow of advice did not begin or end in 1720. Admittedly, the Bubble may have represented a peak in speculative activity, but it was no more than a spectacular hiccup in the regular progress of commerce; an advance that sent an ever-increasing number of business men and entrepreneurs

Directors' Minutes, vol. x), fos. 14–15, 18, 253; ibid., Add. MSS 25504 (South Sea Directors' Minutes, vol. xi), fo. 231; ibid., Add. MSS 25508 (South Sea Directors' Minutes, vol. xv), fos. 17, 42, 51 (references to counsels' opinions at courts of directors, 1721–36). Other counsel were also consulted during these years (ibid., Add. MSS 25500, fos. 39, 48, 97–8, and references cited above). For Bootle see above, p. 137; Gambier was called MT 31 May 1717 (*MT Adm. Reg.*, i. 272).

• [103] BL, Add. MSS 25500, fo. 101: court of directors, 7 Sept. 1721.

[104] Ibid., Add. MSS 22675 (opinion book of Sir Thomas Pengelly), fos. 4–6, 13–14, 22, 57: opinions for the Bank, 1719–21; ibid., Hargrave MS 294 (law cases *temp.* Anne and George I), fos. 54–5; copy case and opinion for the Bank, n.d.

[105] For the act see above, p. 172.

[106] DuBois, *English Business Company*, pp. 3–4; BL, Add. MSS 22675 *passim*.

[107] DuBois, *English Business Company*, p. 286.

to the lawyers for advice. For example, in 1710 Sir Edward Northey gave his opinion as to the rightful beneficiaries of freightage paid by the commissioners of the Royal Navy for carrying stores to Lisbon. Eight years later William Peer Williams was called upon to advise a London bank on the proper means of action for recovering a debt on a bill of exchange drawn upon it, the drawer of the bill in Amsterdam having gone bankrupt. And in 1723 Thomas Reeve advised the master of a ship trading to Seville how he might take action against a London company for recovery of the costs of freight alleged to be owing on a consignment of oranges and lemons.[108] Given the continued expansion of overseas trade and colonial enterprise, it is safe to conclude that counselling of this kind became part of the 'bread and butter' of London-based barristers in the eighteenth century.[109]

The evidence summarized above is sufficient to show that there were considerable opportunities in the late Stuart and early Georgian period for lawyers who could turn their minds to the problems of commerce and industry. It is not possible to say precisely how many London barristers were acting as regular counsellors and advocates for Augustan business men and entrepreneurs, but the narrow range of sources examined to date suggests that every able metropolitan practitioner must have taken on some business of this kind from time to time, while for at least a few it constituted a very large element of their practice. Men like Sir Thomas Pengelly and Thomas Bootle, the two counsel named most frequently among the surviving traces of this incipient 'commercial bar', were preoccupied with the complex problems associated with bills of exchange, charter parties, share dealings, and company organization at least as much as they were involved in the ramifications of the law of real property. And the success of commercial specialists like Pengelly and Bootle must have encouraged recruitment to the bar from among the urban bourgeoisie who were their clients. Indeed, it is possible that they themselves became involved in this kind of work as a consequence of experience derived from their family connections; Pengelly was the son of a Turkey merchant, while Bootle was brought up near the expanding

---

[108] BL, Egerton MS 1074 (legal cases and opinions of counsel, 1639–1757), fos. 55, 71: cases and opinions of Northey and Reeve (copies), 6 Apr. 1710 and 4 May 1723; ibid., Hargrave MS 294, fo. 2: case and opinion (copy) of William Peer Williams, 29 Aug. 1718. Williams was called GI 11 Nov. 1687 (*GIPB* ii. 92); Reeve was called IT 5 June 1698 (*CITR* iii. 339).

[109] See e.g. BL, Hargrave MS, fos. 6–8, 10–11, 56–7; ibid., Egerton MS 1074, fo. 55; ibid., Add. MSS 34729 (West Papers), fos. 338–47 (cases and opinions, 1714–54).

trade centre of Liverpool, and his brother became a director of the East India Company.[110]

The legal profession was much more open to market forces than any of the other 'great' professions. It was liable to react to social and economic changes more quickly than the armed forces or the Church, whose personnel did not sell their services in the market-place. The bar's growing colonization by the middle classes, and the activities of barristers like Pengelly and Bootle, are signs of a positive response to the changing fabric of life and work in Augustan England. The profession may have been experiencing a purge which reduced its quota of part-timers and incompetents as a consequence of the decline in the volume of litigation; but its leaders were rewarded with unprecedented wealth, and they were barristers able to adapt to the changing conditions by taking business wherever it was offered. These conditions encouraged individualists, often men from unconventional backgrounds.

Another example is William Murray, the future Lord Mansfield and the father of modern commercial law. Unlike Bootle and Pengelly, Murray does not seem to have had any familial connections with the 'growth sectors' of English society, but he also took advantage of new developments, because he established his reputation as a parliamentary counsel by representing enterpreneurs and local pressure groups who were seeking private acts to establish new manufactures, or improve communications. It is not a coincidence that Murray had an unusual background and an unconventional career. As a man of Scottish birth, he was a rare bird among English barristers, and he was also remarkable for his broad liberal education, which encouraged his mind to range beyond the narrow confines of the common law to encompass Scots law and international law generally. The period of his professional advancement lies outside the scope of this study, but it is significant that he rose via parliamentary success and government patronage, rather than according to the traditional pattern of progress as bencher and serjeant, because his career symbolizes the way in which the bar élite became liberated from the medieval structure of the profession.[111] Barristers who were able to adapt to the changes in English society tended to be men who were not closely identified with

---

[110] Sedgwick, *House of Commons 1715–54*, i. 473, ii. 334; *Victoria History of the Counties of England: Lancashire*, iii. 253.

[111] Foss, *Judges of England*, viii. 336; Sedgwick, *House of Commons 1715–54*, ii. 285–6; Holdsworth, *History of English Law*, xii. 464–70; Fifoot, *Lord Mansfield*, pp. 27–9.

its ancient institutions, and this explains why the bar was becoming separated from its institutional base in the Augustan period. The increasing attraction of the House of Commons was another force which contributed to this process, and its role is the subject of the following chapter.

7
BARRISTERS IN PARLIAMENT

THE law courts and the High Court of Parliament have always had certain common features, and in consequence men who follow a career at the bar have also found a ready market for their skills as members of the House of Commons. The period covered by this study was no exception to this phenomenon: a sizeable number of barristers were also MPs during these years and they played an important part in the activities of the legislature. Indeed, certain developments peculiar to the Augustan age may have offered unprecedented opportunities for the ambitious lawyer to further his career through a spell in parliament. Moreover, these opportunities were being created at a time when the ancient structures of the profession were in decay, and it is possible that for a growing number of barristers activity in parliament usurped the place which reading and the coif had occupied in the careers of their predecessors. The development of this parliamentary option forms the subject-matter of the present chapter.[1] The first aspect which will be examined is the representation of the inns of court and their barristers in each of the parliaments which sat between 1680 and 1730.

I. NUMBERS

The representation of the inns of court among members of the House of Commons was in decline during the later seventeenth and early eighteenth centuries, in accordance with the falling rolls at the inns themselves.[2] The numbers of inns' men among MPs had probably been at a peak in the late Elizabethan and early Stuart period, when the 'educational revolution' identified by Professor Stone was in full swing,

[1] I am most grateful to Dr Eveline Cruickshanks, editor of the forthcoming volumes on *The House of Commons 1690–1715* and to her research assistant Dr David Hayton, for their kind advice and assistance. This chapter could not have been written without the information derived from draft biographies, constituency articles, and files which they have most generously allowed me to consult.
[2] Comparing Table 7.1 with Fig. 1.1 above.

for at that time 50 per cent or more of the Commons' members had been admitted to an inn.[3] Table 7.1 shows that the later Stuart parliaments still included around 40 per cent inns' men among their members, but this level of representation was not maintained after 1705, as the trough in admissions to the inns which had begun in the 1680s was working its way through to the legislators of the nation. By the time of the first parliament of George II only just over a quarter of the English and Welsh members of the Commons had been admitted to an inn of court, and it seems likely that the proportion of inns' men among MPs fell still further towards the middle of the eighteenth century.[4] Nevertheless, for most of the half-century which is the focus of this study, 30–40 per cent of the House of Commons might have attended one of the inns, and this gives an upper limit of four out every ten English and Welsh members who possibly received some training in the common law.[5]

The distribution of these 'legal' MPs, in terms of their affiliation to the individual inns of court, presents few surprises. Looking at Table 7.1 again, it is apparent that the parliaments elected from 1679 to 1689 represented the final phase of Gray's Inn's numerical supremacy among the four societies, for during those years men from that house formed the largest single group in the Commons, followed by contingents of roughly equal size from the Temple societies, and a smaller body of men who had been admitted to Lincoln's Inn. From 1690 the representation of Gray's diminished steadily, while that of the Temple inns grew; a redistribution which was again mainly a reflection of the changes in aggregate admissions to the inns themselves. This process, together with the first signs of increased representation from Lincoln's Inn in elections to the parliament of 1727, meant that by George II's reign the inns of court contingent among MPs was dominated by Templars, with a fair proportion from Lincoln's Inn but only a smattering of men from Gray's.

[3] L. Stone, 'The Educational Revolution in England, 1560–1640', *P&P* 28 (1964), 41–80; P. W. Hasler, *The House of Commons 1558–1603* (1981), i. 4; J. E. Neale, *The Elizabethan House of Commons* (1949), 302–3; M. F. Keeler, *The Long Parliament, 1640–1641* (Philadelphia, 1954), 27; D. Brunton and D. H. Pennington, *Members of the Long Parliament* (1954), 6.

[4] Adjusting the statistics in Table 7.1 to include the Scots elected after 1707 (none of whom had been admitted to an inn of court) and comparing with Lucas, 'Blackstone', pp. 463, 488.

[5] Although the real proportion was doubtless much lower, given members' non-attendance at the inns and the decline of formal education there (see above, chs. 2, 4 *passim*).

TABLE 7.1. *Those admitted to the inns of court among English and Welsh members of parliament, 1679–1734*[a]

Parliament of	Gray's Inn		Inner Temple		Lincoln's Inn		Middle Temple		Total % all MPs	
	No.	%	No.	%	No.	%	No.	%	No.	%
1679 (Oct.)	74	32.3	58	25.3	42	18.3	55	24.0	229	42.3
1681	69	31.4	56	25.4	38	17.3	57	25.9	220	43.8
1685	52	24.3	63	29.4	37	17.3	62	29.0	214	40.7
1689	75	32.3	61	26.3	35	15.1	61	26.3	232	41.7
1690	70	26.6	71	27.0	42	16.0	80	30.4	263	42.3
1695	54	23.1	58	24.8	43	18.4	79	33.8	234	41.6
1698	45	19.1	65	27.5	44	18.6	82	34.7	236	43.6
1701 (Feb.)	40	17.9	61	27.2	44	19.6	79	35.3	224	42.0
1701 (Dec.)	35	16.3	60	27.9	42	19.5	78	36.3	215	43.3
1702	34	14.7	63	27.3	47	20.3	87	37.7	231	41.5
1705	27	12.1	64	28.7	41	18.4	91	40.8	223	38.6
1708	24	12.3	60	30.8	38	19.5	73	37.4	195	35.6
1710	27	12.3	72	32.7	39	17.7	82	37.3	220	37.1
1713	23	12.2	63	33.5	35	18.6	67	35.6	188	35.2
1715	25	11.1	72	32.0	41	18.2	87	38.7	225	32.8
1722	14	7.5	60	32.3	34	18.3	78	41.9	186	30.0
1727	12	7.0	52	30.2	40	23.3	68	39.5	172	27.2

[a] All MPs admitted to an inn previously or who were admitted in the course of the parliament specified. In the case of MPs admitted to more than one inn they have been attributed to the house of *last* admission.

Sources: Henning, *House of Commons 1660–90*; *HPT* (checklist of MPs 1690–1715); Sedgwick, *House of Commons 1715–54*; *GI Adm. Reg.*; *IT Adm. Reg.*, i, ii; *LI Adm. Reg.*, i; *MT Adm. Reg.*, i.

The four inns' high level of representation in the House of Commons was simply a consequence of the place which the legal societies occupied in the traditional pattern of a gentleman's education.[6] The gentry entered parliament as a matter of course, because they were the natural leaders of their local communities, and a substantial minority also registered at the inns as a formality. However, this chapter is primarily concerned with members of parliament who had been called to the bar of their inns, especially those who practised the

[6] See above, pp. 13–21.

law, and they became MPs for more positive reasons. From their point of view, a seat in parliament was an asset which might pay a rich dividend. In the first place, there was the possibility of preferment: success in the Commons was rewarded with jobs in the gift of the crown which could eventually lead talented lawyers to the judicial bench or even the woolsack.[7] This prospect was probably uppermost in John Locke's mind when he told his protégé Peter King that his election for a Devon borough 'will be much for your advantage in many ways'.[8] Locke may also have been thinking of the young counsel's practice, for the second clear advantage which membership of the Commons conferred upon a lawyer was the opportunity to gain fresh business from among the political élite of the nation. As an MP he would enjoy enhanced prestige which might be turned to account by attracting clients of better quality. Moreover, the affairs of the gentry and aristocracy quite naturally were liable to become the subject of parliamentary attention, and it was therefore of some benefit to them to employ a lawyer who was familiar with MPs and peers. Indeed, some barrister MPs were prepared to use their voices in the Commons to advance a ligitant's cause, as Sir Thomas Pengelly did in 1726, when he was instrumental in securing the expulsion of his client's legal adversary from his own privileged place in St Stephen's Chapel.[9]

How many barristers (as distinct from members of inns who had not gone on to be called) were there in the House of Commons during the period covered by this study? Table 7.2 shows the number and proportion of men who had been called to the bar among English and Welsh MPs in every parliament which sat between 1680 and 1730.[10] Taking a broad view of the figures, it is clear that, with the exception of the parliament of 1689, the house normally included a group of barristers which represented approximately 14 per cent of the total of

---

[7] See below, pp. 210–13, and ch. 8 *passim*.

[8] Bodl., MS Locke c. 40, fo. 94: Locke to King, 20 Jan. 1701; *Correspondence of Locke*, vii. 226; cf. ibid., vii. 231.

[9] Bodl., MS Eng. Lett. c. 17, fos. 54–8: letters of K[atherine, dowager duchess of] Buckingham to [Sir Thomas Pengelly], 4 Feb. 1726 and n.d. The unfortunate opponent of Pengelly's client was John Ward MP, for whom see Sedgwick, *House of Commons 1715–54*, ii. 519–20.

[10] MPs selected for Scottish constituencies after 1707 have been excluded from the totals, since their inclusion would inhibit any chronological perspective of the proportion of barristers in the house, given the fact that English lawyers were very unlikely to stand for Scottish seats (no barrister was returned for a constituency north of the border during this period).

TABLE 7.2. *Barristers/practitioners among English and Welsh members of parliament, 1679–1734*

Parliament of	Barristers		Among whom, practitioners		No evidence of practice		Total MPs
	No.	%	No.	%	No.	%	
1679 (Oct.)	78	14.4	39	7.2	39	7.2	541
1681	69	13.7	28	5.6	41	8.2	502
1685	74	14.1	46	8.7	28	5.3	526
1689	67	12.0	37	6.6	30	5.4	556
1690	88	14.1	45	7.2	43	6.9	622
1695	78	13.9	39	6.9	39	6.9	562
1698	81	15.0	43	7.9	38	7.0	541
1701 (Feb.)	80	15.0	38	7.1	42	7.9	533
1701 (Dec.)	72	14.5	35	7.1	37	7.5	496
1702	86	15.5	41	7.4	45	8.1	556
1705	89	15.4	44	7.6	45	7.8	577
1708	85	15.5	45	8.2	40	7.3	548
1710	98	16.5	53	8.9	45	7.6	593
1713	86	16.1	45	8.4	41	7.7	534
1715	97	14.1	62	9.0	35	5.1	686
1722	82	13.2	60	9.7	22	3.5	620
1727	80	12.7	58	9.2	22	3.5	632

Sources: As in Table 7.1. Also *GIPB* i, ii; *CITR* ii, iii, iv; *LIBB* ii, iii; sources cited in Appendix II.

MPs returned. This proportion rose to 15 per cent or more for the last parliaments of William III and the first three of Anne, and then to 16 per cent or more in 1710–14. Following this crest the *number* of barristers remained much the same in the parliament of 1715–22, but as the length of parliaments (and the number of MPs elected) increased, their proportion in the house declined steadily under the early Hanoverians to a level of around 12–13 per cent, which was more or less maintained throughout the eighteenth century.[11]

These fluctuations in the aggregate of barristers elected to the House of Commons simply reflect the changing numbers of barristers

[11] Adjusting the statistics for barristers in Table 7.2 to represent the proportion of *all* MPs and comparing with Lucas, 'Blackstone', p. 488. The number of *practising* barristers fell by mid-century (see below, pp. 186–7).

created by the inns themselves.[12] Thus the barrister contingent in the house under Charles II and James II was larger than it had been in the parliament of 1614 (when it formed around 10 per cent of the Commons), and the increase represented the rise in the output of barristers from the inns during the mid-seventeenth century: a rise which had been reflected earlier by the large proportion of lawyers among members of the Long Parliament.[13] The subsequent plateau of 1698–1715 corresponds roughly to the spate of barristers produced in the Restoration period, given a time-lag for men to become eligible for the Commons, and the post-1715 decline in the number of barrister MPs clearly parallels the levelling-off of the output of barristers after 1680.

A more important aspect of this question must be considered at greater length. Not all those who were called to the bar ever practised law; in consequence a bare analysis of the quantity of barristers among MPs reveals little about the changing proportion of *career* lawyers in the House of Commons. For this reason, an attempt is made in Table 7.2 to identify the practitioners among barristers returned to each parliament in this period. The resultant figures are conservative estimates which should be treated with some caution, but they reveal a clear trend which seems to override minor fluctuations. Thus, according to the second column of Table 7.2, it appears that the proportion of practising barristers in the House of Commons increased between 1679 and 1734—especially during the early eighteenth century—rising from around 7 per cent at the time of the Exclusion Crisis to 9 per cent or more in the longer parliaments under the first Hanoverians.[14] In terms of numbers there was a one-third increase between 1679 and the 1720s, from around forty to approximately sixty practitioners. The significance for the bar itself becomes quite apparent if the parliament of 1690 is compared with that of 1722. Out of a similar aggregate number of men (622, 620) returned to the Commons in each case there were forty-five practitioners in 1690–5 and no less than sixty in 1722–7. It may not be entirely coincidental that in 1714 an abortive place bill had attempted to limit the number of barristers in the House of Commons to no more

[12] Comparing the levels of barrister MPs with the graph in Prest, 'English Bar, 1550–1700', p. 68, and Fig. 3.1 above.

[13] For the number of barristers in the early 17th-cent. parliaments see Lucas, 'Blackstone', p. 488.

[14] Cf. Holmes, *Augustan England*, p. 123.

than twenty. The reign of Queen Anne and, in particular, the early
Hanoverian period seem to have witnessed a real increase in the
number of professional lawyers who were developing a parliamentary
aspect to their careers, despite the fact that the practising bar itself had
contracted over the previous fifty years.[15]

It is evident that the later Stuart and early Georgian bar enjoyed a
degree of representation in the House of Commons quite disproportionate to its tiny size. Of course a good number of lawyers was
always likely to be found in the Commons, given the fundamental
affinity between parliament in all its aspects and the institutions, forms,
and substance of the common law. During the seventeenth century,
however, the barristers' natural fitness for parliament was augmented
as politics became riddled with legal concepts and practices, to the
extent that the political and constitutional issues of the Restoration
period were fought and settled by men who, whether they were
practising lawyers or not, were armed to the teeth with precedents and
learned arguments to give the 'colour' of law to their actions.[16]
Moreover, the 'settlement' of the great constitutional issues of 1689
was not followed by any diminution of the degree to which politics in
general and parliamentary business in particular was expressed in the
language and lore of the courtroom; on the contrary, eighteenth-
century politicians were obsessed with jurisprudence to a 'disastrous'
extent, according to Sir Lewis Namier.[17] Barristers practising in our
period therefore had every reason to look to the Commons as a forum
for their talents no less appropriate than Westminster Hall.

There is another aspect to this clear consanguinity between law and
parliamentary affairs which was also likely to encourage Augustan
lawyers to contemplate a political career. The parliamentary franchise,
in all its various forms, was fundamentally bound up with the common
law, and this meant that counsel were very likely to become involved
with electoral disputes, especially in the English and Welsh boroughs.
Where the franchise was a matter of burgage tenure, for instance,
control of a borough was acquired via the possession of real property,
and in consequence political rivals often carried their disputes into a
court of law, where they would naturally require the services of a

---

[15] HMC, *House of Lords MSS* (new series), x. 278–9: Lords' proceedings of 12 and 14
Apr. 1714. Cf. Veall, *Law Reform*, pp. 203–6; see above, pp. 123–4.

[16] H. Nenner, *By Colour of Law* (Chicago, 1977), pp. x, 131–54, 198; William
Sacheverell, for instance, greatly valued his collection of constitutional precedents
(Henning, *House of Commons 1660–90*, iii. 370).

[17] L. Namier, *The Structure of Politics at the Accession of George III* (2nd edn., 1957), 42.

barrister. Similarly, in boroughs where the franchise was vested in the freemen or in the corporation alone, quarrels might arise over the corporation's assumed right to create freemen, or there might be a question as to the validity of a municipal election, both of which were likely to result in litigation before the court of King's Bench. For example, in January–February 1729 the sitting members for Harwich, who had found difficulty in securing the election of their own candidate for mayor (a crucial figure in parliamentary elections), resorted to King's Bench for a writ of *mandamus* to compel a fresh municipal election. The arrangements for this process necessitated the employment of no less than five counsel, including two mere barristers, two serjeants at law, and one king's counsel.[18] Cases such as these were a fertile field of opportunity for the Augustan barrister who had parliamentary ambitions.[19]

The common lawyers' natural involvement in the affairs of the parliamentary constituencies was by no means confined to incidental litigation in Westminster Hall: they were also likely to be major actors in parliamentary elections themselves, even when they were not actually candidates. In the first place, it seems that it was not at all uncommon for candidates to retain a barrister as an adviser who would wrangle over knotty points of procedure at the scene of the poll itself. In July 1717 for instance, at the Cockermouth by-election, both candidates were accompanied by their counsel, who duly argued at length over points in dispute between the parties, being principally the alleged minority of one of the candidates.[20] Secondly, if the result of an election was disputed and one of the candidates petitioned, the case would be argued in the House of Commons, either at the bar or, more usually, before the committee of privileges and elections. Despite the evident partiality of final judgements, some borough patrons were prepared to spare no expense for the best legal representation at these hearings, and there were rich pickings for counsel who specialized in

[18] HMC, *Egmont Diary*, iii. 323–48 *passim*; Sedgwick, *House of Commons 1715–54*, i. 242. For the parliamentary franchises generally see E. and A. Porritt, *The Unreformed House of Commons* (Cambridge, 1903), i. ch. 3 *passim*.

[19] e.g. Sir Thomas Pengelly, whose practice developed a bent towards municipal disputes and *quo warranto* proceedings which pre-dated his election to parliament (BL, Add. MSS 19773, fos. 185–93: brief in *R. v. Walter*, 1714; ibid., Add. MSS 19774, fos. 18–19, 22–30: legal documents, 1723–4; Bodl., MS Eng. Lett. c. 17, fos. 8, 33–4, 41–2, 47–8, 59, 66–7, 101, 108–16: correspondence and papers of Pengelly, 1717–26; Sedgwick, *House of Commons 1715–54*, ii. 334–5).

[20] BL, Add. MSS 19773, fos. 117–20: papers in the case of the Cockermouth election of 8 July 1717; cf. *HPT* Ludgershall.

such work.[21] In fact the potential gains were not confined to handsome fees, and these parliamentary counsel often became MPs themselves later in their careers.[22]

It was not only barristers concentrating upon election disputes who found both regular employment and political opportunity in borough affairs. Indeed, the close association between the legal profession and the municipalities was virtually institutionalized in the office of the borough recorder. This officer was normally a practising barrister retained in order to preside over the borough courts; if a non-lawyer was appointed he would invariably nominate a legally trained deputy to act for him. As the next chapter will show, the acquisition of a recordership or deputy recordership was a feature of the careers of many successful counsellors, and such an office may have made an important contribution to their ultimate prosperity. In this respect not the least advantage of a recorder's place was its possible role as an entrée to the House of Commons, for boroughs evidently regarded their recorders or deputy recorders as suitable men to represent them at Westminster, and a handful of the lawyers who sat in each parliament between 1680 and 1730 served their constituencies in that capacity.[23]

It is clear that the close connections between the common law and parliament, both in terms of the legal colour of debate and procedure at the centre and the need for forensic services in the constituencies, meant that practising barristers had a greater chance than most men of finding a natural role among the representatives who sat in the House of Commons. But this organic connection between English law and the English parliament does not sufficiently explain the increase in the number of practising lawyer MPs shown in Table 7.2 for the period from the Glorious Revolution onwards. It is obvious however that any rise in the political temperature was likely to lead to a greater demand for barristers' skills and an enhancement to their opportunities for entry into parliament; and it is surely no coincidence that the early eighteenth-century expansion of the legal contingent in the house, in particular, took place at a time when the political nation was torn asunder by deep divisions, just as the adamantine stability of the middle of the eighteenth century was reflected by a decrease in the

---

[21] See *HPT* Plympton Erle and *HPT* Cockermouth for e.g. of 1691 and 1711.
[22] See below, p. 196.
[23] They ranged from a low of 6 in 1681 and 1713 to a high of 12 in 1685. These are no doubt underestimates (sources as in Table 7.2).

number of lawyer MPs.[24] For the period covered by this study, regular sessions of parliament after 1689 and an unprecedented run of contested elections after 1694 gave rise to a sharpening of debating and procedural skills at Westminster and a bitter and protracted struggle in the constituencies.[25] The role of the lawyers in the cut and thrust of St Stephen's Chapel will be considered later. For the moment it is necessary to turn to the constituency aspect of the picture, in order to explain the *mechanism* by which an increasing proportion of the bar found its way into the House of Commons.

2. CONSTITUENCIES

Practising lawyers who occupied seats in the unreformed parliament have often been associated with the notion of 'carpet-baggers', meaning men who had no legitimate interest in their own constituencies, but rather became MPs via the exploitation of the least democratic aspects of the electoral system. Indeed, some lawyers virtually admitted the charge: Sir John Trevor, sometime master of the rolls and a leading lawyer-parliamentarian during the late seventeenth century, was moved in 1689 to defend Stockbridge, a notoriously venal borough which was under threat of disenfranchisement, on the grounds that constituencies which were entirely influenced by patronage or money were necessary in order to accommodate professional men like himself. Trevor did not then represent a strictly venal borough, but he was nevertheless a carpet-bagger *par excellence*, because he sat for constituencies to which he was an entire stranger in five out of the seven parliaments to which he was returned. On each of these occasions he was brought into parliament on the interest of some other person or persons.[26] Now this is interesting, because Trevor's case serves to connect the demand for lawyers in the Commons with the phenomenon of the carpet-bagger in the constituencies, and implies

---

[24] For party strife 1689–1720 see J. H. Plumb, *The Growth of Political Stability in England 1675–1725* (Harmondsworth, 1973), ch. 5 *passim*. Sir Lewis Namier identified only 40 practising barristers among the House of Commons in 1761 (Namier, *Structure of Politics*, p. 44).

[25] Average number of contests per election (general elections, excluding Scottish constituencies) for parliaments 1679 (Oct.)–1689 inclusive: 68; 1690–1701; 94; 1701–8: 96; 1710–27: 115. (Henning, *House of Commons 1660–90*, i. 107–24); H. Horwitz, *Parliament, Policy and Politics in the Reign of William III* (Manchester, 1977), 328; W. A. Speck, *Tory and Whig: The Struggle in the Constituencies 1701–1715* (1970), 126–31; Sedgwick, *House of Commons 1715–54*, i. 116–22.)

[26] Henning, *House of Commons 1660–90*, iii. 604–6.

that any increase in that demand would be reflected by a corresponding rise in the number of lawyers brought in by borough patrons. In order to test this hypothesis it is necessary to look at the relationship between the lawyers and their constituencies, and the peculiar characteristics of those constituencies, in some detail.

It would be quite wrong to suggest that most barristers who sat in the House of Commons between 1680 and 1730 did not have a natural interest in the constituencies which they represented. In fact examples to the contrary are not difficult to find. For instance the great Restoration barrister, Sir John Maynard, was a borough patron in his own right: he possessed the dominant interest in the tiny Devon borough of Bere Alston, which he only exercised in his own favour when adverse political winds obliged him to retreat from Plymouth, where he also enjoyed considerable influence.[27] A decade after Maynard's death in 1690 Sir Thomas Powys, a former attorney-general to James II, first exploited his powerful interest in the town of Ludlow in order to become an MP, and his influence proved sufficiently durable to maintain his seat throughout most of the reign of Queen Anne.[28] A few barristers enjoyed a degree of power and prestige which stretched even beyond the confines of a mere borough, for they were able to secure election as knight of the shire, as was Thomas Vernon, the leading Chancery counsel and Worcestershire landowner, who was returned for his county to the first Hanoverian parliament in 1715.[29]

Not many lawyers had as good an interest as Vernon or Maynard, but it is likely that men who were absolute strangers to their constituencies were always a minority among barrister MPs. Table 7.3 enumerates the probable carpet-baggers via a breakdown of the barristers in each parliament who neither lived, held property, nor had family ties in the county which included their own constituency. Of course this is a very narrow definition of a 'stranger'; it is certain that some men returned to parliament by the influence of borough patrons—Peter King, for example—had a connection with their constituencies which amounted to no more than birth or residence in the same county. Nevertheless, even if these 'local' men were

---

[27] Henning, *House of Commons 1660–90*, iii. 39–44.

[28] *HPT* Sir Thomas Powys; Shropshire CRO, Bishop of Shipton MSS 3385/2/14, 18–19, 23, 29, 32, 36, 53: letters of [Sir] Thomas and [Sir] Littleton Powys to Henry Mitton, 1700–2, 1707–8, 1710, and n.d. I am obliged to Dr Hayton for drawing my attention to these papers.

[29] Sedgwick, *House of Commons 1715–54*, ii. 499.

TABLE 7.3. *'Strangers' among barrister members of parliament, 1679–1734*[a]

Parliament of	Strangers[b]		Barrister MPs
	No.	%	
1679 (Oct.)	6 (1)	7.7	78
1681	5 (1)	7.2	69
1685	10 (3)	13.5	74
1689	6 (2)	8.9	67
1690	7 (1)	7.9	88
1695	9 (1)	11.5	78
1698	9 (3)	11.1	81
1701 (Feb.)	12 (3)	15.0	80
1701 (Dec.)	9 (2)	12.5	72
1702	13 (3)	15.1	86
1705	14 (4)	15.7	89
1708	16 (3)	18.8	85
1710	18 (3)	18.4	98
1713	16 (—)	18.6	86
1715	30 (2)	30.9	97
1722	21 (1)	25.6	82
1727	15 (2)	18.7	80

[a] Those barristers who had no residential, proprietorial, or familial connection with the county which included their constituency.

[b] The figures before the brackets represent *all* barrister MPs who were strangers to their constituencies, while those in brackets enumerate barristers among them who have *not* been positively identified as practitioners.

Sources: As in Table 7.2; also *HPT* (biographies and constituency articles).

redefined as aliens it remains doubtful whether the strangers would amount to a majority among the legal contingent in the House of Commons, since the figures show that their number as presently defined never even represented a third of the total.

More interestingly, the statistics in Table 7.3 do suggest that the proportion of carpet-baggers among lawyers in the Commons was on the increase during the later Stuart and early Georgian period, for from a mere half-dozen in the Second Exclusion Parliament the number seems to have risen steadily, first only reflecting a unique influx of court lawyers returned by royal influence in 1685, but then expanding regularly after 1700 and manifesting a quantum leap with the Hanoverian succession.[30] Indeed, the barristers returned to the parliaments of 1715 and 1722 included over a quarter who were quite unknown to their constituencies, although the proportion fell again with elections to George II's first parliament. It is worthy of note that the dynamic element in this trend towards more carpet-baggers was mainly confined to the practising barristers, for the number of strangers among those who have not been positively identified as career counsel was small and roughly a constant over the whole period. Thus it seems that the expansion of the professional lawyer contingent in the House of Commons represented a remarkable and possibly unique incursion of men who had no real ties with the constituencies for which they sat. This can be explained in two ways. Either the increasing wealth which was characteristic of the top barristers in the early eighteenth century was facilitating their return for venal boroughs on a considerable scale; or there was indeed a genuine rise in demand for lawyers in the Commons which was satisfied by bringing them in for constituencies which were under the influence of patronage.[31]

There are a few examples of barristers who exploited their purchasing power to gain a seat in the Commons during this period. James Anderton, for instance, one of the practising lawyers among the carpet-baggers quantified above, sat for Ilchester between February 1701 and 1708, and he certainly owed his election there to outright bribery, which built on the support of a section of the corporation.[32] Stockbridge, that borough whose venality brought it to the point of disenfranchisement in 1689, returned at least one practising barrister, in the person of Sir John Hawles, a former solicitor-general, who was elected there in 1705 and 1708, and it is reasonable to suppose that he had to spend considerable sums of money for the privilege.[33] One has the impression, however, that electoral venality was more attractive to merchants and 'monied men' generally than to the habitually cautious lawyers. Thomas Vernon, although he was prepared to spend vast sums on land purchases and house building, seems to have been more

---

[30] Of the 74 barristers returned in 1685, 40 were new to parliament; of these at least 32 were Tories, and a high proportion of them were office-holders. Several had assisted in the surrender of borough charters (Table 7.2 above; Henning, *House of Commons 1660–90*, i. 695, ii. 70, iii. 770 and *passim*; Table 7.7 below). Cf. Cockburn, *Assizes*, pp. 251–2.

[31] For e.g.s of barristers' incomes see above, pp. 154–6.

[32] *HPT* James Anderton.

[33] *HPT* Stockbridge. For Hawles see *DNB* ix. 242–3.

circumspect when it came to parliamentary elections; it is true that he was considered a suitable candidate at Worcester City in 1707, but prospects of success in the seat were dependent upon laying out some money, and the lawyer 'refused to meddle with it'.[34] Furthermore, despite the evident prosperity of leading barristers like Vernon in the early eighteenth century, it is very unlikely that this inclined more of the bar to spend their way into the Commons, given the fact that election expenses had increased considerably since the Revolution, and went through the roof after the Septennial Act made the investment more worth while.[35]

Failing venality, it is necessary to fall back on patronage as an explanation for the trend to carpet-bagging manifested by Table 7.3. But it is not sufficient to rely on mere supposition alone in order to establish this point: rather it is necessary to show that barrister MPs were increasingly associated with pocket boroughs, and for this purpose it is appropriate to turn to an analysis of the lawyers' constituencies. Table 7.4 classifies the constituencies represented by practising barristers between 1679 and 1734 according to the criteria established in Professor Henning's volumes of the *History of Parliament*.[36] The lawyer MPs are divided into three categories, being those who sat for counties, those who represented boroughs which had a relatively democratic franchise or a large electorate, and those who were elected for boroughs which had a restricted franchise or a small electorate, and were therefore most susceptible to the influence of patronage. Before proceeding to interpret the figures, it should be noted that with regard to the boroughs, there were *two* variables which may have contributed to any trends manifested by the analysis; first, of course, there was a natural dynamic created by barrister MPs being elected for different types of constituencies in different parliaments, but there was also a second element of 'artificial' change, caused by alterations in the electorates and franchises of some boroughs over these years, which moved certain constituencies into different categories. In order to provide a rough check on the likely influence of this second dynamic, a

[34] For Vernon's estate see above, p. 160; SCRO, Somers MSS B20 (a): W[illiam] Walsh to [Lord Somers], 26 Oct. 1707.

[35] Plumb, *Growth of Political Stability*, pp. 91–101, 175.

[36] Borough constituencies are classified as follows: large: all boroughs with over 500 electors; medium open: 51–500 electors, franchise extended to freemen, inhabitants, householders, or those paying scot and lot; medium select: 51–500 electors, franchise limited to the corporation or to burgage tenants; small: all boroughs with under 51 electors (Henning, *House of Commons 1660–90*, i. 62–3).

TABLE 7.4*a*. *Constituency types of barrister members of parliament, 1679–1734*[a]

Parliament of	County		Large and medium open		Small and medium select		Total classified	Unclassified
	No.	%	No.	%	No.	%		
1679 (Oct.)	1	2.6	27	71.0	10	26.3	38	1
1681	2	7.4	17	63.0	8	29.6	27	1
1685	2	4.4	26	57.8	17	37.8	45	1
1689	—	—	18	51.4	17	48.6	35	2
1690	2	4.6	29	67.4	12	27.9	43	2
1695	—	—	25	65.8	13	34.2	38	1
1698	1	2.3	25	58.1	17	39.5	43	—
1701 (Feb.)	1	2.7	24	64.9	12	32.4	37	1
1701 (Dec.)	2	5.9	20	58.8	12	35.3	34	1
1702	—	—	22	56.4	17	43.6	39	2
1705	4	9.3	24	55.8	15	34.9	43	1
1708	2	4.5	24	54.5	18	40.9	44	1
1710	2	3.8	29	55.8	21	40.4	52	1
1713	—	—	24	54.5	20	45.4	44	1
1715	1	1.6	30	49.2	30	49.2	61	1
1722	1	1.7	34	56.7	25	41.7	60	—
1727	3	5.2	38	65.5	17	29.3	58	—

[a] Practitioners only, excluding those returned for university seats.

TABLE 7.4*b*. *Classification of all seats in England and Wales (excluding universities)*

Parliament of	County		Large and medium open		Small and medium select		Total classified	Unclassified
	No.	%	No.	%	No.	%		
1679 (Oct.)	92	18.1	272	53.4	145	28.5	509	4
1685	92	18.1	248	48.7	169	33.2	509	4
1689–1700	92	18.1	276	54.2	141	27.7	509	4
1701–15	92	18.1	272	53.4	145	28.5	509	4
1715	92	18.1	280	55.0	137	26.9	509	4

Sources: Barrister MPs: as in Table 7.2. Constituency details: Henning, *House of Commons 1660–90*, i. 125–522 for 1679–89 and applying the details for 1689 to 1690–1700; Speck, *Tory and Whig*, pp. 126–31 for 1701–15; Sedgwick, *House of Commons 1715–54*, i. 189–380 for 1715–34.

breakdown of the proportion of *all* English and Welsh seats in each category has been provided for strategic points within the period covered. This reveals that, with the exception of the gerrymandering which preceded the election of 1685, changes in populations and franchises tended broadly to cancel each other out, as boroughs which became 'open' due to larger electorates were compensated for by those which 'closed' in consequence of restrictions to their franchise. Given this absence of significant change in the electoral map of England and Wales (as it is classified here) over most of the period, it seems reasonable to assume that the trends shown in the table are a reflection of genuine shifts in the pattern of representation among barristers, rather than a product of mutations in the constituencies themselves.

These qualifications do not apply to the statistics in Table 7.4 which represent those barristers who enjoyed the dignity of knights of the shire, and it is therefore possible to state with some confidence that a disproportionately small number of Augustan barristers were elected to serve as MPs for the counties. While county members accounted for 17–19 per cent of *all* MPs who were eligible to sit in the parliaments of 1680, 1681, 1685, and 1689, normally less than 5 per cent of the barrister MPs returned to the Commons during these years were knights of the shire, and the proportion sometimes fell in zero in the subsequent parliaments elected under the last Stuarts and the early Hanoverians.[37] This is a concrete testimony to the ambiguous social position occupied by many lawyers, being men who aspired to a place among the landed élite but who in reality were properly located among the urban bourgeoisie and the lesser gentry in the country.

The strength of the lawyers' natural interest in the larger and more democratic urban areas of England and Wales is revealed by the relatively high proportion of barrister MPs who were returned for boroughs classified as 'large' or 'medium open'. With the single exception of the first Hanoverian parliament, the legal contingent of the House of Commons always included a majority of men who were returned by this type of constituency. Indeed, their representation in these boroughs was quite disproportionately large in the Second and Third Exclusion Parliaments, when the genuinely democratic large boroughs often elected lawyers to serve them in the Commons. While nearly a third of the professional barristers returned to parliament in 1680 and 1681 sat for constituencies classified as 'large', only

---

[37] For the proportions of county members in parliament 1680–9, see Henning, *House of Commons 1660–90*, i. 65–6.

approximately 13 per cent of all MPs in the house at this time represented similar boroughs.[38] It is probably not a coincidence that some of the most prominent Whig lawyers—such as John Trenchard, MP for Taunton, William Williams, MP for Chester, and Sir Francis Winnington, MP for Worcester—were included among the 'great urban' barrister MPs returned to the Exclusion Parliaments, for it was no doubt the strength of the first Whigs among the urban electorates which accounted for the success of the lawyers in the large parliamentary towns.

Despite the enduring strength of the lawyers in the larger and more democratic boroughs, the pattern of representation among barrister MPs changed during the closing years of the seventeenth century as a growing proportion of the legal contingent in the Commons was derived from constituencies of a quite different type from those which had returned the great Whig lawyers. The first signs of this shift were revealed by elections to the parliament of 1685, when the large body of barristers returned to James II's assembly included an unusually high proportion from small or 'select' boroughs. Of course this was probably a reflection of the gerrymandering in the constituencies, but the change outlived the effects of remodelling corporations, and the early eighteenth-century parliaments registered a significant addition to their legal strength which was based upon the less democratic boroughs. Thus, during Anne's reign, four out of every ten lawyer MPs were returned for constituencies of this type, and the trend reached a peak with elections to the first parliament of George I, when almost half the practising lawyers in the House of Commons represented small or close boroughs. It does not seem to have been maintained into the mid-eighteenth century, however, for the pattern of representation among barrister MPs elected in 1727–34 was reminiscent of its Restoration predecessors.

This reversion to type on the part of the legal contingent returned to George II's first parliament is worthy of note, because it matches the downturn in the number of 'strangers' included among the lawyers in the House of Commons at that time. Indeed, it is clear that there was a constant fair parallel between the fluctuating number of barristers returned for small or restricted franchise boroughs during the half-century of this study and the changing level of strangers among the

[38] Of the practising barrister MPs, 28.9% were returned by large boroughs to the parliament of Oct. 1679, and 29.6% were returned for similar boroughs in 1681 (sources as in Table 7.2). Cf. Henning, *House of Commons 1660–90*, i. 65.

lawyer MPs.[39] Of course it is by no means true that every man who sat for a constituency of this type was unknown to his borough, or that every stranger was elected on a small or restricted franchise, but the analogy cannot but suggest that the increase of carpet-bagging lawyers and of barristers who represented the less democratic constituencies were part and parcel of the same phenomenon. This amounted to an incursion of lawyers who had been returned by borough patrons into the early eighteenth-century parliaments, which had the effect of augmenting the overall size of the barrister contingent by adding to the twenty to thirty lawyers who represented the bar's 'natural' constituency in the 'large' and 'medium open' boroughs.

As the statistics imply, subsequent to the Revolution of 1688 the élite members of the political nation seem to have been increasingly likely to nominate practising barristers for the constituencies which they controlled or influenced. Sir Francis Drake and the earl of Stamford, for instance, who together enjoyed the decisive influence at Bere Alston after Sir John Maynard's death, returned a whole crop of lawyers, including Peter King (1701–14), Sir John Hawles (1698–1700), James Montague (1698–1700), Lawrence Carter (1710–22), and the two Cowper brothers, William (1701–5) and Spencer (1705–10).[40] In Cornwall the Boscawen interest also benefited several barristers, such as Montague (1695–8), Sir John Tremaine (1690–4), and Charles Talbot (1720–2) at Tregony, as well as Hawles (1701), Spencer Cowper (1715–27), and Thomas Wyndham (1721–7) at Truro.[41] Other Cornish borough patrons were responsible for returning Henry Poley at West Looe (1703–5) and Sir Clement Wearg at Helston (1724–6).[42] Away from the west country, the duke of Somerset provided seats in the House of Commons for John Fortescue Aland (1715–17) and Thomas Bootle (1734–54) at Midhurst, as well as for Sir Thomas Pengelly at Cockermouth (1717–26); while the greatest

---

[39] Comparing the third column of statistics in Table 7.4 with Table 7.3 above.

[40] *HPT* Bere Alston; DCRO, Drake MSS 346M/F57, F65, F67: Sir Francis Drake to Sir Peter King, Apr.–June 1710; HCRO, Pangshanger MSS D/EP F100, unfol.: draft letters, (Lord) Cowper [to Sir Francis Drake and Lord Stamford], n.d. and 14 Apr. 1708; for the lawyers not previously mentioned see *DNB* iii. 111–12, iv. 1311–12, xiii. 699.

[41] *HPT* Tregony; Sedgwick, *House of Commons 1715–54*, i. 220; for Tremayne, king's serjeant, see Baker, *Serjeants*, p. 541. *HPT* Truro; Sedgwick, *House of Commons 1715–54*, i. 221; for Wyndham see ibid. ii. 560–1.

[42] *HPT* Henry Poley (he was no doubt returned on the Trelawny interest). Helston was controlled by the Godolphin family (Sedgwick, *House of Commons 1715–54*, i. 212); for Wearg see Sedgwick, *House of Commons 1715–54*, ii. 525–6.

borough-monger of all, the duke of Newcastle, returned Philip Yorke, first at Lewes (1719–22), and then at Seaford (1722–33).[43]

The lawyer MPs were direct beneficiaries of the political struggle which preoccupied their betters in the early eighteenth century. Of course the long drawn out contest in the constituencies gave barristers more chances to ingratiate themselves with magnates through fighting the legal battles generated by their divisions. This no doubt explains why two of the four counsel who represented the great borough patron, Lord Wharton, in the celebrated case of *Ashby* v. *White* (1705) were later returned to parliament for constituencies over which he exercised some measure of influence.[44] Likewise Serjeant John Pratt, parliamentary counsel *par excellence*, was elected MP for Midhurst in 1711 after appearing for the duke of Somerset, one of the patrons of the borough, before the bar of the House of Commons.[45] But not all the lawyers were elected upon the initiative of the borough magnates; the level of strife at Westminster had reached such a pitch by the closing years of Queen Anne's reign that the party leaders themselves were prepared to recommend promising lawyers to patrons of their persuasion.[46] After 1714 this process became common, because the Whig government's ability to secure the services of barristers who caught their eye was enhanced, as magnates who had previously enjoyed a degree of independence came much more under the thumb of the ministry.[47] In consequence the early years of the Hanoverian

[43] Sedgwick, *House of Commons 1715–54*, i. 336; for Bootle see ibid. i. 473–4 and for Fortescue Aland ibid. ii. 47. Ibid. i. 222–3, 335, 369; BL, Add. MSS 35584, fos. 179, 249–50: addresses of the electors of Lewes and Seaford respectively to the duke of Newcastle, n.d.; ibid., Add. MSS 32686 (Newcastle Papers), fos. 129–30: letters to the duke of Newcastle and Philip Yorke to Henry Pelham, 15 Apr. 1719; ibid., Add. MSS 32687 (Newcastle Papers), fos. 7–8: Yorke [to Newcastle], 31 Jan. 1724.

[44] Alexander Denton, MP Buckingham 1708–10, 1715–22; Nicholas Lechmere, MP Appleby 1708–10, Cockermouth 1710–17 (E. Cruickshanks, '*Ashby* v. *White*: The Case of the Men of Aylesbury, 1701–4', in C. Jones (ed.), *Party and Management in Parliament, 1660–1784* (Leicester, 1984), 98; *HPT* Nicholas Lechmere; *HPT* Appleby; *HPT* Buckingham). I am grateful to Dr Cruickshanks for bringing this case to my attention.

[45] For Pratt as parliamentary counsel see DCRO, Drake MSS 346M/F70: Richard Duke to Peter King, 6 June 1711; HMC, *13th Report*, app. VI, p. 44: Lord Keeper Somers to Sir G[eorge] Treby, 5 Dec. 1696; HCRO, Panshanger MSS D/EP F149/5–6: Pratt to LCJ Parker, 7 Apr. 1710; *DNB* xvi. 288–9; *HPT* John Pratt; *HPT* Cockermouth.

[46] e.g. Thomas Lutwyche, brought in at Appleby in 1710 by Lord Thanet upon the recommendation of John Ward of Capesthorne and Lord Nottingham; and Robert Raymond, provided with a seat as SG in 1710 upon the recommendation of Robert Harley (*HPT* Thomas Lutwyche; *HPT* Robert Raymond; Sedgwick, *House of Commons 1715–54*, ii. 231, 379–80).

[47] Plumb, *Growth of Political Stability*, pp. 103–4.

monarchy marked the golden age of the legal carpet-baggers, and a remarkable crop of young counsel found its way into the Commons at this time. The most outstanding ministerial nominee was Philip Yorke, who was returned by Newcastle at the behest of Lord Chancellor Macclesfield, but Sir Clement Wearg and Charles Talbot were also elected for their Cornish boroughs upon the initiative of the government.[48]

Dudley Ryder, who was brought in for St Germans in 1733, was also a government nominee, but by the time he entered the commons the demand for lawyer MPs appears to have passed its peak, and the legal contingent in the house was returning to more natural levels, as the temperature of politics cooled down.[49] Stability had arrived, although half a century of partisan strife had not passed without leaving its marks upon the bar and the House of Commons. The 'rage of party' had provided the conditions necessary for the development of the model of the career lawyer MP, and this was of great consequence for the structure of the legal profession. At this point it is appropriate to turn to the activities of this hybrid within the walls of St Stephen's Chapel.

3. ACTIVITY AND PLACES

The close ties of kinship which existed between the common law and parliament suggest that lawyers were not likely to be short of opportunities for employment in the House of Commons. Those barristers who were not sitting on their own interest had presumably been brought in for a purpose, and their patrons, whether magnates, corporations, or the government itself, would no doubt expect a return on their investment in the form of activity on their behalf. Of course the nature of this activity might vary according to the sponsor, and the collective characteristics of the lawyers' involvement in the business of the house were therefore liable to change with the augmentation of the legal contingent by carpet-baggers. For all these reasons, it is apposite to consider the role of the barrister MPs in the Commons in some detail, and it is no less important to examine the patronage distributed among them with a view to controlling their activity, because the chance of preferment made parliamentary service potentially a very rewarding supplement to a barrister's career.

[48] Sedgwick, *House of Commons 1715–54*, i. 212, 220, 335–6, ii. 461, 525–6, 569; cf. Thomas Wyndham, MP Truro 1721–7, Dunwich 1727–34 (ibid. ii. 561).
[49] Ibid. ii. 397.

It had long been customary for the lawyers to preside over the formal conduct of business in the House of Commons.[50] Their activity in this regard was at a peak during the later seventeenth century, for all but one of the eleven speakers chosen between 1660 and 1700 had been called to the bar, and at least seven of these eleven men had practised their profession.[51] Barristers also frequently occupied the chairs of the standing committees of elections and privileges, ways and means, and supply during these years.[52] After 1701 the lawyers' hold over the speakership itself tended to become less constant with the election of several lay speakers such as Robert Harley, John Smith, and William Bromley, but practising barristers continued to be voted into the other chairs; William Cowper, for example, was chairman of the committees of supply and ways and means in the first session of the parliament of 1698.[53] Some early eighteenth-century lawyers virtually made a career out of this activity: John Conyers of the Middle Temple was chairman of supply and ways and means from 1700 to 1708 and from 1710 to 1714, and he was succeeded by another practitioner from that inn—William Farrer—who held these chairs for thirteen years until he left the Commons in 1727.[54] Farrer's presidency then passed to a layman, but by that time the lawyers had regained the speakership and the parliaments of George II witnessed the greatest lawyer chairman of all in the person of Arthur Onslow, who presided over the house for the next thirty years, and first established the model of the career speaker.[55]

Barristers with thriving practices might have thought twice before committing themselves to the regular attendance and activity entailed by chairmanship in the Commons. This was not a problem for the lawyer speaker, for although the president of the assembly was entirely debarred from practice during his tenure of the chair, long-term incumbents were normally given an office to compensate them for loss of fees: the mastership of the rolls was frequently used for this purpose down to the Hanoverian succession.[56] Ordinary lawyer MPs were not

[50] Prest, *Rise of the Barristers*, p. 253.

[51] Henning, *House of Commons 1660–90*, i. 88 and *passim*; P. Laundy, *The Office of Speaker* (1964), 458–9; sources as in Table 7.2 above.

[52] Henning, *House of Commons 1660–90*, i. 89–91 and *passim*.

[53] Laundy, *Office of Speaker*, pp. 458–9; *CJ* xii. 390–687 *passim*, xiii. 9.

[54] *HPT* John Conyers; Sedgwick, *House of Commons 1714–54*, i. 134.

[55] Ibid. ii. 308–9.

[56] HCRO, Panshanger MSS D/EP F199/77–8: draft letter [Mary, Countess Cowper] to Baron Bernstorff [*c*.1717].

always so lucky, however, and it is clear that practising barristers were often torn between the demands of their profession and the claims made upon their time by the House of Commons, especially when the Lent assizes came round. Such decisions became especially difficult after 1689, with the burden of frequent sessions on the one hand and the clear opportunities offered by participation in the internecine warfare at Westminster on the other.[57]

In fact lawyer MPs enjoyed a poor reputation for attendance in the house; according to Lord Cowper 'the cheif lawyers did in all ages & ever will give the preference to their practise, & attend the publick in Parliament but on some great occasions'.[58] This notoriety for absenteeism may have been the reason why 'all the gentlemen of the long robe' were so frequently added to committees appointed to process the business of the Commons.[59] How many duly turned up and took part in the proceedings of these committees will never be known, but it is possible to quantify the representation of lawyers who were specifically named to them, and this may provide some clues as to the level of their activity.

Some words of caution are necessary before proceeding to an analysis of the select committee nominations which appear in the *Commons' Journal*. As suggested above, an individual's appointment to a committee did not mean that he attended its sittings, although it does seem reasonable to assume that members who were frequently nominated were more active in committee than those who were named rarely, or not at all. More positively, throughout the seventeenth century at least, the Commons normally followed the convention that MPs appointed to a committee had to be present in the chamber when it was named. This means that at worst the frequency of appointment to committees probably bore some relation to the level of an individual's attendance in the house, while at best it genuinely reflected his activity with regard to the proceedings of the committees themselves.[60]

[57] Witness the agonizing of Peter King when faced with this choice at assize time in 1701 and 1702 (*Correspondence of Locke*, vii. 226, 229–31, 234–8, 261–2, 280, 564–7, 575–8, 590).
[58] HCRO, Panshanger MSS D/EP F57/124–5: draft letter [Cowper] to [?Bernstorff] [autumn 1716]; cf. M. Landon, *The Triumph of the Lawyers* (Tuscaloosa, Alabama, 1970), 76.   [59] Prest, *Rise of the Barristers*, p. 255.
[60] Cf. T. K. Moore and H. Horwitz, 'Who Runs the House? Aspects of Parliamentary Organisation in the Later Seventeenth Century', *JMH* 43 (1971), 207; for the significance of committee nominations in the Lords see R. W. Davis, 'Committee and Other Procedures in the House of Lords, 1660–1685', *HLQ* 45 (1982), 20–30.

Table 7.5*a* is an analysis of committee nominations in the House of Commons for the whole of the Second Exclusion Parliament, which sat in 1680–1.[61] Within the limitations noted previously, the statistics appear to demonstrate that the lawyers who were MPs were slightly more heavily involved in the business of the house than members who had not been called to the bar, for more than half the barristers were named to a committee, while only just over 40 per cent of the remaining MPs appeared on the lists in the *Journal*. This is a fair testimony to the commitment of the barristers to the affairs of the Commons at this time. More impressive is the fact that a disproportionate number of the *most* active MPs were barristers—nearly a third of the men most frequently named to committees had been called to the bar—and this implies that a significant minority of the legal contingent in the house were prominent among the group of MPs which carried the main burden of business in the Commons. The regular participation of these lawyers is explained by the circumstance that parliament was at this time still in the grip of the mass hysteria generated by the Popish Plot, and the lower house was preoccupied, even in its select committees, with exclusion, the examination of matters relating to the plot, and the impeachment of royal ministers, peers, and judges, rather than more mundane public or private legislation. These affairs naturally demanded the attention of men learned in the law, including several *practising* barristers, most notably Sir Francis Winnington and Sir William Jones, two former law officers, and John Trenchard, later a king's serjeant and secretary of state under William III.[62]

The impression that the legal expertise available to the House of Commons was fully employed at the time of the Exclusion Crisis is reinforced by Table 7.5*b*, which analyses the activity of those men who presented reports to the whole house from the select committees. This activity was important because it was normally the duty of a committee's *chairman* to deliver the report, and the figures therefore represent barristers and others who took the chair in committee. Clearly, the lawyers were much more likely to be called upon to preside over these deliberations than their lay colleagues, because approximately 15 per cent of the barrister MPs sitting in the Commons

[61] The statistics which represent the committee activity of all MPs are broadly in agreement with those presented in Henning, *House of Commons 1660–90*, i. 83.

[62] Of the 13 'very active' barristers, 8 were practitioners (sources as in Table 7.5); Henning, *House of Commons 1660–90*, iii. 597–8, 667, 747.

TABLE 7.5. *Activity in the House of Commons, parliament summoned in 1679 (Oct.)*

a. Nominations to committees

Committees (no. of)	Barrister MPs		Other MPs		All MPs	
	No.	%	No.	%	No.	%
Very active (17+)	13	17.8	27	5.9	40	7.5
Active (10–16)	5	6.8	20	4.4	25	4.7
Moderately active (3–9)	11	15.1	74	16.2	85	16.0
Occasionally active (1–2)	11	15.1	69	15.1	80	15.1
Indefinite activity	—	—	3	0.7	3	0.6
Total nominated	40	54.8	193	42.2	233	44.0
Total (sitting)	73		457		530	

Range: 1–51

Most active barristers

40 Sir Francis Winnington (MT)	31 Sir William Jones (GI)
35 [Henry] Powle (LI)	30 [John] Trenchard (MT)

b. Reporting from committees

Reporters/reports	Barrister MPs	Other MPs	All MPs
Reporters	11	14	25
% of all reporters	44.0	56.0	100.0
% of total MPs	15.1	3.1	4.7
Reports	35	26	61
% of all reports	57.4	42.6	100.0
Total MPs (sitting)	73	457	530

Range (reports per MP): 1–14

Most active barristers

14 [George] Treby (MT)	4 [John] Trenchard (MT)
4 Sir William Pulteney (IT)	3 Sir Francis Winnington (MT)

Table 7.5 (cont.):
c. Participation in debate

Debates (speeches)	Barrister MPs		Other MPs		All MPs	
	No.	%	No.	%	No.	%
Regular (20+)	4	5.5	8	1.7	12	2.3
Frequent (5–19)	6	8.2	21	4.6	27	5.1
Occasional (1–4)	4	5.5	39	8.5	43	8.1
Indefinite activity	—	—	2	0.4	2	0.4
Total speakers	14	19.2	70	15.3	84	15.8
Total (sitting)	73		457		530	

Range: 1–74

Most active barristers
74 Sir Francis Winnington (MT)
50 Sir William Jones (GI)
25 [Sir John] Maynard (king's serjeant)
21 [William] Sacheverell (GI)

Conventions: Barrister MPs: all MPs called to the bar; Committees: all individual nominations to select committees, including the committee of elections and privileges, but excluding nominations which might apply to more than one man of the same name. The classification of 'indefinite activity' relates to individuals nominated to one or more committees by full name, and possibly nominated to more by surname only, but being indistinguishable from namesakes; Debates: every intervention in the recorded debates, classified according to the conventions applied for the committee analysis.

Sources: As in Table 7.2; also *CJ* ix. 636–704; Anchitell Grey, *Debates of the House of Commons, from the Year 1667 to the Year 1694* (1769), vii. 347–477, viii. 1–290.

during 1680–1 delivered a report, while a much smaller proportion of the members who had not been called to the bar did so. It is also remarkable that the eleven barristers who acted as chairmen—most of them practitioners—were together responsible for a majority (over 57 per cent) of all the reports delivered to the house.[63] George Treby and Sir William Pulteney were naturally very active in this regard as chairman and deputy chairman respectively of the elections and

---

[63] Among these 11 reporters only George England and William Sacheverell are not known to have practised the law.

privileges committee, but both were also heavily involved as chairmen in the extraordinary business transacted by the Commons at this time: Treby, in fact, promised to work 'night and day' if the house demanded it of him. Trenchard and Winnington were entrusted with proceedings which were scarcely less important, even if they were less laborious.[64]

Of course the legal contingent of the Commons was more likely to include experienced public speakers than the rest of the house, and these men at least were apt to find a natural role in parliamentary debate.[65] Yet it is by no means true that every barrister MP who was active as a committee man in the Second Exclusion Parliament was active in debate, for twenty-seven of the forty lawyers who were named to committees are not noted as having spoken in the debates recorded by Anchitell Grey.[66] While this apparently high level of inactivity owes at least something to the partial nature of the source, it does imply that there was a significant proportion of silent barristers in the Commons at this time. Still, Table 7.5c shows that the level of participation in the debates of 1680–1 was greater among the lawyers than it was among other MPs, although the representation of the bar was by no means greatly superior, being 19 per cent of their total strength as against around 15 per cent of the non-barristers in the house.[67] The lawyers were especially well represented among the most frequent speakers, just as they were among the regular committee men: four of the twelve MPs who were most active in debate were barristers and three of these were professional advocates.[68] Winnington, indeed, was the most frequent speaker in the House of Commons at this time, and Sir William Jones was also very prominent in debate, remarkably so for a man who was new to parliament.

Considering the activity of the body of barristers in the Second Exclusion Parliament as a whole, certain conclusions may be drawn. With regard to the generality of barrister MPs, the extent of their participation in parliamentary business as represented by select committee appointments seems impressive, given the fact that the law courts must have competed for their time during the Michaelmas term

[64] For the activities of Pulteney and Treby see Henning, *House of Commons, 1660–90*, iii. 303, 581; for Trenchard and Winnington see above, n. 62.

[65] *Lives of the Norths*, iii. 181.

[66] Sources as in Table 7.5

[67] The figures for participation in debate on the part of all MPs broadly correspond to those in Henning, *House of Commons 1660–90*, i. 83.

[68] William Sacheverell is the exception.

in 1680. As has been seen, a majority of these committee men may have been silent in debate, but the average barrister's record with regard to speaking was better than that of his lay colleagues, and it is worthy of note that the most active lawyers in committee were nearly all also participants in the debates.[69] These very prominent lawyer MPs—most notably Winnington, Jones, Trenchard, and Treby—have a real claim to be regarded as some of the leading MPs in the Commons at this time. Thus it seems that the lawyers were influential in the parliament of 1680–1 at all levels, and to an extent which considerably exceeded their numerical strength.

Lawyer MPs were no less prominent in the constitutional debates of the Convention Parliament which gave rise to the Declaration of Rights and the transfer of the crown to William and Mary. This was probably the high point of that process by which seventeenth-century politics became suffused with the form and substance of the common law, and Professor Schwoerer has shown how the common lawyers, including many of the same men who had been active in 1680–1, virtually dominated the proceedings of the committees and the debates which legitimized the Revolution.[70] It should be said, however, that this did not represent the 'triumph of the Whig lawyers' beloved of the Whig historians, because the settlement of 1689 was a compromise document which owed nearly as much to leading Tory lawyers such as Gilbert Dolben, Sir Robert Sawyer, and Heneage Finch as it did to the Whig barristers who had survived from the opposition of the early 1680s.[71] This is important, for it shows that the prominence of the lawyers in parliamentary affairs during the later seventeenth century was not merely a coincidence due to the wealth of legal talent among the first Whigs; rather the constitutional controversy of this period brought leading barrister MPs of *all* persuasions to the forefront of affairs in the House of Commons.

Constitutional issues tended to be less dominant in English politics after 1689, but political strife became more intense, and it is probable

[69] Of the 13 barristers most active in committee, 11 are recorded as speaking by Grey (sources as in Table 7.5).

[70] L. G. Schwoerer, *The Declaration of Rights, 1689* (Baltimore, 1981), chs. 2, 3, 9–13 *passim*, and app. 3; ead., 'A Jornall of the Convention at Westminster begun the 22 of January 1688/9', *BIHR* 49 (1976), 243–63; ead., 'The Transformation of the 1689 Convention into a Parliament', *Parliamentary History*, 3 (1984), 57–8, 60–2, 66. Cf. R. J. Frankle, 'The Formulation of the Declaration of Rights', *HJ* 17 (1974), 266–9.

[71] The Whig interpretation has been resurrected in a rather superficial and one-sided review of the lawyers' involvement in politics during the Restoration period (Landon, *Triumph of the Lawyers*).

that the lawyers' collective influence in parliament was not greatly reduced during the reigns of William and Anne, although their role was not as central as it had been at the time of the Revolution settlement.[72] It is reasonable to expect some change in this position under the early Hanoverians, however, because the heat was going out of politics at Westminster by the 1720s, although the warfare in the constituencies had by no means died down.[73] In order to test this hypothesis, and to give some chronological perspective to the role of the barrister MPs in the House of Commons, it is necessary to turn to further statistics which represent their activity in the first and second sessions of the parliament of 1722.

TABLE 7.6. *Activity in the House of Commons, parliament summoned in 1722*

a. Nominations to committees (2nd sess.)

Committees (no. of)	Barrister MPs		Other MPs		All MPs	
	No.	%	No.	%	No.	%
Very active (16+)	6	7.3	26	4.4	32	4.7
Active (9–15)	5	6.1	42	7.1	47	7.0
Moderately active (3–8)	15	18.3	103	17.4	118	17.5
Occasionally active (1–2)	14	17.1	98	16.6	112	16.6
Indefinite activity	2	2.4	1	0.2	3	0.4
Total nominated	42	51.2	270	45.7	312	46.4
Total (returned)	82		591		673	

Range (committees per MP): 1–48

Most active barristers
39 [William] Farrer (MT)
33 [Arthur] Onslow (MT)
31 [John] Scrope (MT)
30 [John] Conyers (MT)

[72] Horwitz and Moore, 'Who Runs the House?', pp. 224–6.
[73] See above, n. 25.

Table 7.6 (cont.):
b. *Reporting from committees* (2nd sess.)

Reporters/reports	Barrister MPs	Other MPs	All MPs
Reporters	6	28	34
% of all reporters	17.6	82.3	100.0
% of total MPs	7.3	4.7	5.0
Reports	8	37	45
% of all reports	17.8	82.2	100.0
Total (returned)	82	591	673

Range (reports per MP): 1–4

Most active barristers
3 [John] Conyers (MT)
1 [James] Cocks (MT)
1 [John] Scrope (MT)
1 [William] Farrer (IT)

c. *Participation in debate* (1st & 2nd sess.)

Debates (speeches)	Barrister MPs		Other MPs		All MPs	
	No.	%	No.	%	No.	%
Regular (10+)	3	3.7	2	0.3	5	0.7
Frequent (3–9)	8	9.8	12	2.0	20	3.0
Occasional (1–2)	10	12.2	28	4.7	38	5.6
Indefinite activity	—	—	—	—	—	—
Total speakers	21	25.6	42	7.1	63	9.4
Total (returned)	82		591		673	

Range (speeches per MP): 1–20

Most active barristers
13 Sir Joseph Jekyll (LI)
12 [William] Shippen (MT)
10 [John] Hungerford (LI)
 7 [Archibald] Hutcheson (MT)

Conventions: As in Table 7.5.

Sources: As in Table 7.2; also *CJ* xx. 224–330; *The History and Proceedings of the House of Commons from the Restoration to the Present Time* (1742–4), vi. 282–324.

Table 7.6*a* is an analysis of the committee nominations found in the *Commons' Journal* for the proceedings of January to April 1724, which has been compiled on the same basis as the statistics presented for 1680–1. By contrast with the Second Exclusion Parliament, it appears that barrister MPs at this time were not much more active in terms of committee appointments than the generality of the house. This may indeed reflect the developing stability at Westminster, and possibly confirms Lord Cowper's statement of 1716 that the lawyers only turned up at the house on 'great occasions'—few and far between in 1724 due to Walpole's 'mastery' of the Commons.[74] Moreover, the barristers generally were no more prominent in respect of taking the chair in select committee: according to Table 7.6*b* only six barristers delivered reports and they accounted for less than 20 per cent of the total reports delivered to the house, although it is true that they were marginally more likely to preside over these proceedings than the MPs who had not been called to the bar. It may be that this analysis underestimates the influence of John Scrope and William Farrer, respectively secretary to the Treasury and chairman of supply and ways and means (and both practising barristers), because their work was heavily weighted towards committees of the whole house, but there is no doubt that their activity cannot compare with that of their predecessors as lawyer chairmen in 1680–1.[75] It is also clear that Farrer and Scrope were no more than paid servants of the Treasury, while the influence of Treby, Winnington, and the other great lawyer MPs who dominated committees in the Restoration period was a genuine reflection of their leading role in the Commons.

This contrast between the most active barristers of the two sample sessions is confirmed by Table 7.6*c*, which classifies barristers and non-barristers according to their participation in debates published for the first and second sessions of the 1722 parliament in 1722–4.[76] It is remarkable that none of the barristers who were prominent in committee at this time was among the leading lawyers in debate, unlike their predecessors of the Exclusion Crisis. In fact, most of them did not speak at all, which suggests that they were indeed by no means

---

[74] See above, p. 199; J. B. Owen, *The Eighteenth Century 1714–1815* (1974), 27.

[75] Sedgwick, *House of Commons 1715–54*, ii. 26–7, 413–14.

[76] An identical analysis based upon the more limited reports of Sir Edward Knatchbull MP produced broadly similar statistics (for the debates see *The Parliamentary Diary of Sir Edward Knatchbull 1722–1730*, ed. A. N. Newman (Camden Soc., 3rd ser., 94; 1963), 2–30).

natural leaders of the House of Commons.[77] It is true that the barrister MPs generally were relatively active in debate at this time, for three of the five most frequent speakers identified had been called to the bar (although one, William Shippen, had never practised), and a quarter of the MPs who were barristers made at least one intervention in debate, as against only about 7 per cent of the other members. But the collective characteristics of the lawyer speakers give the impression that their prominence, like that of the leading committee men, was somewhat contrived. At the upper levels of activity these debaters were relatively independent men and established leaders of the house—Sir Joseph Jekyll, the master of the rolls, and the prominent Tory John Hungerford are cases in point—but the less regular speakers included several relatively unknown men, as well as a disproportionate number who probably owed their seats to electoral patronage.[78] Edward Lutwyche, for instance, made five recorded speeches, while the attorney-general, Sir Robert Raymond, made four, and his successor Sir Philip Yorke also spoke. None of these lawyers was sitting on his own interest. Of course Lutwyche was a man of some reputation and experience in the Commons, and the law officers would naturally be active in debate, but the participation of inexperienced young barristers such as Richard West (three speeches) and Charles Talbot (two speeches), who both owed their original election to government interest, tends to suggest a connection between speaking and sponsored carpet-bagging which may have been more than coincidence.

Looking at the lawyers' activity in the 1722 parliament generally, and comparing this with 1680–1, two clear points stand out. In the first place, the overall involvement of the lawyers in the business of the Commons, as expressed by committee appointments, was less notable by comparison with the remainder of the house, and this probably represented a lowering of the general demand for legal expertise in response to the decline of political strife at the centre. Secondly, the high profile of barristers in debate appears rather 'artificial' at a time of falling demand, and the characteristics of the lawyer speakers suggest a

[77] Of the 6 barristers who reported from committees in the second session, only 1—Arthur Onslow—is recorded as having spoken either in the published debates or in those summarized by Knatchbull (sources as in Table 7.6 and above, n. 76).

[78] For Jekyll and Hungerford see Sedgwick, *House of Commons 1715–54*, ii. 161–2, 174–6. Eight or 38.1% of the 21 speakers were strangers to their constituencies, and 10 or 47.6% sat for small or restricted franchise boroughs. This compares with proportions of 25.6% strangers and 37.8% returned for 'pocket' boroughs among *all* barrister MPs returned to the parliament of 1722–7 (sources as in Tables 7.3, 7.4, and 7.6).

degree of dependence not observed in their predecessors of the Restoration period. This last contrast is a true reflection of the development of eighteenth-century methods of parliamentary management: some of the lawyers who spoke in 1722–4, like the barristers who were employed at that time to organize the business of supply in the house, were 'professional' barrister MPs in a way that their predecessors most certainly were not. In short, they were careerists.

The apogee of the careerist lawyer MP is represented by a man like Dudley Ryder, who was simply brought into parliament to act as the paid lackey of the Walpolean ministry.[79] The origins of the breed, however, must be sought in the years after 1689, when regular parliaments and the party struggle generated great opportunities for gifted advocates who were by no means absolute dependants of the major factions, but were nevertheless not averse to putting their skills at the disposal of the party leaders, especially if they were rewarded with preferment. In 1694 Lord Keeper Somers drew the king's attention to 'a want of Lawyers to carry on Your service, both in the House of Commons & in Westminster Hall', and in order to remedy the former problem he recommended the employment of John Hawles, who had been an effective speaker in a previous parliament.[80] Hawles was subsequently made solicitor-general, and was active as a spokesman for the ministry in the Commons during the remainder of the decade, sitting by dint of government influence in the last parliaments of William III.[81] William Cowper also took a prominent part in parliamentary debates during the later 1690s, although he followed a rather more independent line than Hawles.[82] His talents as a speaker were likewise recognized by the Whig leaders, and in 1701, after his own interest at Hertford had collapsed, Cowper was brought in for Bere Alston by the influence of the Junto, in acknowledgement of 'your known Integrity & Great Abilitys for the service of this Government [i.e. the fallen Whig ministers]'.[83] Within a few weeks of returning to the Commons he was called upon to defend Lord Somers

[79] *Diary of Dudley Ryder*, pp. 21–3.

[80] New York Public Library, Hardwicke MSS 33, 64: copy letter [Lord Somers] to [King William] [31 July 1694]; cf. *CSPD 1694–1695*, 246.

[81] *HPT* John Hawles.

[82] Cowper spoke in support of the government at the time of the Fenwick attainder in 1696, but 'left' the ministry over the standing army controversy in 1698 (Foss, *Judges*, viii. 21; HCRO, Panshanger MSS D/EP F36 unpag.: copy of Cowper's speech in defence of Lord Somers [?28 Mar. 1701]).

[83] Ibid., D/EP F54: Sir Francis Drake to Cowper [Feb. or Mar. 1701].

from the attacks being launched against him in the Tory-dominated house, and he continued to speak on behalf of the Junto until he became lord keeper in 1705.[84]

It is not suggested that these men were simply time servers who sold their professional services to the highest bidder. On the contrary, Cowper and Hawles were both committed Whigs. But as lawyer MPs they were in a different class from their predecessors of the Exclusion Parliaments, because they were clearly subordinate politicians, and their activity in the Commons was an enduring and constant aspect of their careers which led directly to preferment. Peter King is another case in point. King was an even more thoroughgoing lawyer politician, for he was an MP during virtually all his career at the bar, and he was regularly active as a leading spokesman in the house. Like Cowper, he had his phases of independence, but he was taken into the employment of the ministry as recorder of London in 1708, and in this capacity he functioned as a leading representative of the Junto in the Commons for the remainder of his parliamentary career.[85] Besides King, Simon Harcourt, Joseph Jekyll, Nicholas Lechmere, and James Montague might be instanced as examples of the same type, and together they testify to the emergence of the careerist lawyer in the ideal conditions of the post-Revolutionary House of Commons.[86]

An important aspect of these conditions was the provision of adequate rewards for the services of the lawyer politician, beyond the mere possession of a seat in the Commons. In the long term, the lawyers might be rewarded with a place on the judicial bench as a consequence of their work in parliament, but that is the subject of another chapter; in the short term, their spoils took the form of some office or rank which was compatible with their status as MPs. Following the establishment of the legislature's permanency in 1689

[84] HCRO, Panshanger MSS D/EP F55: Sir J[oseph] Jekyll to Cowper [Mar. 1701]; ibid., D/EP F63/1: draft letter [Cowper] to [John Churchill], duke of Marlborough, 6 Oct. 1705; Foss, *Judges*, viii. 21. For Cowper's speech in defence of Somers see above, n. 82.

[85] King was leader of the 'whimsical' Whigs during the middle years of Queen Anne's reign (D. Hayton, 'The Country Interest and the Party System, 1698–*c*.1720', in C. Jones (ed.), *Party and Management in Parliament, 1660–1784* (Leicester, 1984), 51). For his role as Junto spokesman see *DNB* xi. 144–5; Foss, *Judges*, viii. 134–5; BL, Add. MSS 61460 (Blenheim Papers), fos. 24–5, 32–4, 36–7, 108–10, 129–32: correspondence [Arthur Mainwaring to the duchess of Marlborough, Apr. and Nov. 1708]. I am grateful to Dr Hayton for referring me to these letters.

[86] *DNB* viii. 1206–9, x. 724–5, xi. 776–7, xiii. 699; Foss, *Judges*, viii. 34–7, 42–3, 128–30; *The Harcourt Papers*, ed. E. W. Harcourt (Oxford, 1880–1905), ii. 7–28; *HPT* Nicholas Lechmere.

there was naturally a tendency to concentrate patronage on the House of Commons as a means to ensure political control, and the lawyer MPs shared fully in this augmentation of booty. Table 7.7 demonstrates the nature of the patronage made available to them by means of an analysis of places in the gift of the crown which were held by barristers returned to parliament between 1679 and 1734.[87] Not all these, of course, were acquired as a consequence of a seat in the Commons: some men had been preferred before they were elected, and others would no doubt have gained places even if they had not become MPs. But there is no doubt that certain offices were increasingly becoming identified with service in parliament. Places as crown counsel are an obvious example: John Hawles was made a KC in 1694 specifically because he was likely to become an MP, and of nineteen men who were similarly honoured down to 1730, fourteen were then members of parliament.[88] Several other barrister MPs became king's or queen's serjeants, and Welsh judgeships were also looked upon as a legitimate field of patronage for the legal contingent of the House of Commons, to the extent that there were several shufflings with the ebb and flow of the parties at Westminster.[89] All these offices were of great advantage to the lawyer MP, for they enhanced his prestige and were likely to increase his practice, while for the government they provided a means of controlling the barristers in the house.[90] By the time of the accession of George II, their deployment for this last purpose was commonplace, and the new monarch simply followed the established procedure in renewing appointments, as Lord Chancellor King related:

I gave him a list of all the Judges, both in England and Wales, King's Serjeants, and [king's] Council, and other subordinate offices in the law, in his invariable

[87] The recordership of London was not strictly in the gift of the crown, but the government undoubtedly had great influence over appointments to the office (HMC, *15th Report*, app. IV, p. 246: Sir John Buckworth [Lord Mayor] to Robert Harley, 11 Sept. 1705; BL, Add. MSS 61459 (Blenheim Papers), fos. 36–7: [Arthur Mainwaring] to [the duchess of Marlborough] [?26 Apr. 1708]).

[88] *CSPD 1694–1695*, p. 246; details of crown counsel appointments 1680–1730 kindly supplied by Sir John Sainty.

[89] Of the 23 KSs/QSs identified as MPs 1679 (Oct.)–1734, 13 were promoted as sitting members (sources as in Table 7.7). In 1711 John Pocklington, a Whig, was turned out from the Welsh judiciary, while John Ward and Edward Winnington (alias Jeffreys), two Tories, were brought in. Robert Harley's friend Charles Coxe lost his Welsh judgeship at the hands of the Whigs in 1715 (W. R. Williams, *The History of the Great Sessions in Wales 1542–1830* (Brecknock, 1899), 64, 144–5; HCRO, Panshanger MSS D/EP F60/21: Harley to [Lord Cowper], 25 Apr. 1707; ibid., D/EP F149/19–23: C[harles] Coxe to [Cowper], 11 and 28 Dec. 1714, 8 Jan. 1715).

[90] Holmes, *Augustan England*, pp. 122–3.

nomination, and told him, that as to those which were not Judges in England, they were many of them Parliament men, and some now stood again. So he ordered me to make out fiats for such of them as were like to be Parliament men.[91]

The statistics in Table 7.7 show that this legal patronage was most liberally applied in the early eighteenth century, although James II had anticipated such Walpolean parliamentary management in 1685. There were more crown counsel and Welsh judges among the barrister MPs after 1710, and the number of 'mere' serjeants suggests that even ordinary coifs might have been used to suborn or reward some lawyers in the Commons at this time.[92] The figures are difficult to interpret because of the varying length of parliaments and changes in particular offices during their lifetimes, but it appears that between 1710 and 1727 an average of one in every four barrister MPs might enjoy some place or rank, which amounts to a proportion of perhaps four out of every ten practitioners in the Commons. Evidently the bar was well rewarded for its activities on behalf of the politicians, and an enduring connection between parliamentary service and professional preferment had been forged by the time of the Walpolean oligarchy.[93] How far this circumstance influenced the collective political alignment of the lawyers, and how far it allowed governments to depend upon their support, is the subject of the final section of this chapter.

4. VOTES AND PERSUASIONS

Enough has been said to show that there were great opportunities for ambitious barristers to enhance their careers via service in parliament during the period covered by this study. Obviously, however, there was a price to be paid: governments did not bestow offices on their opponents—crown patronage was deployed among MPs for the purpose of managing the Commons after all—and candidates for preferment would have to deliver the political goods, in terms of support for the appropriate measures and policies. This sobering thought might have concentrated the minds of aspiring lawyers as they

---

[91] Peter, Lord King, *Life of Locke* (2nd edn., 1830), ii: 'Notes of Domestic and Foreign Affairs', 48. I owe this reference to the kindness of Dr Jeremy Black of the University of Durham.

[92] Cf. Henning, *House of Commons 1660–90*, iii. 334, 501–3.

[93] Cf. Plumb, *Growth of Political Stability*, pp. 129–30.

Parliament of	MR or CGS judge	Welsh/Irish/Scots judge	Crown law officer	Royal law officer	Government counsel	Recorder CS London	KC/QC	KS/QS	'Mere' Serjeant	Irish/Welsh law officer	Duchy counsel/law officer	Total/Preferred	% practisers preferred	% barristers preferred
1679 (Oct.)	1	2	—	—	—	1	4	4	4	1	2	14 (14)	35.9 (35.9)	17.9 (17.9)
1681	1	1	—	—	—	1	3	2	—	—	—	8 (8)	28.6 (28.6)	11.6 (11.6)
1685	2	4	1	3	—	2	7	4	6	1	1	22 (22)	47.8 (47.8)	29.7 (29.7)
1689	2	2	3	1	—	1	2	4	2	—	—	14 (14)	37.8 (37.8)	20.9 (20.9)
1690	4	4	3	3	—	1	2	5	2	2	—	19 (19)	42.2 (42.2)	21.6 (21.6)
1695	—	3	2	2	—	—	4	2	2	—	1	14 (14)	35.9 (35.9)	17.9 (17.9)
1698	—	4	1	1	—	—	2	2	3	—	2	13 (13)	30.2 (30.2)	16.0 (16.0)
1701 (Feb.)	—	2	2	2	—	—	2	1	2	—	1	10 (10)	26.3 (26.3)	12.5 (12.5)
1701 (Dec.)	—	5	2	2	—	—	3	4	1	—	1	16 (15)	45.7 (42.9)	22.2 (20.8)
1702	—	4	1	2	—	—	3	3	2	—	1	15 (15)	36.6 (36.6)	17.4 (17.4)
1705	—	4	2	1	—	—	5	4	3	—	1	18 (17)	40.9 (38.6)	20.2 (19.1)
1708	—	5	3	—	1	1	3	4	3	1	—	17 (17)	37.8 (37.8)	20.0 (20.0)
1710	—	8	3	—	1	1	6	3	7	—	1	29 (26)	54.7 (49.0)	29.6 (26.5)
1713	—	5	2	—	1	1	6	2	5	1	1	20 (20)	44.4 (44.4)	23.3 (23.3)
1715	1	6	6	2	1	1	7	2	5	—	3	21 (16)	33.9 (25.8)	21.6 (16.5)
1722	1	10	4	2	1	1	8	1	5	—	2	28 (26)	46.7 (43.3)	34.1 (31.7)
1727	1	4	3	4	2	1	7	2	1	—	—	17 (16)	29.3 (27.6)	21.2 (20.0)

Note: Some individuals are counted more than once in different columns and the totals are cumulative figures for the whole of each parliament. The figures and percentages in brackets represent the maximum number of placemen who were members of the parliament in question at any one time.

Sources: As in Table 7.2; also Foss, *Judges*, vii. 28, 207, 300–1, 379, viii. 10–11, 88; W. R. Williams, *The History of the Great Sessions in Wales 1542–1830* (Brecknock, 1899), id., *Official Lists of the Duchy and County Palatine of Lancaster* (Brecknock, 1901); R. Somerville, *Office-Holders in the Duchy and County Palatine of Lancaster from 1603* (1972); Baker, *Serjeants*; F. E. Ball, *The Judges in Ireland, 1221–1921* (1926), *Recorders of the City of London 1298–1850* (1850); information on KCs supplied by Sir John Sainty; J. C. Sainty, *Office-Holders in Modern Britain: Treasury Officials 1660–1870* (1972), i. 97–8; id., *Office-Holders in Modern Britain: Officials of the Board of Trade 1660–1870* (1974), iii. 37.

rose to speak, or registered their vote in a division, and it leads the historian to expect a relative lack of independence among barrister MPs as reflected in their collective political alignments.

But perhaps this is too simplistic. Not all lawyers in parliament were careerists, and it is over-cynical to regard interest as the only factor which affected the political actions of men in the House of Commons, even if they had a living to earn. Principle might also have some bearing on their behaviour. Indeed, strongly held convictions might well override the constraints of advantage at times of great controversy, when passions ran high—at the time of the Exclusion Crisis, for instance. Moreover, there was certainly greater room for the exercise of independence during periods when governments of different persuasions changed places frequently, for there was always the chance of finding favour with the reversionary interest, if not with the ministry *in situ*. Clearly such a pattern could well be appropriate to the reign of Queen Anne, when ministries were regularly changed in the course of party strife, but it would be incongruous during the years of the Walpolean supremacy.

This raises the question of the political ideology most characteristic of barristers during this period. Professors Holmes and Speck have drawn attention to 'a natural Whig bias in the lay professions' which they say had been established by the late seventeenth century, and have bracketed the lawyers within this tendency.[94] But this seems a trifle crude: Professor Pocock has written more sensitively of 'the common law mind' and has identified its characteristics in notions of immemorial custom and an 'ancient constitution' which included a parliament independent of the crown.[95] The ideology of the ancient constitution was widely accepted by the opponents of Stuart 'absolutism' in the seventeenth century, and survived in an ossified form to be employed by Whig lawyers who helped to legitimize the Revolution of 1688; for these reasons it may indeed be appropriate to anticipate some elements of 'Whiggism' in the politics of the lawyers.[96] However, this does not necessarily translate into support for the *court* Whigs of Queen Anne's reign, and still less does it promise a favourable view of the establishment of Whig oligarchy under the Hanoverians. On the

[94] *The Divided Society: Party Conflict in England 1694–1716*, ed. G. Holmes and W. A. Speck (1967), 58.

[95] J. G. A. Pocock, *The Ancient Constitution and the Feudal Law* (Cambridge, 1957), ch. 2 *passim*.

[96] Ibid., chs. 8–9 *passim*; H. T. Dickinson, *Liberty and Property: Political Ideology in 18th-Century Britain* (1977), 61–75.

contrary, there is no reason why men who continued to adhere to the theory of the ancient constitution in its *pure* form might not be found supporting 'country' measures under William III, or be numbered among Tories and opposition Whigs in the early eighteenth century.[97]

In the light of these considerations as to the lawyers' complex motivation and shifts in the ideological ground on which they stood, it is best to turn to the evidence of their alignments in parliament with a relatively open mind. Table 7.8 is an analysis of the barrister MPs' politics as reflected in a collection of parliamentary lists covering 1679–98. Looking first at the statistics which represent voting on the Exclusion Bill, it is no surprise to see that a majority of the barristers were in favour of that measure, bearing in mind what has been said previously on the subject of the common law case against Stuart 'absolutism'.[98] In fact, the lawyer MPs seem to have been more

TABLE 7.8. *Political alignment of members of parliament, 1679–98*[a]

a. 21 May 1679: 1st Exclusion Bill

	Barrister MPs		All MPs	
	No.	%	No.	%
For	34 (15)	47.9	219	43.0
Against	17 (11)	23.9	124	24.4
Absent	20 (11)	28.2	166	32.6
Total listed	71 (37)		509	

b. 5 Feb. 1689: Transfer of the crown

	Barrister MPs		All MPs	
	No.	%	No.	%
For Lords' motion	19 (10)	31.7	151	29.4
Total sitting	60 (30)		513	

[97] See Dickinson, *Liberty and Property*, pp. 102–18; Hayton, ' "Country" Interest and Party System', pp. 45–6.

[98] For commentary on the division, see Browning and Milne, 'An Exclusion Bill Division List', pp. 205–7.

Table 7.8 (cont.):

c. Jan. 1690: Sacheverell clause

	Barrister MPs		All MPs	
	No.	%	No.	%
For clause	14 (6)	25.0	147	28.6
Total sitting	56 (28)		513	

d. Spring 1693: Grascombe's List

	Barrister MPs		All MPs	
	No.	%	No.	%
Court supporters	26 (15)	36.6	201	39.2
Opposition placemen/ pensioners	3 (2)	4.2	25	4.9
'Quere'	—	—	4	0.8
Total sitting	71 (38)		513	

e. Jan. 1696: Forecast on council of trade

	Barrister MPs		All MPs	
	No.	%	No.	%
For court	24 (12)	33.8	240	47.6
Against court	43 (22)	60.6	236	46.8
Doubtful	4 (1)	5.6	28	5.5
Total listed	71 (35)		504	

enthusiastic for the exclusion of James than the generality of the house, although those identified as practitioners were less heavily supportive of the measure. Subsequent lists present a rather different pattern, however. According to two lists which classify some of the members of the Convention of 1689, the barristers who were MPs at this time were

Table 7.8 (cont.):

f. Feb.–Mar. 1696: Price of guineas

	Barrister MPs		All MPs	
	No.	%	No.	%
For court	24 (10)	42.9	204	54.0
Against court	32 (18)	57.1	174	46.0
Total listed	56 (28)		378	

g. Feb.–Mar. 1696: Association

	Barrister MPs		All MPs	
	No.	%	No.	%
Refused association	19 (9)	26.4	94	18.3
Total sitting	72 (36)		513	

h. 25 Nov. 1696: Fenwick attainder

	Barrister MPs		All MPs	
	No.	%	No.	%
For attainder	19 (10)	34.5	188	53.9
Against attainder	36 (9)	65.4	161	46.1
Total listed	55 (29)		349	

not at all more inclined collectively to support Whig policies and principles than the other members. In the first place, the legal contingent divided in roughly similar proportions to the house as a whole on the question of agreeing with the lords that the throne had not become vacant with James II's flight. This motion was designed to force Tories who were against the transfer of the crown to declare themselves, and over 30 per cent of the barristers voted accordingly.[99]

[99] For the motion see Cruickshanks, Ferris, and Hayton, 'The House of Commons Vote on the Transfer of the Crown', pp. 37–47.

Table 7.8 (cont.):

i. *c*.Sept. 1698: Standing army forecast

	Barrister MPs		All MPs	
	No.	%	No.	%
For standing army	29 (12)	39.7	227	48.5
Against standing army	44 (26)	60.3	241	51.5
Total positively classified	73 (38)		468	

[a] Where the lists give only one side of the house the figures have been compared against the total of sitting MPs; this has been estimated for all MPs where precise figures are not available. In these cases the percentage which represents all MPs listed may be a slight underestimate. The figures before the brackets represent *all* barrister MPs, while those in brackets enumerate those among them who have been identified as practitioners.

Sources: Lists: *a*. A. Browning and D. J. Milne, 'An Exclusion Bill Division List', *BIHR* 23 (1950), 207–25; *b*. E. Cruickshanks, J. Ferris, and D. Hayton, 'The House of Commons Vote on the Transfer of the Crown, 5 February 1689', *BIHR* 52 (1979), 41–7; *c*. A. Browning, *Thomas Osborne Earl of Danby and Duke of Leeds 1632–1712* (Glasgow, 1944–51), iii. 164–72; *d–i*. HPT. Barrister MPs: as in Table 7.2.

Secondly, the lawyer MPs may have included proportionately fewer *extreme* Whigs than the Commons as a whole, since only about a quarter of them (as against nearly 29 per cent of the house) voted for the misnamed 'Sacheverell clause' of January 1690, which had the object of excluding from municipal office all the Tories who had played a part in the surrender of borough charters under Charles II and James II.[100] These two lists together suggest that there was a sizeable body of Tory lawyers in the Convention. Perhaps this might be explained by the fact that nearly two hundred members of James II's parliament had been re-elected in 1689, because in 1685 the king's electoral agents had been especially successful in returning practising barristers of a Tory bent.[101] Moreover, it is by no means certain that the royal campaign which preceded elections to the Convention itself was entirely without effect, and it may be that some of the barristers

[100] See Browning, *Danby*, i. 461–2, iii. 164; R. R. Walcott, 'Division Lists of the House of Commons, 1689–1715', *BIHR* 14 (1936–7), 25–6.
[101] See above, n. 30.

had been returned by processes originally set in motion during the reign of the exiled king.[102]

Under the new regime major ideological divisions were partially blunted and partisan groupings tended to become more fluid, especially during the middle years of William's reign. In this period some political questions fell more naturally into a court/country dichotomy rather than that of Whig and Tory, although party loyalty remained never far from the surface, and asserted itself upon occasion.[103] Despite this confused situation, the lists of the 1690s continue to have relevance for the purpose in hand because they indicate at least how far the legal contingent of the Commons was prepared to support the policies of the court. The list which was compiled by Samuel Grascombe in the spring of 1693 is instructive in this regard, because it shows that the lawyer MPs may have been proportionately less inclined to adhere to the government of the day than the house as a whole.[104] According to three further lists (council of trade, price of guineas, and Fenwick attainder), this antipathy to the court was even more marked among the barristers elected to the 1695–8 parliament, and that is particularly striking, given the fact that the 1695 election was regarded as a Whig victory, and a Whig dominated ministry was in place after 1694.[105] Notwithstanding the Whig government, the lawyers appear to have been heavily against the court over the issues of the proposed council of trade and the recoinage, by contrast with the complexion of the house generally.[106] Moreover, the controversy which arose over the attainder of Sir John Fenwick, who was implicated in the assassination plot against William III, also gave rise to a majority among the legal MPs against the overall division in the Commons, although this is less surprising, because the measure was quite unorthodox in regard to the common law. The attorney-general himself admitted as much, and the scruples of other lawyers may account for some of the large number of barristers who voted against the attainder.[107]

---

[102] J. H. Plumb, 'The Elections to the Convention Parliament of 1689', *Cambridge Historical Journal*, 5 (1935), 235–44; H. Horwitz, 'Parliament and the Glorious Revolution', *BIHR* 47 (1974), 41–2.

[103] Horwitz, *Parliament, Policy and Politics*, pp. 94–100, 208–18, 316–18.

[104] For commentary on the list see ibid. 339.

[105] Ibid. 132–9.

[106] For these issues see I. F. Burton, P. W. J. Riley, and E. Rowlands, *Political Parties in the Reigns of William III and Anne: The Evidence of Division Lists (BIHR*, special suppl. 7; 1968), 6–19.

[107] Ibid. 20–6.

In spite of the special circumstances of the Fenwick division, it is clear that the lawyers sitting in parliament during 1696 included a majority who were habitually opposed to the government. A few were probably country Whigs, although the majority were no doubt outright Tories.[108] More precisely, it is possible to identify a disproportionately large group of *extreme* Tory lawyers, for nineteen of the barristers refused the association to William III at the time of the assassination plot.[109] This preponderance of Tories and country Whigs seems to have been maintained into the next parliament, according to a list of September 1698, when the lawyer MPs elected were heavily prejudiced against the court's policy of maintaining a standing army in peacetime.[110]

Table 7.9 summarizes a further series of parliamentary lists which contrast the alignment of the lawyer MPs with the rest of the house during the years between 1701 and 1713, when political divisions returned to a clear Whig/Tory split. The first list details those Tories who signalled themselves as being opposed to making preparations for war with France by their votes in the short parliament of 1701.[111] The house at this time included a clear majority of Tories, but the voting of the barristers implies that as a body they were still more Tory-inclined than the Commons as a whole.[112] The subsequent election of December 1701 possibly went some way towards a redressal of the balance in the house between the two parties, and Robert Harley's classification of the new parliament suggests that the legal contingent may have been diluted with Whigs (and therefore opponents of Harley) accordingly, although it is possible that a slight Tory bias remained.[113] Indeed, it is notable that a clear majority of the barristers in this parliament were among the Tories who declared themselves not satisfied with the House of Lords' acquittal of the impeached Whig leaders.[114] Naturally this predominance of Tories among barristers in

---

[108] A modern party classification of the individuals who appeared on the 1696 lists gives 32 Whig barristers (16 identified as practitioners), among whom 9 are described as being opposed to the court over at least 1 of the 3 issues (council of trade, price of guineas, and Fenwick attainder). Of the 71 lawyers on the list 39 (and 19 of the 35 practitioners) have been classified as outright Tories after 1696 (ibid. 41–51 col. 13).

[109] See Browning, *Danby*, iii. 187; Horwitz, *Parliament, Policy and Politics*, pp. 175–6.

[110] See H. Horwitz, 'Parties, Connections and Parliamentary Politics, 1689–1714: Review and Revision', *JBS* 6 (1966), 60–1; Burton, Riley, and Rowlands, *Political Parties*, p. 33, n. 3.

[111] See Walcott, 'Division Lists', pp. 26–7.

[112] For the Commons generally see Horwitz, *Parliament, Policy and Politics*, p. 295.

[113] Ibid. 298–9, 339.

[114] See Walcott, 'Division Lists', p. 27.

the Commons increased after the 1702 election, when the Tories secured a large majority.[115] Nevertheless, it is remarkable that the lawyer MPs once more included a disproportionate number of extremists, for as a body they voted heavily against the Whig lords' efforts to enforce the oath abjuring the pretender, and an unusually large number of them supported the famous 'Tack' of the bill against

TABLE 7.9. *Political alignment of members of parliament, 1701–13* [a]

a. Feb./May 1701: Opposed to war

	Barrister MPs		All MPs	
	No.	%	No.	%
Opposed to war	32 (15)	41.0	167	32.5
Total sitting	78 (38)		513	

b. *c.*Dec. 1701: Harley list of new parliament

	Barrister MPs		All MPs	
	No.	%	No.	%
Harley supporters	37 (17)	52.9	253	51.0
Harley opponents	31 (16)	44.3	229	46.2
Uncertain	2 (1)	2.9	14	2.8
Total listed	70 (34)		496	

c. 26 Feb. 1702: Impeachments

	Barrister MPs		All MPs	
	No.	%	No.	%
For impeachments	37 (18)	52.9	223	43.5
Total sitting	70 (34)		513	

[115] *Divided Society*, p. 27; Speck, *Tory and Whig*, p. 123.

Table 7.9 (cont.):
d. 13 Feb. 1703: Abjuration Act

	Barrister MPs		All MPs	
	No.	%	No.	%
For Lords' 1st amendment	15 (7)	36.6	118	50.2
Against Lords' 1st Amendment	26 (11)	63.4	117	49.8
Total listed	41 (18)		235	

e. 28 Nov. 1704: The 'Tack'

	Barrister MPs		All MPs	
	No.	%	No.	%
For 'Tack'	30 (11)	38.0	134	26.1
Total sitting	79 (39)		513	

f. 22 Oct. 1705: Choice of speaker

	Barrister MPs		All MPs	
	No.	%	No.	%
For Smith	37 (21)	54.4	248	54.7
For Bromley	31 (13)	45.6	205	45.2
Total listed	68 (34)		453	

g. Feb.–Mar. 1709: Naturalization Bill

	Barrister MPs		All MPs	
	No.	%	No.	%
For bill	35 (21)	43.2	249	44.6
Total sitting	81 (42)		558	

Table 7.9 (cont.):

h. Feb.–Mar. 1710: Sacheverell impeachment

	Barrister MPs		All MPs	
	No.	%	No.	%
Against impeachment	34 (18)	41.5	193	37.6
Total sitting (English)	82 (44)		513	

i. 3 Nov. 1710: New parliament

	Barrister MPs		All MPs	
	No.	%	No.	%
Tory	55 (29)	74.3	304	62.4
Whig	14 (11)	18.9	145	29.8
Doubtful	5 (3)	6.8	38	7.8
Total listed	74[b](43)		487	

j. 7 Dec. 1711: 'No peace without Spain'

	Barrister MPs		All MPs	
	No.	%	No.	%
For motion	14 (12)	16.5	106	19.0
Total sitting	85 (44)		558	

k. Feb. 1712: October Club

	Barrister MPs		All MPs	
	No.	%	No.	%
Member of club	23 (11)	26.4	159	28.5
Total sitting	87 (45)		558	

Table 7.9 (cont.):
l. 18 June 1713: French commercial treaty

	Barrister MPs		All MPs	
	No.	%	No.	%
For treaty	35 (20)	55.6	187	48.8
Against treaty	28 (14)	44.4	196	51.2
Whigs against	15 (10)	23.8	120	31.3
'Whimsicals' against	7 (4)	11.1	36	9.4
Total listed	63 (34)		383	

[a] As in Table 7.8 n.
[b] Including 2 men who were not finally returned.

Sources: Lists: all *HPT*; Barrister MPs: as in Table 7.2.

occasional conformity to the land tax, a High Tory measure designed to strike at the dissenting interest among the Whigs.[116] It may be significant that the barristers in the house who are known to have practised the law seem to have been less enthusiastic about the 'Tack'; perhaps their professional ambitions made them more susceptible to the extreme pressure which the government exerted to dissuade members from supporting it? Their votes in favour of the impeachments of the Whig peers and against enforcing the abjuration oath suggest that the majority of practitioners were committed to Tory principles and policies, however, along with the generality of barristers in parliament.

Thus it seems that the anti-court majority among the barrister MPs during the 1690s had been succeeded by a regular preponderance of Tories in the parliaments of 1701–5. The division on the speakership contest for the new parliament of 1705 presents a different pattern, since the barrister MPs split roughly in proportion to the house over this question, and the greater number supported the Whig/court candidate Smith.[117] This parliament is unique as the only one since the Convention which probably included a majority of Whigs and court Tories among the barristers. The reason for this is clear: government interest in and influence over the 1705 general election had been applied specifically in order to exclude as many as possible of the 134

[116] For these divisions see Walcott, 'Division Lists', pp. 28–9.
[117] See W. A. Speck, 'The Choice of a Speaker in 1705', *BIHR* 37 (1964), 20–35.

'Tackers' among the Tories, and forty-four of them had not been returned. Given the large number of lawyers who had voted for the 'Tack', this government campaign probably had a disproportionate effect on Tory strength among the barrister MPs.[118]

This partial purge of High Church barristers was exceptional, and Queen Anne's last three parliaments witnessed a return to the pattern by which the legal contingent of the house had been dominated by Tories. It is not clear from the lists how far this reversion to type was established in the parliament of 1708–10: the elections of 1708 went heavily in favour of the Whigs, and the lawyers in the Commons were broadly in line with other MPs with regard to the 1709 Whig bill for naturalizing foreign protestants, although they displayed a slightly more Tory tendency to oppose the impeachment of Sacheverell, the High church divine.[119] But the new parliament of 1710 certainly included a heavy majority of Tories among the barrister MPs, according to an analysis made as the election results appeared in the press.[120] It is therefore not surprising that relatively few barristers were prepared to support the diehard Whigs in calling for 'no peace without Spain', although it may seem strange that the lawyers were relatively under-represented in the 'October Club' of High Tories.[121] It appears that the 'backwoods' brand of extreme Toryism which characterized the Octobrist revolt was not especially attractive to Tory lawyers; and a few participated in the rebellion of the 'Whimsicals' or Hanoverian Tories over the commercial treaty with France, caused in part by a taint of jacobitism which was fast attaching itself to government policy.[122] Nevertheless, such a stigma was not sufficient to prevent the lawyer MPs who voted on the issue from recording a majority in favour of the treaty, against the division in the house as a whole.[123] A majority of the

[118] Of the 30 'Tackers' among the barrister MPs 9 men were not re-elected, while only 4 of the 42 lawyers who were said to have voted *against* the 'Tack' were not returned again (excluding those incapacitated from standing; sources as in Table 7.9). For the election campaign of 1705 see Speck, *Tory and Whig*, pp. 98–102.

[119] *Divided Society*, pp. 27–8; Speck, *Tory and Whig*, p. 123; Walcott, 'Division Lists', pp. 33–4.

[120] For the list see BL, Stowe MSS 223 (Hanover Papers), fos. 453–4.

[121] For 'no peace without Spain' see G. S. Holmes, 'The Commons' Division on "No Peace without Spain", 7 December 1711', *BIHR* 33 (1960), 223–33.

[122] For the Octobrists see H. T. Dickinson, 'The October Club', *HLQ* 33 (1969–70), 158–9.

[123] See Walcott, 'Division Lists', pp. 35–6. For the complex issues and alignments involved in the commercial treaty see G. S. Holmes, *British Politics in the Age of Anne* (1967), 280; D. Szechi, *Jacobitism and Tory Politics 1710–14* (Edinburgh, 1984), 124–5, 136–7.

practising barristers who voted in the division likewise supported the
measure, but it should be noted that over a quarter of the practitioners
sitting in the house in December 1711 had declared themselves
opposed to the Tory government's policy of negotiating peace with
France. It seems that an aggressive minority of committed Whig
lawyers (such as Peter King, Nicholas Lechmere, Sir Joseph Jekyll,
and James Montague, all of whom voted for 'no peace without Spain')
survived the Tory landslide at the polls in 1710; although the analysis
of members elected by 3 November of that year and the vote on the
commercial treaty itself show that most of the practitioners, like the
majority of their fellow barristers, were Tories through and through.

It is noteworthy that the legal faction of the House of Commons may
even have preserved some bias towards Toryism into the Hanoverian
period, in spite of the tide of Whig triumph at the polls. The evidence
for this belief is presented in Table 7.10, which continues the analysis
of parliamentary lists from 1715 to the second parliament of George II.
The first list is a breakdown of the new parliament of 1715, and it
shows that the lawyer MPs still included a substantial proportion of
Tories, by contrast with the decimated Tory strength in the Commons
at large.[124] This residual Toryism, combined no doubt with the
presence of some opposition Whigs among the lawyers, may explain
the remarkable anti-court votes recorded by the body of barristers over
the Septennial Bill and the repeal of the Occasional Conformity and
Schism Acts: votes which were quite contrary to the tide of opinion in
the house.[125] It is possible that the opposition's strength among
barrister MPs at this time was concentrated among independent
members who were barristers in name only, however. During these
years they were becoming more outnumbered than before by
professional barristers who were not at all independent, as the
government and its client magnates returned an increasing number of
rising lawyers. This may explain why a majority of the *practising
barristers* who voted in the divisions over the Septennial Bill and the
repeal of the Occasional Conformity and Schism Acts supported the
court over these issues, and why the practitioners were more
supportive of the government than the other barristers when presented
with the Peerage Bill in 1719. But government influence was not

---

[124] See H. L. Snyder, 'Party Configurations in the Early 18th-Century House of
Commons', *BIHR* 45 (1972), 51–3, 67.

[125] See Sedgwick, *House of Commons 1715–54*, i. 19–20, 25–8, 81–3, 126–7.

TABLE 7.10. *Political alignment of members of parliament, 1715–34*[a]

a. Early 1715: New parliament

	Barrister MPs		All MPs	
	No.	%	No.	%
Whigs	28 (18)	42.4	270	57.6
Tories	30 (18)	45.4	158	33.7
'Whimsical' Whigs	6 (3)	9.1	30	6.4
'Whimsical' Tories	2 (1)	3.0	11	2.3
Total listed	66 (40)		469	

b. Apr. 1716: Septennial Bill

	Barrister MPs		All MPs	
	No.	%	No.	%
For Bill	31 (24)	43.7	295	53.6
Against Bill	33 (18)	46.5	186	33.8
Absent	7 (3)	9.9	69	12.5
Total listed	71 (45)		550	

c. Jan. 1719: Repeal of Occasional Conformity and Schism Acts

	Barrister MPs		All MPs	
	No.	%	No.	%
For repeal	30 (20)	41.1	259	46.6
Against repeal	34 (17)	46.6	204	36.7
Absent	9 (7)	12.3	93	16.7
Total listed	73 (44)		556	

over/

Table 7.10 (cont.):
d. 28 Feb. 1719: Craggs's forecast for Peerage Bill

	Barrister MPs		All MPs	
	No.	%	No.	%
For Bill	13 (9)	18.0	194	35.1
Against Bill	43 (22)	59.7	233	42.1
Doubtful	16 (11)	22.2	126	22.8
Total listed	72 (42)		553	

e. Mar.–Apr. 1719: Sunderland's forecast for Peerage Bill

	Barrister MPs		All MPs	
	No.	%	No.	%
For Bill	14 (9)	19.2	211	38.0
Against Bill	41 (21)	56.2	223	40.2
Doubtful	8 (14)	24.7	121	21.8
Total listed	73 (44)		555	

f. Dec. 1719: Peerage Bill

	Barrister MPs		All MPs	
	No.	%	No.	%
For Bill	17 (13)	25.4	191	39.5
Against Bill	50 (28)	74.6	293	60.5
Total listed	67 (41)		484	

sufficient to persuade a majority of the professionals to support a measure which would limit their natural ambitions, and the level of opposition to the bill among barristers which appears from the forecasts and the division itself is quite striking by comparison with reaction among the house generally.[126]

[126] See Sedgwick, *House of Commons 1715–54*, i. 29, 84–5, 128.

Table 7.10 (cont.):
g. 23 Apr. 1729: Civil list arrears

	Barrister MPs		All MPs	
	No.	%	No.	%
For motion	25 (21)	53.2	241	67.7
Against motion	22 (15)	46.8	115	32.3
Total listed	47 (36)		356	

h. 4 Feb. 1730: Hessian troops

	Barrister MPs		All MPs	
	No.	%	No.	%
For motion	24 (19)	45.3	249	59.3
Against motion	29 (22)	54.7	171	40.7
Total listed	53 (41)		420	

i. 26 Jan. 1732: Army estimates

	Barrister MPs		All MPs	
	No.	%	No.	%
For motion	24 (19)	48.0	241	58.5
Against motion	26 (20)	52.0	171	41.5
Total listed	50 (39)		412	

j. 14 Mar. 1733: Excise Bill

	Barrister MPs		All MPs	
	No.	%	No.	%
For Bill	28 (21)	50.0	266	56.5
Against Bill	28 (18)	50.0	205	43.5
Total listed	56 (39)		471	

Table 7.10 (cont.):
k. 13 Mar. 1734: Repeal of Septennial Act

	Barrister MPs		All MPs	
	No.	%	No.	%
For motion	21 (13)	51.2	186	42.8
Against motion	20 (13)	48.8	249	57.2
Total listed	41 (26)		435	

^a As in Table 7.8.

Sources: Lists: *a.* H. L. Snyder, 'Party Configurations in the Early 18th-Century House of Commons', *BIHR* 45 (1972), 67–71; *b–k. HPT* (voting records compiled for Sedgwick, *House of Commons 1715–54*, kindly provided by Dr Cruickshanks). Barrister MPs: as in Table 7.2 n.

There are no lists extant for George I's second parliament, but there are four divisions which have been recorded for the parliament of 1727–34, and these continue to imply the presence of a significant body of lawyer MPs who were opposed to the Whig ministry, although their strength may have declined since 1719, because even more of the barristers in the house were now professional lawyers who were susceptible to government influence. It is therefore not surprising that the lawyers present supported the court over the issue of the civil list arrears and divided equally on the Excise Bill, but three of the lists— those for the divisions over the Hessian troops, the army estimates, and the proposed repeal of the Septennial Act—show a small anti-court majority among the barristers who voted.[127] The turnout of lawyers for these votes was low, but all the divisions demonstrate that the legal contingent remained collectively less supportive of government policies and proposals than members of parliament generally.

The overall picture of the political characteristics of Augustan lawyer MPs which these lists present is quite remarkable. Far from manifesting a 'natural Whig bias', it seems very likely that after 1689, and with only a brief interlude in the parliament of 1705 (and possibly that of 1708), most of the barristers sitting in the House of Commons exhibited an abiding attachment to Toryism. Of course it is true that some of the anti-court majorities registered in the late 1690s had an

[127] For these divisions and the political background to them see ibid. i. 39–42, 86–7, 128–9.

element of country Whiggism, and opposition Whigs may have been present among the lawyers who voted against the government after 1715. On the other hand, an excessively large number of barrister MPs were included on High Tory lists, such as the list of MPs who refused the association in 1696, the list of 'Tackers' in 1704, and the supporters of the French commercial treaty in 1713; while there was a relative scarcity of keen Whig lawyers in the house, according to lists which relate to the 'Sacheverell clause' of 1690, the Naturalization Bill in 1709, and 'no peace without Spain' in 1711. This can only suggest that a hard core of Tories was present invariably among the generality of barristers in the House of Commons between 1689 and 1714, while the early Hanoverian divisions testify to its resilience in the face of strong adverse political winds.

Taking account of the behaviour of *practising* as opposed to merely nominal barristers tends to modify this conclusion, although it does not overturn it entirely. The professionals were just as Tory or 'country' as the rest of the barristers in the parliaments of William III. Moreover, their reluctance to vote for the 'Tack' in 1705 and the appearance of a group of diehard Whig practitioners who voted for 'no peace without Spain' in 1709 does not detract much from the general impression of their Toryism created by most of the parliamentary lists which survive for the reign of Queen Anne. Only in the first parliament after the accession of George I is there a fairly consistent discrepancy between the alignment of those barristers identified as practitioners and the other barristers whose votes are recorded. And this was a sign of the times: after 1714 government power and influence were used systematically to turn a natural Tory majority in the country into a Whig stranglehold on the House of Commons. In the long term, proscription from office and electoral management were bound to reduce the number of Tories among barrister MPs generally by limiting the proportion of independents who neither practised their profession nor were subject to government influence. But in 1715–22 the immediate impact of the Whig supremacy on the barristers was confined to an increase in the number of careerist lawyer MPs among the professionals: men whose adherence to their employers in the ministry contrasted with the tendency to opposition manifested by the majority of barristers in the house.

The increased distribution of jobs among the lawyers in the early eighteenth century shows how Walpolean methods of parliamentary management were making the most of available sources of patronage to attract legal talent, just as the ministry's growing electoral influence was being applied to return more lawyers who would be *predisposed* to support the court. There were more crown counsel and Welsh judges in the House of Commons after 1715 than there had been at any time since James II's parliament of 1685.[128] In most cases these honours were applied to encourage barrister MPs to *favour* the government, rather than to make them outright dependants. The policy applied was the same as that articulated by Lord Somers in 1694, when he recommended John Hawles to the King for a KC's place because 'it would be a good way to engage him to your service, by making him the compliment beforehand'.[129] Some of the beneficiaries did not feel bound by the honour they received, for there were times when crown counsel opposed the court, as in 1696, when three KCs and Prince George's attorney voted against the government over the price of guineas issue.[130] But potential recalcitrants were intimidated by the possibility of dismissal, reinforced by the occasional example, such as that of Sir William Williams, who was discharged from his place as king's counsel in 1696 after turning against the government and compounding the offence by refusing the association to William III.[131] Some crown counsel were not inclined to take such risks: rather they resorted to 'sneaking', or abstaining from crucial divisions where they were opposed to the government, as did Sir Thomas Powys king's serjeant and John Conyers KC in 1705, when they withdrew before the speakership vote.[132] And most legal placemen were undoubtedly 'engaged' to the crown by their promotion. With only one exception, a majority of the legal office-holders supported the court in every division between 1679 and 1722 where a clear government policy was apparent, despite the frequent anti-court votes among the barristers generally. The exception was the Peerage Bill: a uniquely divisive measure which provoked eight of the thirteen legal placemen in the house to vote with the opposition (including Sir William Thompson, the solicitor-general, who was discharged shortly afterwards). As far as can be ascertained in the absence of division lists for the 1722–7 parliament, there was no recurrence of this rebellion; and the legal office-holders who sat in the House of Commons between 1727 and 1734 were mostly docile followers of the court: men who failed even

---

[128] See Table 7.7 above.   [129] See above, n. 88.
[130] Sources as in Table 7.8 above.
[131] Information from Sir John Sainty; *HPT* Sir William Williams.
[132] Speck, 'Choice of a Speaker in 1705', p. 23.

to respond to the opposition's campaign against Walpole's hated Excise Bill.

Legal placemen may have been compliant and numerous in the early eighteenth century, but patronage was never available in sufficient quantity to suborn a majority of the barrister MPs. The government therefore had to find ways of influencing the lawyers in parliament who were beholden to no one. The lists which record forecasts of opinion among MPs on the Peerage Bill in 1719 show how the ministers who compiled them intended to arrange for influential people to speak with waverers with a view to gaining their support for the measure. This kind of lobbying was typical of early Georgian methods of parliamentary management, and the barristers were subject to the attention of the whips like everyone else in the house. Indeed, there is some evidence that special arrangements were made for them, as a body of members united by their profession. In the aftermath of the Septennial vote Lord Chancellor Cowper received ministerial complaints 'that the Lawyers in Parliament, have not so much exerted themselves, as they ought in Parliament & that it is to be laid at my Door'. It seems that Cowper was expected to supplement the limited effect of patronage by using his personal influence with the lawyer MPs in order to persuade them to turn up and support the government. He certainly made some efforts in this regard, for he insisted 'that on all great occasions I did prevail on more of the profession to attend & serve in the debates, then any one man of the age, though in my place could have done'.[133]

Although the combined effect of electoral influence, place, and ministerial lobbying were not enough entirely to overcome what may well have been a natural Tory bias among the lawyer MPs, these methods were no doubt turning more and more heads by the time of George II's reign, as the prospect of perpetual exile in the wilderness loomed before erstwhile Tories. Some of the more ambitious or realistic men had compromised their principles and accepted office under the Whigs before this time—Sir Robert Raymond and John Comyns are cases in point—and their example must have been a salutary one.[134] Yet the lists clearly suggest that others continued to remain alienated from or unacceptable to the Hanoverian regime. Indeed, there are examples of eminent Tory barristers who were never distinguished by office, such as Nicholas Fazackerley and Abel

[133] DCRO, Panshanger MSS D/EP F57/124–5: draft letter [Cowper] to [?Bernstorff] [autumn 1716].
[134] Sedgwick, *House of Commons 1715–54*, i. 569, ii. 378–80.

Ketelby.[135] This chance of being left on the beach after the political tide had ebbed was one of the more negative aspects of the lawyer MPs' lot during the Augustan age. For the ultimate positive advantages, it is necessary to turn to the next chapter.

[135] For the parliamentary careers of Ketelby and Fazackerley see ibid. i. 27–8, 189; for their eminence in KB during 1720 see Apps. III and IV below.

8

THE PATTERN OF PREFERMENT

THE emergence of the professional lawyer politician in the hothouse
conditions of post-Revolutionary England was bound to affect the
structure of the bar itself. Successful lawyer MPs were rewarded with
legal office, and this was one factor which helped to transform the
traditional pattern of advancement within the profession. Medieval
common lawyers had ascended a hierarchy of status and power which
began with call to the bench of their inn of court and passed through
reading and practice as a serjeant before final promotion to the
Westminster Hall bench. It is well known that this structure was
already changing from the mid-sixteenth century with the rise of the
crown counsel.[1] This final chapter is designed to show how the
increasing attraction which parliament exercised for up-and-coming
barristers after 1689 was a major element of the process by which the
track of preferment to the judiciary was shifted into a quite different
course, far removed from the old institutions of the bar.

For this purpose it is necessary to trace the career landmarks of
barristers and judges active in this period. The discussion follows the
promotional hierarchy from mid-career to the judicial bench, concentrating upon the different prospects of crown counsel as against
serjeants at law. In this way it is possible to identify a 'high' and a 'low'
road to the top of the profession, and the characteristics of the
barristers who followed these different routes are compared with
respect to their affinity with the inns of court on the one hand, and the
House of Commons on the other. Of course all barristers had some
association with the inns, and it is appropriate, therefore, to begin by
attempting to assess the significance of promotion within the societies
of law for Augustan counsel against the background of the career
experience of their medieval and Tudor/Stuart predecessors.

---

[1] Holdsworth, *History of English Law*, vi. 457–81; Baker, *Introduction to English Legal
History*, pp. 72–3; id., *Serjeants*, pp. 111–14; Harding, *Social History of English Law*,
pp. 175, 182–3.

1. STEPS TO SUCCESS?

A lengthy career at the inns of court which included service at a senior level was an essential prerequisite for ultimate promotion among the common lawyers of pre-Reformation England. While external preferment was not linked formally to standing within the inns, the ladder of promotion was so organized that those who reached the top at this time had all served a prolonged apprenticeship in their societies. Only readers (normally those who had read twice) were eligible to become serjeants and judges, and, because seniority governed the date of call to the bench or appointment to read, those who had read were necessarily men who had attained considerable standing in their houses. This meant that the medieval and early Tudor judiciary was composed of lawyers who were all steeped in the forms and customs of the inns of court.[2]

This state of affairs had already undergone a partial change by the Elizabethan and early Stuart period, in so far as rising barristers no longer *depended* upon promotion within the inns for ultimate success; rather their advancement to the bench and the place of reader was becoming *incidental* to their eminence. By 1600 benchers of the inns were not necessarily senior men who had already delivered a reading, for it was possible to gain early access to the governing body via appointment to office.[3] But most of them read eventually, and it is significant that all but one of the serjeants and judges created during the half-century before the Civil War had been benchers.[4] Even if the relationship between senior service at the inns and professional success was no longer one of cause and effect, the basic identity between them was not greatly diminished, and the élite of the early seventeenth-century bar and bench was probably no less wedded to its professional base than the great lawyers of Fortescue's day.

In this respect the generation of successful barristers who reached a senior level in their profession between 1680 and 1730 makes a great contrast, and it appears that regular election to the bench of an inn of court was a feature of diminishing importance to the careers of post-Restoration barristers. The figures speak for themselves: 61 per cent

[2] Ives, *Common Lawyers*, pp. 42–8; id., 'Promotion in the Legal Profession of Yorkist and early Tudor England', pp. 348–9, 353–4.

[3] Prest, *Inns of Court*, pp. 60–70.

[4] Ibid. 60; Prest, *Rise of the Barristers*, p. 136. All the judges of Westminster Hall in 1640 had been benchers and readers (S. F. Black, 'The Judges of Westminster Hall during the Great Rebellion, 1640–1660' (Oxford Univ. M.Litt. thesis, 1970), 9).

of the serjeants created between 1680 and 1730 had not been benchers before they were summoned to take the coif, and even the judges in office during these years included a third who had not been called to the bench—a remarkable proportion when it is considered that many of the two-thirds who had sat on the governing bodies of their inns had been called there simply by virtue of appointment to office.[5] In fact, there was no longer any natural identity between the leaders of the profession and the men who ran the inns of court. This explains why the benchers lost their former privilege of pre-audience in Westminster Hall during the mid-seventeenth century.[6] Their remaining honours were confined merely to the enjoyment of precedence and extra comfort within their own societies. By 1700 any barrister could expect to be called to the bench and enjoy these privileges, if only he lived long enough; indeed, it was not even necessary to be a practising counsellor.[7] The degree of professional prestige associated with membership of the bench had diminished accordingly, and this may be the reason why some senior barristers continued to refuse promotion to their governing bodies after the readings had ceased.[8] The obligation to read had been a burden, but the demise of the readings stripped the rank of bencher of the remnants of the external significance that it had once enjoyed. In this sense the Restoration period was a watershed which terminated with the appointment of Sir Nicholas Lechmere to the judicial bench in May 1689, for he was the last English judge who had delivered a reading at the inns of court.[9]

Henceforth only ranks and offices *external* to the legal societies were

[5] Of the 132 serjeants created 1680–1730, 81, and of the 94 judges in office 1680–1730, 31, had not been called to the bench of their inn (Baker, *Serjeants*, pp. 198–209; Foss, *Judges*, vii. 5–6, 10–15, 202–6, 292, 295–8, 374–5, 377–9, viii. 4–10, 78–85; *GIPB* i, ii; *CITR* ii, iii, iv; *LIBB*, ii, iii; *MT Adm. Reg.*, i).

[6] Prest, *Inns of Court*, pp. 62–3; Prynne, *Brief Animadversions*, preface, sig. A.2.

[7] Narcissus Luttrell, who abandoned practice at an early stage, was invited to the bench of GI on 11 Feb. 1706 (F. E. Ball, 'Narcissus Luttrell', *N&Q* 152 (1927), 111; *GIPB* ii. 145). Cf. above, pp. 41–2.

[8] GI, MS Orders ii. 297–8, 339, 361, 384, 428; IT, MS Acts 1665–87, fos. 123–7; ibid., MS Orders 1685–91, fo. 54; ibid. 1691–8, fo. 6; ibid. 1699–1714, fo. 110; *CITR* iii. 329; LI, MS Black Book ix, fo. 231, x, fos. 156, 212; MT, MS Orders E5, 303, 306, 308, 385, 387–9, 440, 442–3, 447–9, 456, 459–60, H(8), 22, 25, 27–8, 30, 34–5, 44, 48–50, 52, 57–61, 64, 66, 96, 105, 112, 115, 137, 139, 222, 353–4.

[9] For Lechmere see Foss, *Judges*, vii. 322–5; he had read at MT in Lent 1669 (see Table 4.1 above). Only 1 of the common law judges appointed under James I and Charles I had not read (H. H. A. Cooper, 'Promotion and Politics among the Common Law Judges of the Reigns of James I and Charles I' (Liverpool Univ. MA thesis, 1964), 25).

of any real importance to the career prospects of practising barristers. Appointments as fee'd counsel or recorders of English and Welsh boroughs were often of value, although their precise contribution to the eventual success of individual counsel is difficult to assess. Much depended upon the stage in his career at which a barrister obtained such a place. For Thomas Greene, a candidate for the recordership of Colchester in 1714, that office would have been a significant preferment, because 'the Salary . . . is greater than in Most Boroughs, and Yeilds a tolerable livelihood for one newly come to the Barr'.[10] On the other hand, the recordership of Gloucester, which Sir John Somers obtained in 1690, was no more than his due, and probably conferred more honour on the borough than the recorder, because Somers was already solicitor-general and in a few short years would be lord keeper.[11] The importance of a recordership to a barrister's career also depended upon the nature of the town or city concerned: the recordership of Colchester might have increased Counsellor Greene's standing at Westminster, but it was small game compared to similar positions in the great city corporations. Of these the recordership of London was by far the most important; indeed, it must be considered as being almost on a par with the offices of attorney- and solicitor-general by reason of its prestige and the regular preferment of incumbents to the judicial bench. Nine men enjoyed this office between 1680 and 1730, among whom no less than seven later became English judges, four in the capacity of a common law chief justice. Two of these four (Jeffreys and King) became lord chancellor.[12] Occupants of the office were marked men in legal and governmental circles, and it is no wonder that there was great competition among leading barristers in order to obtain it.[13] No other recordership was so valuable, but all provided early judicial experience, together with income which could well be crucial before a counsel became established in practice, and, of course, the chance of a parliamentary seat. Considering all these possible benefits, it is probably not a coincidence that at least thirty-eight of the ninety-four English judges

[10] HCRO, Panshanger MSS D/EP F179/3: T[homas] Greene to [Lord Cowper], 3 Nov. 1714. Greene had in fact been called LI on 20 Nov. 1697, and was a native of Colchester (LI, MS Admissions Book x, fo. 138; *Alumni Cantabrigienses*, pt. I, ii. 258, 525).

[11] Foss, *Judges*, vii. 356.

[12] *Recorders of the City of London*, pp. 14–16; Foss, *Judges*, vii, viii, *passim*. Cf. Cooper 'Promotion and Politics', p. 60.

[13] HMC, *15th Report*, app. IV, p. 494: E. Lewis to [Robert] Harley, 24 June 1708.

who were on the bench between 1680 and 1730 had served as recorders or deputy recorders, and it is reasonable to conclude that the careers of at least some of them had been materially advanced in consequence.[14]

If the acquisition of a borough recordership was a common feature among barristers destined to become judges, admission to the order of the coif was an invariable one, although the connection between the serjeants and the common law bench was becoming increasingly formal rather than genuine by the eighteenth century, as the degree ceased to function as a real passport to a judge's place. Nevertheless, until the Victorian law reforms only barristers who had been invested with the coif were eligible for appointment to commissions of assize or the common law judiciary, and the serjeants and judges lived communally at their own inns located in Fleet Street and/or Chancery Lane, rather than among the utter barristers and benchers of the inns of court.[15] As has been seen, this association between the coif and the judiciary had been established in medieval times, when the serjeants were a few pleaders distinguished as élite members of their profession who were earmarked for advancement to the bench.[16] Professor J. H. Baker has shown that the order was progressively inflated and debased during the later sixteenth and seventeenth centuries owing to the decline of the court of Common Pleas (where the serjeants enjoyed a monopoly), the sale of coifs, and the increasing tendency for top barristers to prefer appointments as crown counsel rather than practice as a serjeant. In consequence, the serjeants were effectively relegated; a development which received official sanction in 1671, when Charles II ruled that all his counsel should enjoy precedence (which was taken to mean pre-audience in court) before ordinary members of the coif.[17] Henceforth the degree of serjeant at law became more and more a characteristic of second-rank members of the bar.

After the ruling of 1671 the serjeants could not claim to represent the élite of their profession, and the order could no longer hope

---

[14] E. Foss, *Biographica Juridica: A Biographical Dictionary of the Judges of England from the Conquest to the Present Time* (1870); Henning, *House of Commons 1660–90*; Sedgwick, *House of Commons 1715–54*.

[15] The Fleet Street inn was abandoned by the serjeants in 1733, the lease having expired (H. C. King, *Records and Documents Concerning Serjeants' Inn Fleet Street* (1922), 246).

[16] See above, p. 2.

[17] Baker, *Serjeants*, pp. 108–114, 488–90; id., 'A History of the Order of Serjeants at Law' (London Univ. Ph.D. thesis, 1968), i. 398–403.

virtually to monopolize appointments to the judiciary. The formality of insisting that every judge should have been a serjeant was preserved by coifing judges appointed from outside the order pro forma at their elevation to the bench, but in reality the extent of preferment from among the ranks of *practising* serjeants diminished significantly in the later Stuart and early Hanoverian period.[18] Under the first two Stuart monarchs, of ninety-six serjeants created, fifty-two men or 54 per cent had eventually become common law judges.[19] This was admittedly a decline from the serjeants' zenith in the fifteenth century, but these men were more fortunate than their successors who joined the order of the coif between 1680 and 1730, for Table 8.1 shows that only thirty-six of these serjeants—just over a quarter of the total created in this period—found their way eventually to the judicial bench.[20] Indeed, the breakdown of creations during these years into three distinct periods suggests that the decline of the order was quite precipitate at this time, because each successive cohort contained proportionately fewer future judges. By the early Georgian years a newly created serjeant's chance of becoming an English judge was less than one in five, and his prospects of gaining a senior judgeship were almost non-existent. It is true that some serjeants became judges of jurisdictions outside England (mainly in Wales) and others became king's serjeants. But many of the latter received their royal patents at the same time as they were admitted to the coif, and the promotional prospects of 'mere' serjeants became steadily worse throughout the period, to the point where nearly half of all the serjeants created between 1715 and 1730 received no further preferment.

The decline in importance of the order of the coif as a stepping-stone to the judicial bench should not be taken to apply in equal measure to the king's serjeants, the members of the order who were retained by the monarch as his representatives in Common Pleas. The two senior king's serjeants enjoyed precedence over the law officers of the crown until the early nineteenth century, and all the king's serjeants continued to precede the king's counsel extraordinary after Charles II's order of 1671.[21] The crown serjeants had originally performed certain functions of advocacy as part of their office, and

---

[18] Baker, *Serjeants*, pp. 113–14.

[19] Cooper, 'Promotion and Politics', pp. 49–50.

[20] Over two-thirds of the serjeants created in the 15th cent. became judges, and most of the others probably died before a vacancy occurred (Baker, 'History of the Order of Serjeants', i. 265–6).

[21] Baker, 'History of the Order of Serjeants', i. 275, 283–4, 301–2.

TABLE 8.1. *Preferments of serjeants created 1680–1730*[a]

Preferment	1680–8		1689–1714		1715–30		Total 1680–1730	
	No.	%	No.	%	No.	%	No.	%
Senior English judges[b]	4	9.1	7	12.3	2	6.4	13	9.8
All English judges	14	31.8	16	28.1	6	19.3	36	27.3
Welsh/Scots/Irish judges	15	34.1	10	17.5	7	22.6	32	24.2
KS/other royal counsel	17	38.6	16	28.1	9	29.0	42	31.8
Recorder London/ common serjeant London	4	9.1	—		1	3.2	5	3.8
No higher preferment[c]	13	29.5	24	42.1	15	48.4	52	39.4
Total serjeants created	44		57		31		132	

[a] Excluding serjeants created pro forma upon appointment to the bench. Some serjeants are included in more than 1 row, and the percentages in each column therefore exceed 100%.
[b] Chief justices of CP and KB, chief barons of the Exchequer, masters of the rolls, and lord chancellors/keepers.
[c] Excluding minor offices.

Sources: Baker, *Serjeants*, pp. 198–209 and *passim*; Foss, *Judges*, vii, viii; *Recorders of the City of London*, pp. 14–22; Williams, *Great Sessions*; Ball, *Judges in Ireland*, i, ii; Henning, *House of Commons 1660–90*; Sedgwick, *House of Commons 1715–54*.

even in the later Stuart period they were retained to prosecute for the crown at the assizes and in state trials, although they could not act without the instructions of the attorney-general.[22] By this time the office was in reality inferior to that of a law officer, but patents as king's serjeants continued to be eagerly sought after, and some men of real eminence were appointed throughout the period covered by this study; most notably Sir George Jeffreys, Sir John Holt, Sir Thomas Parker,

[22] Ibid. 289–92; HMC, *15th Report*, app. IV, pp. 393–4: Chief Baron Sir Edward Ward and Baron Sir Thomas Bury to [Robert] Harley, 14 Mar. 1707; *Lives of the Norths*, iii. 138.

Sir Thomas Powys, Sir Thomas Pengelly, and Sir John Cheshire.[23] All except the last became English judges, and four of them were presidents of their courts, including two (Jeffreys and Parker) who went on to the woolsack.[24] Indeed, the king's serjeants generally were much more successful in terms of ultimate preferment than their undistinguished brethren of the coif, for of forty serjeants created between 1680 and 1730 who also received royal patents, nineteen became judges, and eight of these were senior members of the judiciary.[25] In fact the crown serjeants should be regarded as the real heirs of the medieval order of the coif, because they were always a small, select body, and they were by no means inferior to the king's counsel extraordinary. Notwithstanding their pre-eminence in the Augustan period they were ultimately destined to decline with the rest of the coif, however, for the rank was neglected in the nineteenth century and has not survived to the present day.[26]

Despite the enduring superiority of the king's serjeants, the decline in quality of the order of the coif generally meant that judges were increasingly appointed from among barristers who had not practised as serjeants.[27] From the later sixteenth century an alternative source of supply for the judiciary had appeared in the form of the crown counsel. First and foremost among these men were the law officers, and it was therefore entirely appropriate that incumbents of the places of attorney- and solicitor-general, the *de facto* leaders of the bar by the early seventeenth century, were invariably promoted to the highest stations on the judicial bench. Four of Elizabeth's five attorneys-general became judges and no less than eight of the nine attorneys appointed by the first two Stuarts reached the judiciary, seven of them in a senior capacity. The early Stuart solicitors-general were not much less successful, some being appointed to the bench directly from that office and others being promoted via the attorney-generalship.[28]

Thus by 1640, although the law officers had by no means achieved a *prescriptive* right to the highest positions on the bench, it is clear that

[23] For applications to become KS, see SCRO, Somers MSS L1: J[ohn] Darnell to [Lord Keeper Somers], 26 Feb. 1694; HMC, *15th Report*, app. IV, p. 159: James Mundy to Robert Harley, 2 Feb. 1705.

[24] For the judges see Foss, *Biographica Juridica*; for Cheshire see *DNB* iv. 200–1, pp. 155–6 above, and App. VII below. The Whig assessment of Jeffreys as a lawyer is revised (perhaps with some exaggeration) in Keeton, *Jeffreys*.

[25] Sources as in Table 8.1.

[26] Baker, *Serjeants*, pp. 116–17; id., 'History of the Order of Serjeants', i. 281–4.

[27] Id., *Serjeants*, pp. 113–14, and p. 114 nn. 2–3.

[28] Cooper, 'Promotion and Politics', p. 1 n. 1 and pp. 54–5.

any man who became solicitor or attorney to the king had an excellent chance of becoming a judge, and a fair prospect of gaining one of the collars of SS (worn by the chiefs of the common law benches) or even the woolsack. This state of affairs was broadly maintained after the Restoration, although the increased incursion of politics into the law and legal preferment from the 1670s meant that some king's attorneys and solicitors ended up on the wrong side of the political fence after 1689, and were proscribed for the rest of their careers. Sir Robert Sawyer, for instance, attorney-general between 1681 and 1687, never became a judge at all, and Sir Thomas Powys, James II's last attorney and one of the prosecutors of the Seven Bishops, had to be content with only a brief spell as a puisne judge under Queen Anne, in spite of a valiant attempt to excuse his conduct with King William's ministers after the Revolution.[29] In total only two of the five barristers who served as attorney- or solicitor-general between 1680 and 1688 reached the judiciary, and neither of them rose beyond a puisne judgeship.[30] No doubt these disappointed counsel found some consolation in the purely financial benefits of their places, which amounted to £4,000–£7,000 a year in the reign of Charles II.[31] Their successors were more fortunate with regard to promotion; after 1689 the law officers resumed their regular progress to the upper reaches of the bench, to the extent that nine of the eleven attorneys- or solicitors-general employed under William and Anne became judges, and all of them eventually sat as chiefs or lord chancellor. Over the whole period 1680–1730, of twenty-two law officers, fifteen reached the judiciary, and no less than eleven became senior judges.[32]

Appointments to the judiciary from outside the order of serjeants were not, of course, confined to the law officers of the crown, for the king's counsel extraordinary provided a further supply of highly eligible men. Table 8.2 shows that, of forty-three KCs appointed between 1680 and 1730, eighteen, or over 40 per cent, became judges

---

[29] For Sawyer see Henning, *House of Commons 1660–90*, iii. 399–403; for Powys see Foss, *Judges*, viii. 55–6; Dorset CRO, Trenchard MSS, D. 60 x 8: 'Sir Thomas Powys's case' [*c*.1692–5]. Cf. Bodl. MSS Tanner 28/2, fo. 313: Powys to [Archbishop Sancroft], Jan. 1689. In 1710 Powys applied to become AG again, and in 1714, following his dismissal from the bench, he was reappointed KS after appealing to LC Cowper (HMC, *15th Report*, app. IV, pp. 614–15: Powys to [Robert Harley], 16 Oct. 1710; HCRO, Panshanger MSS D/EP F149/12–16: Powys to Cowper, 21, 23, and 25 Oct. 1714).

[30] Foss, *Judges*, vii. 28, 207, 251–4, viii. 55–7.

[31] See above, pp. 154–5; *Lives of the Norths*, i. 125.

[32] Foss, *Judges*, vii. 28, 207, 300–1, 379, viii. 10–11, 88, and *passim*.

TABLE 8.2. *Preferments of KCs/QCs appointed 1680–1730*[a]

Preferment	1680–8		1689–1714		1715–30		Total 1680–1730	
	No.	%	No.	%	No.	%	No.	%
Senior English judges[b]	2	18.2	4	22.2	5	35.7	11	25.6
All English judges	5	45.4	4	22.2	9	64.3	18	41.9
Welsh/Scots/Irish judges	2	18.2	2	11.1	5	35.7	9	20.9
AG/SC/other royal counsel	3	27.3	7	38.9	10	71.4	20	46.5
Recorder London/ common serjeant London	2	18.2	—		—		2	4.6
No higher preferment[c]	1	9.1	8	44.4	—		9	20.9
Total KCs/QCs appointed	11		18		14		43	

[a] Some KCs/QCs are included in more than 1 row, and the percentages in each column therefore exceed 100%.
[b] As in Table 8.1 n.b.
[c] Excluding minor offices.

Sources: As in Table 8.1; also information from Sir John Sainty.

and eleven reached the upper levels of the judiciary.[33] If these figures are compared with the promotional record of the serjeants as quantified in Table 8.1, it is quite apparent that a patent as KC was a far more certain path to the bench for this generation of lawyers than the degree of the coif. As yet the alternative route was not more heavily trodden, because twice as many practising serjeants became judges as KCs, but it is worthy of note that the king's counsel extraordinary supplied almost as many *senior* judges as the serjeants, despite the numerical inferiority of their order, and it is clear that the pattern of preferment shifted decisively in favour of the KCs during the early

[33] KC is used in the text as a generic term to represent the crown counsel extraordinary, in order to avoid the tedious repetition of devices to denote king's and queen's counsel.

eighteenth century. Nine of the fourteen king's counsel appointed between 1715 and 1730 became judges, as compared with only six of the thirty-one serjeants created in these years. Moreover, *all* these early Georgian KCs secured some further appointment, if only as a law officer to a member of the royal family, or as a Welsh or Irish judge, which contrasts greatly with the large number of their counterparts among the serjeants who languished as undistinguished members of the coif. Evidently, by this time the crown counsel were men who were in the fast lane of preferment within the legal profession, and the serjeants were mere plodders by comparison.

2. SERJEANTS AND KCS: DIFFERENT EXPERIENCES

This change in promotional patterns is especially important because the crown counsel of 1680–1730 were a qualitatively different breed of lawyers from the barristers who became serjeants during these years. It is clear that the serjeants were more senior men who had been passed over in the race for preferment. The average seniority of KCs appointed in this period, calculated from their dates of call to the bar, was less than sixteen years, while the serjeants who received the coif at this time were barristers of an average of twenty-two years' standing. Even the law officers were more junior than serjeants at law in point of seniority from call.[34] It is no wonder that the order of the coif had lost its attraction for rising members of the bar, when all the ordinary serjeants could be leap-frogged with regard to precedence and pre-audience by king's counsel who were much their junior in experience and standing.

Moreover, the accelerated promotion of the KCs was also subversive of the time-honoured system of internal advancement at the inns of court, and this implies a second distinction between the crown counsel and the serjeants, in that the former probably had less respect for the practices and customs of the ancient societies. It has been seen that call to the bench of an inn was a factor of diminishing significance for the career prospects of practising lawyers in the seventeenth century,

---

[34] The average standing of 42 KCs (the call of 1 man has not been identified) was 15.6 years, while that of 131 serjeants (excluding those appointed pro forma upon becoming judges and one whose call to the bar has not been found) was 22.1 years. The 22 AGs and SGs in office 1680–1730 were men of an average of 17.6 years' seniority from call (list of KCs supplied by Sir John Sainty; Baker, *Serjeants*, pp. 198–209; Foss, *Judges*, vii. 28, 207, 300–1, 379, viii. 10–11, 88; *GIPB* i, ii; *CITR* ii, iii, iv; *LIBB* ii, iii; *MT Adm. Reg.*, i).

and even the Augustan serjeants themselves included a majority who had not been benchers, but it is noteworthy that at least 39 per cent of them *had* been regularly elected by dint of seniority to the governing bodies of their inns. By contrast less than 20 per cent of the KCs had been senior enough to be called to the bench before they received their patents from the crown.[35] It is true that almost all the king's counsel were subsequently elected to the bench by virtue of their newly acquired status, but this meant that the KCs became senior members of their societies as a mere formality, while the future serjeants only did so after a long period as utter barristers, if at all. The consequence of this was resentment on the part of the benchers who had worked their passage, and seeming indifference towards the inns and their concerns among the KCs at the bench. The latter could not be expected to attach much importance to an honour which they had gained as a matter of course, and they appear to have been less active than the ordinary benchers in their capacity as governors of the inns— appropriately enough for men who were busy advocates and invariably members of parliament.[36] Roger North, who was both a KC and an MP, rarely failed to touch a humorous note when he mentioned the privileges taken so seriously by many of his fellow benchers, and it may be significant that he did not trouble to make any comment in his autobiography on the subject of his tenure of the treasurership of the Middle Temple.[37]

It is possible that the crown counsel were discouraged from full participation in the affairs of their societies, because their undistinguished fellows had made it very clear that they were not welcome members of the inns' governing bodies, and refused them precedence in matters of ceremony and the choice of bench chambers.[38] In the Restoration

[35] Of the 132 serjeants created 1680–1730, 51 had been benchers before they were summoned to take the degree of serjeant, while only 8 of the 43 KCs were benchers before they received their royal patents (sources as cited for KCs, serjeants, and inns' proceedings above, n. 34).

[36] At IT the crown counsel among the benchers had a poor record of attendance at the meetings of the governing parliament: John Ward QC MP and Thomas Lutwyche QC MP never attended during the last years of Queen Anne's reign (for attendance 1689–1715 see *CITR* iii. 259–442 passim, iv. 1).

[37] BL, Add. MSS 32501, fo. 142: North to North Foley, 25 Nov. 1717; *Lives of the Norths*, iii. 46–7.

[38] GI, MS Orders iii. 26: IT, MS Orders 1699–1714, fos. 94, 99; ibid. 1715–1733 fos. 18, 89, 100; *CITR* iii. 265, 274–6, iv. 46; MT, MS Orders E5, 367, 423, 501, H(8), 385, 387. LI alone seems to have accorded KCs precedence before ordinary benchers (LI, MS Black Book xi. 267). All the inns called the AG and SG to the bench without demur and accorded them precedence before all other benchers.

period the benchers had resisted accepting the principle that KCs were entitled to be called to their fellowship by virtue of their appointment, for it was felt that this would enable the crown to take over the governance of the inns. The classic case here was that of Francis North KC, who was only elected to the Middle Temple bench in 1668 after extreme pressure had been exerted on his behalf by the lord chief justice.[39] Following this capitulation crown counsel were regularly elected to the bench until the Revolution, but from that time the inns reasserted their freedom of choice and occasionally refused to call newly made KCs. Thus in 1689 John Conyers KC and William Cowper KC were not granted admission to the governing body of the Middle Temple.[40] Both men subsequently appealed to the lord keeper for redress of their grievances, but Conyers did not become a bencher until 1702, and Cowper never did; a remarkable omission for a lord high chancellor of England.[41] It may not be a coincidence that the future chancellor, who was clearly a marked man from a very early stage in his career, had little time for the petty pride of the ordinary benchers, and he appears to have written a piece of crude doggerel entitled 'On the Benchers bog house looking to the Water Side' which made his feelings plain:

> Here poor mean Common and exceeding high
> In Common nastiness lie
> Here the proud Bencher takes his Airy Seat
> And freely shits what he as freely Eats.
> Here the house stock (for this way most on't goes)
> Stinks and offends the Rogue Consumers Nose
> But not his conscience that I humbly think
> Is too Corrupt to smell another stink.[42]

---

[39] *Lives of the Norths*, i. 50–1. More traditional members of the profession were also upset by the fact that North wore a tufted gown like that of a reader in court. This later became the full dress appropriate to KCs (Baker, 'History of the Order of Serjeants', p. 403; id., 'The Origin of the Bar Gown', *Law Guardian*, 49 (1969), 17–18); id., 'History of the Gowns worn at the English Bar', *Costume*, 9 (1975), 17).

[40] MT, MS Orders E5, 368, 371–2, 375, 397, 417, 451.

[41] Ibid. 422, 500, 506. William Clarke KC (1690) was also refused promotion to the bench—at GI—and John Aglionby KC (1690) seems to have been passed over by the same society (GI, MS Orders ii. 346; *GIPB* ii. 346 and *passim*; *CITR* iii. 321–2). At MT Edward Winnington (alias Jeffreys) KC (1710), Thomas Reeve KC (1717), and Alexander Denton KC (1715) were only made benchers some years after their appointments (MT, MS Orders H(8), 105, 107, 152; *MT Adm. Reg.*, i. 220). Cf. *Master Worsley's Book*, p. 110.

[42] Cowper became KC by virtue of his family's connections in 1689, when he had been at the bar for little more than a year (HCRO, D/EP F24/17, 20–5:

Cowper, like North, was a member of parliament, and this is important, because the third and most significant distinction between the crown counsel and the serjeants was the fact that the former were more likely to occupy a seat in the House of Commons. Forty-nine of the 132 barristers who became serjeants between 1680 and 1730 were MPs at some point in their careers, but this represents less than 40 per cent of the total, whereas over three-quarters of the KCs appointed during this period sat in parliament, and over 90 per cent of the law officers did.[43] As was seen in the last chapter, patents as king's counsel and other legal offices were liberally deployed after 1689 in order to control the legal contingent of the Commons. In consequence, the crucial distinguishing feature of the crown counsel became their activity in parliament.

This parliamentary option was the real foundation of the alternative career structure which was transforming promotion among barristers in the later seventeenth and early eighteenth centuries. The shift in the pattern of preferment which has been observed was not simply a product of the bar élite's tendency to prefer crown service to practice as a serjeant. After 1689 a more fundamental change had accelerated the trend, and the next generation of rising barristers were further drawn away from the inns and the coif by the pull of parliament and the patronage available there. In consequence the leadership of the bar passed to men who were necessarily parliamentarians as well as common lawyers—counsel whose outlook was not bounded by the medieval structure of the profession. How far this process was apparent in the career characteristics of the judges who sat on the bench between 1680 and 1730 will be considered in the final section of this chapter.

---

correspondence of Lady Sarah Cowper, Rachel, Lady Russell, and [Sir George Savile, Marquis of] Halifax, 1689 and n.d.; ibid., D/EP F94: Sir Robert Howard to [Charles Talbot], earl of Shrewsbury, 26 July 1689; ibid., D/EP F63/1: draft letter, William Cowper to [John Churchill], duke of Marlborough, 16 Oct. 1705). Ibid., D/EP F36 unpag.: copy poem by 'W.C.'.

[43] Of the practising serjeants, 37.1% were MPs, while 33 (76.7%) of the 43 KCs and 20 (90.9%) of the 22 law officers sat in parliament (sources for serjeants, KCs, and law officers as above, n. 34; Henning, *House of Commons 1660–90*; *HPT* checklist of MPs 1690–1715; Sedgwick, *House of Commons 1715–54*). There were objections to the law officers (especially the AG) being MPs in the 17th cent., but these were settled by 1689 (J. Ll. J. Edwards, *The Law Officers of the Crown* (1964), 4, 32–9, 44–5).

3. JUDGES

Much of what has been said in this chapter relies upon the implicit assumption that early modern English barristers saw the judicial bench as the summit of their professional ambitions. This was no doubt broadly true, but it is in need of some qualification. By the early eighteenth century, as has been seen, a leading crown counsel could well be earning £3,000 or £4,000 per annum from his practice at the bar.[44] Against this a puisne judgeship was worth £1,100 to £1,400 before 1714 and only £500 more after the accession of George I.[45] Thus a distinguished counsel at the height of his powers was not likely to abandon his practice for a puisne judgeship too readily, although an older man—especially one whose health was in decline—might find the prospect of retirement to a junior seat on the bench more attractive.[46] This should be borne in mind when considering the statistics in Table 8.3, which represent the career characteristics of English judges in office between 1680 and 1730 who never rose beyond the level of puisne justice. It is also important to realize that this body of men was not entirely contemporary with the mid-career barristers considered in the earlier sections of this chapter; the judges were lawyers of a slightly earlier generation. These factors no doubt explain why the king's counsel extraordinary were not well represented among the puisne judges. Indeed, there were fewer ex-KCs among the puisnes than there were former practising serjeants, for the latter accounted for no less than 61 per cent of the appointments summarized here. It is significant, however, that the representation of the practising serjeants at this level showed a clear decline over the period, from 75 per cent of the puisnes on the bench between 1680 and 1688 to just over half in the reigns of William and Anne and under a third of the junior judges who were in office during the first years of the Hanoverian period. It is also clear that most of these men had been king's serjeants, and no more than a quarter of the puisnes had been

---

[44] See above, pp. 155–6.

[45] That is, £1,000 salary plus fees until 1714 and £1,500 plus fees after George I's accession. In the 1690s Mr Justice Rokeby's fees amounted to slightly more than the estimate (HCRO, Panshanger MSS D/EP F147/21–2: memorial of LCJ Parker on the salaries of the judges, [c.1714]; Foss, *Judges*, v. 299, viii. 10). Dr Duman's figures for the salaries of the puisne judges 1715–59 are not correct (Duman, *English Judicial Bench*, pp. 112, 115).

[46] HCRO, Panshanger MSS D/EP F147/21; cf. Holmes, *Augustan England*, p. 129.

TABLE 8.3. *Career patterns of English puisne judges, 1680–1730*[a]

Preferment	1680–8		1689–1714		1715–30		Total 1680–1730	
	No.	%	No.	%	No.	%	No.	%
Welsh/Scots/Irish judge	7	29.2	7	30.4	2	28.6	16	29.6
AG/SG	1	4.2	1	4.3	1	14.3	3	5.5
KC/QC	4	16.7	—		4	57.1	8	14.8
KS/QS	11	45.8	5	21.7	2	28.6	18	33.3
Other royal counsel	—		—		4	57.1	4	7.4
Recorder London/ common serjeant London	2	8.3	1	4.3	1	14.3	4	7.4
'Mere' serjeant[b]	7	29.2	8	34.8	—		15	27.8
'Mere' barrister	2	8.3	7	30.4	—		9	16.7
Total with crown service	18	75.0	11	47.8	6	85.7	35	64.8
Total practising serjeants	18	75.0	13	56.5	2	28.6	33	61.1
MP	10	41.7	10	43.5	6	85.7	26	48.1
Total judges	24		23		7		54	

[a] Common law puisnes (excluding cursitor barons) and commissioners of the great seal appointed during each period specified, plus those incumbent on 1 Jan. 1680. Excluding puisnes who later became chief justices or chief barons, masters of the rolls, or lord chancellor/keeper. Some judges are included in more than 1 row, and the percentages in each column therefore exceed 100%.
[b] Serjeants who never received a patent as KS, excluding those created pro forma upon appointment to the bench.

Sources: As in Table 8.2; also *HPT* (checklist of MPs, 1690–1715).

undistinguished members of the coif. The outlook for the 'mere' serjeants was bleak indeed.

Patents as king's counsel had not been issued ih sufficient numbers to overcome the preponderance of practising serjeants among later Stuart and early Georgian puisne justices. But it is evident from the statistics that crown service in *some* capacity was a very important factor in the selection of the judiciary, because two-thirds of the puisnes had

been distinguished in this way.[47] Of course, few puisne judges had
reached the heights of a law officership; the only three examples in this
period were two of James II's unfortunate attorneys-general and Sir
John Fortescue-Aland, who was regarded as a failure in the office of
solicitor-general under George I.[48] The puisnes were more typically
former king's serjeants, or had been junior judges of some non-
English jurisdiction, most likely in Wales. The Welsh judgeships in
particular were popular with English barristers as a valuable and
convenient supplement to advocacy at the bar.[49] They were equally
useful to the government, not only as a form of patronage appropriate
to lawyer MPs, but for a ready-made supply of mature candidates to fill
the lesser places on the English bench.[50] As the duke of Bolton pointed
out (with pardonable exaggeration) when recommending his cousin
Serjeant Powlett for an English judgeship in 1695, the serjeant was
suitably experienced, for 'he hath served almost an Apprenticeship as
one of his Majestyes Justices of Wales from whence such Translations
of Persons of Meritt have been usuall in former tymes'.[51]

Patrons such as Bolton never failed to draw attention to their clients'
'fidelity to the Governmentt' when writing on their behalf, and there
is no doubt that politics was a significant element in the choice of
men for the bench, although it was by no means pre-eminent in
the appointment of mere puisne judges. James II had been most
concerned with this aspect of selecting men for the judiciary, to the
extent that he subsequently removed many for their contumacy, but
after 1689 governments did not insist on a similar degree of political
conformity at this level.[52] Of course it remained the case that
individuals who were suspected of outright opposition to the regime
were rarely appointed, and this was the reason for the proscription of
James's law officers. Moreover, even after the Revolution the judiciary
was liable to be the subject of political purges upon the demise of the
monarch, and the reshuffles occasionally descended to the grade of the

[47] Cf. Cooper, 'Promotion and Politics', p. 61; Black, 'Judges of Westminster Hall',
p. 11.
[48] HCRO, Panshanger MSS D/EP F57/122: draft letter [Cowper] to [?Bernstorff]
[autumn 1717].
[49] Williams, *Great Sessions in Wales*, p. 25: *CSPD 1689*, p. 208: [Charles Talbot] earl
of Shrewsbury to the commissioners of the great seal, 2 Aug. 1689.
[50] See above, p. 211.
[51] SCRO, Somers MSS L13: [Charles Powlett] duke of Bolton to Lord Keeper
[Somers], 13 July 1695.
[52] A. F. Havighurst, 'James II and the Twelve Men in Scarlet', *LQR* 69 (1953),
522–46.

puisnes, as Sir John Turton and Sir William Banister discovered, the former in 1702 and the latter in 1714.[53] Nevertheless, at this level of the judiciary it was not *essential* for successful candidates to have proved themselves by faithful service in the House of Commons, and a majority of the puisne judges had not been MPs. But the presence of twenty-six ex-MPs among the fifty-four judges analysed here does suggest that many may have come to the attention of the government because of their presence in the Commons, and the chronological perspective implies that promotion via parliament and crown service rather than through the order of the coif was increasingly important, even among the lesser members of the Augustan judiciary.

Although a parliamentary career may have been the decisive factor in the ultimate promotion of many counsel between 1680 and 1730, this does not mean that governments of the period were normally prepared to dispense with the basic requirement for judges to be competent and learned members of their profession. Only in the last five years of Charles II's reign and under James II is it possible to identify many incompetent lawyers among the occupants of the judicial bench.[54] Certainly after 1689 it appears that political service of the highest order was not *by itself* a sufficient recommendation for a judgeship: Sir John Hawles, solicitor-general under William III, was debarred from the bench because the lord chief justice did not think he was 'orthodox' in the criminal law.[55] Legal experience, on the other hand, was invariably a requirement for promotion to the judiciary: the puisne judges appointed in the years covered by this study were men of an average of nearly twenty-nine years' seniority at the bar, and even the senior judges, who might have been expected to proceed up the ladder of promotion rather more rapidly, were barristers of an average of nearly twenty-five years' standing.[56] Indeed, a parliamentary career

---

[53] Foss, *Judges*, vii. 405, viii. 14; HCRO, D/EP F147/19: Lord Cowper's memorial to George I on the judges [1714]; John, Lord Campbell, *The Lives of the Lord Chancellors and Keepers of the Great Seal of England* (1845–69), vi. 349–50; cf. D. A. Rubini, 'The Precarious Independence of the Judiciary, 1688–1701', *LQR* 83 (1967), 343–5; HMC, *Finch MSS* iii. 138, 396.

[54] Havighurst, 'The Judiciary and Politics in the Reign of Charles II', p. 249; id., 'James II and the Twelve Men in Scarlet', p. 543.

[55] New York Public Library, Hardwicke MSS 33, 44: marginal note to copy letter [Lord Somers] to [King William] [31 July 1694], said to be in the hand of the 2nd earl of Hardwicke.

[56] The average standing of 53 puisne judges (the call of one has not been identified) was 28.9 years, and that of the 40 senior judges (upon first reaching the bench) was 24.7 years. These latter judges reached a senior level at an average of 27.6 years from call

did not make much difference in this respect, and judges who had
been MPs did not reach the bench much earlier than their non-
political brethren.[57]

While high-flying judges of this period were generally very
experienced barristers, the discrepancy between the length of their
pre-judicial careers and those of the puisnes is significant, and this
represents a major distinction, both in terms of the characteristics of
the two groups and of the remuneration and honour of their offices.
Ambitious and successful counsel were unlikely to leave the bar in
mid-career for the sake of a puisne judgeship, but they were liable to
be tempted by the offer of a chief's collar of SS, the rolls, or the
woolsack, even if this was made only on the condition that they accept a
junior place in the first instance. The senior positions were generally
more profitable and certainly more prestigious than the office of an
ordinary judge, which meant that they were a greater compensation
for the loss of private practice.[58] The lord chancellor or keeper, for
example, might receive £8,000 per annum in total emoluments during
this period, and the chief justiceships of King's Bench and Common
Pleas were also very profitable (especially the latter).[59] It is true that the
mastership of the rolls and the post of chief baron of the Exchequer
were not so well remunerated, and in consequence these two offices

(sources as for puisne and senior judges in Tables 8.3 and 8.4; *GIPB* i, ii; *CITR* ii, iii, iv;
LIBB ii, iii; *MT Adm. Reg.*, i).

[57] The average standing of the 56 judges (puisnes and seniors) in office 1680–1730
who had been MPs was 27.1 years, while that of 37 non-MPs (1 unknown) was 27.2
years (sources as above, n. 56).

[58] This applied in some measure even to the office of chief baron of the Exchequer,
which was probably the least attractive senior judgeship (BL, Add. MSS 32686, fo. 383:
copy letter [Thomas Pelham-Holles, duke of] Newcastle to [Charles, Viscount]
Townshend, 1 Nov. 1723).

[59] LC Cowper received £7,500–£8,000 a year from his office between 1705 and 1710
(HCRO, Panshanger MSS D/EP F69, end of volume, unpag.: notes of income
appended to original diary of Earl Cowper, 1705–14; cf. *The Private Diary of William,
First Earl Cowper, Lord Chancellor of England* (Eton, 1833), 59). LC Harcourt received
£8,000 plus per annum in 1711–14 (BL, Stowe MSS 416, fos. 5–6: Edward Dupper to
[?] n.d. [?1718] with an account of the profits of the seal). No doubt LC Macclesfield's
income was even larger (Foss, *Judges*, viii. 3–4). In 1716 Parker, LCJ of KB (who may
well have been a special case) had a salary of £2,000 per annum plus a yearly pension of
£1,200, together with his fees and considerable patronage income. Lord Cowper said
that Parker's income then exceeded the chancellor's, although Parker himself had
insisted in 1714 that the profits of his office were much diminished. He stated then that
the office of LCJ of CP was worth twice as much in profits as the chief's place in KB
(HCRO, Panshanger MSS D/EP F57/126–7; ibid., D/EP F147/21). Roger North said
that the chief justiceship of CP was not worth more than £4,000 per annum when his
brother was appointed to it in 1674 (*Lives of the Norths*, i. 125).

did not excite as much competition as the others, but *all* the senior judgeships were considered suitable preferments for the leaders of the bar.[60]

Barristers who were appointed to the best places in the judiciary were collectively an eminent and distinguished body of men by comparison with their puisnes. This is apparent from Table 8.4, which summarizes the career patterns of the forty occupants of the bench between 1680 and 1730 who attained the heights of a senior judgeship. Certainly, some had found their way through appointment as a puisne in the first instance, but they too were by no means second rank counsel, because eleven of the seventeen former puisnes had been employed by the crown, three in the capacity of a law officer, four as king's serjeants, two as king's counsel extraordinary, and one as counsel to the prince of Wales. No doubt several of these judges had been promised further promotion when they were first appointed to the bench.[61] Although preferment by translation was not universal among the top judges, it is evident that previous service of some kind was almost a *sine qua non* for appointment at this level, for no less than 90 per cent of all the senior members of the judiciary had already held places under the crown, whether as puisne justices in England, judges in Wales or Ireland, law officers, or other royal counsel. Moreover, many of them, unlike the mere puisnes, served in a senior capacity, to the extent that eleven of the forty had been attorney- or solicitor-general, six others had been chief justices in Wales and Ireland, and one had been the king's premier serjeant at law. It is manifest that the governments of this period did not take many chances when they filled the upper reaches of the judicial bench, and successful candidates for these jobs had been tried and tested more generally and at a higher level than counsel who never progressed beyond a junior place.

It is worthy of note, however, that crown service in the form of

[60] The *profits* of the chief baron's place did not exceed those of the puisnes in the other courts, although incumbents were sometimes given extra allowances (HCRO, Panshanger MSS D/EP F147/21; LI, MS Misc. 582, loose papers: letters and memoranda of Sir Edward Ward, 1693–1703; HMC, *14th Report*, app. II, p. 478: Robert Harley to Sir Edward Harley, 24 Oct. 1691). Sir John Strange, the incumbent SG, rejected the mastership of the rolls in 1738 because of its poor remuneration. He did accept in 1750, after over 30 years at the bar (BL, Add. MSS 35586, fo. 83: Strange to [Lord Hardwicke], 28 Aug. 1738; Foss, *Judges*, viii. 166–9).

[61] Sir Thomas Reeve, who was first appointed to the bench in 1733, was only induced to accept a puisne judgeship 'by the vague promise of higher advancement'. He was LCJ of CP 1736–7 (BL, Add. MSS 35585, fos. 307–8: draft letter [Lord Hardwicke] to [Alexander Denton], 22 Dec. 1735; Foss, *Judges*, viii. 158–9).

TABLE 8.4. *Career patterns of English senior judges, 1680–1730*[a]

Preferment	1680–8		1689–1714		1715–30		Total 1680–1730	
	No.	%	No.	%	No.	%	No.	%
Puisne English judge	6	42.9	1	8.3	10	71.4	17	42.5
Welsh/Irish judge	4	28.6	—		3	21.4	7	17.5
AG/SG	2	14.3	6	50.0	3	21.4	11	27.5
KC/QC	6	42.9	3	25.0	3	21.4	12	30.0
KS/QS	6	42.9	3	25.0	2	14.3	11	27.5
Other royal counsel	4	28.6	2	16.7	3	21.4	9	22.5
Recorder London/ common serjeant London	1	7.1	2	16.7	1	7.1	4	10.0
'Mere' serjeant[b]	—		—		5	35.7	5	12.5
'Mere' barrister	—		2	16.7	1	7.1	3	7.5
Total with crown service	14	100.0	10	83.3	12	85.7	36	90.0
Total practising serjeants	6	42.9	3	25.0	7	50.0	16	40.0
MP	10	71.4	10	83.3	10	71.4	30	75.0
Total judges	14		12		14		40	

[a] Chief justices and chief barons, masters of the rolls, and lord chancellors/ keepers appointed in their senior capacity during each period specified plus those incumbent on 1 Jan. 1680, and the puisnes who later became senior judges.
[b] Serjeants who never received a patent as KS, excluding those created pro forma upon appointment to the bench.

Sources: As in Table 8.3.

previous appointment as a king's serjeant was a diminishing characteristic of the senior judges, and it appears that the order of the coif generally was less well represented among the top judges at this time than it was at the level of puisne justice. Only a minority of the men appointed to the upper levels of the judiciary had practised as a serjeant, and very few of these had not been distinguished by a patent from the crown. It is remarkable that five of the presiding judges who were appointed in the early years of the Hanoverian monarchy had been ordinary members of the coif, but all except two of them were only promoted after many years' service as junior justices.[62] Former KCs, by contrast, were more common among the senior judges than they were among the puisnes, and they were generally appointed outright, rather than by translation.[63] Unlike the serjeants, they had not been forced to rely upon extreme longevity and stamina for ultimate promotional success. A comparison between the careers of William Cowper and Sir John Comyns—two contemporary barristers—is telling with regard to this point. Cowper was catapulted to the very head of his profession from the ranks of the crown counsel, and had served two terms on the woolsack and died before Comyns reached the judiciary from the coif. Furthermore, Comyns only finally became chief baron of the Exchequer after twelve years on the bench and earnest supplication to the lord chief justice of England, who had himself been called to the bar twenty-five years *after* the aged judge.[64] It is clear that serjeants such as Sir John clawed their way to the top of the legal profession against all the odds, and a career which included service as a KC or law officer was much the more natural route by the early eighteenth century.

As has been seen, that route usually passed through the House of Commons as a major stopping-point along the way. It is not surprising, therefore, that the senior judges were more political animals than their inferior brethren, and three-quarters of them had been MPs before they were promoted to the judiciary. Of course top judges were necessarily able lawyers, but it seems that political reliability was often the deciding factor in appointments and dismissals, especially with regard to the sensitive posts of chief justice in King's Bench and Common Pleas, and lord chancellor or keeper. Historians have traditionally emphasized the 'independence' of the judiciary from the crown after 1689, and it is true that senior judges were rarely

[62] The exceptions were Sir John Pratt, who was a puisne judge of KB 1714–18 and LCJ of KB 1718–25, and James Reynolds, judge of KB 1725–30 and LCB of Exchequer 1730–8 (Foss, *Judges*, viii. 57–60, 160–2).

[63] Only 4 of the 12 former KCs among the senior judges had served as puisnes: Sir Robert Atkins, Sir Robert Eyre, Sir James Montague, and Sir William Lee (Foss, *Judges*, vii. 306–10, viii. 4–41, 121–3, 139–42).

[64] Cowper: called MT 1688, KC 1689, LK 1705–7, LC 1707–10 and 1714–18, died 1723, aged 58; Comyns: called LI 1690, serjeant 1705, baron of Exchequer 1726–36, judge of CP 1736–8, LCB of Exchequer 1738–40, died 1740, aged 73 (sources as in Table 8.2 and above, n. 56; *Victoria History of the Counties of England: Hertfordshire Genealogical Volume*, ed. D. Warrand (1907) 138–9). For Comyns's application to the LCJ see BL, Add. MSS 35584, fo. 309: Comyns to [Hardwicke], 3 Jan. 1736. Hardwicke had been called MT 27 May 1715 (MT, MS Orders E5, 70).

dismissed, although Sir Thomas Trevor was removed from his place as lord chief justice of Common Pleas in 1714, upon Lord Cowper's advice that he had been a zealous supporter of the late Tory administration.[65] In fact the comparative rarity of purges at this level was a consequence of the altered conditions of promotion throughout the upper branch of the legal profession, at least as much as it was owing to forebearance on the part of the crown. For after the Revolution governments could be fairly sure that their appointments to senior positions in the judiciary were 'safe' politically, because aspiring candidates had to prove themselves publicly by loyal service in parliament. Before 1689 the careers of Pemberton, Scroggs, Saunders, and Jeffreys demonstrate that it was perfectly possible for a barrister who was not an MP to aspire to the highest places on the bench, but only six of the twenty-six judges in office from 1689 to 1730 who reached a senior place had not been MPs, and all except one of them remained in the less sensitive place of chief baron of the Exchequer.[66] As in the case of appointments at the level of puisne justice, a successful career in parliament was no *guarantee* of eventual preferment, and a lawyer politician might well fall foul of political change, but after 1689 it undoubtedly placed a barrister in a quite different category from his fellows, for he was much more likely to be considered as suitable material for the very highest positions on the judicial bench.

Thus it appears that the pattern of preferment within the legal profession was shifting at all levels between 1680 and 1730. The new structure became fully established in the course of the eighteenth century, and this implies that the dynamic elements of the English bar were alienated from the institutions which had fashioned their medieval predecessors.[67] The élite of the profession became identified with the court and the House of Commons as their main avenue of advancement, retaining only formal connections with the inns of court and the order of serjeants at law. This was one of the clearest expressions of the transformation outlined in this work, and it only remains, by way of conclusion, to summarize all its features.

[65] HCRO, Panshanger MSS D/EP F147/19: Cowper's advice to George I on the judges [1714]; cf. BL, Add. MSS 32686, fos. 383–8: Newcastle to Townshend, 1 Nov. 1723, and Newcastle to Robert Walpole, 2 Nov. 1723.

[66] The exception was Sir Nathan Wright, who was appointed LK as a desperate measure in 1700 after the leaders of the profession had declined to succeed Lord Somers in his office (*Bishop Burnet's History of His Own Time* (2nd edn., Oxford, 1833), iv. 446).

[67] For promotional patterns of the 18th-cent. judges see Duman, *English Judicial Bench*, pp. 72–96 *passim*.

CONCLUSION

THE inns of court entered a period of steep decline in the later seventeenth century. This was not so much a result of the loss of their role as academies for educating the gentry: rather it was a consequence of their diminishing function as institutional centres for the training, regulation, and accommodation of the English bar itself. It is true that there was a limited 'flight of the gentry' from the four societies after 1660, but this was neither so rapid nor so complete as has been thought. More serious was the fact that every inn experienced a crisis of non-residence which owed a great deal to increasing reluctance among committed law students and barristers to study and practise as a community within the precincts of their societies. This in turn precipitated a crisis of insolvency which was only resolved by the benchers' acquiescence in the partial transformation of their houses from hostels for common lawyers to places of abode and employment for a broad cross-section of Londoners not connected with the administration of the law. Financial problems and falling rolls also made the inns willing to accept the practical erosion of the formal qualifications prescribed for admission to the bar, so that country gentlemen who had no intention of practising the law were encouraged to acquire the status of a barrister, and 'the degree of the utter bar' became less synonymous with the practising bar itself. These qualifications became increasingly irrelevant to the real business of becoming a lawyer, just as the empty forms which survived the parallel decay of readings and moots had no bearing on legal education in a real sense. By 1730, many counsellors and law students must have been members of their societies in a formal way only: their professional activities were separate from the remnants of those customs and traditions which had moulded the minds and bounded the actions of their predecessors.

The regime of the inns of court had developed in response to the requirements of medieval England and the lawyers who serviced it. By 1700 at least, the structure of a medieval guild organization was inappropriate to the demands of a society which was experiencing rapid economic change in the context of free market capitalism.

Indeed, it was a check to individual enterprise. Enterprise and initiative were essential to survive and prosper in a world where the general conditions of life and work were changing with bewildering rapidity, and where the aggregate of business available for barristers in particular was diminishing. The evidence suggests that the bar experienced an invigorating purge. In 1720 it was leaner, fitter, more professional, and more respected than it had been in 1680. It is surely no coincidence that the bar was now less firmly attached to the inns of court, and to that other feature of the profession's ancient structure, the order of serjeants at law. Those lawyers who were equipped to prosper in the challenging environment of the early eighteenth century were not likely to be men whose outlook had been narrowed by a career immersed in the enervating atmosphere of the legal inns; rather they tended to be individualists who were most active elsewhere—for example among politicians in the House of Commons or business men in the City of London. They were successful because they were attuned to their times and flexible enough to respond to them, and they gained wealth and preferment at the expense of lawyers cast in a more traditional mould, who languished as benchers and serjeants in their empty fiefdoms of the inns of court and the court of Common Pleas.

The evidence presented in this book suggests that the inns decayed because the logic of the market (economic *and* political) insisted that the dynamic elements of the English bar should be separate from its ancient institutions, and the profession's centre of gravity shifted accordingly. Progressively liberated from the restrictions of the inns and the coif, by 1730 the bar should have been in a position to play a full part in the creation of the new world which was opening up before English men and women. Moreover, its potential role was not limited to meeting the demand for legal services. Practice as a barrister was also important as a career which might absorb the energies and ambitions of men who sprang from the expanding sectors of society. And entry to the élite of Hanoverian England was truly 'open' for those who were able to take advantage of the opportunities available. Thus, at the same time as the bar seemed to be adapting itself to the requirements of a society moving towards industrialization, the profession was equipped to operate as a career open to the talents which might absorb some of the social pressures engendered by that momentous change. Another book will have to be written before it is possible to say how far the eighteenth-century barristers fulfilled the potential manifested by their Augustan predecessors.

APPENDIX I. Minimum qualifications prescribed for the bar, 1680–1730

All inns (judges' orders of 1664 and statutes)

Standing:	7 years.
Exercises:	to have kept the exercises in the house and at the inns of chancery.
Commons:	to have been frequently in commons according to the orders of the house.
Oaths:	to take the oath of supremacy (1563); to take the oaths of allegiance and supremacy (1689).

Gray's Inn

Standing:	7 years, allowing up to 2 years for time spent at Staple Inn or Barnard's Inn.
Exercises:	6 grand moots in the house and 3 at the inns of chancery, plus certain exercises after call.
Commons:	5 years, being 2 weeks in every term (including the grand weeks) and 4 weeks in every long vacation.
Chamber:	to be admitted to a chamber in the house, or to deposit £50 in lieu (example of 1692), or £20 in lieu (from 1725). Not to assign the chamber for at least 5 years after call (from 1690).
Sacrament:	to produce a certificate of having received the sacrament in the chapel during the term when called.
Oaths:	to take the oaths of allegiance and supremacy upon publication.
Payments:	to pay all outstanding duties and give a new bond.
Attorneys and solicitors:	no person to be called who has practised as an attorney or solicitor within the previous 5 years.

Inner Temple

Standing:	7 years.
Exercises:	8 grand moots at the inns of chancery, and such other exercise 'as they ought to performe' (1664); several grand moots, petty moots, library moots, clerks' commons cases and imparlances (1665); 1 imparlance, 1 library moot, 6 petty moots, 6 clerks' commons cases, and, in case of 'Grand Readings', 4 grand moots (1683); 2 imparlances, 2 library moots, 6 petty moots, 4 clerks' commons cases (c.1687); 1 imparlance, 1 library

moot, and a 'competent number' of other exercises (1699); 1 imparlance, 2 library moots, 6 petty moots, 4 clerks' commons cases (1709); 1 imparlance, 2 library moots, 6 clerks' commons cases (1736 and 1738).

Commons: 4 years, being 2 weeks in each term, or (by 1709) to pay 30*s.* for each term lacking; plus 4 vacations (excepting those specially admitted).

Chamber: to have a chamber in the house or to deposit £20 as a caution to buy one. ? To be retained for 3 years after call (proposal of 1733).

Sacrament: to have received the sacrament before being sworn a barrister.

Oaths: to take the oaths of supremacy and allegiance.

Payments: to pay all duties and enter into a new bond.

Attorneys and
solicitors: no practising attorneys or solicitors to be called.

Lincoln's Inn

Standing: 7 years, allowing up to 2 years for time spent at an inn of chancery.

Exercises: at least 4 moots (1678); 4 bolts besides other exercises (1699); also a 'bar moot' upon call.

Commons: unspecified continuance in commons; to keep under-bar vacations.

Chamber: to be admitted into a chamber (or part of a chamber) in the house, or to deposit £20 in lieu of having a chamber.

Sacrament: to receive the sacrament before publication.

Payments: to pay all duties and to enter into a new bond.

Attorneys and
solicitors: no practising attorneys or solicitors to be called.

Middle Temple

Standing: 7 years (1660); 6 years (1682); 7 years (1689); 6 years (1710, 1719, 1726, and 1733). Up to 2 years allowed for time spent at an inn of chancery.

Exercises: 4, of which 3 at least were to be performed in the house (1660); 15 exercises in the house and at the inns of chancery (1671); 8 exercises, of which 4 were to be performed in the house (1673, 1689); 8 exercises, of which 2 were to be performed at New Inn (1699, 1708); 9 exercises, including 2 at New Inn (1733). Junior barristers to perform a number of 'assignments' after call. The sons of benchers were excused from all obligations of exercise.

Commons: to have been in commons for 2 years before call, being 2 weeks in each term, plus 1 vacation. Benchers' sons excused from all these obligations.

Chamber:	to have a chamber in the house or to give a deposit (examples of £50 and £100) in lieu.
Sacrament:	to present a certificate of having received the sacrament in the Temple Church during the year preceding call (1667); to present a certificate of having received the sacrament 'in some protestant Congregation' (1694); to present a certificate of having received the sacrament in the Temple Church and in no other place (1726).
Oaths:	to take the oaths of supremacy and allegiance upon publication.
Payments:	to pay all outstanding duties.
Attorneys and solicitors:	to have discontinued practice as an attorney or solicitor for 7 years before call (1679, 1704); besides attornies and solicitors, no clerks in the chancery or clerks and attornies of the exchequer, to be called to the bar (1707).

Sources: all inns: Richardson, *History of the Inns of Court*, p. 450; 5 Eliz., c. 1; 1 Wm. & M., c. 8. Gray's Inn: BL., Harleian MSS 1912, fo. 237; GI, MS Orders i, fos. 537, 543, 545, ii. 43, 58–9, 67, 141–2, 164, 175–6, 210, 291, 295, 302, 329, 641, 646, 691. Inner Temple: IT, MS Acts 1638–64, fos. 146, 175–7; ibid., MS Acts 1665–87, fos. 8, 26, 32, 45, 51, 86, 119, 125, 131–2; ibid., MS Orders 1685–91, fos. 35, 67, 81–2, 94, 112; ibid., MS Orders 1691–8, fos. 22, 106; ibid., MS Orders 1699–1714, fos. 2–4, 6, 8, 10, 23, 31, 39, 61; ibid., MS Orders 1715–33, fo. 129; ibid., MS Miscellanea ii, fos. 40, 130, xxiv, fos. 114–15, xxviii, fo. 3, xxix, fo. 11; *CITR* iii. 260, 296, iv. 382. Lincoln's Inn: LI, MS Black Book viii, fos. 671, 730, ix, fos. 26, 49, 90, 95, 170, 179, 206, 226–7, 230–1, 234, 236, 244, 316, 325, x, fos. 16–17, 85, xi. 245, 301; *LIBB* iii, pp. iii–iv. Middle Temple: MT, MS Orders E5, 22, 37–8, 100, 118–19, 137, 139, 160–1, 174, 180, 193, 199, 216, 284, 296, 298, 316, 321, 325–6, 354, 361, 365, 370, 397, 403, 406, 460, 463, 473–4, 488–9, H(8), 3, 25, 28–9, 31, 39, 127, 254, 297; IT, MS Miscellanea xxiv, fos. 117–18, xxviii, fo. 7, xxix, fo. 35; *Master Worsley's Book*, pp. 131–6; Downing, *Observations on the Middle Temple*, p. 79.

APPENDIX II. The practising bar: sources and methodology of quantification

In order to understand the nature and significance of the quantitative analysis of practising counsel for the sample years of 1680 and 1720, it is necessary here to describe the sources used and the methodology applied. The primary sources from which the information was derived were the records of the central courts as they are preserved in the Public Record Office, together with rough minutes of proceedings in the House of Lords during these years.[1] For the King's Bench and Exchequer, the documents used were the rule or order books and minute books: these consist in the main of interlocutory orders made upon the motion of named counsel appearing before the court, although the minute books also include applications to the court which were unsuccessful, in that they led to no order.[2] In the case of the Common Pleas, recourse was had to the remembrance rolls of the prothonotaries, or chief clerks, from which the bills of pleas provided records of interlocutory orders, together with the names of the serjeants who moved them.[3] The sources used for the analysis of the Chancery and House of Lords were of a slightly different nature; because of the sheer bulk of the entry book of decrees and orders it was necessary to utilize the registers' minute books, which are rough records of day to day proceedings in the equity side of the chancellor's court, including the name of counsel who participated.[4] The manuscript minute books of the House of Lords provided similar information with regard to the appearances of counsel in appeals and writs of error to the peers.[5]

The surnames of counsel found in the records signify the motions or speeches they made on behalf of litigants. Bearing this in mind, the records which have been specified were examined for all proceedings which took place between 1 January and 31 December for both 1680 and 1720, and for each court the surnames of counsel were extracted, together with the number of

---

[1] I am most grateful to Professor J. H. Baker for his kind advice on the subject of the legal records in the PRO.

[2] PRO, KB21 (KB crown side rule or order books), supplemented with PRO, KB36 (rough drafts of KB crown side rule or order books); PRO, KB125 (KB plea side entry books of rules); PRO, E11 (Exchequer of pleas minute books), checked against PRO, E12 (Exchequer of pleas order books); PRO, E161 (Exchequer king's remembrancer common minute books), supplemented with PRO, E127 (Exchequer king's remembrancer order books).

[3] PRO, CP45 (Common Pleas remembrance rolls).

[4] PRO, C37 (Chancery registers' minute books). The entry books of decrees and orders are at PRO, C33.

[5] HLRO, MS Minutes, HL.

times each occurred. Repeated motions or speeches made by counsel at the same hearing were not counted separately. The cumulative totals of nominations therefore represent an aggregate of distinct appearances made by individual counsel at each bar. Of course they do not represent the number of cases for which each barrister was retained, because many cases would have involved separate motions or arguments over many weeks and months of the year. However, advocacy was remunerated on the basis of individual appearances, and it seems reasonable to suggest that data of this nature do crudely reflect the work-load of each barrister, in terms of court work only, during each of the sample years. Moreover, although the correlation between the frequency of appearances in court and professional success was not exact, the work-load of a barrister was naturally a concomitant of his eminence at the bar. Indeed, comparison between the lists of the most active barristers in 1680 and 1720 and the published law reports for those years shows that the great counsel of the day were indeed those most frequently named in the original records, and these men have therefore been designated as the leaders of the bar.[6]

For the individual courts, it may be assumed that a surname which occurs several times represents the same barrister, because the clerks generally entered an initial when two or more men of the same surname appeared at the bar. Thus the data collected are adequate to fulfil at least one of the aims of the exercise: to estimate the number of barristers appearing at each individual bar and to assess the distribution of business among them during the two years in question. The other objective of the exercise was to gauge the size of the *total* Westminster bar for each sample, and to adumbrate some of the characteristics of the collective body of practitioners. For this purpose the surnames extracted were checked against the admissions registers and benchers' minutes of the four inns, in order to identify them and to establish the vital facts with regard to background and career.[7] It should be said that twenty-one names were found for 1680, and twenty-four for 1720, which could not be traced among the records of persons who had been called to the bar during the relevant period. These represent 4.7 per cent and 6.6 per cent respectively of the total number of names found for each sample year. There are various possible explanations for the anomaly: on the one hand, the names may have been original errors made by the clerks, who cannot have been infallible, or they may be slips on the part of the researcher, who is no less subject to human error. More interestingly, it may be that records of calls to the bar were not complete during the period covered by this study, or it is even possible that some judges deviated from the convention that only barristers might appear as

---

[6] See Apps. III–X below. *The English Reports* (1900–30), i, ii, iii, lxxxiii, lxxxiv, lxxxvi, lxxxviii, lxxxix, xcii, xciii, cxlv, all *passim* for 1 Jan.–31 Dec. 1680/1720.

[7] *GIPB* i, ii; *GI Adm. Reg.*; *CITR* ii, iii, iv; *IT Adm. Reg.*, i, ii; *LIBB* ii, iii; *LI Adm. Reg.*, i; *MTR* ii, iii; *MT Adm. Reg.*, i. Serjeants and future judges were identified via Baker, *Serjeants*, Foss, *Judges*, vii, viii.

advocates before them. It should be remembered that the monopoly of advocacy in the central courts which barristers of the inns of court enjoyed was a comparatively recent innovation, and it is certainly true that mere attorneys were heard at the side bars of the common law courts.[8]

In the absence of any proof as to the authenticity of the attributed names, they have been excluded from the entire analysis, along with Dr Henchman, the civilian, who was heard in Chancery in 1720, and two Scots advocates who appeared in the House of Lords during the same year. This leaves 424 names for 1680 and 338 for 1720 which have been traced among the lists of men called to the bar at the inns. Unfortunately, these can be regarded only as *minimum* figures for the size of the total bar in each case. Since the records of the courts invariably give only the *surnames* of counsel, it has not been possible to identify all the names, and a 'Mr Smith' which occurs several times in the records of *different* courts might represent more than one barrister.[9] However, it is doubtful if the underestimate is a serious one, and the figures remain useful for the purposes of assessing changes in the size of the bar between 1680 and 1720, because it can be assumed that the multiplication factor for common names remained a constant. More seriously, the large proportion of unidentified names does devalue some of the statistics which relate to social origins and the other characteristics of practising barristers, because the sample of men which has been identified is not strictly random. On the other hand, there is no reason to believe that these men were not representative of the bar in general, for they have been identified only because their names were not common among the lists of men called to the bar during the period. Like most exercises in historical quantification, there are problems in the processing and interpretation of this data, because it involves using ancient records for a purpose quite different from their original function, but, if used critically, they may make a useful contribution to our understanding of the early modern bar.

[8] See above, p. 5, BL, Add. MSS 32510, fos. 85–6; *Lives of the Norths*, i. 132–3, iii. 104–5.

[9] First names or first initials are only given for barristers of the same surname appearing in the same court, together with the law officers, the recorder/common serjeant of London, and knights or baronets.

APPENDIX III. King's Bench (crown side) bar:
dimensions and distribution of business, 1680 and 1720

1680

No. of barristers			No. of appearances per barrister	Total appearances		
No.	%	Cum%		No.	%	Cum%
1	0.6	99.7	44	44	5.6	100.0
1	0.6	99.1	42	42	5.4	94.4
1	0.6	98.5	39	39	5.0	89.0
1	0.6	97.9	32	32	4.1	84.0
1	0.6	97.3	30	30	3.8	79.9
1	0.6	96.7	29	29	3.7	76.1
1	0.6	96.1	27	27	3.5	72.4
1	0.6	95.5	24	24	3.1	68.9
1	0.6	94.9	17	17	2.2	65.8
1	0.6	94.3	16	16	2.0	63.6
2	1.2	93.7	13	26	3.3	61.6
3	1.8	92.5	12	36	4.6	58.3
2	1.2	90.7	11	22	2.8	53.7
3	1.8	89.5	10	30	3.8	50.9
3	1.8	87.7	9	27	3.5	47.1
3	1.8	85.9	8	24	3.1	43.6
5	3.0	84.1	7	35	4.5	40.5
4	2.4	81.1	6	24	3.1	36.0
11	6.7	78.7	5	55	7.0	32.9
7	4.3	72.0	4	28	3.6	25.9
20	12.2	67.7	3	60	7.7	22.3
23	14.0	55.5	2	46	5.9	14.6
68	41.5	41.5	1	68	8.7	8.7
164[a]	100			781	100	

[a] 38.7% of minimum bar.

Leaders, 1680

44 [? Sir William] Jones (GI)
42 [Henry] Pollexfen (IT)
39 [William] Scroggs [jun.] (GI)
32 [Sir Creswell Levinz] AG (GI)
30 [Edmund] Saunders (MT)

29 [John] Holt (GI)
27 Sir George Jeffreys
(king's serjeant)
24 [William] Williams (GI)

1720

No. of barristers			No. of appearances per barrister	Total appearances		
No.	%	Cum%		No.	%	Cum%
1	0.8	99.5	38	38	6.9	100.0
1	0.8	98.7	31	31	5.7	93.1
1	0.8	97.9	21	21	3.8	87.4
1	0.8	97.1	20	20	3.7	83.6
1	0.8	96.3	18	18	3.3	79.9
1	0.8	95.5	15	15	2.7	76.6
1	0.8	94.7	14	14	2.6	73.9
2	1.7	93.9	13	26	4.7	71.3
1	0.8	92.2	11	11	2.0	66.6
2	1.7	91.4	10	20	3.7	64.6
5	4.3	89.7	9	45	8.2	60.9
1	0.8	85.4	8	8	1.5	52.7
6	5.1	84.6	7	42	7.7	51.2
9	7.7	79.5	6	54	9.9	43.5
7	6.0	71.8	5	35	6.4	33.6
7	6.0	65.8	4	28	5.1	27.2
11	9.4	59.8	3	33	6.0	22.1
29	24.8	50.4	2	58	10.6	16.1
30	25.6	25.6	1	30	5.5	5.5
117[b]	100			547	100	

[b] 34.6% of minimum bar.

Leaders, 1720

38 [Thomas] Reeve KC (MT)
31 [Nicholas] Fazackerley (IT)
23 [Clement] Wearg (IT)
20 [Sir Thomas] Pengelly
(king's serjeant)

18 [John] Darnell (serjeant)
15 [John] Baines (IT)
14 [Edward] Corbett (LI)
13 [Abel] Ketelby (MT)

Sources: As specified in Appendix II.

APPENDIX IV. King's Bench (plea side) bar: dimensions and distribution of business, 1680 and 1720

1680						
No. of barristers			No. of appearances per barrister	Total appearances		
No.	%	Cum%		No.	%	Cum%
1	0.4	100.0	110	110	5.3	99.8
1	0.4	99.6	96	96	4.6	94.5
2	0.8	99.2	84	168	8.0	89.9
1	0.4	98.4	81	81	3.9	81.9
1	0.4	98.0	80	80	3.8	78.0
1	0.4	97.6	60	60	2.9	74.2
1	0.4	97.2	50	50	2.4	71.3
1	0.4	96.8	46	46	2.2	68.9
1	0.4	96.4	45	45	2.1	66.7
1	0.4	96.0	28	28	1.3	64.6
1	0.4	95.6	27	27	1.3	63.3
1	0.4	95.2	26	26	1.2	62.0
2	0.8	94.8	25	50	2.4	60.8
2	0.8	94.0	22	44	2.1	58.4
1	0.4	93.2	21	21	1.0	56.3
2	0.8	92.8	20	40	1.9	55.3
2	0.8	92.0	19	38	1.8	53.4
5	1.9	91.1	18	90	4.3	51.6
3	1.2	89.2	17	51	2.4	47.3
2	0.8	88.0	16	32	1.5	44.9
5	1.9	87.2	15	75	3.6	43.4
5	1.9	85.3	14	70	3.3	39.8
1	0.4	83.4	13	13	0.6	36.5
5	1.9	83.0	12	60	2.9	35.9
4	1.6	81.1	11	44	2.1	33.0
6	2.3	79.5	10	60	2.9	30.9

1680

No. of barristers			No. of appearances per barrister	Total appearances		
No.	%	Cum%		No.	%	Cum%
5	1.9	77.2	9	45	2.1	28.0
7	2.7	75.3	8	56	2.7	25.9
7	2.7	72.6	7	49	2.3	23.2
11	4.3	69.9	6	66	3.2	20.9
19	7.4	65.6	5	95	4.5	17.7
15	5.9	58.2	4	60	2.9	13.2
18	7.0	52.3	3	54	2.6	10.3
45	17.6	45.3	2	90	4.3	7.7
71	27.7	27.7	1	71	3.4	3.4
256[a]	100			2091	100	

Leaders, 1680
110 [Edmund] Saunders (MT)
 96 [William] Thompson (MT)
 84 Sir George Jeffreys (king's serjeant)
 81 [John] Holt (GI)
 80 [John] Tremaine (IT)
 60 [Charles] Bonython (GI)

1720

No. of barristers			No. of appearances per barrister	Total appearances		
No.	%	Cum%		No.	%	Cum%
2	12.0	100.3	68	136	1.2	100.0
1	4.8	99.1	55	55	0.6	88.0
1	4.5	98.5	51	51	0.6	83.2
1	4.0	97.9	45	45	0.6	78.7
1	3.7	97.3	42	42	0.6	74.7
1	3.4	96.7	39	39	0.6	71.0
1	3.3	96.1	37	37	0.6	67.6
1	2.8	95.5	32	32	0.6	64.3
1	2.5	94.9	28	28	0.6	61.5
1	2.1	94.3	24	24	0.6	59.0
2	3.5	93.7	20	40	1.2	56.9
1	1.7	92.5	19	19	0.6	53.4
1	1.5	91.9	17	17	0.6	51.7
1	1.3	91.3	15	15	0.6	50.2
1	1.2	90.7	14	14	0.6	48.9
2	2.3	90.1	13	26	1.2	47.7
2	2.1	88.9	12	24	1.2	45.4
7	6.8	87.7	11	77	4.1	43.3
2	1.8	83.6	10	20	1.2	36.5
2	1.6	82.4	9	18	1.2	34.7
10	7.0	81.2	8	80	5.8	33.1
3	1.8	75.4	7	21	1.7	26.1
4	2.1	73.7	6	24	2.3	24.3
10	4.4	71.4	5	50	5.8	22.2
12	4.2	65.6	4	48	7.0	17.8
14	3.7	58.6	3	42	8.1	13.6
25	14.5	50.5	2	50	4.4	9.9
62	36.0	36.0	1	62	5.5	5.5
172[b]	100			1136	100	

[a] 60.4% of minimum bar.
[b] 50.9% of minimum bar.

Leaders, 1720
68 [John] Baines (IT)
68 [Clement] Wearg (IT)
55 [Nicholas] Fazackerley (IT)
51 [Edward] Whittaker (serjeant)
45 [William] Branthwaite (serjeant)
42 [Abel] Ketelby (MT)

Sources: As specified in Appendix II.

APPENDIX V. Exchequer (plea side) bar: dimensions and distribution of business, 1680 and 1720

1680

No. of barristers			No. of appearances per barrister	Total appearances		
No.	%	Cum%		No.	%	Cum%
1	1.0	99.6	69	69	11.7	100.0
1	1.0	98.6	59	59	10.0	88.3
1	1.0	97.6	47	47	8.0	78.3
1	1.0	96.6	36	36	6.1	70.3
1	1.0	95.6	32	32	5.4	64.2
1	1.0	94.6	26	26	4.4	58.8
1	1.0	93.6	25	25	4.2	54.4
2	2.1	92.6	22	44	7.5	50.2
2	2.1	90.5	18	36	6.1	42.7
2	2.1	88.4	12	24	4.1	36.6
1	1.0	86.3	11	11	1.9	32.5
3	3.1	85.3	8	24	4.1	30.6
3	3.1	82.2	6	18	3.1	26.5
2	2.1	79.1	5	10	1.7	23.4
6	6.2	77.0	4	24	4.1	21.7
10	10.4	70.8	3	30	5.1	17.6
16	16.7	60.4	2	32	5.4	12.5
42	43.7	43.7	1	42	7.1	7.1
96[a]	100			589	100	

[a] 22.6% of minimum bar.

Leaders, 1680

69 [Giles or Francis] Duncombe (IT)
59 [Edward] Ward (IT)
47 [William] Williams (GI)
36 Sir Robert Sawyer KC (IT)

32 [William] Wogan (GI)
26 —— Powell (—)
26 [Anthony or William] Ettricke (MT)

1720

No. of barristers			No. of appearances per barrister	Total appearances		
No.	%	Cum%		No.	%	Cum%
1	2.3	100.1	95	95	30.4	99.9
1	2.3	97.8	22	22	7.0	69.5
1	2.3	95.5	16	16	5.1	62.5
2	4.5	93.2	15	30	9.6	57.4
1	2.3	88.7	14	14	4.5	47.8
1	2.3	86.4	12	12	3.8	43.3
1	2.3	84.1	11	11	3.5	39.5
2	4.5	81.8	9	18	5.7	36.0
2	4.5	77.3	8	16	5.1	30.3
1	2.3	72.8	7	7	2.2	25.2
1	2.3	70.5	6	6	1.9	23.0
4	9.1	68.2	5	20	6.4	21.1
4	9.1	59.1	3	12	3.8	14.7
12	27.3	50.0	2	24	7.7	10.9
10	22.7	22.7	1	10	3.2	3.2
44[b]	100			313	100	

[b] 13.0% of minimum bar.

Leaders, 1720
95 [Thomas] Bootle (IT)
22 [Maurice or Thomas] Lewis (MT)
16 Sir Constantine Phipps (MT)
15 [William] Bunbury (IT)
15 —— Owen (—)

Sources: As specified in Appendix II.

APPENDIX VI. Exchequer (equity side) bar: dimensions and distribution of business, 1680 and 1720

1680

No. of barristers			No. of appearances per barrister	Total appearances		
No.	%	Cum%		No.	%	Cum%
1	0.6	100.0	311	311	19.2	100.1
1	0.6	99.4	173	173	10.7	80.9
1	0.6	98.8	170	170	10.5	70.2
1	0.6	98.2	94	94	5.8	59.7
1	0.6	97.6	66	66	4.1	53.9
1	0.6	97.0	61	61	3.8	49.8
1	0.6	96.4	58	58	3.6	46.0
1	0.6	95.8	47	47	2.9	42.4
1	0.6	95.2	41	41	2.5	39.5
1	0.6	94.6	34	34	2.1	37.0
1	0.6	94.0	28	28	1.7	34.9
2	1.2	93.4	23	46	2.8	33.2
1	0.6	92.2	19	19	1.2	30.4
1	0.6	91.6	18	18	1.1	29.2
1	0.6	91.0	14	14	0.9	28.1
4	2.3	90.4	12	48	3.0	27.2
1	0.6	88.1	11	11	0.7	24.2
5	2.9	87.5	9	45	2.8	23.2
4	2.3	84.6	8	32	2.0	20.7
5	2.9	82.3	6	30	1.8	18.7
7	4.1	79.4	5	35	2.2	16.9
12	7.1	75.3	4	48	3.0	14.7
24	14.1	68.2	3	72	4.4	11.7
28	16.5	54.1	2	56	3.4	7.3
64	37.6	37.6	1	64	3.9	3.9
170[a]	100			1621	100	

[a] 40.1% of minimum bar.

Leaders, 1680

311 [Edward] Ward (IT)
173 [Thomas] Jenner (IT)
170 Sir Robert Sawyer KC (IT)
 94 [Nicholas] Lechmere (MT)
 66 —— Smith (—)
 61 [Henry] Montague (MT)

1720

No. of barristers			No. of appearances per barrister	Total appearances		
No.	%	Cum%		No.	%	Cum%
1	0.7	99.8	200	200	11.2	100.0
1	0.7	98.9	168	168	9.4	88.8
1	0.7	98.2	166	166	9.3	79.4
1	0.7	97.5	162	162	9.1	70.1
1	0.7	96.8	138	138	7.8	61.0
1	0.7	96.1	100	100	5.6	53.2
1	0.7	95.4	90	90	5.1	47.6
1	0.7	94.7	55	55	3.1	42.5
1	0.7	94.0	44	44	2.5	39.4
1	0.7	93.3	43	43	2.4	36.9
1	0.7	92.6	37	37	2.1	34.5
1	0.7	91.9	33	33	2.0	32.4
2	1.4	91.2	27	54	3.0	30.4
1	0.7	89.8	26	26	1.5	27.4
1	0.7	89.1	21	21	1.2	25.9
1	0.7	88.4	20	20	1.1	24.7
1	0.7	87.7	19	19	1.1	23.6
1	0.7	87.0	15	15	0.8	22.5
1	0.7	86.3	14	14	0.8	21.7
4	2.8	85.6	12	48	2.7	20.9
1	0.7	82.8	11	11	0.6	18.2
1	0.7	82.1	10	10	0.6	17.6
4	2.8	81.4	9	36	2.0	17.0
3	2.1	78.6	8	24	1.3	15.0
4	2.8	76.5	7	28	1.6	13.7
3	2.1	73.7	6	18	1.0	12.1
7	5.0	71.6	5	35	2.0	11.1
5	3.5	66.6	4	20	1.1	9.1
10	7.1	63.1	3	30	1.7	8.0
33	23.4	56.0	2	66	3.7	6.3
46	32.6	32.6	1	46	2.6	2.6
141[b]	100			1777	100	

[b] 41.7% of minimum bar.

Leaders, 1720

200 Sir Constantine Phipps (MT)

168 [Thomas] Bootle (IT)

166 [?Paul] Foley (LI)

162 [John] Brown (LI)

138 [?John] Ward (?IT)

100 [Henry] Stephens (serjeant)

Sources: As specified in Appendix II.

APPENDIX VII. Common Pleas bar: dimensions and distribution of business, 1680 and 1720

1680

No. of serjeants			No. of appearances per serjeant	Total appearances		
No.	%	Cum%		No.	%	Cum%
1	2.8	99.8	226	226	12.9	99.9
1	2.8	97.0	151	151	8.6	87.0
1	2.8	94.2	131	131	7.5	78.4
1	2.8	91.4	129	129	7.4	70.9
1	2.8	88.6	113	113	6.5	63.5
1	2.8	85.6	94	94	5.4	57.0
1	2.8	83.0	86	86	4.9	51.6
1	2.8	80.2	65	65	3.7	46.7
1	2.8	77.4	53	53	3.0	43.0
1	2.8	74.6	48	48	2.7	40.0
1	2.8	71.8	47	47	2.7	37.3
1	2.8	69.0	45	45	2.6	34.6
1	2.8	66.2	44	44	2.5	32.0
1	2.8	63.4	43	43	2.5	29.5
2	5.5	60.6	42	84	4.8	27.0
1	2.8	55.1	40	40	2.3	22.2
2	5.5	52.3	39	78	4.5	19.9
1	2.8	46.8	35	35	2.0	15.4
1	2.8	44.0	32	32	1.8	13.4
1	2.8	41.2	23	23	1.3	11.6
1	2.8	38.4	22	22	1.3	10.3
1	2.8	35.6	19	19	1.1	9.0
1	2.8	32.8	18	18	1.0	7.9
1	2.8	30.0	15	15	0.9	6.9
4	11.1	27.8	14	56	3.2	6.0
1	2.8	16.7	12	12	0.7	2.8
2	5.5	13.9	10	20	1.1	2.1

1680

No. of serjeants			No. of appearances per serjeant	Total appearances		
No.	%	Cum%		No.	%	Cum%
1	2.8	8.4	8	8	0.5	1.0
1	2.8	5.6	5	5	0.3	0.5
1	2.8	2.8	4	4	0.2	0.2
36[a]	100			1746	100	

[a] 8.5% of minimum bar.

Leaders, 1680
226 [Sir] G[eorge] Strode (king's serjeant)
151 [Samuel] Baldwyn (serjeant)
131 T[homas] Strode (serjeant)
129 [Sir Thomas] Stringer (king's serjeant)
113 [Sir Francis] Pemberton (serjeant)

1720

No. of serjeants			No. of appearances per serjeant	Total appearances		
No.	%	Cum%		No.	%	Cum%
1	3.8	99.1	213	213	12.8	99.8
1	3.8	95.3	180	180	10.3	87.6
1	3.8	91.5	147	147	8.4	77.3
1	3.8	87.7	122	122	7.0	68.9
2	7.7	83.9	117	234	13.4	61.9
1	3.8	76.2	113	113	6.5	48.5
1	3.8	72.4	111	111	6.3	42.0
1	3.8	68.6	109	109	6.2	35.7
1	3.8	64.8	94	94	5.4	29.5
1	3.8	61.0	74	74	4.2	24.1
1	3.8	57.2	72	72	4.1	19.9
1	3.8	53.4	63	63	3.6	15.8
1	3.8	49.6	53	53	3.0	12.2
1	3.8	45.8	44	44	2.5	9.2
1	3.8	42.0	42	42	2.4	6.7
1	3.8	38.2	33	33	1.9	4.3
1	3.8	34.4	13	13	0.7	2.4
1	3.8	30.6	9	9	0.5	1.7
1	3.8	26.8	7	7	0.4	1.2
1	3.8	23.0	6	6	0.3	0.8
1	3.8	19.2	3	3	0.2	0.5
2	7.7	15.4	2	4	0.2	0.3
2	7.7	7.7	1	2	0.1	0.1
26[b]	100			1747	100	

[b] 7.7% of minimum bar.

Leaders, 1720

213 [James] Grove (serjeant)
180 [James] Selby (serjeant)
147 [Sir John] Cheshire
      (king's serjeant)

122 [William] Branthwaite (serjeant)
117 [John] Comyns (serjeant)
117 [William] Hall (serjeant)

Sources: As specified in Appendix II.

APPENDIX VIII. House of Lords bar: dimensions and distribution of business, 1680 and 1720

1680

No. of barristers			No. of appearances per barrister	Total appearances		
No.	%	Cum%		No.	%	Cum%
1	4.2	100.0	11	11	14.3	100.0
2	8.3	95.8	8	16	20.3	85.8
3	12.5	87.5	6	18	23.4	65.0
1	4.2	75.0	4	4	5.2	41.6
2	8.3	70.8	3	6	7.8	36.4
7	29.2	62.5	2	14	18.2	28.6
8	33.3	33.3	1	8	10.4	10.4
24[a]	100			77	100	

[a] 5.7% of minimum bar.

Leaders, 1680
11 [Charles] Porter (MT)
 8 Sir John Churchill KC (LI)
 8 [George] Hutchins (GI)
 6 [Hon. Heneage Finch] SG (IT)
 6 [Ambrose] Phillips (IT)
 6 Sir Robert Sawyer KC (IT)

1720

No. of barristers			No. of appearances per barrister	Total appearances		
No.	%	Cum%		No.	%	Cum%
I	4.8	100.4	35	35	23.3	99.8
I	4.8	95.6	23	23	15.3	76.5
I	4.8	90.8	19	19	12.7	61.2
I	4.8	86.0	14	14	9.3	48.5
I	4.8	81.2	9	9	6.0	39.2
I	4.8	76.4	8	8	5.3	33.2
2	9.5	71.6	7	14	9.3	27.9
I	4.8	62.1	6	6	4.0	18.6
I	4.8	57.3	5	5	3.3	14.6
I	4.8	52.5	4	4	2.7	11.3
I	4.8	47.7	3	3	2.0	8.6
I	4.8	42.9	2	2	1.3	6.6
8	38.1	38.1	I	8	5.3	5.3
21[b]	100			150	100	

[b] 6.2% of minimum bar.

Leaders, 1720
35 Sir Robert Raymond (GI)
23 [Samuel] Mead (LI)
19 Sir Constantine Phipps (MT)
14 [William] Hamilton (LI)
9 [Thomas] Lutwyche KC (IT)
8 [Spencer] Cowper KC (LI)

Sources: As specified in Appendix II.

APPENDIX IX: Chancery bar: dimensions and distribution of business, 1680

No. of barristers			No. of appearances per barrister	Total appearances		
No.	%	Cum%		No.	%	Cum%
1	0.34	99.87	1197	1197	9.64	99.98
1	0.34	99.53	997	997	8.03	90.34
1	0.34	99.19	836	836	6.73	82.31
1	0.34	98.85	766	766	6.17	75.58
1	0.34	98.51	648	648	5.22	69.41
1	0.34	98.17	609	609	4.90	64.19
1	0.34	97.83	576	576	4.64	59.29
1	0.34	97.49	538	538	4.33	54.65
1	0.34	97.15	458	458	3.69	50.32
1	0.34	96.81	397	397	3.20	46.63
1	0.34	96.47	366	366	2.95	43.43
1	0.34	96.13	262	262	2.11	40.48
1	0.34	95.79	258	258	2.08	38.37
1	0.34	95.45	228	228	1.84	36.29
1	0.34	95.11	225	225	1.81	34.45
1	0.34	94.77	179	179	1.44	32.64
1	0.34	94.43	148	148	1.19	31.20
1	0.34	94.09	138	138	1.11	30.01
1	0.34	93.75	122	122	0.98	28.90
1	0.34	93.41	120	120	0.97	27.92
1	0.34	93.07	119	119	0.96	26.95
1	0.34	92.73	102	102	0.82	25.99
1	0.34	92.39	95	95	0.76	25.19
1	0.34	92.05	83	83	0.67	24.41
2	0.69	91.71	81	162	1.30	23.74
1	0.34	91.02	78	78	0.63	22.44
1	0.34	90.68	74	74	0.60	21.81
1	0.34	90.34	73	73	0.59	21.21

No. of barristers			No. of appearances per barrister	Total appearances		
No.	%	Cum%		No.	%	Cum%
2	0.69	90.00	71	142	1.14	20.62
1	0.34	89.31	69	69	0.55	19.48
1	0.34	88.97	67	67	0.54	18.93
1	0.34	88.63	63	63	0.51	18.39
1	0.34	88.29	61	61	0.49	17.88
1	0.34	87.95	60	60	0.48	17.39
1	0.34	87.61	58	58	0.47	16.91
2	0.69	87.27	51	102	0.82	16.44
1	0.34	86.58	49	49	0.39	15.62
1	0.34	86.24	48	48	0.39	15.23
2	0.69	85.90	44	88	0.71	14.84
2	0.69	85.21	43	86	0.69	14.13
1	0.34	84.52	41	41	0.33	13.44
2	0.69	84.18	40	80	0.64	13.11
1	0.34	83.49	39	39	0.31	12.47
1	0.34	83.15	37	37	0.30	12.16
1	0.34	82.81	36	36	0.29	11.86
2	0.69	82.47	35	70	0.56	11.57
1	0.34	81.78	34	34	0.27	11.01
1	0.34	81.44	32	32	0.26	10.74
1	0.34	81.10	31	31	0.25	10.48
1	0.34	80.76	29	29	0.23	10.23
2	0.69	80.42	26	52	0.42	10.00
1	0.34	79.93	23	23	0.19	9.58
2	0.69	79.39	21	42	0.34	9.39
3	1.03	78.70	20	60	0.48	9.05
2	0.69	77.67	19	38	0.31	8.57
4	1.37	76.98	18	72	0.58	8.26
2	0.69	75.61	17	34	0.27	7.68
3	1.03	74.92	16	48	0.39	7.41
3	1.03	73.89	15	45	0.36	7.02
2	0.69	72.86	14	28	0.22	6.66
2	0.69	72.17	13	26	0.21	6.44
5	1.72	71.48	12	60	0.48	6.23
5	1.72	69.76	11	55	0.44	5.75
10	3.44	68.04	10	100	0.80	5.31

No. of barristers			No. of appearances per barrister	Total appearances		
No.	%	Cum%		No.	%	Cum%
8	2.75	64.60	9	72	0.58	4.51
5	1.72	61.85	8	40	0.32	3.93
5	1.72	60.13	7	35	0.28	3.61
15	5.15	58.41	6	90	0.72	3.33
11	3.78	53.26	5	55	0.44	2.61
16	5.50	49.48	4	64	0.51	2.17
23	7.90	43.98	3	69	0.56	1.66
31	10.65	36.08	2	62	0.50	1.10
74	25.43	25.43	1	74	0.60	0.60
291[a]	100			12420	100	

[a] 68.6% of minimum bar.

Leaders

1197 [Anthony] Keck (IT)
 997 [George] Hutchins (GI)
 836 [William] Rawlinson (GI)
 766 [Ambrose] Phillips (IT)
 648 [Charles] Porter (MT)
 609 [?Anthony] Collins (?MT)
 576 Sir John Churchill KC (LI)
 538 [Hon. Heneage Finch] SG (IT)
 458 [William] Whitelocke (MT)
 397 [Robert] Holford (LI)
 366 Sir Francis Winnington (MT)

Sources: As specified in Appendix II.

APPENDIX X. Chancery bar: dimensions and distribution of business, 1720

No. of barristers			No. of appearances per barrister	Total appearances		
No.	%	Cum%		No.	%	Cum%
1	0.39	100.10	835	835	7.91	99.94
1	0.39	99.71	655	655	6.20	92.03
1	0.39	99.32	539	539	5.11	85.83
1	0.39	98.93	486	486	4.60	80.72
1	0.39	98.54	444	444	4.21	76.12
1	0.39	98.15	440	440	4.17	71.91
1	0.39	97.76	411	411	3.89	67.74
1	0.39	97.37	377	337	3.19	63.85
1	0.39	96.98	271	271	2.57	60.66
1	0.39	96.59	240	240	2.27	58.09
1	0.39	96.20	239	239	2.26	55.82
1	0.39	95.81	238	238	2.25	53.56
1	0.39	95.42	223	223	2.11	51.31
1	0.39	95.03	220	220	2.08	49.20
1	0.39	94.64	219	219	2.07	47.12
1	0.39	94.25	205	205	1.94	45.05
1	0.39	93.86	174	174	1.65	43.11
1	0.39	93.47	173	173	1.64	41.46
1	0.39	93.08	152	152	1.44	39.82
1	0.39	92.69	143	143	1.35	38.38
1	0.39	92.30	133	133	1.26	37.03
1	0.39	91.91	127	127	1.20	35.77
1	0.39	91.52	125	125	1.18	34.57
1	0.39	91.13	117	117	1.11	33.39
1	0.39	90.74	108	108	1.02	32.28
1	0.39	90.35	104	104	0.98	31.26
1	0.39	89.96	98	98	0.93	30.28
1	0.39	89.57	94	94	0.89	29.35
1	0.39	89.18	92	92	0.87	28.46

No. of barristers			No. of appearances per barrister	Total appearances		
No.	%	Cum%		No.	%	Cum%
1	0.39	88.79	84	84	0.80	27.59
1	0.39	88.40	81	81	0.77	26.79
1	0.39	88.01	76	76	0.72	26.02
1	0.39	87.62	74	74	0.70	25.30
1	0.39	87.23	73	73	0.69	24.60
1	0.39	86.84	70	70	0.66	23.91
1	0.39	86.45	69	69	0.65	23.25
1	0.39	86.06	65	65	0.62	22.60
2	0.77	85.67	63	126	1.19	21.98
1	0.39	84.90	62	62	0.59	20.79
1	0.39	84.51	61	61	0.58	20.20
1	0.39	84.12	58	58	0.55	19.62
1	0.39	83.73	56	56	0.53	19.07
1	0.39	83.34	54	54	0.51	18.54
2	0.77	82.95	52	104	0.98	18.03
1	0.39	82.18	48	48	0.45	17.05
1	0.39	81.79	47	47	0.44	16.60
2	0.77	81.40	46	92	0.87	16.16
1	0.39	80.63	45	45	0.43	15.29
1	0.39	80.24	44	44	0.42	14.86
1	0.39	79.85	43	43	0.41	14.44
3	1.16	79.46	41	123	1.16	14.03
1	0.39	78.30	40	40	0.38	12.87
1	0.39	77.91	38	38	0.36	12.49
2	0.77	77.52	37	74	0.70	12.13
1	0.39	76.75	35	35	0.33	11.43
1	0.39	76.36	32	32	0.30	11.10
1	0.39	75.97	29	29	0.27	10.80
1	0.39	75.58	27	27	0.26	10.53
1	0.39	75.19	25	25	0.24	10.27
1	0.39	74.80	24	24	0.23	10.03
1	0.39	74.41	23	23	0.22	9.80
1	0.39	74.02	21	21	0.20	9.58
1	0.39	73.63	20	20	0.19	9.38
3	1.16	73.24	19	57	0.54	9.19
3	1.16	72.08	18	54	0.51	8.65
2	0.77	70.92	17	34	0.32	8.14

No. of barristers			No. of appearances per barrister	Total appearances		
No.	%	Cum%		No.	%	Cum%
5	1.94	70.15	16	80	0.76	7.82
6	2.33	68.21	15	90	0.85	7.06
1	0.39	65.88	14	14	0.13	6.21
4	1.55	65.49	13	52	0.49	6.08
2	0.77	63.94	12	24	0.23	5.59
7	2.71	63.17	11	77	0.73	5.36
4	1.55	60.46	10	40	0.38	4.63
4	1.55	58.91	9	36	0.34	4.25
6	2.33	57.36	8	48	0.45	3.91
8	3.10	55.03	7	56	0.53	3.46
6	2.33	51.93	6	36	0.34	2.93
7	2.71	49.60	5	35	0.33	2.59
16	6.20	46.89	4	64	0.61	2.26
21	8.14	40.69	3	63	0.60	1.65
27	10.46	32.55	2	54	0.51	1.05
57	22.09	22.09	1	57	0.54	0.54
258[a]	100			10556	100	

[a] 76.3% of minimum bar.

Leaders

835 [Samuel] Mead (LI)
655 [Thomas] Lutwyche KC (IT)
539 [Sir Robert Raymond] AG (GI)
486 [Spencer] Cowper KC (LI)
444 [——] Williams (—)
440 [Charles] Talbot (IT)
411 [?John] Brown (?LI)
337 [Thomas] Bedford (MT)
271 [Marmaduke] Horseley (GI)
240 [Sir Philip Yorke] SG (MT)

Sources: As specified in Appendix II.

APPENDIX XI. Fees paid to counsel in
Carrington v. *Cantillon*, 1721–9 (Chancery)

Breviates

To: Mr Solicitor-General [1727–8] 3g. × 1, 2g. × 2 Charles Talbot, called IT 1711.
Mr [Nicholas] Fazackerley 2g. × 2 Called MT 1707.
Mr [Robert] Fenwick 2g. × 2 Called GI 1715.
Mr [Knightley] Danvers 2g. × 1 Called IT 1696.
Mr [Cavendish] Ford 1g. × 1 Called IT 1721.

Retainers

To: Mr Solicitor-General [1727] 2g. × 1 (for House of Lords) Sir Philip Yorke, called MT 1715.
  1g. × 1

Mr Attorney-General [1727] 1g. × 1 Called IT 1698, serjeant 1724.
Mr Serjeant [Fettiplace] Nott 1g. × 2 (retainers in a related cause)
Mr Danvers 1g. × 1 (retainers in a related cause)
Mr [John] Willes 1g. × 1 Called LI 1713, KC 1718.
Mr Serjeant [Giles] Eyre 1g. × 1 Called MT 1706, serjeant 1724.
Mr [William] Fortescue 1g. × 1 Called IT 1715.

Refreshers

To: Mr Willes 3g. × 1 Called MT 1695, serjeant 1715.
Serjeant [Sir John] Darnell 3g. × 1
Mr Fazackerley 3g. × 1
Mr [William] Wynne 2g. × 1 Called MT 1718.
Mr [?John] Browne 2g. × 1 Probably John Brown of LI, called 1698 and bencher 1717.

Mr [Paul] Foley 2g. × 1 Called LI 1708.
Mr [Abel] Kettleby 2g. × 1 Called MT 1699, bencher 1724.

Refreshers (cont.):

Mr [Robert] Kettleby, jun.	1g. × 1	
Mr Solicitor-General [1728]	1g. × 1	
Mr Ford	1g. × 1	Robert Johnston alias Kettleby, called MT 1724.

Motions

To: Mr Serjeant [Sir Thomas] Pengelly	3g. × 1, 2g. × 3, 1g. × 1	Called IT 1700, serjeant 1710, king's premier serjeant 1719.
Mr Kettleby	3g. × 1, 2g. × 1, 1g. × 4	
Sir Constantine Phipps	2g. × 1, 1g. × 5, ½g. × 3	Called MT 1684, bencher 1708, lord chancellor of Ireland 1710–14.
Mr Browne	2g. × 1, 1g. × 10, ½g. × 1	
Mr [?John] Ward	2g. × 1, 1g. × 4, ½g. × 1	Probably John Ward, called GI 1693, bencher IT 1711, QC 1711–15.
Mr Fazackerley	1g. × 3	
Mr Solicitor-General [1727]	1g. × 2	
Mr Willes	1g. × 1	
Mr Fenwick	1g. × 2	
Mr Wynne	1g. × 5	
[Unspecified counsel]	½g. × 2, 13s. × 1	

Defences

To: Mr Browne	2g. × 1, 1g. × 6, ½g. × 2
Sir Constantine Phipps	1g. × 6, 10s. × 1
Mr Ward	2g. × 1, 1g. × 1
Mr Kettleby	1g. × 1

Arguments

To: Mr Willes   5g. × 1
Mr Fazackerley   5g. × 1
Mr Browne   4g. × 1
Mr Wynne   3g. × 1
Sir Constantine Phipps   2g. × 1
Mr Kettleby   2g. × 1
Mr Kettleby, jun.   2g. × 1

Consultations, advice, opinions

To: Mr Willes   3g. × 1, 2g. × 2
Mr Wynne   3g. × 1, 2g. × 1, 1g. × 2
Mr Serjeant Pengelly   2g. × 1, 1g. × 2
Mr Fazackerley   2g. × 3, 1g. × 1
Mr Ward   2g. × 1, 1g. × 4
Mr Browne   2g. × 3, 1g. × 4
Sir John Darnell   2g. × 1
Mr Kettleby   2g. × 2
Mr Foley   2g. × 2
Sir Constantine Phipps   1g. × 3, 10s. × 1

Perusing, settling, signing documents

To: Mr [?Richard] Agar   3g. × 1
Mr Wynne   2g. × 1, 1g. × 3
Mr Fenwick   2g. × 1, 1g. × 3
Mr Kettleby   2g. × 1, 1g. × 1

?Richard Agar, called MT 1700, bencher 1721.

Perusing, settling, signing documents (cont.):

Mr Browne	2g. × 1	
Mr Serjeant [William] Branthwaite	1g. × 1	Called GI 1691, serjeant 1715.
Sir Constantine Phipps	1g. × 1	
Mr [?Edmond] Sawyer	1g. × 1	?Edmond Sawyer, called IT 1713.
Mr Ward	1g. × 1	
[Unspecified counsel]	1g. × 1	

Unspecified fees [?arguments]

To: Mr Serjeant Pengelly	10g. × 1	
Mr Fazackerley	10g. × 1	
Mr Ward	10g. × 1	
Mr Wynne	10g. × 1	
Mr Browne	10g. × 1	

Sources: BL, Add. MSS 28251 (Miscellaneous law papers, accounts etc.), fos. 111–14, 121–4, 130–6, 152–3, 156–7, 164–5, 168, 170–1: solicitors' bills in *Carrington* v. *Cantillon*, 1722–9; *GIPB* iii; *CITR* iii, iv. *LIBB* iii; *MT Adm. Reg*, i.; Baker, *Serjeants*; Ball, *The Judges in Ireland, 1221–1921*, ii. 70–1; information on crown counsel from Sir John Sainty; Foss, *Judges*, viii. 10–11, 88.

BIBLIOGRAPHY

(Including material cited in the footnotes only.)

I. MANUSCRIPT SOURCES

Gray's Inn

MS Admittance Book ii
MS Books of Orders i, ii, iii
MS Ledgers A, B
MS Commons Rolls G(a) 8 Box 1, 2, 3
MS House Rolls G(a)9 Box 1

Inner Temple

MS Acts of Parliament 1638–64, 1665–87
MS Bench Table Orders 1685–91, 1691–8, 1699–1714, 1715–33
MS Miscellanea ii, vii, xi, xxiv, xxviii–xxx
Miscellaneous or Additional MSS iv
MS General Account Books 1682–4, 1684–94, 1694–1702, 1702–10, 1710–18, 1719–25, 1725–31, 1732–7, 1737–42
Barrington MSS 60–3, 71–4, 78, 80

Lincoln's Inn

MS Admission Books ix, x
MS Black Books viii–xi
MS Red Books i–ii
MS Misc. 582

Middle Temple

MS Admissions to House and Chambers 1658–95, 1695–1735
MS Orders of Parliament E5 (1658–1703), H(8) (1704–48)

Bodleian Library, Oxford

MSS Ballard 10–11, 22 (Arthur Charlett)
MSS Eng. Lett. c. 17 (Sir Thomas Pengelly)
MSS Locke c. 12, c. 30 (John Locke)
MSS North c. 5 (Lord Guilford)
MSS Rawlinson B. 374, D. 862
MSS Tanner 28

British Library London

Additional MSS
  4472 (Thomas Birch)
  19773–4 (Sir Thomas Pengelly)
  22185
  22263
  22675 (Sir Thomas Pengelly)
  25500, 25503–8 (South Sea Company)
  28251
  32501, 32506, 32508–11 (Roger North, Lord Guilford)
  32686–7 (duke of Newcastle)
  34729
  35584–6, 35988–90 (earl of Hardwicke)
  36134, 36137 (earl of Hardwicke)
  36707 (James Harrington)
  41843 (William Wynne)
  50116–17 (Sir Thomas Raymond, William Longueville)
  61459–60 (Arthur Mainwaring, duchess of Marlborough)
  61469
Egerton MSS 1074
Harleian MSS 1912
Hargrave MSS 294, 319 (?Roger North)
Lansdowne MSS 1105 (Sir Bartholomew Shower)
Stowe MSS 223, 416750 (earl of Macclesfield)

Public Record Office, Chancery Lane, London

Chancery
  C33/255
  C37/314–15, 318–29, 334–5, 1027–49
  C113/38
Common Pleas
  CP45/515, 519–27, 734–7
Exchequer
  E11/11, 22, 26
  E12/26, 34–5
  E126/13, 21
  E127/11–12, 32
  E161/45–6, 71
King's Bench
  KB21/20, 31
  KB36/14–17
  CB125/113, 137–8

Probate
  PROB11/370, 489

House of Lords Record Office
MS Minutes, HL, 22, 62–4

Devon County Record Office, Exeter
Drake of Buckland Abbey MSS (Sir Francis Drake, Peter King)
Exeter City Library MSS

West Devon Record Office, Plymouth
Bastard of Kitley MSS (Edmund Pollexfen)

Dorset County Record Office, Dorchester
Trenchard MSS (Sir John Trenchard)

East Sussex County Record Office, Lewes
Frewen MSS (Henry Turner)

Guildford Muniment Room
Loseley MSS (Thomas Molyneux)
Midleton MSS (Alan Brodrick, St. John Brodrick)

Guildhall Library, London
MS 18760 (Johnson, Cobb, Pearson & Co., solicitors)

Hereford and Worcester County Record Office, Worcester
Vernon MSS (Thomas Vernon)

Hertfordshire County Record Office, Hertford
Panshanger MSS (Earl Cowper)
Lawes-Wittewronge MSS (James Wittewronge)

Kent Archives Office, Maidstone
Papillon MSS (Papillon family, Philip Yorke)

New York Public Library
Hardwicke MSS 33 (microfilm) (Lord Somers)

University of Nottingham
Mellish of Hodsock MSS (William Mellish)

Sandon Hall, Stafford
Harrowby MSS (Dudley Ryder)

Shropshire County Record Office, Shrewsbury
Bishop of Shipton MSS (Sir Thomas Powys, Sir Littleton Powys)

Surrey County Record Office, Kingston
Somers MSS (Lord Somers)

2. UNPUBLISHED WORK

BAKER, J. H., 'A History of the Order of Serjeants at Law' (London Univ. Ph.D. thesis, 1968).

BLACK, S. F., 'The Judges of Westminster Hall during the Great Rebellion, 1640–1660' (Oxford Univ. M.Litt. thesis, 1970).

BROOKS, C. W., 'Interpersonal Conflict and Social Tension. Civil Litigation and Court Usage in England, 1640–1830' (forthcoming).

COOPER, H. H. A., 'Promotion and Politics among the Common Law Judges of the Reigns of James I and Charles I' (Liverpool Univ. MA thesis, 1964).

CROFT, C. E., 'Philip Yorke, 1st Earl of Hardwicke: An Assessment of his Legal Career' (Cambridge Univ. Ph.D. thesis, 1983).

CRUICKSHANKS, E., _The House of Commons 1690–1715_ (forthcoming—draft biographies, constituency articles, lists, and files).

LEMMINGS, D., 'The Inns of Court and the English Bar, 1680–1730' (Oxford Univ. D.Phil. thesis, 1986).

LLOYD, R. L., 'Admissions to the Inner Temple, 1505–1850' (typescript in the office of the librarian of the Inner Temple, 1954–60).

MacLEOD, C., 'Patents for Invention and Technical Change in England 1680–1753' (Cambridge Univ. Ph.D. thesis, 1982).

MILES, M., ' "Eminent Attorneys": Some Aspects of West Riding Attorneyship _c._1750–1800' (Birmingham Univ. Ph.D. thesis, 1982).

SAINTY, J. C., 'King's Counsel 1604–1820' (part copy of list of KCs).

3. PRINTED PRIMARY SOURCES

ALEXANDER, J. J., 'Exeter Members of Parliament, Part III, 1537 to 1688', _Report and Transactions of the Devonshire Association_, 61 (1929), 193–215.

BAKER, J. H., _The Order of Serjeants at Law_ (Selden Soc., suppl. ser. 5; 1984).

BALL, F. E., _The Judges in Ireland, 1221–1921_ (1926).

BLACKSTONE, W., _Commentaries on the Laws of England_ (Oxford, 1765–9).

The Autobiography of Sir John Bramston, KB, ed. R. G. Neville, Lord Braybrooke (Camden Soc., old ser., 32; 1845).

BURKE, B., and BURKE, A. P., _A Geneological and Heraldic History of the Peerage and Baronetage_ (89th edn., 1931).

Bishop Burnet's History of His Own Time (2nd edn., Oxford, 1833).

The Letters of Thomas Burnet to George Duckett 1712–1722, ed. D. N. Smith (Oxford, 1914).

H.C., 'The Character of an Honest Lawyer' (1676), in *Somers Tracts* (1748), pt. I, iv. 305–8.

Calendar of State Papers Domestic, 1689

Calendar of State Papers Domestic, 1694–1695

CAMPBELL, JOHN, Lord, *The Lives of the Lord Chancellors and Keepers of the Great Seal of England* (1845–69).

CAMPBELL, R., *The London Tradesman* (1747).

Alumni Cantabrigienses, ed. J. and J. A. Venn, pt. I (Cambridge, 1922–7).

CHAMBERLAYNE E./CHAMBERLAYNE, J., *Angliae Notitia, or the Present State of England/Magnae Brittaniae Notitia, or the Present State of Great Britain*, pts. I and II (38 edns., 1669–1748).

CHAUNCY, H., *The Historical Antiquities of Hertfordshire* (1700).

'Fee-Book of Serjeant Sir John Chesshyre', *N&Q*, 2nd ser. (1859), 492–3.

The Pension Book of Clement's Inn, ed. C. Carr (Selden Soc., 78; 1960).

The Reports of Sir Edward Coke Kt. (1738).

Commons' Journals, ix, xii–xiii, xx–xxi.

COOKSEY, R., *Essay on the Life and Character of John Lord Somers, Baron of Evesham: Also Sketches of an essay on the Life and Character of Philip Earl of Hardwicke* (Worcester, 1791).

Corona Civica: A Poem to the Right Honourable Lord Keeper of the Great Seal of England (1706).

The Private Diary of William, First Earl Cowper, Lord Chancellor of England, ed. E. C. Hawtrey (Eton, 1833).

DAVIES, Sir John, *Le Primer Report des cases and matters en ley* (Dublin, 1615).

DEFOE, D., *The Compleat English Gentleman*, ed. K. D. Buldring (1890).

Dictionary of National Biography.

The Divided Society: Party Conflict in England 1694–1716, ed. G. Holmes and W. A. Speck (1967).

DOWNING, W., *Observations on the Constitution Customs and Usuage of the Honourable Society of the Middle Temple* (1896).

Alumni Dublinenses, ed. G. D. Burtchaell and T. U. Sadleir (2nd edn., Dublin, 1935).

DUGDALE, W., *Origines Juridiciales* (2nd edn., 1680).

ELIOTT-DRAKE, Lady, *The Family and Heirs of Sir Francis Drake* (1911).

ELYOT, Sir THOMAS, *The Boke Named the Gouernour*, ed. H. H. S. Croft (1880).

English Legal Manuscripts, ed. J. H. Baker (Zug, Switzerland, 1975–8).

The English Reports (1900–30).

EVANS, K., 'Eighteenth-Century Caernarvon, Il., Burgesses—Resident and Non-Resident', *Carnarvonshire Historical Society: Transactions*, 8 (1947), 44–80.

The Diary of John Evelyn, ed. E. S. De Beer (Oxford, 1955).

FORTESCUE, Sir JOHN, *De Laudibus Legum Angliae*, ed. S. B. Chrimes (Cambridge, 1942).

FOSS, E., *The Judges of England* (1848–69).

—— *Biographica Juridica: A Biographical Dictionary of the Judges of England from the Conquest to the Present Time 1066–1870* (1870).

FOWLER, D. B., *The Practice of the Court of Exchequer upon Proceedings in Equity* (1795).

[GILBERT, Sir GEOFFREY], *The Law of Evidence* (1761 [written before 1726]).

The Register of Admissions to Gray's Inn, 1521–1889, ed. J. Foster (1889).

The Pension Book of Gray's Inn, ed. R. J. Fletcher (1901–10).

GREY, A., *Debates of the House of Commons, from the Year 1667 to the Year 1694* (1769).

HALE, M., 'Considerations Touching the Amendment or Alteration of Lawes', in F. Hargrave (ed.), *A Collection of Tracts Relative to the Law of England* (1787), 249–89.

—— 'A Discourse concerning the Courts of King's Bench and Common Pleas', in F. Hargrave (ed.), *A Collection of Tracts Relative to the Law of England* (1787), 357–76.

—— preface to H. Rolle, *Un abridgement des plusieurs cases et resolutions del common ley* (1668).

The Harcourt Papers, ed. E. W. Harcourt (Oxford, 1880–1905).

HASLER, P. W., *The House of Commons 1558–1603* (1981).

HATTON, E., *A New View of London or, an Ample Account of that City* (1708).

HENNING, B. D., *The House of Commons 1660–1690* (1983).

Historical Manuscripts Commission

    5th Report, app.

    13th Report, app. VI, Fitzherbert MSS.

    14th Report, app. II, Portland MSS.

    15th Report, app. IV, Portland MSS.

    Egmont Diary, iii.

    Finch MSS, iii.

    House of Lords MSS, x.

    Portland MSS, v.

    Various Collections, viii.

The History and Proceedings of the House of Commons from the Restoration to the Present Time (1742–4).

HOLME, R., *The Academy of Armory, or a Storehouse of Armory and Blazon* (Chester, 1688).

A Calendar of the Inner Temple Records, ed. F. A. Inderwick and R. A. Roberts (1896–1936).

JACOB, G., *The Student's Companion: Or the Reason of the Laws of England* (2nd edn., 1734).

KING, H. C., *Records and Documents Concerning Serjeants' Inn Fleet Street* (1922).

A Memoir of the Life and Death of Sir John King, Knight, ed. G. H. Sawtell (1855 [written 1677]).

KING, PETER, Lord, *Life of Locke* (2nd edn., 1830).

Select Cases in the Court of King's Bench under Edward I, i, ed. G. O. Sayles (Selden Soc., 55; 1936).

The Parliamentary Diary of Sir Edward Knatchbull 1722–1730, ed. A. N. Newman (Camden Soc., 3rd ser., 94; 1963).

The Law and Lawyers Laid Open in Twelve Visions (1737).

LE NEVE, J., *Monumenta Anglicana 1650–1718* (1719).

The Records of the Honourable Society of Lincoln's Inn: Admissions and Chapel Registers (1896).

The Records of the Honourable Society of Lincoln's Inn: The Black Books, ed. W. P. Baildon (1897–1977).

A List of the Names of all the Subscribers to the Bank of England [1694].

A List of the Names of the Members of the United Company of Merchants of England, Trading to the East-Indies, who are also Members of the General Society, the 7th of April, 1709 (1709).

The Correspondence of John Locke, ed. E. S. De Beer (Oxford, 1976–82).

London Visitation Pedigrees 1664, ed. J. B. Whitmore and A. W. Hughes (1940).

Lords' Journals, xv, xxiv.

LUTTRELL, N., *A Brief Historical Relation of State Affairs from September 1678 to April 1714* (Oxford, 1857).

MASTERS, B. R., 'The Common Serjeant', *Guildhall Miscellany*, 2 (1967), 379–89.

Bibliotheca Illustris Medii Templi Societatis (1700).

Catalogus Librorum Bibliothecae Honorabilis Societatis Medii Templi Londini (1734).

A Calendar of the Middle Temple Records, ed. C. H. Hopwood (1903).

Middle Temple Records: Minutes of Parliament of the Middle Temple, ed. C. T. Martin (1904–5).

The Middle Temple Bench Book, ed. A. R. Ingpen (1st edn., 1912).

The Middle Temple Bench Book, ed. J. B. Williamson (2nd edn., 1937).

Registers of Admissions to the Honourable Society of the Middle Temple from the 15th Century to the Year 1944, ed. H. A. C. Sturgess (1949).

MIÈGE, G., *The New State of England under their Majesties K. William and Q. Mary/Queen Anne* (6 edns., 1691–1707).

—— *The Present State of Great Britain* (11 edns., 1707–48).

Letters on Various Subjects to and from William Nicholson D.D., ed. J. Nichols (1809).

NORBURIE, G., 'The Abuses and Remedies of Chancery', in F. Hargrave (ed.), *A Collection of Tracts Relative to the Law of England* (1787), 425–48.

The Autobiography of the Hon. Roger North, ed. A. Jessopp (1887).

NORTH, R., *A Discourse on the Study of the Laws* (1824).

—— *The Lives of the Right Hon. Francis North, Baron Guilford; The Hon. Sir*

Dudley North; And the Hon. and Rev. Dr. John North, ed. A. Jessopp (1890).
Lord Nottingham's Chancery Cases, ed. D. E. C. Yale (Selden Soc., 73; 1957).
Lord Nottingham's 'Manual of Chancery Practice' and 'Prolegomena of Chancery and Equity', ed. D. E. C. Yale (Cambridge, 1965).
Alumni Oxonienses, ed. J. Foster (Oxford, 1887–92).
Some Private Passages of the Life of Sir Thomas Pengelly, late Chief Baron of the Exchequer, written by a Lady, his Intimate Friend (1733).
The Diary of Samuel Pepys, ed. R. Latham and W. Matthews (1970–83).
PEVSNER, N., *The Buildings of England: Worcester* (Harmondsworth, 1968).
PHILIPPS, H., *The Grandeur of the Law* (1684).
PHILLIPS, W., *Studii Legalis Ratio or Directions for the Study of the Law* (1675).
Private Memoirs of John Potenger, Esq. . . ., ed. C. W. Bingham (1841).
PRYNNE, W., *Brief Animadversions on . . . the Fourth Part of the Institutes of the Lawes of England . . . by Sir Edward Cooke* (1669).
Recorders of the City of London 1298–1850 (1850).
'Lord Chief Justice Reeve's Instructions to his Nephew Concerning the Study of the Law', in *Collectanea Juridica*, ed. F. Hargrave (1791–2), i. 79–81.
The Diary of Dudley Ryder 1715–16, ed. W. Matthews (1939).
SAINTY, J. C., *Office-Holders in Modern Britain: Treasury Officials 1660–1870* (1972).
—— *Office-Holders in Modern Britain: Officials of the Board of Trade 1660–1870* (1974).
—— *The Parliament Office in the 17th and 18th Centuries* (House of Lords Record Office, 1977).
SEDGWICK, R., *The House of Commons 1715–1754* (1970).
SOMERVILLE, R., *Office-Holders in the Duchy and County Palatine of Lancaster from 1603* (1972).
The Prose Writings of Jonathan Swift, ed. H. Davies (Oxford, 1939–68), xii. *Irish Tracts, 1728–33*.
Victoria History of the Counties of England: Hertfordshire Geneological Volume, ed. D. Warrand (1907).
Victoria History of the Counties of England: Lancashire (1906–14).
WILLIAMS, W. R., *The History of the Great Sessions in Wales 1542–1830* (Brecknock, 1899).
—— *Official Lists of the Duchy and County Palatine of Lancaster* (Brecknock, 1901).
'Sir Francis Winnington's Fee-Book', *N&Q*, 2nd ser., 7 (1859), 65.
WOOD, T., *Some Thoughts Concerning the Study of the Laws of England* (2nd edn., 1727).
Master Worsley's Book on the History and Constitution of the Honourable Society of the Middle Temple, ed. A. R. Ingpen (1910).

4. SECONDARY SOURCES

The Agrarian History of England and Wales, v. *1640–1750*, ed. J. Thirsk (Cambridge, 1984–5).

BAKER, J. H., 'The Origin of the Bar Gown', *Law Guardian*, 49 (1969), 17–18.

—— 'The Status of Barristers', *LQR* 85 (1969), 334–8.

—— 'History of the Gowns worn at the English Bar', *Costume*, 9 (1975), 15–21.

—— *An Introduction to English Legal History* (2nd edn., 1979).

—— *A Manual of Law French* (Amersham, 1979).

—— 'The English Legal Profession, 1450–1550', in W. Prest (ed.), *Lawyers in Early Modern Europe and America* (1981).

—— *The Legal Profession and the Common Law: Historical Essays* (1986).

—— 'Counsellors and Barristers', in id., *The Legal Profession and the Common Law*.

—— 'The Inns of Court in 1388', in id., *The Legal Profession and the Common Law*.

—— 'Learning Exercises in the Medieval Inns of Court and Chancery', in id., *The Legal Profession and the Common Law*.

—— 'Readings in Gray's Inn, their Decline and Disappearance', in id., *The Legal Profession and the Common Law*.

—— 'Solicitors and the Law of Maintenance, 1590–1640', in id., *The Legal Profession and the Common Law*.

BALL, F. E., 'Narcissus Luttrell', *N&Q* 152 (1927), 111.

BEATTIE, J. M., *Crime and the Courts in England 1660–1800* (Oxford, 1986).

BECKETT, J. V., 'English Landownership in the Later 17th and 18th Centuries: The Debate and the Problems', *Econ. HR*, 2nd ser., 30 (1977), 567–81.

—— 'The Pattern of Landownership in England and Wales, 1660–1880', *Econ. HR*, 2nd ser., 37 (1984), 1–22.

BELLOT, H. H. L., *The Inner and Middle Temple* (1902).

—— 'The Exclusion of Attorneys from the Inns of Court', *LQR* 26 (1910), 137–45.

—— 'The Jurisdiction of the Inns of Court over the Inns of Chancery', *LQR* 26 (1910), 384–99.

—— *Gray's Inn and Lincoln's Inn* (1925).

BENNETT, G. V., 'University, Society and Church, 1688–1714', in *The History of the University of Oxford*, v: *The Eighteenth Century*, ed. L. S. Sutherland and L. G. Mitchell (Oxford, 1986).

—— 'Against the Tide: Oxford under William III', in *The History of the University of Oxford*, v: *The Eighteenth Century*, ed. L. S. Sutherland and L. G. Mitchell (Oxford, 1986).

BERG, M., *The Age of Manufactures: Industry, Innovation and Work in Britain 1700–1820* (1985).

BLACKWOOD, B. G., *The Lancashire Gentry and the Great Rebellion 1640–60* (Chetham Soc., 3rd ser., 25; 1978).

BOND, M. F., 'Clerks of the Parliaments, 1509–1953' *EHR* 78 (1958), 78–85.

BORSAY, P., 'The English Urban Renaissance: The Development of Provincial Urban Culture *c.*1680–*c.*1760', *Social History*, 2 (1977), 581–603.

BRAND, P., 'Courtroom and Schoolroom: The Education of Lawyers in England prior to 1400', *Historical Research*, 60 (1986), 147–65.

BRAUER, G. C., *The Education of a Gentleman* (New York, 1959).

BROOKS, C. W., 'The Common Lawyers in England, *c.*1558–1642', in W. Prest (ed.), *Lawyers in Early Modern Europe and America* (1981).

—— *Pettyfoggers and Vipers of the Commonwealth: The 'Lower Branch' of the Legal Profession in Early Modern England* (Cambridge, 1986).

BROWNING, A., *Thomas Osborne Earl of Danby and Duke of Leeds 1632–1712* (Glasgow, 1944–51).

—— and MILNE, D. J., 'An Exclusion Bill Division List', *BIHR* 23 (1950), 205–25.

BRUNTON, D. and PENNINGTON, D. H., *Members of the Long Parliament* (1954).

BRYSON, W. H., *The Equity Side of the Exchequer* (Cambridge, 1975).

—— 'The Equity Jurisdiction of the Exchequer', in D. Jenkins (ed.), *Legal History Studies 1972* (Cardiff, 1975).

BURTON, I. F., RILEY, P. W. J., and ROWLANDS, E., *Political Parties in the Reigns of William III and Anne: The Evidence of Division Lists* (*BIHR*, special suppl., 7; 1968).

CHALKLIN, C. W., *The Provincial Towns of Georgian England: A Study of the Building Process 1740–1820* (1974).

CHARLTON, K., *Education in Renaissance England* (1965).

CLAY, C., 'Marriage, Inheritance and the Rise of Large Estates in England, 1660–1815', *Econ. HR*, 2nd ser., 21 (1968), 503–18.

—— 'Property Settlements, Financial Provision for the Family, and Sale of Land by the Greater Landowners, 1660–1790', *JBS* 21 (1981), 18–38.

COCKBURN, J. S., *A History of English Assizes, 1558–1714* (Cambridge, 1972).

COLEMAN, D. C., *The Economy of England 1450–1750* (Oxford, 1977).

CRUICKSHANKS, E., 'Ashby v. White: The Case of the Men of Aylesbury, 1701–4', in C. Jones (ed.), *Party and Management in Parliament, 1660–1784* (Leicester, 1984).

—— FERRIS, J., and HAYTON, D., 'The House of Commons Vote on the Transfer of the Crown, 5 February 1689', *BIHR* 52 (1979), 37–47.

DAVIS, R. W., 'Committee and Other Procedures in the House of Lords, 1660–1685', *HLQ* 45 (1982), 20–35.

DICKINSON, H. T., 'The October Club', *HLQ* 33 (1969–70), 155–73.

—— *Liberty and Property: Political Ideology in 18th-Century Britain* (1977).

DICKSON, P. G. M., *The Financial Revolution in England* (1967).

DOLLAR, C. M. and JENSEN, R. J., *Historian's Guide to Statistics: Quantitative Analysis and Historical Research* (New York, 1971).

DOUTHWAITE, W. R., *Gray's Inn: Its History and Associations* (1886).

DUBOIS, A. B., *The English Business Company after the Bubble Act 1720–1800* (New York, 1938).

DUMAN, D., 'The English Bar in the Georgian Era', in W. Prest (ed.), *Lawyers in Early Modern Europe and America* (1981).

—— *The Judicial Bench in England 1727–1875: The Reshaping of a Professional Elite* (1982).

—— 'The English and Colonial Bars in the Nineteenth Century (1983).

EDWARDS, J. Ll. J., *The Law Officers of the Crown* (1964).

FIFOOT, C. H. S., *Lord Mansfield* (Oxford, 1936).

FRANKLE, R. J., 'The Formulation of the Declaration of Rights', *HJ* 17 (1974), 265–79.

HABBAKUK, H. J., 'English Landownership, 1680–1740', *Econ. HR*, 10 (1939–40), 2–17.

—— 'The Rise and Fall of English Landed Families, 1600–1800', *TRHS*, 5th ser., 29 (1979), 187–207; 30 (1980), 199–221; 31 (1981), 195–217.

HANS, N., *New Trends in Education in the 18th Century* (1966).

HARDING, A., *A Social History of English Law* (Harmondsworth, 1966).

HAVIGHURST, A. F., 'The Judiciary and Politics in the Reign of Charles II', *LQR* 66 (1950), 62–78, 229–52.

—— 'James II and the Twelve Men in Scarlet', *LQR* 69 (1953), 522–46.

HAYTON, D., 'The "Country" Interest and the Party System, 1689–*c.*1720', in C. Jones (ed.), *Party and Management in Parliament, 1660–1784* (Leicester, 1984).

HOLDEN, J. M., *The History of Negotiable Instruments in English Law* (1955).

HOLDERNESS, B. A., 'The English Land Market in the 18th Century: The case of Lincolnshire', *Econ. HR*, 2nd ser., 27 (1974), 557–76.

—— *Pre-industrial England: Economy and Society 1500–1750* (1976).

HOLDSWORTH, W. S., *A History of English Law* (1922–72).

HOLLINGSWORTH, T. H., *The Demography of the British Peerage* (suppl. to *Population Studies*, 18; 1965).

HOLMES, G., 'The Commons' Division on "No Peace without Spain", 7 December 1711', *BIHR* 33 (1960), 223–34.

—— *British Politics in the Age of Anne* (1967).

—— 'Gregory King and the Social Structure of Pre-Industrial England', *TRHS*, 5th ser., 27 (1977), 41–68.

—— 'The Professions and Social Change in England, 1680–1730', *PBA* 65 (1979), 313–54.

—— *Augustan England: Professions, State and Society, 1680–1730* (1982).

—— 'The Achievement of Stability: The Social Context of Politics from the 1680s to the Age of Walpole', in id., *Politics, Religion and Society in England, 1670–1742* (1986).

HORWITZ, H., 'Parties, Connections and Parliamentary Politics, 1689–1714: Review and Revision', *JBS* 6 (1966), 45–69.

—— 'Parliament and the Glorious Revolution', *BIHR* 47 (1974), 36–52.

—— *Parliament, Policy and Politics in the Reign of William III* (Manchester, 1977).

HUGHES, E., *North Country Life in the 18th Century* (Oxford, 1952–65).

—— 'The Professions in the 18th Century', in D. A. Baugh (ed.), *Aristocratic Government and Society in 18th-Century England* (New York, 1975).

INNES, J., and STYLES, J., 'The Crime Wave: Recent Writing on Crime and Criminal Justice in Eighteenth-Century England', *JBS* 25 (1986), 380–435.

IVES, E. W., 'Promotion in the Legal Profession of Yorkist and Early Tudor England', *LQR* 75 (1959), 348–63.

—— 'The Reputation of the Common Lawyers in English Society, 1450–1550', *University of Birmingham Historical Journal*, 7 (1959–60), 130–61.

—— *The Common Lawyers of Pre-Reformation England* (Cambridge, 1983).

KEELER, M. F., *The Long Parliament, 1640–1641* (Philadelphia, 1954).

KEETON, G. W., *Lord Chancellor Jeffreys and the Stuart Cause* (1965).

LANDON, M., *The Triumph of the Lawyers* (Tuscaloosa, Alabama, 1970).

LAUNDY, P., *The Office of Speaker* (1964).

LEMMINGS, D., 'The Student Body of the Inns of Court under the Later Stuarts', *BIHR* 58 (1985), 149–66.

LEVACK, B. P., 'The English Civilians, 1500–1750', in W. Prest (ed.), *Lawyers in Early Modern Europe and America* (1981).

LUCAS, P., 'Blackstone and the Reform of the Legal Profession', *EHR* 77 (1962), 456–89.

—— 'A Collective Biography of Students and Barristers of Lincoln's Inn, 1680–1804: A Study of the "Aristocratic Resurgence" of the 18th Century', *JMH* 46 (1974), 227–61.

McINNES, A., *The English Town, 1660–1760* (Historical Association, 1980).

MALLET, C. E., *The History of the University of Oxford* (1924–7).

MILES, M., ' "Eminent Practitioners": The New Visage of Country Attorneys c.1750–1880', in G. R. Rubin and D. Sugarman (eds.), *Law, Economy and Society 1750–1914* (Abingdon, 1984).

MOORE, T. K., and HORWITZ, H., 'Who Runs the House? Aspects of Parliamentary Organisation in the Later Seventeenth Century', *JMH* 43 (1971), 205–27.

NAMIER, L., *The Structure of Politics at the Accession of George III* (2nd edn., 1957).

NEALE, J. E., *The Elizabethan House of Commons* (1949).

NENNER, H., *By Colour of Law* (Chicago, 1977).

OWEN, J. B., *The Eighteenth Century 1714–1815* (1974).

PALMER, R. C., 'The Origins of the Legal Profession in England', *Irish Jurist*, 11 (1976), 126–46.

PEARCE, R. R., *A History of the Inns of Court and Chancery* (1848).

PLUMB, J. H., 'The Elections to the Convention Parliament of 1689', *Cambridge Historical Journal*, 5 (1935), 235–54.

—— *Sir Robert Walpole* (1956–60).

—— *The Growth of Political Stability in England 1675–1725* (Harmondsworth, 1973).

POCOCK, J. G. A., *The Ancient Constitution and the Feudal Law* (Cambridge, 1957).

POLLOCK, F., and MAITLAND, F. W., The History of English Law before the Time of Edward I (2nd edn., Cambridge, 1898).

PORRITT, E., and PORRITT, A., *The Unreformed House of Commons* (Cambridge, 1903).

PREST, W. R., 'The Learning Exercises at the Inns of Court 1590–1640', *Journal of the Society of Public Teachers of Law*, 9 (1967), 300–13.

—— 'Legal Education of the Gentry at the Inns of Court, 1560–1640', *P&P* 38 (1967), 20–39.

—— *The Inns of Court under Elizabeth I and the Early Stuarts* (1972).

—— 'Counsellors' Fees and Earnings in the Age of Sir Edward Coke', in J. H. Baker (ed.), *Legal Records and the Historian* (1978).

—— 'The English Bar, 1550–1700', in W. Prest (ed.), *Lawyers in Early Modern Europe and America* (1981).

—— 'Why the History of the Professions is Not Written', in G. R. Rubin and D. Sugarman (eds.), *Law, Economy and Society 1750–1914* (Abingdon, 1984).

—— *The Rise of the Barristers: A Social History of the English Bar, 1590–1640* (Oxford, 1986).

PRICE, J. M., 'Sheffield v. Starke: Institutional Experimentation in the London–Maryland Trade *c*.1696–1706', *Business History*, 28:3 (1986), 19–39.

RICHARDSON, W. C., *A History of the Inns of Court* (Baton Rouge, La., n.d. [1977]).

ROBSON, R., *The Attorney in 18th-Century England* (Cambridge, 1959).

RUBINI, D. A., 'The Precarious Independence of the Judiciary, 1688–1701', *LQR* 83 (1967), 343–5.

SCHOECK, R. J., 'The Libraries of Common Lawyers in Renaissance England: Some notes and a Provisional List', *Manuscripta*, 6 (1962), 155–67.

SCHWOERER, L. G., 'Roger North and his Notes on Legal Education', *HLQ* 22 (1958–9), 323–43.

—— 'A Jornall of the Convention at Westminster begun the 22 of January 1688/9', *BIHR* 49 (1976), 243–63.

—— *The Declaration of Rights, 1689* (Baltimore, 1981).

—— 'The Transformation of the 1689 Convention into a Parliament', *Parliamentary History*, 3 (1984), 57–76.

SCOTT, W. R., *The Constitution and Finance of English, Scottish and Irish Joint-Stock Companies to 1720* (Cambridge, 1910–12).

SHARPE, J. A., *Crime in Early Modern England 1550–1750* (1984).

SIMPSON, A. W. B., *The History of the Common Law of Contract: The Rise of the Action of Assumpsit* (Oxford, 1975).

SNYDER, H. L., 'Party Configurations in the Early 18th-Century House of Commons', *BIHR* 45 (1972), 38–72.

SPECK, W. A., 'The Choice of a Speaker in 1705', *BIHR* 37 (1964), 20–46.

—— *Tory and Whig: The Struggle in the Constituencies 1701–1715* (1970).

—— *Stability and Strife: England, 1714–60* (1977).

STONE, L., 'The Educational Revolution in England, 1560–1640', *P&P* 28 (1964), 41–80.

—— 'The Size and Composition of the Oxford Student Body 1580–1909', in id. (ed.), *The University in Society* (Princeton, 1974), i.

—— and STONE, J. C. F., *An Open Elite? England 1540–1880* (Oxford, 1984).

SZECHI, D., *Jacobitism and Tory Politics 1710–14* (Edinburgh, 1984).

THORNE, S. E., 'The Early History of the Inns of Court with Special Reference to Gray's Inn', in id., *Essays in English Legal History* (1985).

VEALL, D., *The Popular Movement for Law Reform 1640–1660* (Oxford, 1970).

WALCOTT, R. R., 'Division Lists of the House of Commons, 1689–1715', *BIHR* 14 (1936–7), 25–36.

WARD, W. R., *The English Land Tax in the 18th Century* (Oxford, 1953).

—— *Georgian Oxford* (Oxford, 1958).

WILLIAMSON, J. B., *The History of the Temple, London* (1924).

WINDER, W. H. D., 'The Courts of Requests', *LQR* 207 (1936), 369–94.

WINFIELD, P. H., *The Chief Sources of English Legal History* (Cambridge, Mass., 1925).

WRIGLEY, E. A., and SCHOFIELD, R. S., *The Population History of England, 1541–1871* (1981).

YORKE, P. C., *The Life and Correspondence of Philip Yorke, Earl of Hardwicke, Lord High Chancellor of Great Britain* (Cambridge, 1913).

INDEX

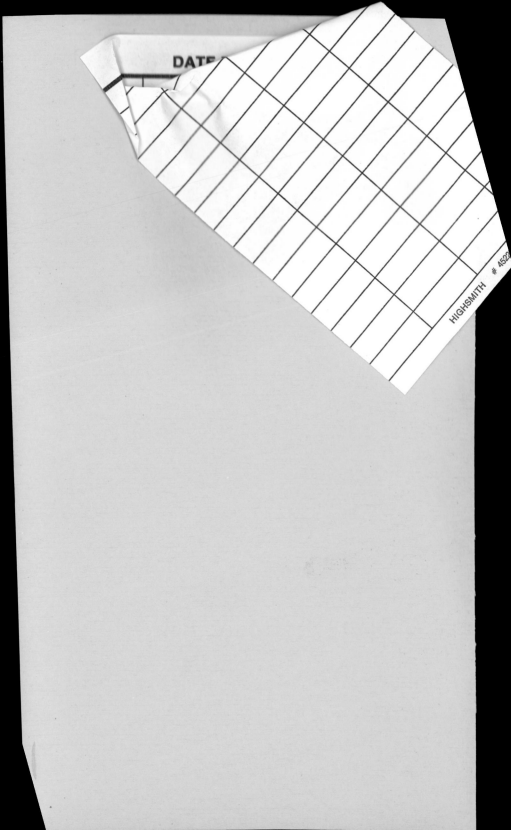